UMBRACO USER'S GUIDE

Umbraco User's Guide

Umbraco User's Guide

Nik Wahlberg
Paul Sterling

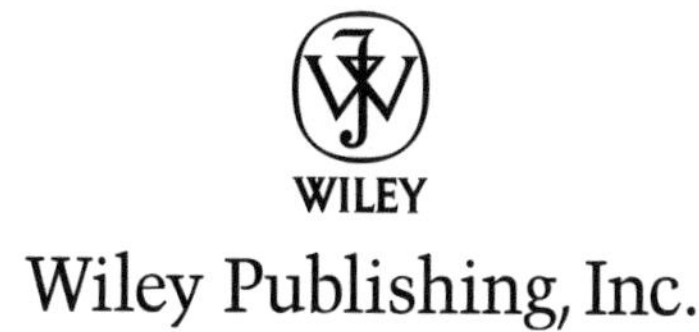

Wiley Publishing, Inc.

Umbraco User's Guide

Published by
Wiley Publishing, Inc.
10475 Crosspoint Boulevard
Indianapolis, IN 46256
www.wiley.com

Published simultaneously in Canada

ISBN: 978-0-470-56082-2
ISBN: 978-1-118-10808-6 (ebk)
ISBN: 978-1-118-10809-3 (ebk)
ISBN: 978-1-118-10807-9 (ebk)

Manufactured in the United States of America

10 9 8 7 6 5 4 3 2 1

Library of Congress Control Number: 2011924906

To my wife, Amy. You are the backbone of our family and I thank you with sincerity for your patience and undying support through my ventures.

To my kids, Olivia and Lukas. You are the light of my life and the force that encourages me to grow and continue the pursuit of a fulfilling life.

To my parents, Sture and Carola. It's because of your tireless patience and efforts that I have made something of my life and have reached the successes that I only dreamed of as a child. Thank you!

—Nik Wahlberg

To Kristin and Tate who showed more patience than I thought possible.

—Paul Sterling

CREDITS

ACQUISITIONS EDITOR
Paul Reese

PROJECT EDITOR
Maureen Spears

TECHNICAL EDITOR
Chris Houston

PRODUCTION EDITOR
Daniel Scribner

COPY EDITOR
Paula Lowell

EDITORIAL DIRECTOR
Robyn B. Siesky

EDITORIAL MANAGER
Mary Beth Wakefield

FREELANCER EDITORIAL MANAGER
Rosemarie Graham

ASSOCIATE DIRECTOR OF MARKETING
David Mayhew

PRODUCTION MANAGER
Tim Tate

VICE PRESIDENT AND EXECUTIVE GROUP PUBLISHER
Richard Swadley

VICE PRESIDENT AND EXECUTIVE PUBLISHER
Barry Pruett

ASSOCIATE PUBLISHER
Jim Minatel

PROJECT COORDINATOR, COVER
Katie Crocker

PROOFREADER
Publication Services, Inc.

INDEXER
Ron Strauss

COVER DESIGNER
LeAndra Young

COVER IMAGE
© iStock / Xavier Arnau

ABOUT THE AUTHORS

NIK WAHLBERG (West Greenwich, RI) was born and raised in Sweden. After graduating with a B.S. in Computer Science, he quickly found himself in the Web development landscape working as a Technical Consultant at a firm in Providence, RI. This eventually led to him founding Scandia Consulting, a full-service consultancy specializing in custom Web application development, with a focus on CMS, CRM, and business-process-to-tech solutions. In 2007 he was introduced to Umbraco as a development framework, and the marriage was an instant success. Since then, his firm has deployed numerous Umbraco installations over the years. He has been, and continues to be, an active Umbraco community supporter and unofficial evangelist. He is a Level 2 Certified Umbraco Professional. In his spare time, Nik loves spending time with his two children, wife, and Penny and Palmer (the English Mastiffs), enjoys the occasional round of golf, and likes to catch up on the latest in tech news and innovation.

PAUL STERLING (Bellingham, WA) is a member of the Umbraco Core Team, a member of the company behind the open-source project, and has built several businesses based on Umbraco. He is committed to making Umbraco easy to use for web developers while keeping Umbraco's unlimited flexibility. Paul lives in Bellingham, WA where being a runner, beer drinker, and web geek does not attract much attention.

ABOUT THE TECHNICAL EDITOR

CHRIS HOUSTON is the Founder and Sr. Architect of Vizioz. Vizioz was established as one of the first dedicated Umbraco consultancies in the UK and was one of the first Umbraco Gold Partners. Chris studied Electronics and Communications at Plymouth University. Since then, Chris has worked for 15 years in the web and mobile sector, initially as a developer for the first UK online bookshop and then as an Intranet consultant. More recently, he worked for six years as a CTO for Mobile Message Centre PLC, which later became the Messaging Solutions division of Carphone Warehouse. Chris first registered the Vizioz.com name while at University, and 12 years later he founded the company. When Chris is not head deep in technology, you can usually find him dancing modern jive at his local Rotary club where he met his French fiancée Marie, or on the ski slopes with a vin chaud.

ACKNOWLEDGMENTS

I want to thank Wrox for the opportunity to write this title. It's been a long time coming, and I am proud to have my name on a Wrox product. I'd like to extend a special thank you to Maureen Spears for her tremendous support and patience throughout the project.

Last, but not least, a collective thank you to the Umbraco community for working hard to keep Umbraco alive and thriving. **High five, you rock!**

CONTENTS

INTRODUCTION

IT'S NOT ENOUGH these days to have a website. As a business or individual in today's technology landscape, you must be able to adapt and change with new emerging technologies that seemingly pop up every day. There are thousands of solutions and implementation to consider, but only a select few are worth your precious time. Over the years, I've discovered that building custom, one-off content management system (CMS) solutions for clients isn't time well spent for me and, in most cases, not money well spent for the client; by the time the project is complete, it's obsolete.

I've spent considerable time working with licensed CMSs as well as a handful of other open source products. Umbraco is the best fit for me and my clients, bar none. The flexibility and extensibility of the product allows us to implement custom applications with Umbraco as a foundation. In addition, we're never out of date with the undying support of the Umbraco community and the core team constantly working to improve and extend the product.

So, for my part, I wanted to write this book as a contribution to the Umbraco project and, of course, to help you become proficient and effective when working with Umbraco for your CMS needs. Welcome aboard.

WHO THIS BOOK IS FOR

You are a professional who is just starting to work with Umbraco and need someone to show you the ropes. This book takes you from installation all the way through more advanced concepts like working with Microsoft .NET user controls so you can add dynamic functionality to your site. In addition, it also describes, in detail, how to plan the content for your site and how you work with it once it's in Umbraco.

You should be familiar with technologies such as Extensible Stylesheet Language (XSL) to work with Umbraco's cached content, the concepts of relational databases, and how to work with HTML and CSS. Finally, you should have a general understanding of CMS concepts.

WHAT THIS BOOK COVERS

This book primarily focuses on Umbraco 4.5.2 and 4.6. However, XSLT code snippets are also provided for the previous version of the Umbraco XML schema in version 4.0.x. The .NET code samples and Umbraco installations will all require .NET Framework 4.0. You should also have access to IIS6 or IIS7 for installing your copy of Umbraco.

HOW THIS BOOK IS STRUCTURED

The content structure of this book is very linear in terms how you should approach working with Umbraco. It starts by providing you with various options for installing Umbraco for the first time, and then, how to build your content structure, how to implement your content, extending your Umbraco installation using advanced output methods and adding functionality for your website users. Finally, you will get a chance to see all of the concepts implemented in a sample application to tie it all together. Additionally, you will find plenty of references and how-to's in the appendices.

WHAT YOU NEED TO USE THIS BOOK

The installation and deployment of Umbraco as discussed in this book will require you to have access to the following:

- Microsoft Windows XP/Vista/7/2003/2008 (Windows 7 is used in the examples)
- IIS 6 or IIS 7 (IIS 7 is used in the examples)
- SQL Server Express 2005/2008 or SQL Server Standard 2005/2008
- Visual Studio 2010 (Optional. To take full advantage of sample projects.)

CONVENTIONS

To help you get the most from the text and keep track of what's happening, we've used a number of conventions throughout the book.

Boxes with a warning icon like this one hold important, not-to-be forgotten information that is directly relevant to the surrounding text.

The pencil icon indicates notes, tips, hints, tricks, and asides to the current discussion.

As for styles in the text:

- We *italicize* new terms and important words when we introduce them.
- We show keyboard strokes like this: Ctrl+A.
- We show file names, URLs, and code within the text like so: `persistence.properties`.
- We present code in two different ways:

```
We use a monofont type with no highlighting for most code examples.
We use bold to emphasize code that's particularly important in the present context.
```

SOURCE CODE

As you work through the examples in this book, you may choose either to type in all the code manually or to use the source code files that accompany the book. All of the source code used in this book is available for download at `www.wrox.com`. You will find the code snippets from the source code are accompanied by a download icon and note indicating the name of the program so you know it's available for download and can easily locate it in the download file. Once at the site, simply locate the book's title (either by using the Search box or by using one of the title lists) and click the Download Code link on the book's detail page to obtain all the source code for the book.

Because many books have similar titles, you may find it easiest to search by ISBN; this book's ISBN is 978-0-470-56082-2.

Once you download the code, just decompress it with your favorite compression tool. Alternately, you can go to the main Wrox code download page at `www.wrox.com/dynamic/books/download.aspx` to see the code available for this book and all other Wrox books.

ERRATA

We make every effort to ensure that there are no errors in the text or in the code. However, no one is perfect, and mistakes do occur. If you find an error in one of our books, like a spelling mistake or faulty piece of code, we would be very grateful for your feedback. By sending in errata you may save another reader hours of frustration, and at the same time you will be helping us provide even higher quality information.

To find the errata page for this book, go to `www.wrox.com` and locate the title using the Search box or one of the title lists. Then, on the book details page, click the Book Errata link. On this page you can view all errata that has been submitted for this book and posted by Wrox editors. A complete book list including links to each book's errata is also available at `www.wrox.com/misc-pages/booklist.shtml`.

If you don't spot "your" error on the Book Errata page, go to `www.wrox.com/contact/techsupport.shtml` and complete the form there to send us the error you have found. We'll check the information and, if appropriate, post a message to the book's errata page and fix the problem in subsequent editions of the book.

P2P.WROX.COM

For author and peer discussion, join the P2P forums at `p2p.wrox.com`. The forums are a Web-based system for you to post messages relating to Wrox books and related technologies and interact with other readers and technology users. The forums offer a subscription feature to e-mail you topics of interest of your choosing when new posts are made to the forums. Wrox authors, editors, other industry experts, and your fellow readers are present on these forums.

At `http://p2p.wrox.com` you will find a number of different forums that will help you not only as you read this book, but also as you develop your own applications. To join the forums, just follow these steps:

1. Go to `p2p.wrox.com` and click the Register link.
2. Read the terms of use and click Agree.
3. Complete the required information to join as well as any optional information you wish to provide and click Submit.
4. You will receive an e-mail with information describing how to verify your account and complete the joining process.

You can read messages in the forums without joining P2P but in order to post your own messages, you must join.

Once you join, you can post new messages and respond to messages other users post. You can read messages at any time on the Web. If you would like to have new messages from a particular forum e-mailed to you, click the Subscribe to this Forum icon by the forum name in the forum listing.

For more information about how to use the Wrox P2P, be sure to read the P2P FAQs for answers to questions about how the forum software works as well as many common questions specific to P2P and Wrox books. To read the FAQs, click the FAQ link on any P2P page.

PART I
Creating Your First Site with Umbraco

Installing for the First Time

- What are the steps for installing Umbraco?
- How do you upgrade your current site?
- Which Umbraco starter kit should you use and how do you install it?
- How do you apply and manipulate Umbraco skins?
- How do you find and install Umbraco modules?

Users have installed Umbraco literally hundreds of thousands of times in a variety of environments — everywhere from an entry-level Windows XP machine, to multiserver load-balanced sites, and even to Microsoft Windows Azure. In the vast majority of these cases the installations complete successfully and take no more than a few minutes. The first section of this chapter contains the Umbraco quick start instructions for facilitating a successful install. Read it, install Umbraco, and then continue reading for additional considerations.

You can always find the latest released version of Umbraco on the Umbraco CodePlex home at `http://umbraco.codeplex.com/` from the Downloads tab. The latest version of Umbraco is also available via Microsoft's Web Platform Installer and Web Application Gallery (`http://www.microsoft.com/web/gallery/umbraco/`). This chapter offers a detailed overview for installing Umbraco with both the Microsoft Web Platform Installer and directly from the Umbraco installation file downloaded from the Umbraco CodePlex home.

INSTALLING UMBRACO

The text in this chapter, as well as the rest of the book, assumes that you have a PC running Windows Vista or Windows 7 and have user permissions sufficient enough to allow for administrative actions. If this is not the case, or if you are installing to a different environment (such as to a shared-hosting account) skip this section for now and refer to Chapter 14, which has troubleshooting tips. One important item to note is that Umbraco is best installed as a website root rather than as a virtual directory under a web root, so plan on running Umbraco from a web root. All current versions of Internet Information Server (IIS) support multiple web roots so running from a web root is not an issue unless you are using IIS5 on Windows XP. See Chapter 14 if this is the case.

Installing Umbraco using the Microsoft Web Platform Installer

The best way to begin your Umbraco installation is by using the Microsoft Web Platform Installer (a free installation tool developed and supported by Microsoft). Some advantages to using the Microsoft Web Platform Installer (shown in Figure 1-1) are that the tool can:

- Automatically detect and install required dependencies.
- Create a Microsoft SQL database or Microsoft SQL CE database prior to installing Umbraco.
- Create and configure new websites in IIS.

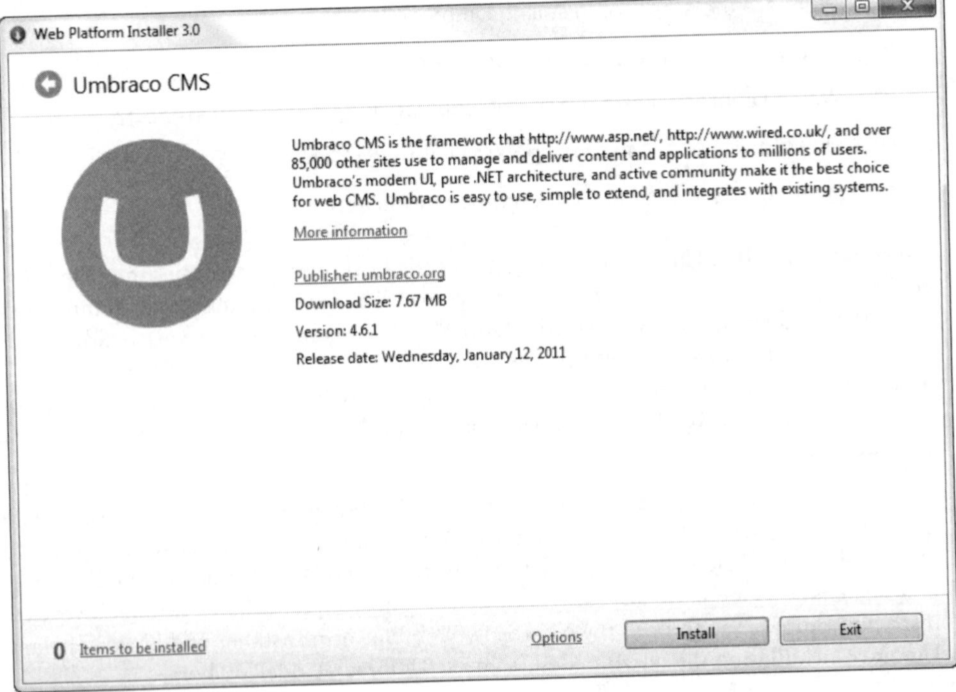

FIGURE 1-1

You can find the Microsoft Web Platform Installer at `www.microsoft.com/web/` along with the latest versions of Umbraco and other web applications as well as any required dependencies. In addition, the Microsoft Web Platform Installer is available as an IIS extension at `www.iis.net/extensions/WebPI/` and is integrated into web hosting control panels such as cPanel and DotNetPanel. Using a web host's control panel to install Umbraco in a shared hosting environment can greatly simplify the installation process.

Use the following steps to install Umbraco with the Web Platform Installer:

1. Launch the Web Platform Installer from the Microsoft Web Application Gallery (`http://www.microsoft.com/web/gallery/Umbraco`).
2. Review the list of files that the Web Platform Installer will download and install.

The list of installation files that the Web Platform Installer presents may only include the Umbraco Content Management System (CMS) component if you already have the required dependencies, such as SQL Server and the .NET Framework, installed.

3. Select the Microsoft SQL Server CE database option as shown in Figure 1-2.

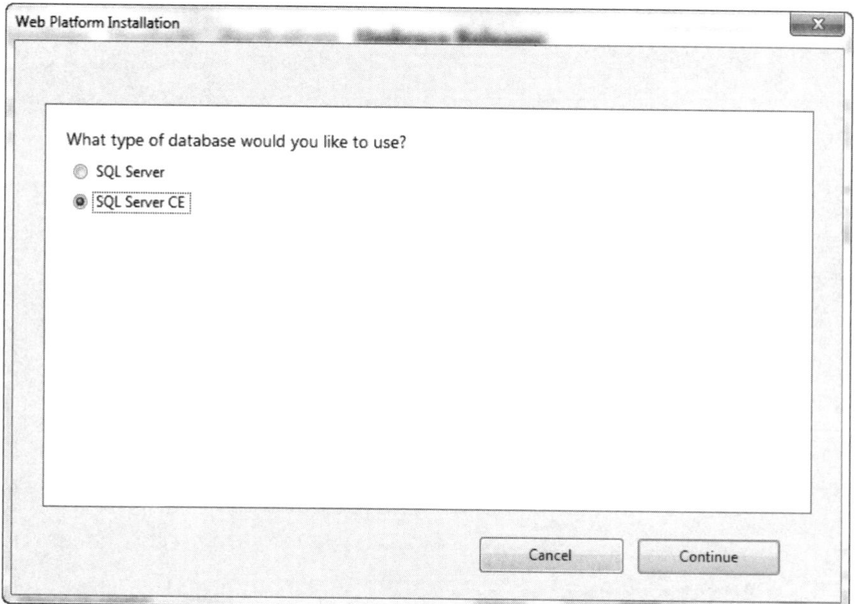

FIGURE 1-2

4. Select New Web Site from the Web Site drop-down menu as shown in Figure 1-3.
5. Enter the site information for Site Name, Path, Port, Home Directory, and Host Name.

The author recommends leaving the Umbraco CMS Application Name blank, as shown in Figure 1-4.

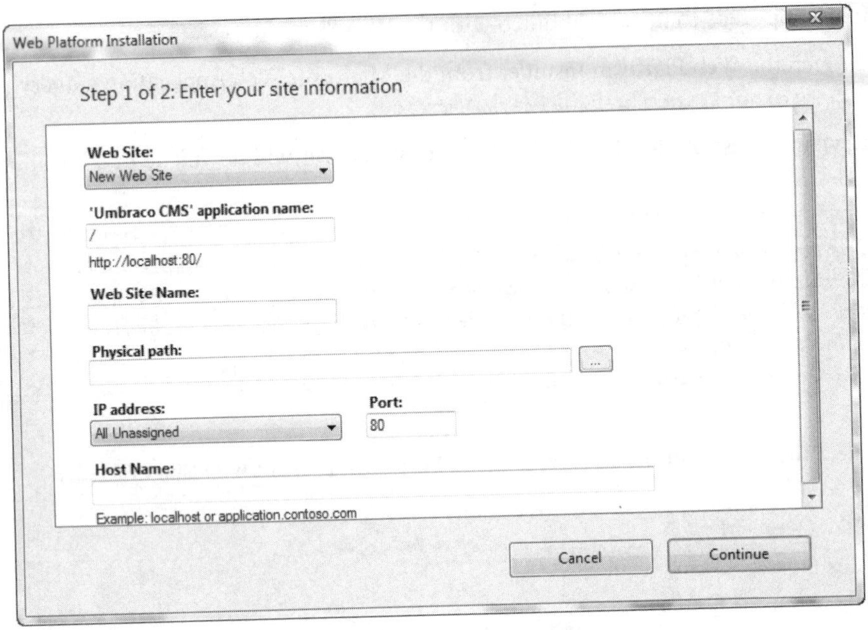

FIGURE 1-3

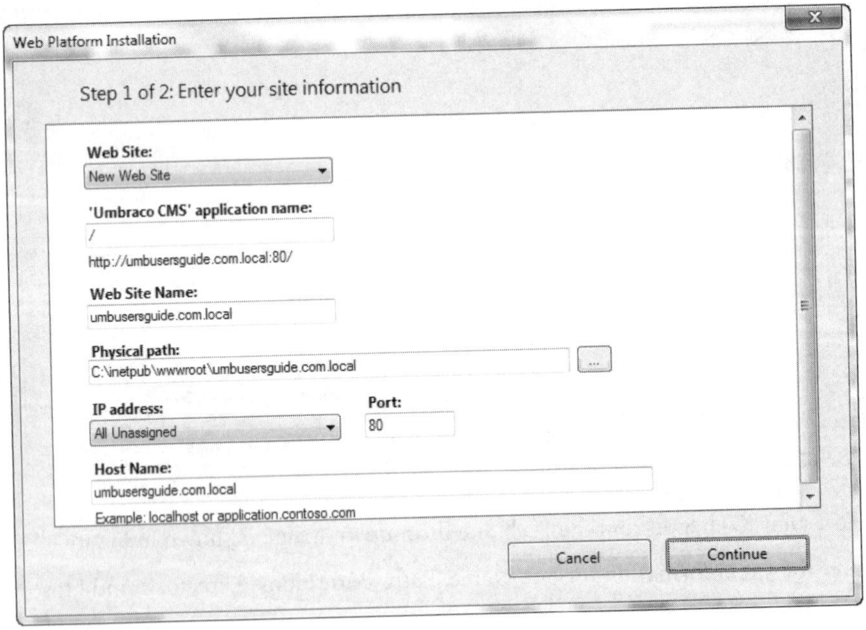

FIGURE 1-4

6. When the Web Platform Installer completes the installation process, click the Launch Umbraco CMS link to launch the Umbraco Installation Wizard.

7. When the Umbraco Installation Wizard loads in your browser, you see the Welcome screen (Figure 1-5). Click the Let's get started! button to complete the steps required to configure your Umbraco installation.

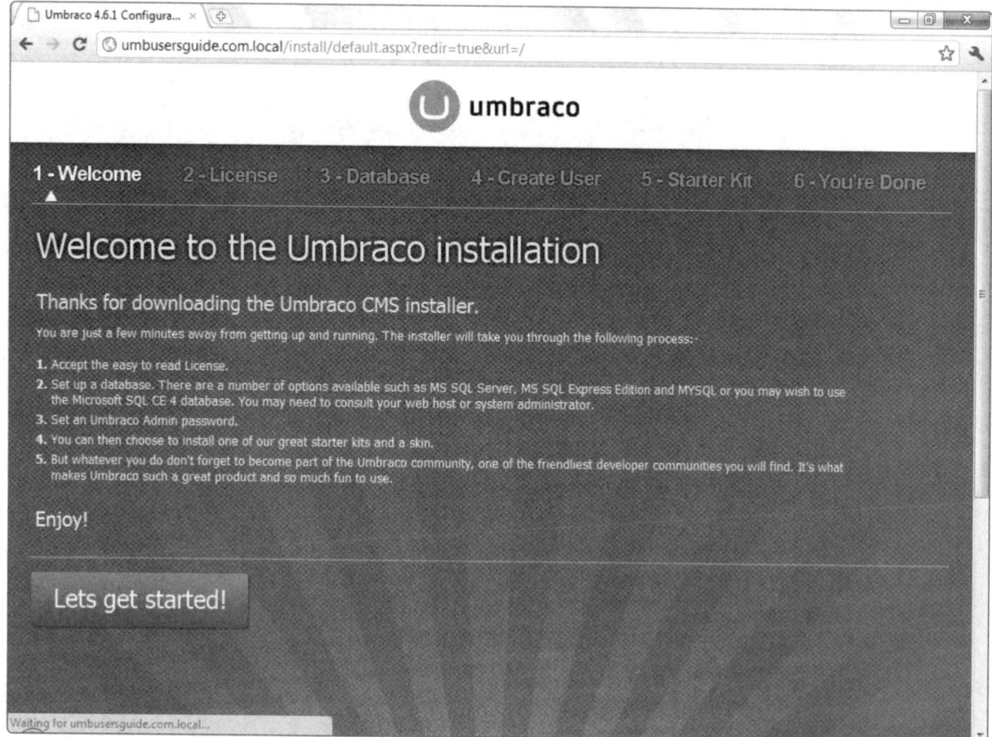

FIGURE 1-5

8. To continue, read and accept the Umbraco license by clicking the Accept and Continue button as shown in Figure 1-6.

9. Because you selected Microsoft SQL CE from the Web Platform Installer, the correct database options will already be set. Click the Install button to complete the Umbraco database configuration as shown in Figure 1-7.

10. Once the database is installed and configured completely, click the Continue button as shown in Figure 1-8.

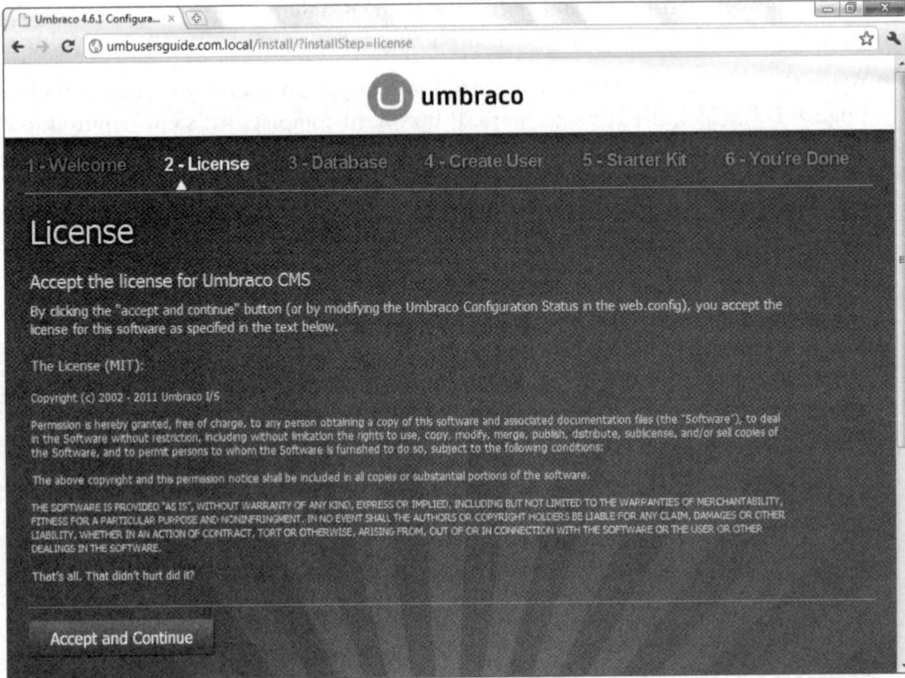

FIGURE 1-6

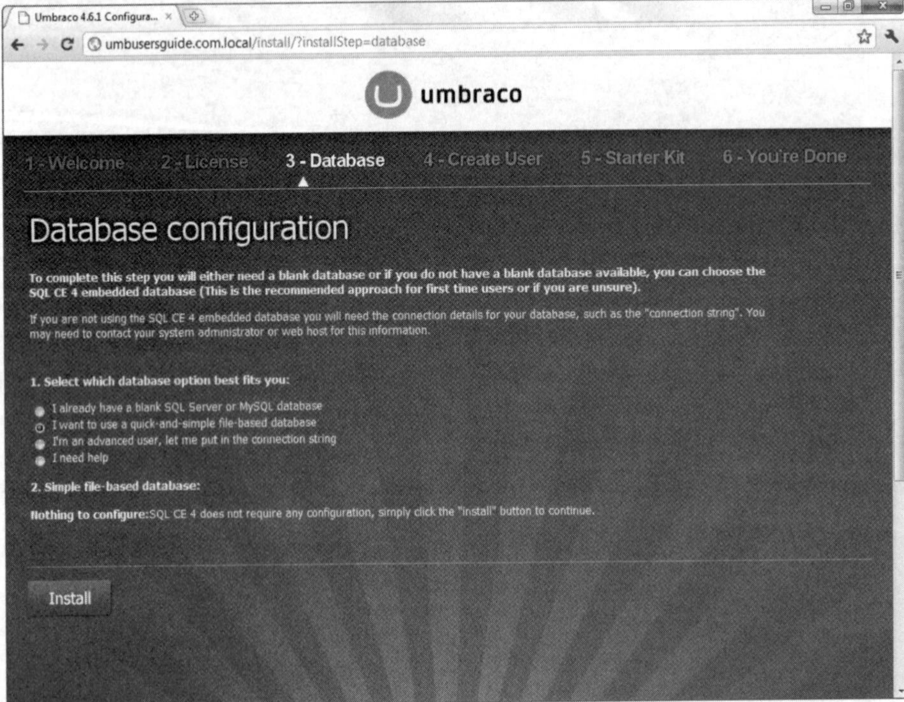

FIGURE 1-7

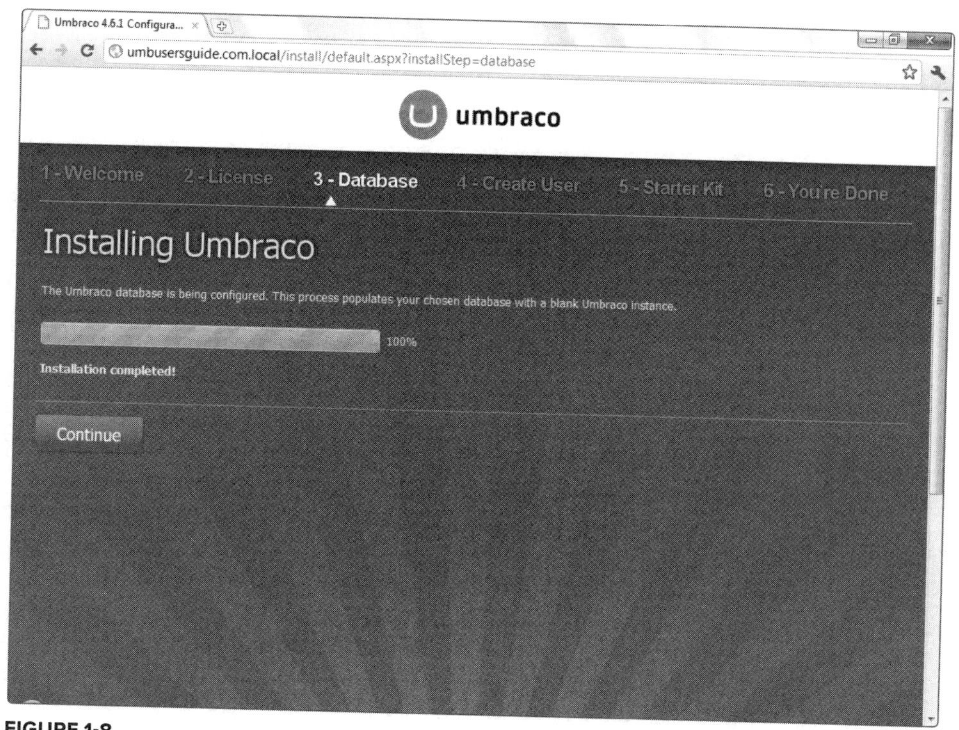

FIGURE 1-8

11. Create an Umbraco user by providing a username, email, and password and then clicking the Create User button. You can also register for the Umbraco newsletter using the email address you provide by selecting the Sign up for our monthly newsletter check box as shown in Figure 1-9.

12. From the Starter Kits screen, you can browse descriptions of each of the Starter Kits by hovering over their icons. To install a Starter Kit, simply click one of the Install this kit buttons.

If this is your first time installing Umbraco, the author recommends selecting the Simple Starter Kit as shown in Figure 1-10. You can find more detailed information about the Starter Kits in the "Utilizing Umbraco Starter Kits" section later in this chapter.

13. Once the Starter Kit is installed, you have the option of installing a skin from the Install a Skin screen. Umbraco Skins are a simple way to make your Starter Kit beautiful. You can preview a skin by hovering over the skin icon and install a skin by clicking the Install button as shown in Figure 1-11.

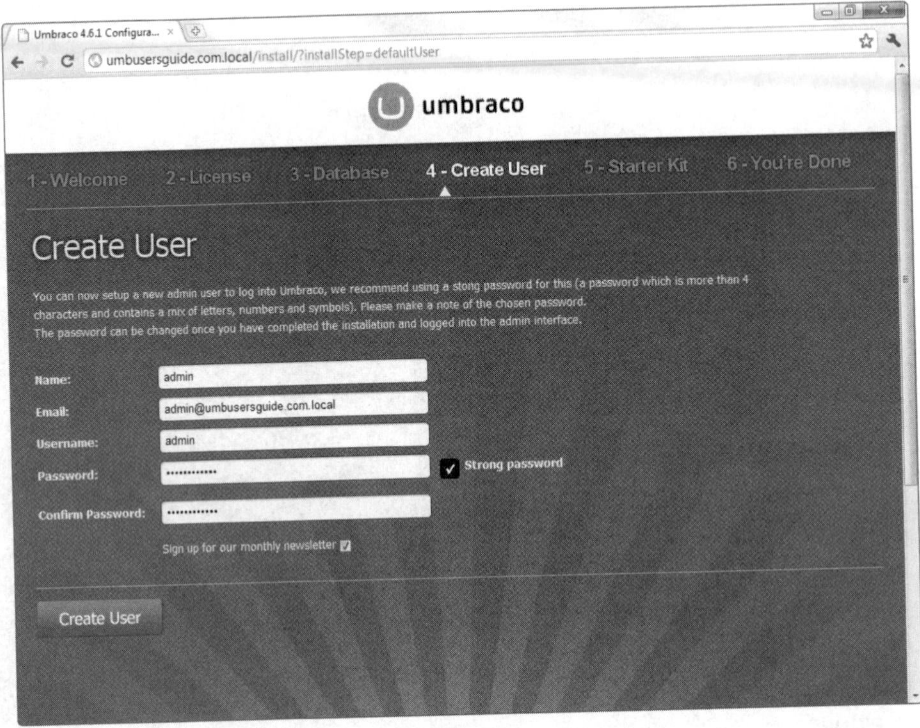

FIGURE 1-9

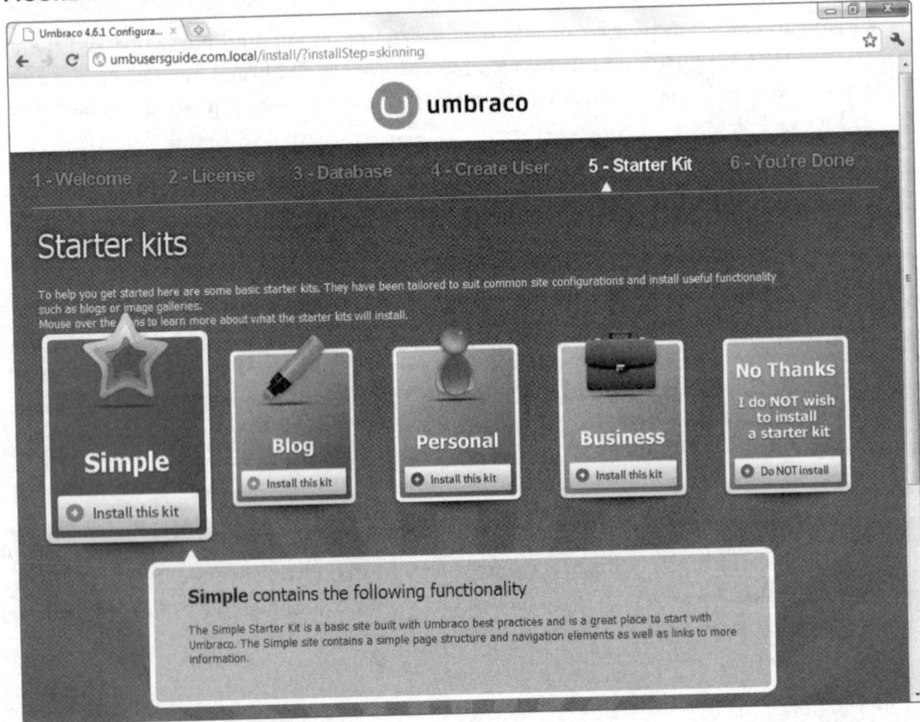

FIGURE 1-10

FIGURE 1-11

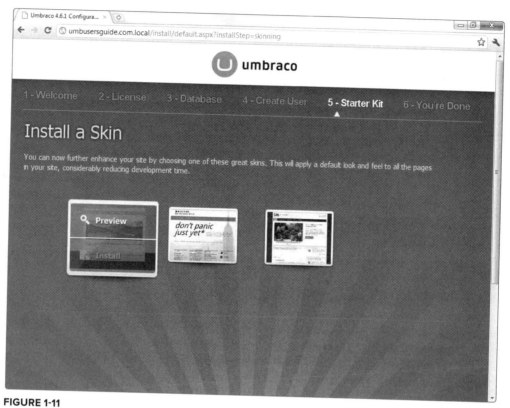

14. Once the skin is installed you will see the You're done screen as show in Figure 1-12. From this screen click the Preview your new website button to launch the skin editor or the Set up your new website button to launch the Umbraco backoffice. This screen also has a collection of useful links to additional information about getting started working with Umbraco.

You're all done and Umbraco is ready for use, complete with a fully functional web site and beautiful skin! As you can see, when you compare the process to a manual installation as discussed in the next section, using the Web Platform Installer greatly simplifies the setup and configuration of the website and database requirements for Umbraco.

A limitation of using the Microsoft Web Platform Installer to install Umbraco is that only Microsoft SQL databases are supported. If you want to install Umbraco using a MySQL database, you must configure the database prior to running the installation from the Microsoft Web Platform Installer. You then provide the database connection information during the Umbraco Installation Wizard database configuration step rather than during the Web Platform Installer configuration step.

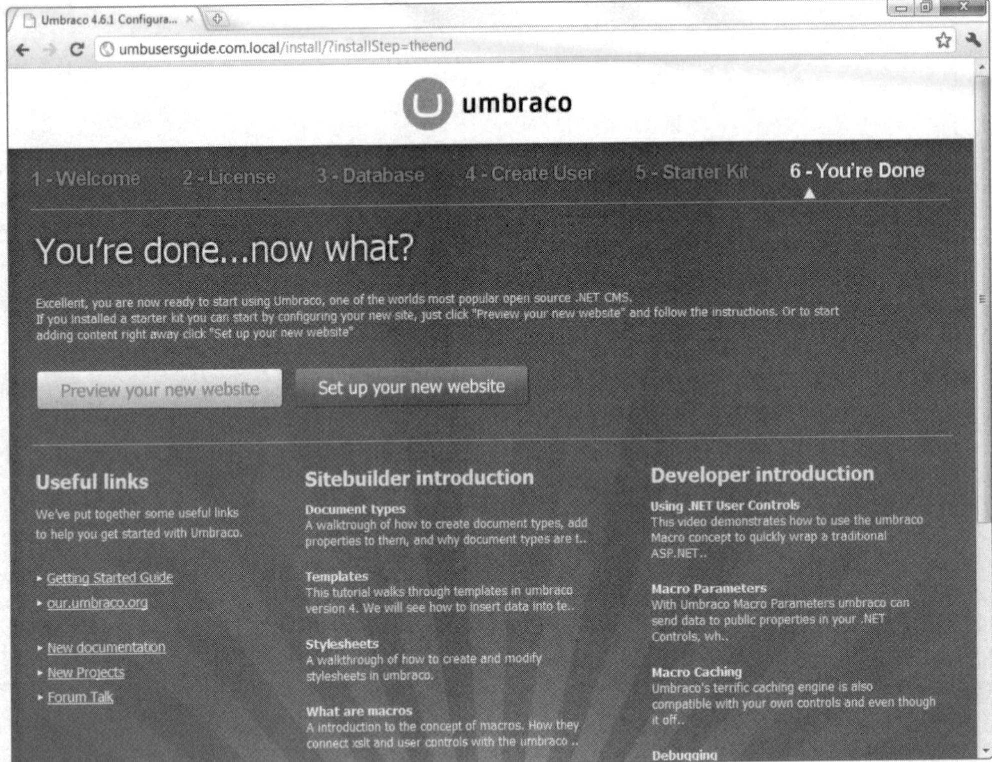

FIGURE 1-12

Installing Umbraco Manually

Although using the Microsoft Web Platform Installer to install Umbraco is strongly advised, cases may exist where a manual installation is desired. In such a case, you must manually complete the steps to create the IIS website, create the database, and set required permissions. The following are the steps to complete a manual installation of Umbraco: If you find yourself stuck on one of these steps, try installing Umbraco using the Quick Start steps first and then return to this section later.

1. Create a new folder with a unique name for your Umbraco installation on your local hard drive.
2. From IIS Manager create a new site and set the home directory to be the new folder; leave the remaining settings at the default.
3. Set permissions on the new folder to allow the new site's application pool identity (usually this is the Network Service or Application Pool Identity account) to Modify, Read & Execute, and Write.
4. From SQL Management Studio create a new database and assign a login to the dbo role for the database. Make a note of the SQL instance name (such as ./SQLEXPRESS), the database name, and the login name and password.

You may skip step 4 if you want to use the Microsoft SQL CE option later in the installation.

5. Download the latest Umbraco release from the Umbraco CodePlex home Downloads tab (`http://umbraco.codeplex.com/`).
6. Copy the Umbraco files from the .zip archive into the new folder. Make sure to unblock the .zip file from the Windows File Property dialog before extracting the contents.
7. Open a web browser and navigate to the root of the new site.
8. When the Umbraco Installation Wizard loads in your browser, you will see the Welcome screen (Figure 1-13). Click the Let's get started! button to complete the steps required to configure your Umbraco installation.

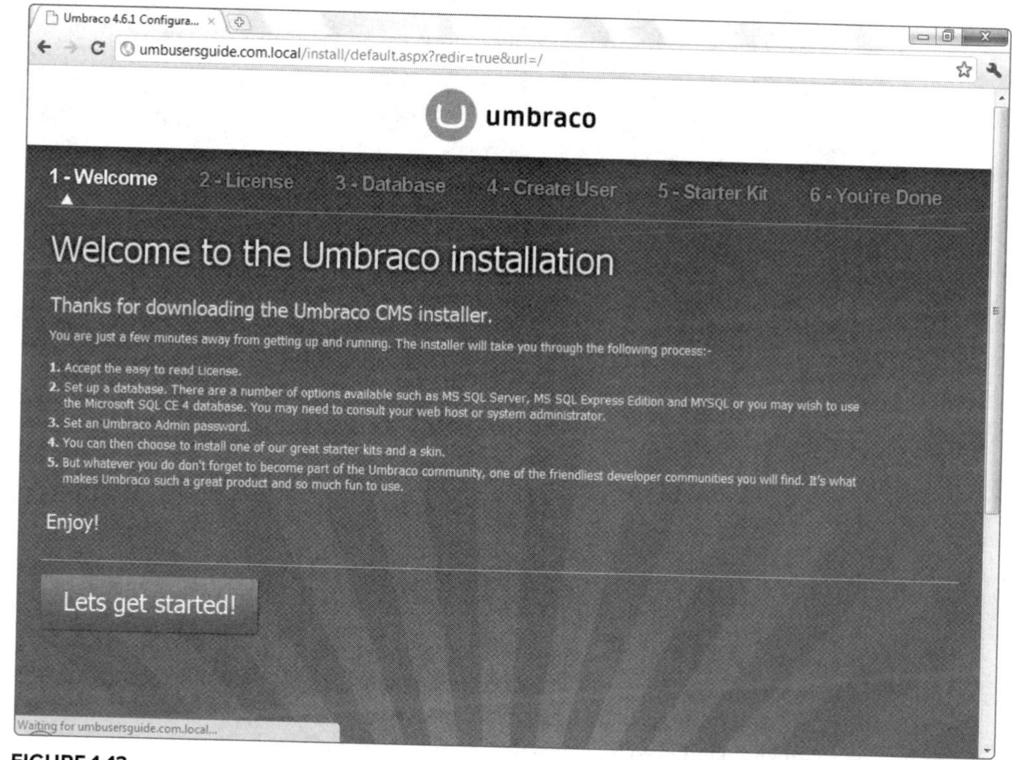

FIGURE 1-13

9. To continue, read and accept the Umbraco license by clicking the Accept and Continue button as shown in Figure 1-14.

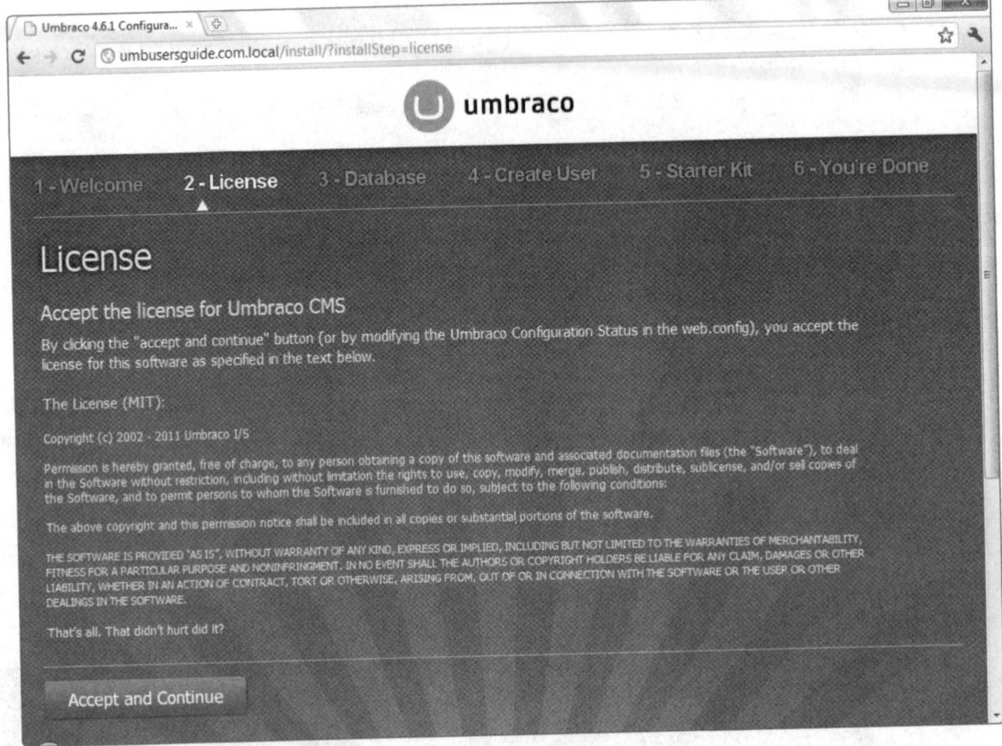

FIGURE 1-14

10. Select the Microsoft SQL Server option in the Database Type drop-down list and enter the Connection Details you created in step 4 (see Figure 1-15). Click the Install button to create and configure the Umbraco database.

11. Once the database is installed and configured completely, click the Continue button as shown in Figure 1-16.

12. Create an Umbraco user by providing a username, email, and password and then clicking the Create User button. You can also register for the Umbraco newsletter using the email address you provide by selecting the Sign up for our monthly newsletter check box as shown in Figure 1-17.

13. From the Starter Kits screen you can browse descriptions of each of the Starter Kits by hovering over the Starter Kit icons. To install a Starter Kit click one of the Install this kit buttons as shown in Figure 1-18. You can find more detailed information about the Starter Kits in the "Utilizing Umbraco Starter Kits" section later in this chapter.

14. Once the Starter Kit is installed you have the option of installing a skin from the Install a Skin screen. You can preview a skin by hovering over the skin icon and install a skin by clicking the Install button as shown in Figure 1-19.

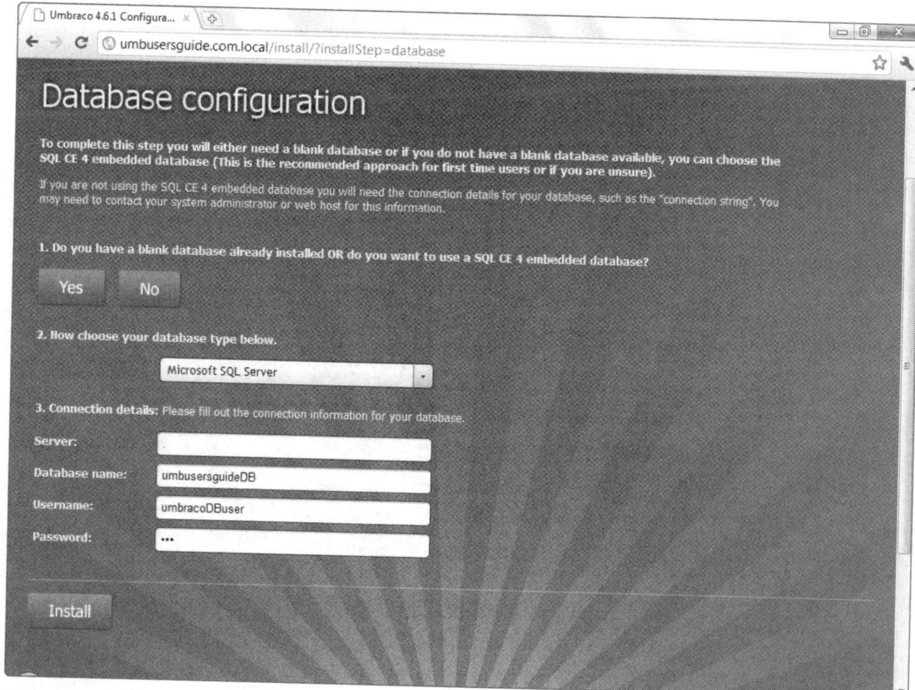

FIGURE 1-15

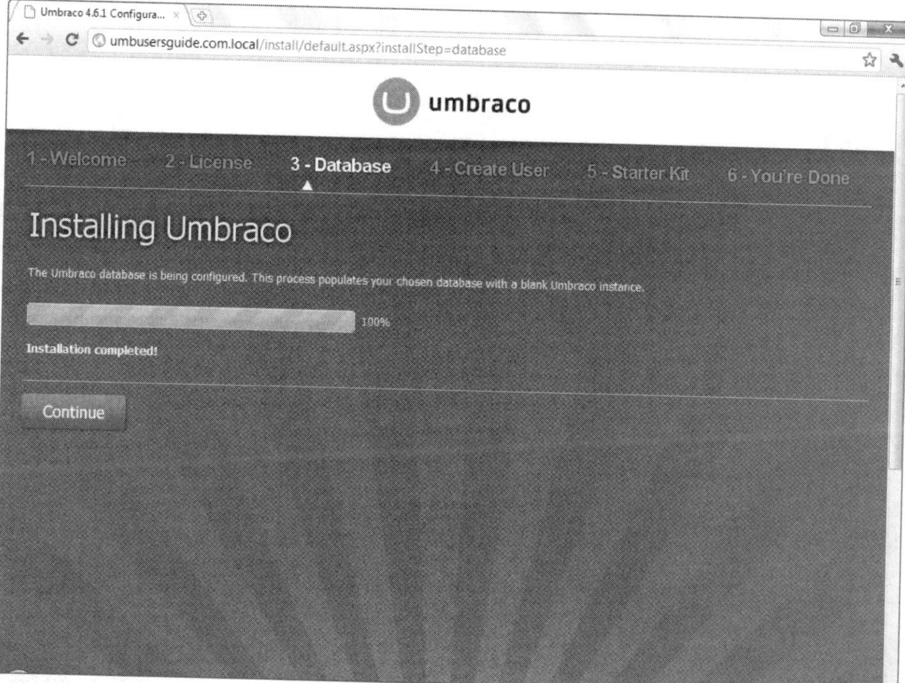

FIGURE 1-16

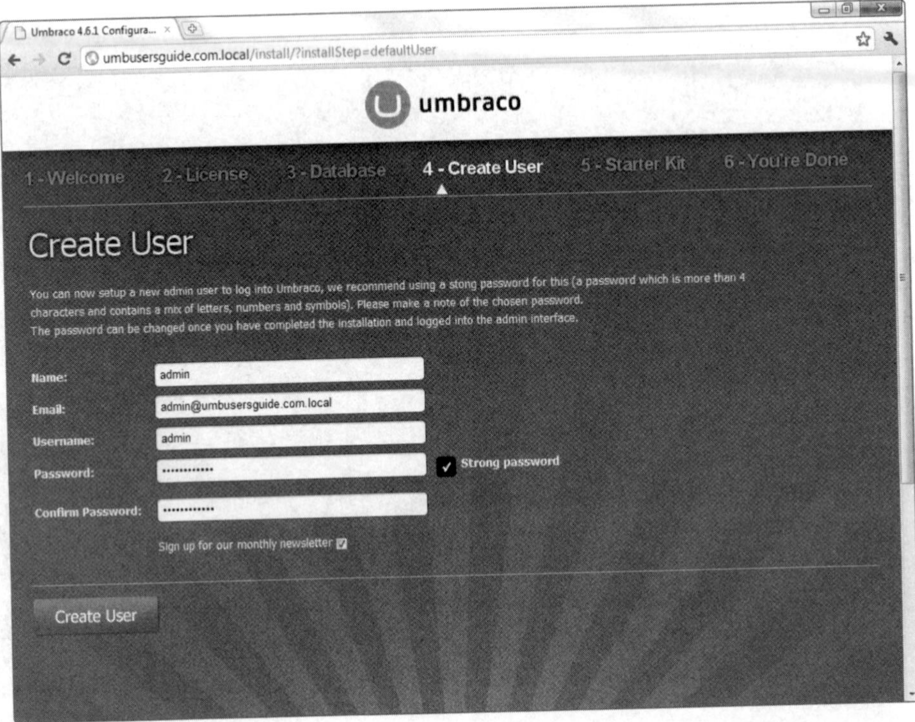

FIGURE 1-17

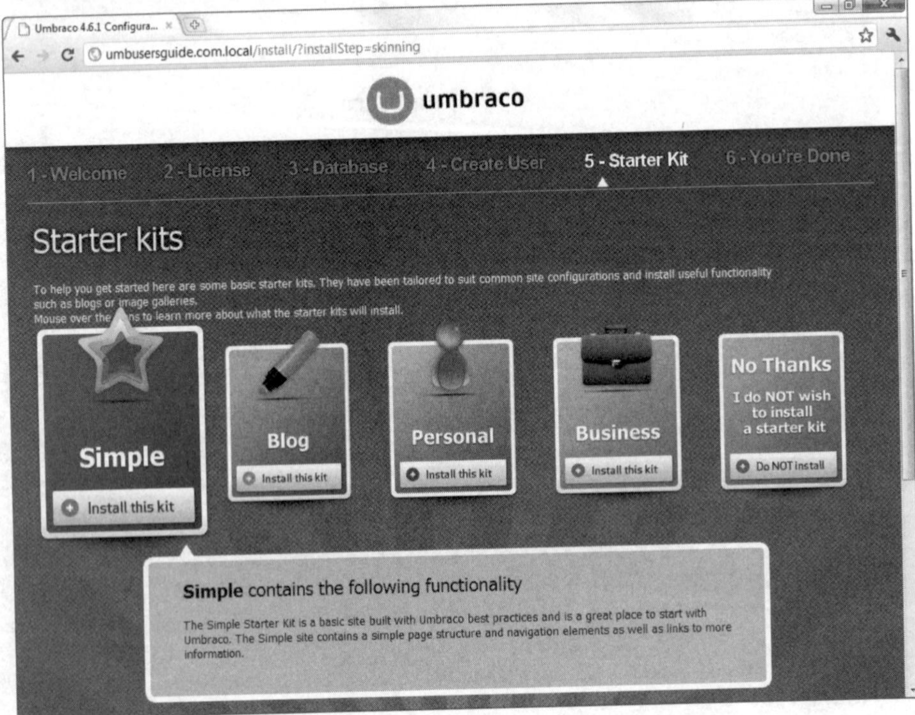

FIGURE 1-18

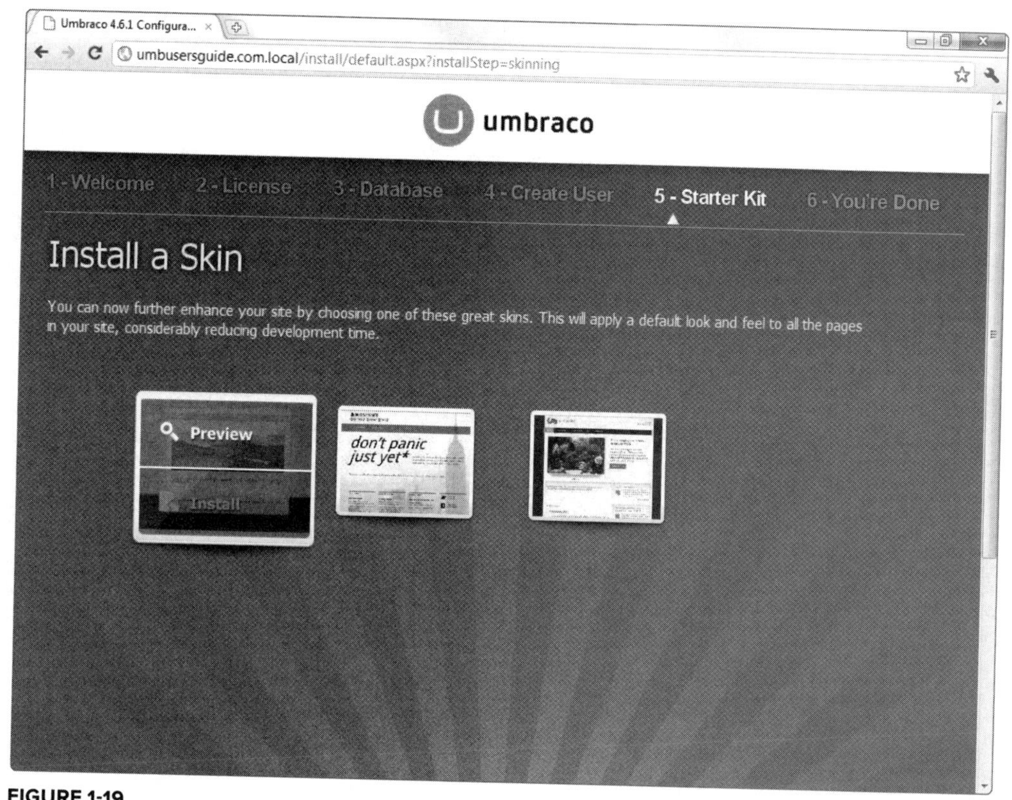

FIGURE 1-19

15. Once the skin is installed you will see the You're done screen as show in Figure 1-20. From this screen click the Preview your new website button to launch the skin editor or the Set up your new website button to launch the Umbraco backoffice. This screen also has a collection of useful links to additional information about getting started working with Umbraco.

You now have everything you need to successfully run, build, and extend Umbraco. Obviously not all Umbraco installations will fit into the preceding step-by-step instructions. The remainder of this chapter covers additional considerations for other installation scenarios and environments.

A NOTE ON SECURITY

One item that some readers will no doubt notice is that the permissions settings in the preceding manual installation are less than optimal from a security perspective. For a production or public-facing website, you will likely make some additional, more finely grained adjustments to a site's home folder and files. The website `http://our.umbraco.org/wiki/` is a good starting point on what settings to adjust.

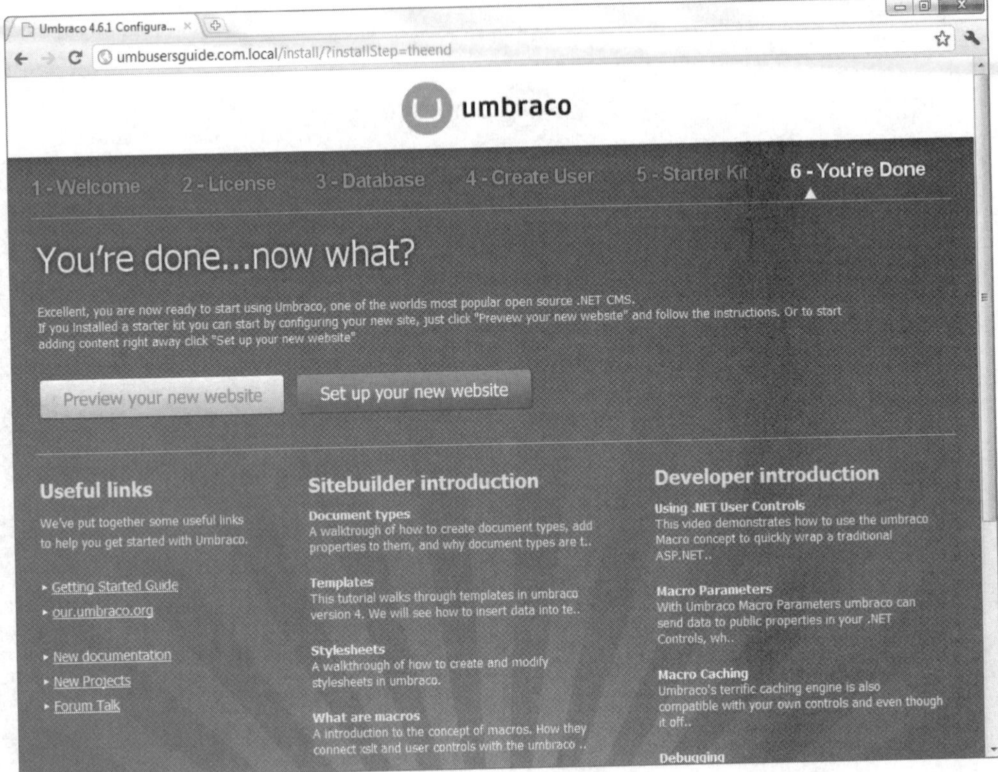

FIGURE 1-20

Tips for Installing Umbraco in Special Environments

One of the great strengths of Umbraco is its simple architecture, which enables it to adapt to a variety of installation and usage scenarios. Certainly the earlier quick start is a simple scenario intended for use on a single machine — most likely a web builder's desktop or laptop — but you can use this same procedure to install Umbraco on a netbook running Windows 7 or a web server running Windows 2008. This procedure is also appropriate for installing an evaluation instance, for an install used to "test" a feature or to reproduce a defect, as well as for a fresh start when building websites with Umbraco.

Debugging in a Development Environment

For web developers, especially those working with .NET user controls integrated with Umbraco, the ability to debug code while running Umbraco is important. You can easily do this debugging by installing Umbraco onto the same physical machine that has Visual Studio installed. This can be on a local development laptop, a virtual machine, or a remote development machine accessed via remote desktop. You can also debug .NET code in a running Umbraco instance on domain-joined machines with the appropriate debugging tools installed and configured, but that is beyond the scope of this book. For this scenario, check out the advanced developer sections of the Umbraco wiki (`http://our.umbraco.org/wiki`).

Security Settings in a Production Environment

When installing to a production environment, you must take some additional considerations into account, and not the least of these are the security and access settings for the Umbraco site and related files (see the earlier A Note on Security sidebar in the "Installing Umbraco Manually" section). In addition you will likely create a backup routine for your Umbraco instance. Including both your Umbraco database and your Umbraco files in your backup is important to have a complete snapshot. The author recommends reviewing the current backup documentation on the Umbraco wiki (`http://our.umbraco.org/wiki`).

Other Installation Scenarios

Of course, other scenarios exist in which you might install Umbraco, such as load balancing, cloud installation (Amazon EC2 or Microsoft Windows Azure), distributed publishing, and others. These scenarios are supported but are outside the scope of this book. For more information on them refer to the Umbraco wiki, the Umbraco forum, and Umbraco.tv for more information.

UPGRADING UMBRACO

The Umbraco Installation Wizard can manage patch upgrades (e.g., 4.5.1 to 4.5.2) and single major version upgrades (e.g., 4.0 to 4.5) gracefully and is the recommended approach for upgrading an installation. With all upgrades, knowing whether your installation contains any modified source or files from the original distribution is important. If so, take care to make backup copies of these files. In addition, if your installation contains a customized `web.config` file, or other configuration file, creating a backup of your configuration files for later use is essential.

Performing a Patch Upgrade

Typically, a patch upgrade contains no new functionality and requires no changes to configuration files. Reading the notes associated with a new Umbraco release prior to installing or upgrading an installation is good practice because any changes to configuration files will be documented in the notes.

The process to complete a patch upgrade is generally as follows:

1. Extract the patch release from the archive.
2. Copy new or altered files to your installation.
3. Run the Umbraco Upgrade Wizard (see Figure 1-21).

You can always find the latest release of Umbraco at the Umbraco home on CodePlex at `http://umbraco.codeplex.com/releases`.

Unless specified in the release notes, you will only copy the following directories to your installation:

- `/app_data`
- `/bin`
- `/install`

- /umbraco
- /umbraco_client

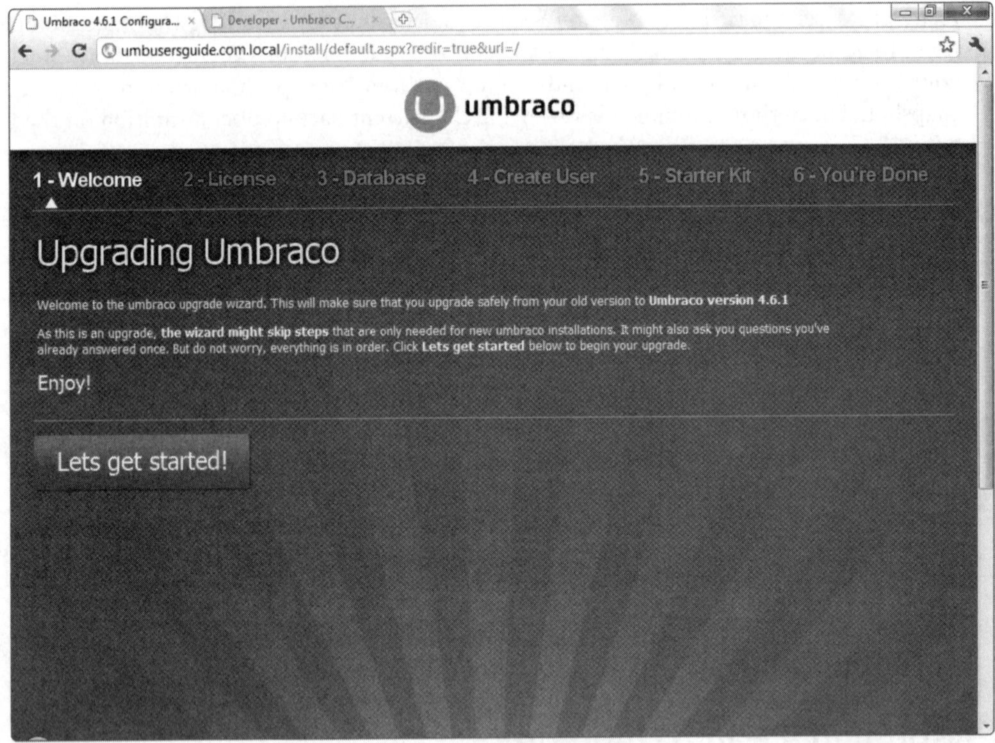

FIGURE 1-21

After the files are copied, open a browser and navigate to your Umbraco instance. The Umbraco Upgrade Wizard launches and guides you through the process to complete the site upgrade.

In addition, you must remove any cache files located in the `/app_data/TEMP/` folder, such as those generated by the client dependency loader, the Examine Search indexer, and the Umbraco document cache.

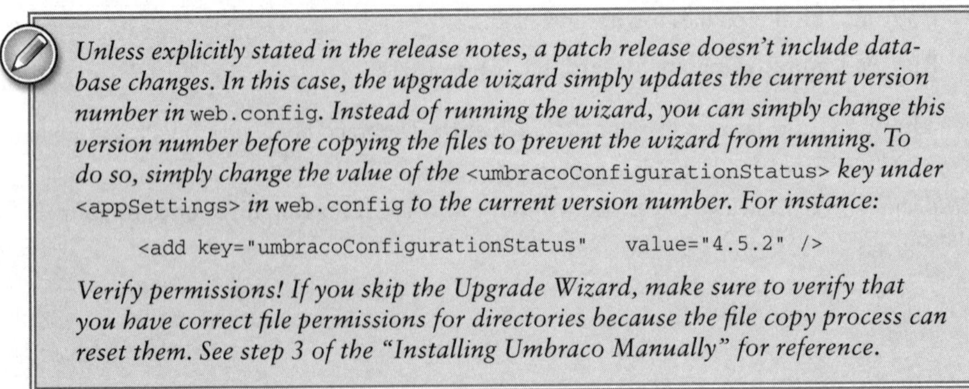

Unless explicitly stated in the release notes, a patch release doesn't include database changes. In this case, the upgrade wizard simply updates the current version number in `web.config`. *Instead of running the wizard, you can simply change this version number before copying the files to prevent the wizard from running. To do so, simply change the value of the* `<umbracoConfigurationStatus>` *key under* `<appSettings>` *in* `web.config` *to the current version number. For instance:*

```
<add key="umbracoConfigurationStatus"   value="4.5.2" />
```

Verify permissions! If you skip the Upgrade Wizard, make sure to verify that you have correct file permissions for directories because the file copy process can reset them. See step 3 of the "Installing Umbraco Manually" for reference.

Performing a Version Upgrade

When upgrading between single major versions, identifying all third-party components and Umbraco version-specific features is important. Breaking changes are noted in the major version's release notes and in Umbraco-provided installation and upgrade guides. Aside from verifying that third -party components are compatible with the version to which you are upgrading, creating a backup of all modified files, dependent assemblies, ASP.NET user controls, and all configuration files is essential.

The process to complete a version upgrade is generally:

1. Gather information about changes to configuration files.
2. Identify third-party components and related files.
3. Extract the version release from the archive.
4. Copy new or altered files to your installation.
5. Apply changes to configuration files.
6. Run the Umbraco Upgrade Wizard.

After the files are copied and the configuration files are updated, open a browser and navigate to your Umbraco instance. The Umbraco Upgrade Wizard launches and guides you through the process to complete the site upgrade.

Updating your installation's configuration files to properly contain both a new version's required settings and your specific settings is tricky at best. Most users have the most success by using a file difference and merge tool to create new configuration files based on the new file and adding the settings from the older version where no conflict exists.

Some settings will need to be determined based on your specific requirements and the specific version being used for the upgrade — for example, XML schema changes from version 4.0 to version 4.5 and Umbraco user password format — set in `web.config` *— from version 4.5.0 to version 4.5.1.*

UTILIZING UMBRACO STARTER KITS

Umbraco comes with four starter kits to help you get up and running quickly with your Umbraco installation. These include the Simple starter kit, the Blog starter kit, the Personal starter kit, and the Business starter kit. Each of these starter kits contains a collection of document types, templates, and modules that make up a simple but complete site. In addition, you can customize each starter kit with a skin and additional modules (discussed later). You can either install Umbraco starter kits when you install Umbraco or at a later time from the Developer Packages section of the Umbraco backoffice as shown in Figure 1-22.

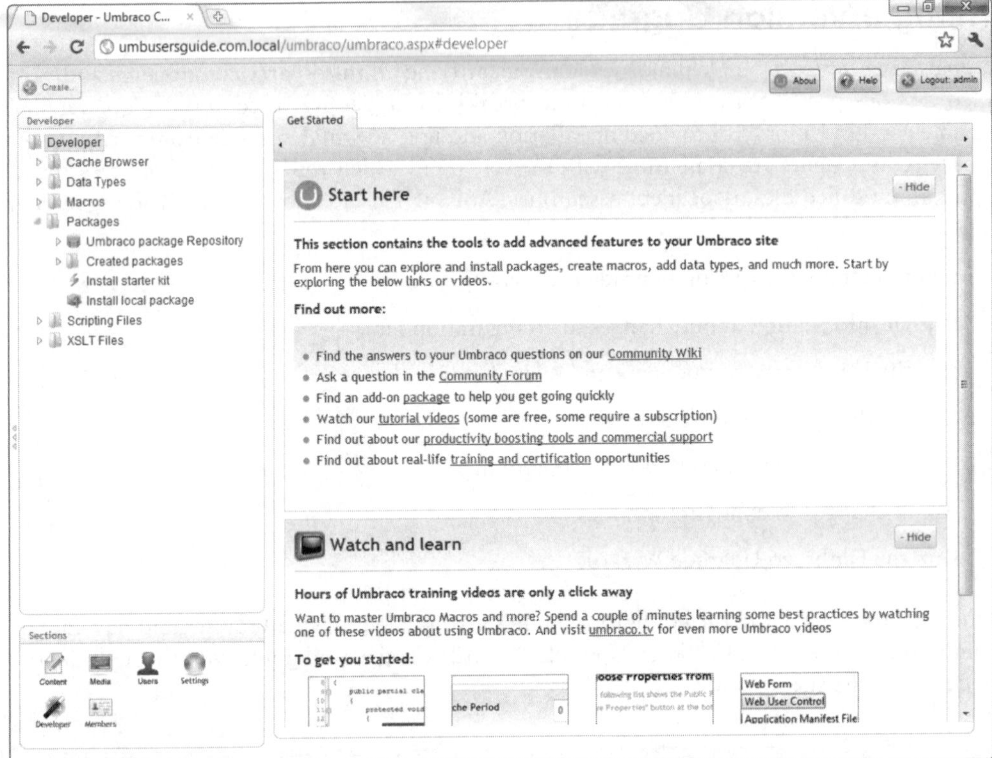

FIGURE 1-22

Installing a Starter Kit

Umbraco starter kits take a best practices approach to site structure. Although the rest of this book deals with the Umbraco building blocks — document types, templates, and such — in great detail, after Umbraco has been installed, the Umbraco starter kits give a simple example of how you should structure a site, which is especially helpful for new Umbraco users. If you didn't install a Starter Kit when you installed Umbraco, don't worry; this section details how to install a starter kit and modules to an existing Umbraco installation.

If you've already installed a starter kit, you made a good choice! With a starter kit installed you have a great starting point with some basic content, templates, document types, and a macro or two. One of the best ways to familiarize yourself with Umbraco, other than reading this book, is to dive in and inspect the structure of the document types, the markup in the templates, and the code in the XSLT macros. Although the included starter kit samples are quite simple, they also represent Umbraco best practices for creating a simple site and its structure.

If you didn't install a starter kit and have now decided you want to install one, simply access the Install Starter Kit option from the Packages tree in the Umbraco Developer section (see Figure 1-23). You can install skins from this section as well.

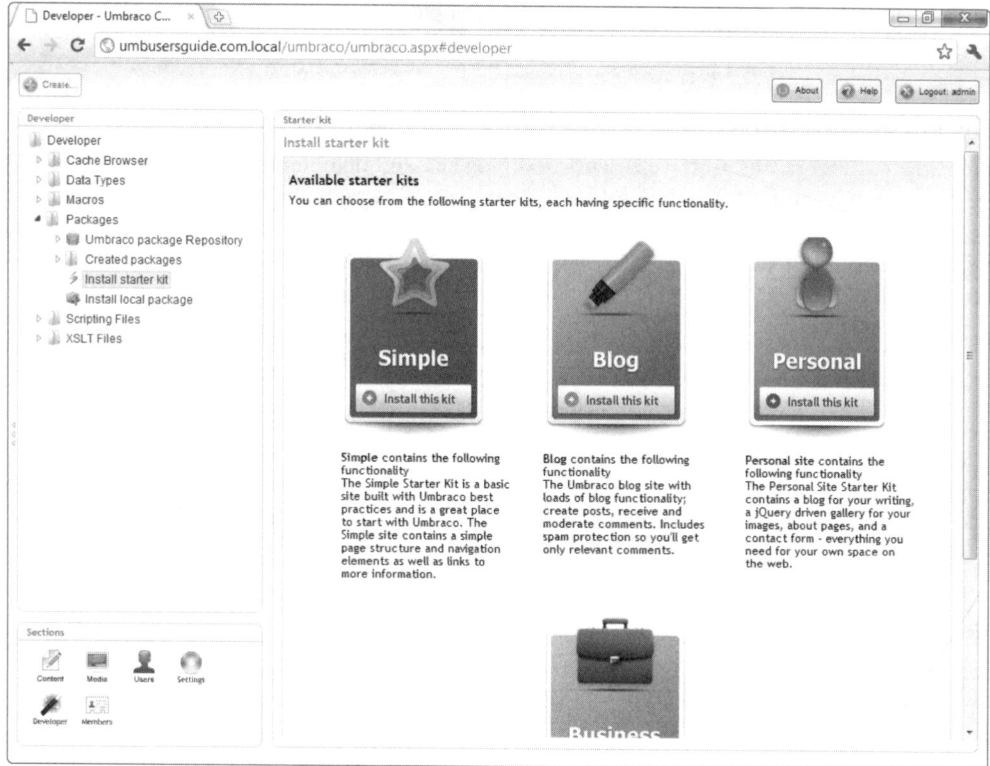

FIGURE 1-23

If you've opted to skip installing a starter kit and want to dive right in, it is best to start by creating a simple document type, template, and content structure to familiarize yourself with Umbraco's structure. Read on in this book for more on how to use Umbraco to create and manage your content. Remember though: the strongest recommendation for new Umbraco users is to install a starter kit and skin when installing Umbraco. Installing and investigating any of the starter kits gives you an overview of how you might structure your own site.

The following sections discuss the various starter kits in detail.

Simple Starter Kit

The *Simple* starter kit is the simplest and most semantically strict starter kit. It has a generic structure and is the prerequisite for many modules and other Umbraco packages. If you are new to web CMS, and Umbraco in particular, you should begin with this starter kit.

The Simple starter kit contains a home page and several subpages along with a navigation module. The Simple starter kit is intentionally missing styling and images in order to focus on the structure. A few minutes spent looking over the Homepage document type and template is time well spent understanding the Umbraco approach to defining data storage and layout.

Blog Starter Kit

The Blog starter kit contains all the elements of a blog site and demonstrates the Umbraco approach to keeping content organized in a date folder format. You can create a new blog post to see this feature in action. After you have given your blog a name, right-click the blog site's home page and select Create, then select Blog Post. Notice that Umbraco creates the folders for year, month, and day automatically.

The Blog starter kit also contains macros that list the latest blog posts on the blog site's home page, list the blog posts in the archive, and allow site visitors to submit comments related to a blog post. The kit even applies a spam filter to submitted comments so your blog site is not inundated with comment spam.

The Blog starter kit is a great example of how you can allow user-generated content, comments in this case, on your site. It's robust enough for you to install and start blogging today without any changes required, or you can use it as the basis for a blog site you customize further.

Personal Starter Kit

The Personal starter kit is a complete site for your own personal home on the web with a summary Homepage and subpages for more about you. The kit also includes a Gallery section where you can feature photos or images you provide in a web-friendly gallery format. The Personal starter kit is also a great starting place for a portfolio site as well where you might feature your own work, whether it is photography, graphics, or poetry.

Business Starter Kit

The Business starter kit is the starting point for a business presence on the web. With the Business starter kit as a beginning, a business can build a meaningful website in almost no time. The Business starter kit includes a blog section, with blog comment moderation tools, a news section, and a built-in contact form. As with all the Umbraco starter kits, you can easily add new functionality or change the default functionality to create the Umbraco site that perfectly fits your needs.

Extending the Starter Kits

The Umbraco starter kits are only a starting point. Each is licensed with the MIT open source license, which allows you to change, add, and remove any feature, code, or layout you want. When you combine the Umbraco starter kits with the knowledge you gain from this book, there are no limits to what you can accomplish.

With the addition of a skin and modules, which are discussed later, creating a complete website without writing one line of code is entirely possible. After you add in some of the advanced techniques discussed later in this book, you will have the platform for building a myriad variety of websites.

APPLYING AND MANIPULATING UMBRACO SKINS

Umbraco skins are created by the Umbraco community members and can be installed from the Developer Packages section of the Umbraco back office. Basically, Umbraco skins enable you to change the look and feel of an Umbraco starter kit simply by applying the skin to a starter kit site. In addition, you can customize skins with user-defined text, colors, and images. Umbraco skins build on the best practices approach of Umbraco starter kits by demonstrating the best way to implement styling and layout control in your site.

When you apply a skin to an Umbraco starter kit site, the skin's styles are used in place of the existing starter kit site's styles. The skin simply provides a unique Cascading Style Sheet (CSS) file, including any images required to achieve the layout defined by the CSS. A skin can also add or change small portions of the starter kit site's HTML templates if needed. You can roll back all CSS, images, and HTML changes to the starter kit's default skin for a site because Umbraco creates a backup of the starter kit's default skin when you apply a different skin.

By default, you can only apply skins to the Umbraco starter kits as opposed to an arbitrary Umbraco site as skins depend on the starter kit's layout. Umbraco automatically determines which skins you can apply to the currently installed starter kit and presents these in the skin selector.

You can select and apply a skin (see Figure 1-24) either when you install an Umbraco starter kit or you can do so at a later time.

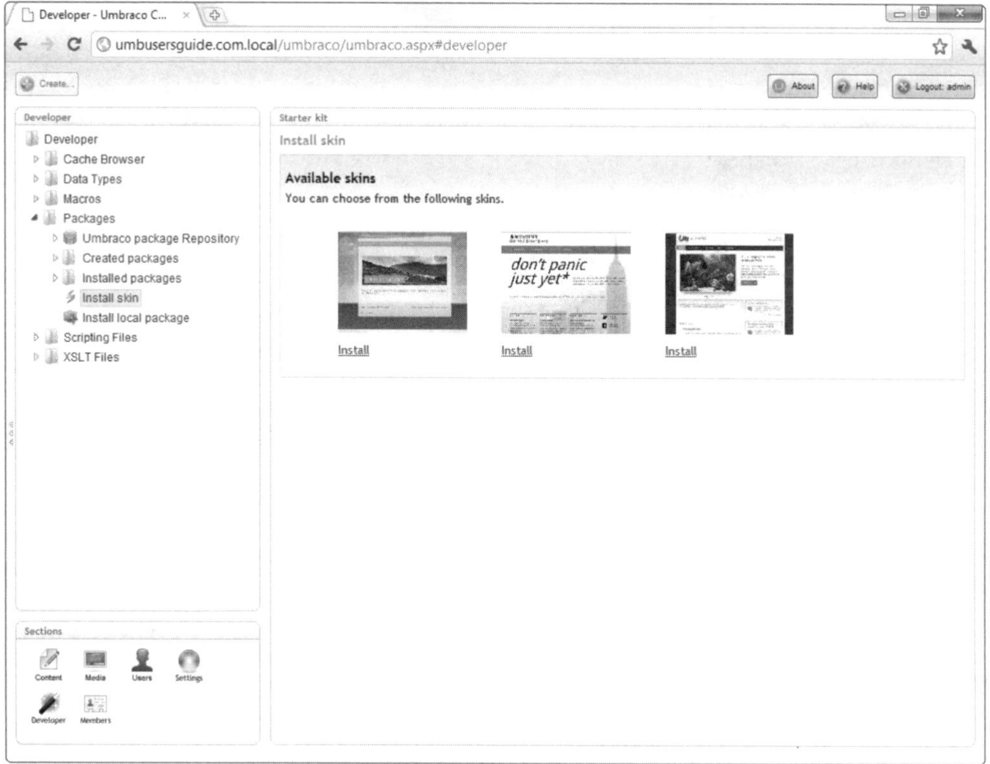

FIGURE 1-24

To access, install, and customize a skin, follow these steps:

1. Navigate to the Developer section, expand the Packages tree and click the Install skin icon. The available skins display in the right pane.

Umbraco skins are stored in a central Internet repository so they can be kept current. An Internet connection is required to browse and install a skin.

2. To install a skin, click the skin icon.
3. To customize an installed skin, navigate to the Settings section, expand the Templates tree, select the Starterkit Master template, and then click the Modify Template Skin button on the right pane toolbar. The Umbraco Customize Skin editor will be launched and you can customize the skin with your own text, colors, and images (see Figure 1-25).

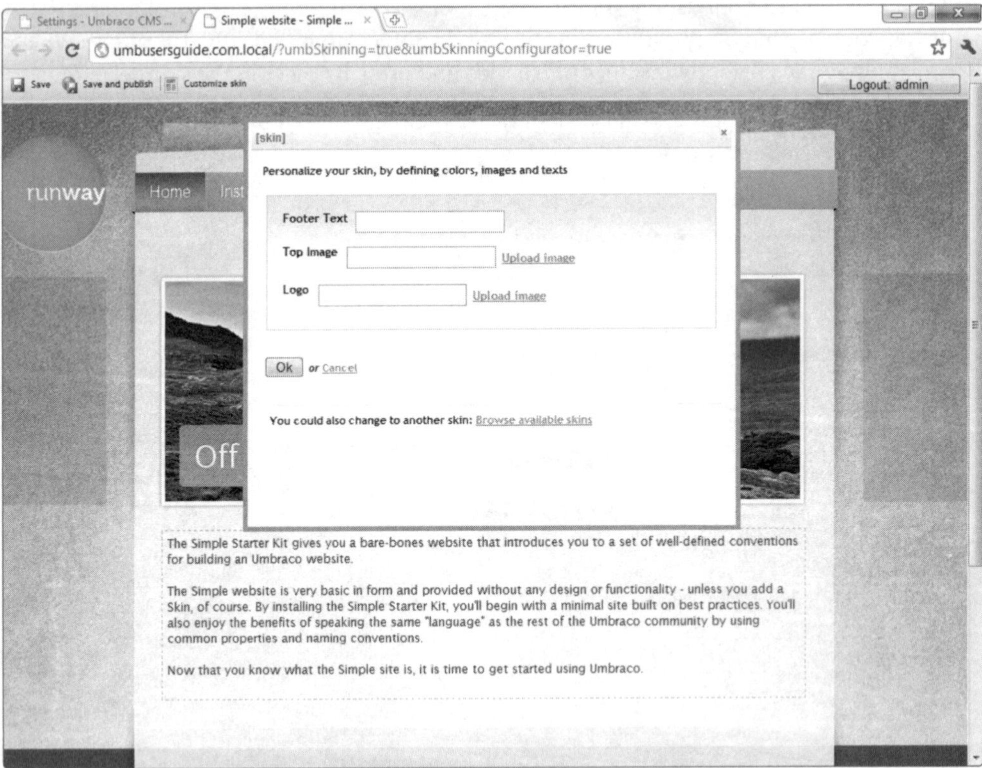

FIGURE 1-25

Customizing a Skin

You can customize an Umbraco skin using only the Umbraco Skin editor with no code required. An Umbraco skin may contain dependencies. Think of these as options that enable you to customize the skin for your own site's use. You can use Umbraco skin dependencies to customize a starter kit site's text, colors, and images. In this way a single skin applied to a single starter kit can be unique from every other Umbraco site with the same starter kit and skin because of the customized text, colors, and images.

When you install a skin, the dependencies defined by the skin author can be set using the Umbraco Skin editor. After a skin has been installed it can be customized.

To customize an installed skin:

1. Navigate to the Settings section, expand the Templates tree, and select the "Starterkit Master" template.
2. Click the Modify Template Skin button on the right-pane toolbar. The Umbraco Customize Skin editor launches.
3. You can customize the skin with your own text, colors, and images. Using the Customize Skin editor you can enter text for text dependencies, choose colors for color dependencies, and choose and edit images for image dependencies (see Figure 1-26).

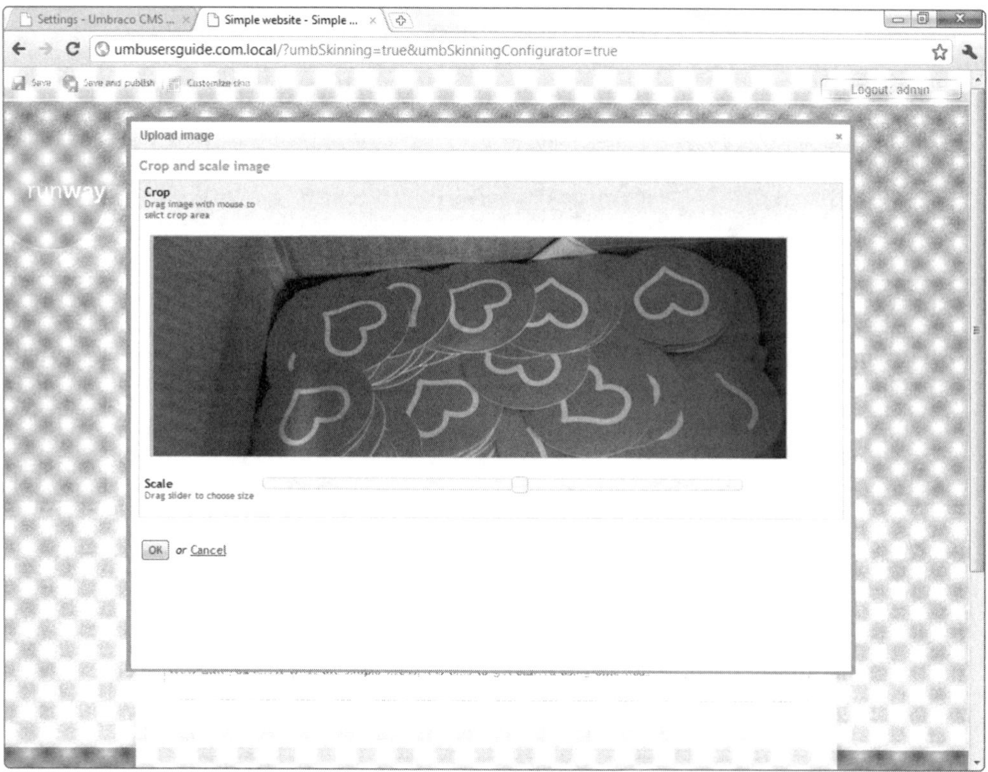

FIGURE 1-26

Modifying a Simple Umbraco Skin

If you're comfortable editing HTML and CSS you can modify a skin further for your own use. At its most basic, an Umbraco skin contains only CSS to achieve the desired changes to a starter kit site's styles. You simply include a reference to the skin's unique CSS file in the starter kit's *MasterPage* template. Don't worry about the terminology yet; this is just an example and all terms you see now are explained fully a bit later in this book. Using this simple example, you can include the following line in the starter kit's MasterPage template so that any styles defined in the referenced CSS file will automatically apply to the starter kit site:

```
<link ref="stylesheet" type="text/css"  src="/css/new_skin.css"></link>
```

When you modify a skin, you may need to add additional elements to a starter kit's MasterPage template in order to apply the desired layout control. To do this, the skin alters the starter kit's default MasterPage template, in this case by adding a single `<div>` element.

The default Runway starter kit MasterPage template contains this markup:

```
<asp:contentplaceholder id="cp_top" runat="server">
 <div id="top">
<h1 id="siteName">
   <a href="/">
    <umbraco:Item runat="server"
                  field="siteName"
                  recursive="true" />
    </a>
   </h1>
   <h2 id="siteDescription">
     <umbraco:Item runat="server"
                   field="siteDescription"
                   recursive="true" />
   </h2>
    <umbraco:Macro Alias="RunwayTopNavigation" runat="server" />
 </div>
</asp:contentplaceholder>
```

A skin might add a `<div>` element, the `<div id="menu" class="container">`, to apply a particular style to the starter kit's navigation sections, as follows:

```
<asp:contentplaceholder id="cp_top" runat="server">
<div id="top">
  <h1 id="siteName">
   <a href="/">
    <umbraco:Item runat="server"
                  field="siteName"
                  recursive="true" />
    </a>
   </h1>
   <h2 id="siteDescription">
    <umbraco:Item runat="server"
                  field="siteDescription"
                  recursive="true" />
   </h2>
```

```
    <div id="menu" class="container">
      <umbraco:Macro Alias="RunwayTopNavigation" runat="server" />
    </div>
  </div>
  </asp:contentplaceholder>
```

In this way an Umbraco skin can insert the HTML needed to achieve the desired styling without affecting the function of the starter kit site in any way.

Typically, a skin should only change the CSS and related images and script for a site. If needed, a skin may also change small snippets of HTML, such as to add an ID to an HTML element or create a new `<div>` for layout control. In this way, skins are kept as independent of a starter kit site's markup as possible and maintain maximum flexibility. A skin may also introduce a unique set of scripts, generally JavaScript, to add functionality related to the skin. In addition, a skin may include images used for layout and styling.

FINDING AND INSTALLING UMBRACO MODULES

Umbraco modules are small pieces of functionality that are compatible with the Umbraco starter kits and are open-source licensed so that you may change the way the modules work if you want. When you install an Umbraco starter kit, such as the Simple starter kit, some modules are installed for you. The top navigation, contact form, and feed viewer are all examples of Umbraco modules.

Umbraco modules are simply Umbraco macros specifically designed to work seamlessly with Umbraco starter kits. The modules may have dependencies on specific starter kit markup, such as an HTML element `id` or a content placeholder `id`. In most cases, you can also use Umbraco modules with Umbraco sites that are not based on Umbraco starter kits. Most Umbraco modules are created without compiled code, which allows you to investigate the module or to alter it for your own specific use. Some modules use XSLT, which you can find in the `/xslt/` folder in your Umbraco site's root. Other modules use ASP.NET, generally C#, code, which is either in the `/app_code/` or `/usercontrols/` folder in your Umbraco site's root.

Some Umbraco modules are installed when you install an Umbraco starter kit.

You can install Umbraco modules directly from the Umbraco Skin editor. When working with the Skin editor for an Umbraco starter kit, do the following:

1. Click the Insert Module button from the toolbar. A list of available modules appears as shown in Figure 1-27.
2. Select a module and then click the area on the page labeled with Module Placeholder where you want to locate the module.

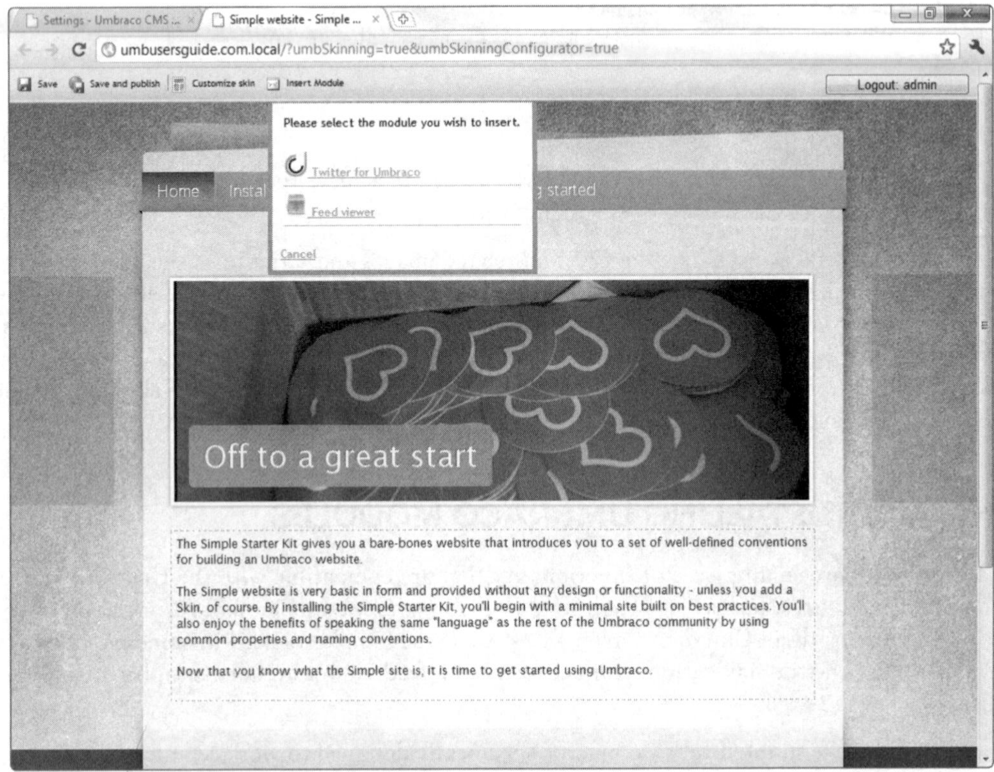

FIGURE 1-27

You can learn more about Umbraco macros in Chapter 5.

TAKE HOME POINTS

After reading this chapter, you should feel comfortable installing Umbraco for the first time. Besides knowing how to install Umbraco using the Web Platform Installer or manually, you should know what to do in special environments and how to upgrade Umbraco. In addition, you should understand the purpose of a Starter Kit and a skin. The following list outlines what you should be "taking home."

- You should use the Microsoft Web Platform Installer for an error-free installation.
- You must pay close attention to your website's user permissions during manual installation.
- You should use the sample checklist provided when upgrading
- Installing a Starter Kit is a quick way to get your site installed.
- You can install a Skin to make your site beautiful.
- Skins are easy to customize for your own use.
- Modules are small features that you can easily add to a Starter Kit.

The Umbraco Approach

- How do you effectively separate content from structure?
- How is the Umbraco backoffice set up?
- How is Umbraco's XML cache structured?
- What's the difference between new and legacy XML schema?
- How do you use the Umbraco admin panel and sections?

This chapter discusses and explores how Umbraco works under the hood. Umbraco's many features make it an especially efficient content engine. The most prominent feature is how it caches the content and makes it available at lightning speeds to the end user. This is all done using an XML cache and the .NET XSLT transformation engine.

If you want to extend the functionality of your XSLT output you can easily do so using XSLT extensions. Also, the .NET XSLT parser is based on the XSL 1.0 specification. Although you can extend your .NET installation using libraries, such as Saxon, to gain access to XSLT 2.0, there is a good chance that you do not need those libraries for working in Umbraco. Chapter 5 covers both XSLT stylesheets and XSLT extensions in depth.

This chapter also provides a detailed overview of the Umbraco backoffice, how and why it's set up the way it is, and best practices examples.

SEPARATING CONTENT AND STRUCTURE

Before you learn about the details of how Umbraco ultimately presents the content, take a look at what it means to separate content from structure. Umbraco has a very clear separation of tools and responsibilities when it comes to maintaining content and layout — structure, design, and media assets. Although Chapter 4 discusses the separation of layout and structure in greater detail, right now the focus is primarily on Umbraco's toolsets and interface.

Understanding the Umbraco Backoffice Structure

The *backoffice*, also known as the admin user interface, is made up of sections, as shown in Figure 2-1. A *section* is an area of the backoffice that contains specific functionality targeted at predefined roles, such as for a developer, an editor, and the like. A set of standard sections comes with every Umbraco installation. However, given the extensibility of the Umbraco application programming interface (API) you, as a developer, can also create your own custom sections (covered in the samples starting in Chapter 15). The following discussion breaks down and covers the backoffice sections.

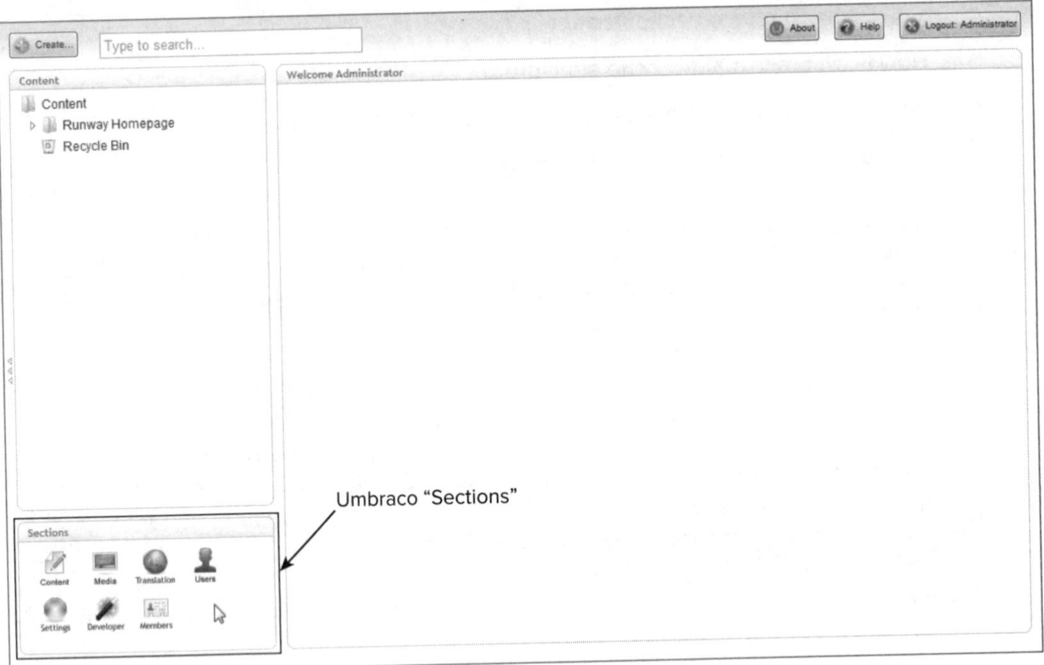

FIGURE 2-1

Each and every section within the Umbraco backoffice is made up of *trees*. These trees contain *nodes* that are made up of the various types of content — media items, content pages, users, permissions, and so on.

WHAT IS A NODE?

This book refers to the various pieces of content as *nodes*. These, in their respective contexts, are pages, users, folders, images, files, templates, and so on.

The benefit of dividing the interface into these sections is that now you can have multiple roles working within the same site and assign the specific sections to them that they need, or rather should, have access to. For example, a content editor and non-technical person should not have access to the Developer section, ever! If you allow that type of access, you're introducing a host of problems for yourself, including a potential site crash!

If you change a template, stylesheet, script, or XSLT macro in the backoffice, you have no way to undo that change after you have navigated away from the window/section. Also, a save to any of these files is instantaneously available to the end user (no save versus publish feature is available on styles, scripts, master pages, or XSLT files). A negligent change can cause you to end up with a trashed site. So, tread carefully.

The author advises, and discusses in detail in this book, that you do not maintain styles, scripts, masterpages, and XSLT files directly within your installation; rather, that you manage these files in a source control environment such as SVN, CVS, or Visual SourceSafe. Appendix C covers the methods and best practices of this type of file management.

Creating a User with Restricted Access

In this section, you create a new user and restrict the sections to which she has access. Follow these steps:

1. Log in using the administrator (admin) account that you created as part of the setup process in Chapter 1 and navigate to the Users section, available in the lower-left corner of the backoffice interface as shown in Figure 2-2.
2. Right-click the Users node in the tree and click the Create menu item.
3. In the Create dialog, type in **Content Editor** as the user's name, as shown in Figure 2-3.
4. Click the Create button.
5. Set all the various user properties for the user's details (discussed in detail in the following sections), as shown in Figure 2-4.

6. Set the start node for both the Content and Media sections. This setting determines where and what the user can access when she logs in. Setting the start node is helpful if you have specific authors for specific areas of the Content and Media trees.

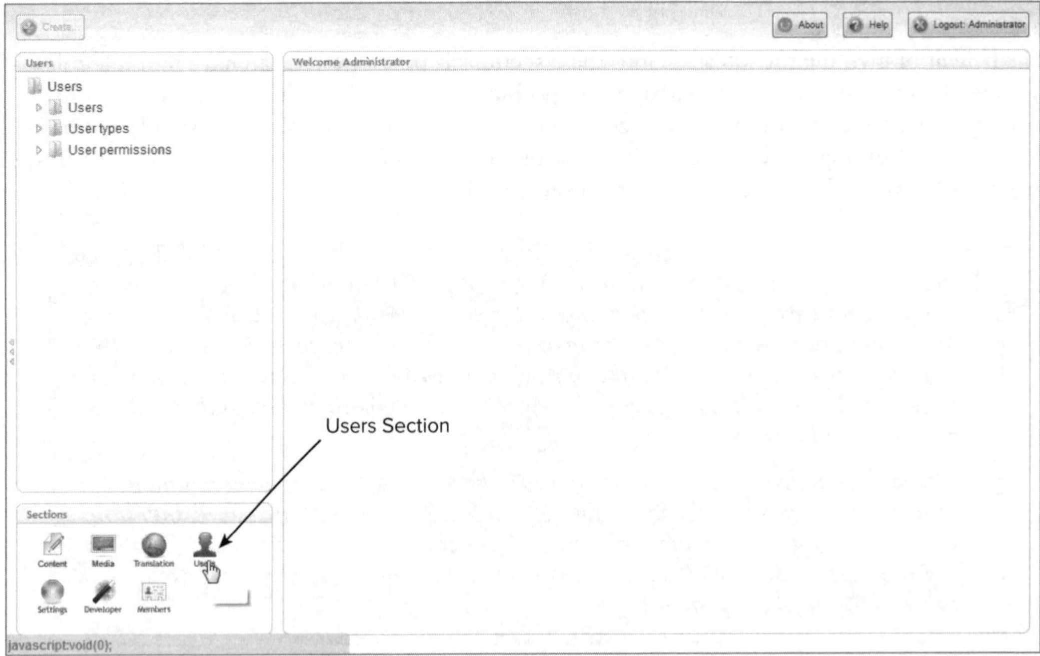

FIGURE 2-2

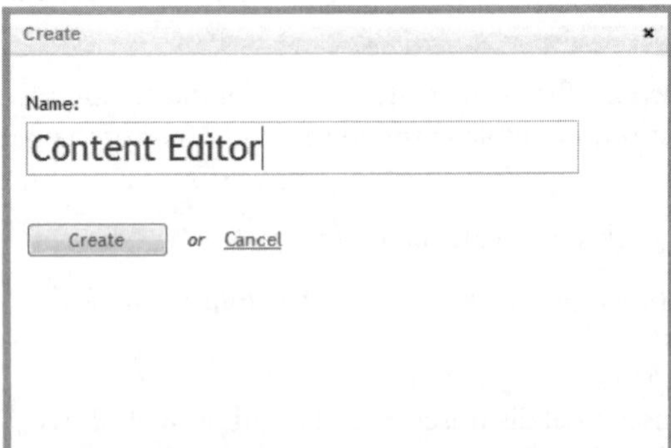

FIGURE 2-3

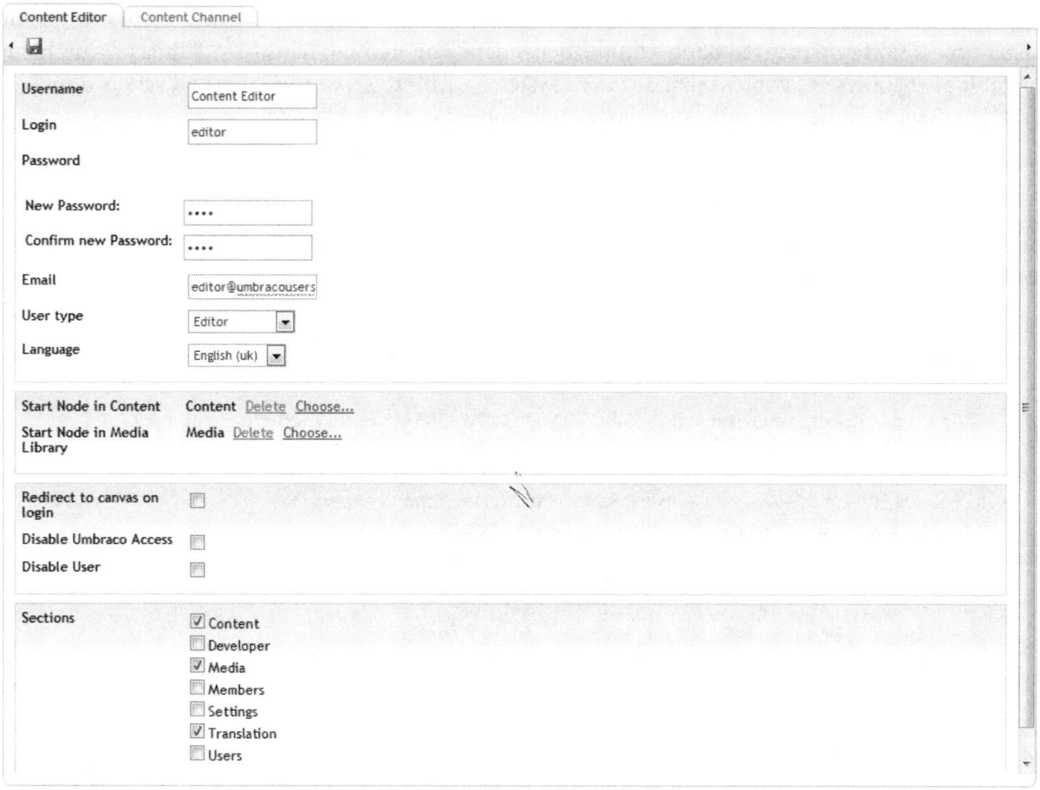

FIGURE 2-4

UMBRACO CONTENT TREE

The Umbraco data model is supported by a number of *relational* databases. Out of the box, the data layer supports Vista DB, SQL CE, SQL Server, and MySQL databases. As of this writing, it does not support Oracle. Having the properties stored in a relational database makes persisting data convenient and provides developers with an industry standard for working with data. The Umbraco backoffice works directly with the installed database when saving and retrieving content nodes, media items, document types, users, and more. Because the authoring environment will not receive thousands of requests by hundreds of users at the same time, interacting directly with the database is not a performance consideration. If you had a very high-trafficked backoffice, you could run Umbraco in a distributed load-balanced environment. Chapter 13 briefly covers this topic.

Even though the supported databases are all *multi-threaded*, with thousands of requests coming in at the same time, the serving of content would eventually be hampered, resulting in a slow-responding website — not a desired outcome. Umbraco has a way to resolve this issue by providing the content and media items via a file-based, in-memory XML cache. This cache allows for much faster access to the structured data, and the dependency on making trips to a database is no longer there. It also allows the content management system (CMS) to separate published versus unpublished content because only published nodes will appear in the XML cache.

As of Umbraco version 4.5, the XML schema changed drastically from older versions. Now the XML output is a closer representation of your document types and content structure.

In Listing 2-1 you can see a representation of the legacy schema XML. This is what the XML cache looks like in versions prior to Umbraco 4.5.

LISTING 2-1: LegacySchemaSample.xml

```
<node id="1188" version="d45e540f-3162-417d-9861-fb49b13c567a" parentID="1130"
level="2" writerID="0" creatorID="0" nodeType="1052" template="1045"
sortOrder="1" createDate="2010-10-01T12:00:00" updateDate="2010-10-
01T12:01:00" nodeName="Sample Page" urlName="sample-page"
writerName="Administrator" creatorName="Administrator"
nodeTypeAlias="ContentPage" path="-1,1130,1188">
    <data alias="pageTitle">Page Title</data>
    <data alias="umbracoNaviHide">0</data>
    <data alias="pageHeading">Page Heading</data>
    <data alias="bodyText"><![CDATA[<p>HTML content here.</p>]]></data>
</node>
```

Listing 2-2 is a sample, using the same data as in Listing 2-1, of the new XML schema. As you can see, the tags now represent the property names as opposed to Listing 2-1 where the `<data>` tag was used for all fields. It may not look like much of a change, but it makes a big difference when working with XSLT files in your macros (covered in Chapter 5 and Chapter 11).

LISTING 2-2: CurrentSchemaSample.xml

```
<Textpage id="1188" parentID="1130" level="2" writerID="0" creatorID="0"
nodeType="1052" template="1051" sortOrder="1" createDate="2009-11-20T15:50:02"
updateDate="2010-08-30T13:12:27" nodeName="Sample Page" urlName="sample-page"
writerName="Administrator" creatorName="Administrator" path="-1,1130,1188"
isDoc="">
    <pageHeading>Page Heading</pageHeading>
    <bodyText><![CDATA[<p>HTML content here.</p>]]></bodyText>
    <pageTitle>Page Title</pageTitle>
    <umbracoNaviHide>0</umbracoNaviHide>
</Textpage>
```

When upgrading from a version prior to 4.5, you can choose to set Umbraco to read the legacy schema so that you are not forced to update XSLT macros and other custom functionality. See Appendix B for more details on upgrading and settings.

So, how does this difference matter in how you work with the XML cache? In short, it improves the readability of your code while also reducing the amount of data that's in memory because it reduces the number of attributes for a given tag. Listings 2-3 and 2-4 show the difference between the 4.x schema stylesheet and the 4.5 schema stylesheet.

LISTING 2-3: OutputTextPageOldSchema.xsl

Available for download on Wrox.com

```
<ul>
    <xsl:for-each select="$currentPage/node [@nodeTypeAlias =
string('TextPage') and string(data [@alias='umbracoNaviHide']) != '1']">
        <li>
            <a href="{umbraco.library:NiceUrl(@id)}">
                <xsl:value-of select="@nodeName"/>
            </a>
        </li>
    </xsl:for-each>
</ul>
```

LISTING 2-4: OutputTextPageNewSchema.xsl

Available for download on Wrox.com

```
<ul>
    <xsl:for-each select="$currentPage/* [name() = string('TextPage') and
 string(umbracoNaviHide) != '1']">
        <li>
            <a href="{umbraco.library:NiceUrl(@id)}">
                <xsl:value-of select="@nodeName"/>
            </a>
        </li>
    </xsl:for-each>
</ul>
```

You may not notice a big difference between the two preceding listings, but you will notice that instead of cluttering the code with the extra attribute selectors, you can simply target the various properties or tags as defined in the document type that supports this content. Chapters 5 and 11 provide far more detailed examples of the differences.

The code listings in this chapter are partial and incomplete. To get more complete solutions, please review Chapters 5 and 11 or see the XSLT templates provided in your Umbraco installation by choosing Developer ➪ XSLT Files and then right-clicking Create menu item.

UMBRACO BUILDING BLOCKS

Umbraco consists of several different sections that, together, make up the comprehensive tool that Umbraco is. The following section discusses what each one of these does and how to appropriately assign them to users.

Understanding the semantic and functional split between these sections is important to you as a developer and implementer of the CMS. You can think of it like the process of building a house where each phase of the project has dedicated roles and responsibilities. Much like it is up to the mason to build a strong and lasting foundation, your job is to do the same with templates, layouts, document types, and styles for the editor to leverage for saving and publishing content.

RESTRICTING ACCESS IS BOTH IMPORTANT AND NECESSARY

I have found in numerous projects that keeping non-technical editors and writers away from the more advanced sections within the Umbraco backoffice is important. Providing access to templates and document types to someone who "knows enough to be dangerous" inevitably leads to a disaster because it allows them to make real-time changes to the website's infrastructure and integrity. How to restrict access should be part of your training phase when deploying your implementation at the client site.

To paint a picture, imagine in the earlier house building analogy that you, as the homeowner, were allowed to mix the concrete for the foundation. Unless you're an expert at concrete, chances are your foundation might crumble with time!

Content

You guessed it! The Content section is where all the content is managed within Umbraco and where most of your admin users will spend their time. In the Content section, content types that you have set up as a developer become available for the editor and/or writer to use for content creation.

You must give special attention to the content Properties tab, which you will always see as part of the right pane for all document types. Figure 2-5 shows that you can control a number of settings for the node in the Properties tab:

- **Name:** This setting controls not only the name of your node but also the URL of the page on the front end of your site. So, if you change it, you also change the URL for the page.
- **Created by:** This is the user who created the node in the first place.
- **Created:** This indicates when the node was created.
- **Id:** This is the internal ID of the node. In Umbraco, various methods use this ID; for example, `NiceUrl(id)`, which generates a search engine optimization (SEO)-friendly URL.
- **Document Type:** This indicates with which document type this node is associated.

After a node has been created, you cannot change the document type because different document types will have, in most cases, vastly different properties. This means that if you filled in a value for the First Name field in one document type, it may not exist in the next, rendering the ability to change document types after node creation useless. Instead, if you need the ability to have different output for similar content, consider creating a document type that supports common properties and instead allow multiple templates for that document type. Chapter 4 discusses this approach in detail.

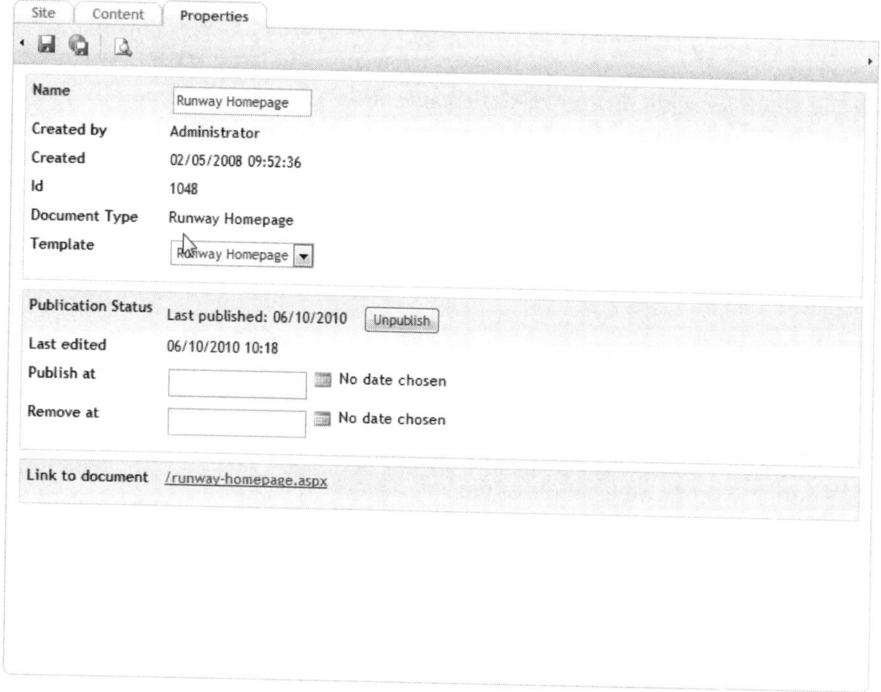

FIGURE 2-5

- **Template:** This shows the template associated with the page. This field can have multiple values because a page could take on multiple shapes based on the specified template (covered in Chapter 4).
- **Publication Status:** If the node is published, then the date when the node was last published is displayed, along with a button to Unpublish the node.

If you unpublish the node that you're currently on, the entire site becomes unpublished and rendered inaccessible to the end user. Be careful where you use this function.

- **Last edited:** The date when the node was last saved.
- **Publish at:** You can specify when a particular node should be published. This allows you to be on vacation and still have that critical press release go live right on time!
- **Remove at:** Similar to Publish at, this setting automatically unpublishes the node at the specified date and time.
- **Link to document:** This provides you with the various links through which this page is accessible.

The link to document field would have multiple entries if you had specified more than one entry in the hostnames setting for the Umbraco website. This setting can be managed by right-clicking the homepage node of your website and is discussed in detail in Chapter 7.

Most of the options in the context menu (shown in Figure 2-6) on the Content nodes are self-explanatory. However, some deserve your attention for further explanation:

- **Edit in Canvas:** This option allows you to edit the content node within the template. A menu bar is provided at the top of the screen and you can edit the content inline. This feature is useful if users want to be able to see how the changes directly affect the page while editing. Figure 2-7 shows an example of this interface.
- **Manage hostnames:** This option allows you to set the node's root domain. It is typically used in a multisite environment or subdomain situation for multilingual sites.
- **Permissions:** The next section discusses permissions in detail, but here you can limit the actions for particular users on individual nodes. Items left unselected will not be available to the user in this context menu. See Figure 2-8 for an example.

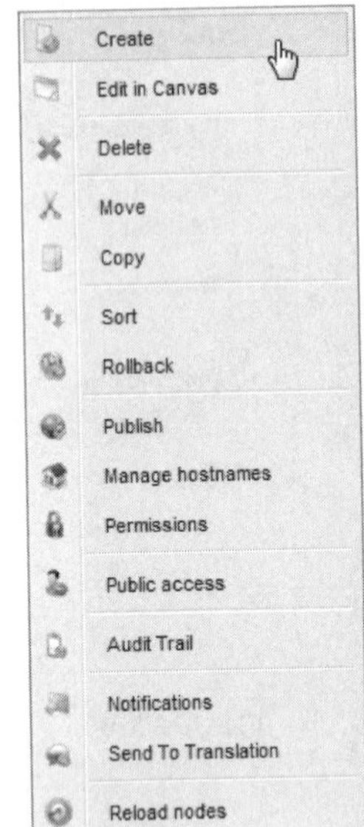

FIGURE 2-6

Furthermore, you can configure a user to automatically start editing in canvas mode if that is his or her preference.

- **Public access:** This function allows you to set up which member groups are allowed to access the node from the front end. You manage members and member groups in the Members section. The beauty of this is that Umbraco leverages the standard .NET Membership Provider for this. See the "Members" section in this chapter for more details.
- **Notifications:** You can set up notifications based on several different events, as shown in Figure 2-9. The notifications are sent automatically to the email address configured as part of your user details.

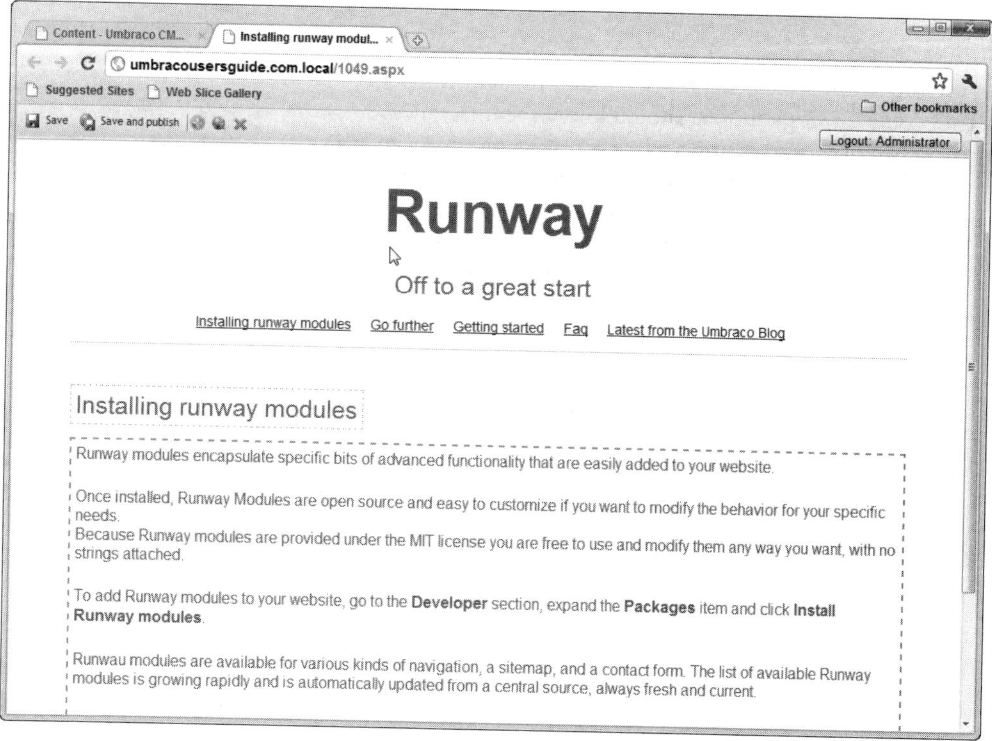

FIGURE 2-7

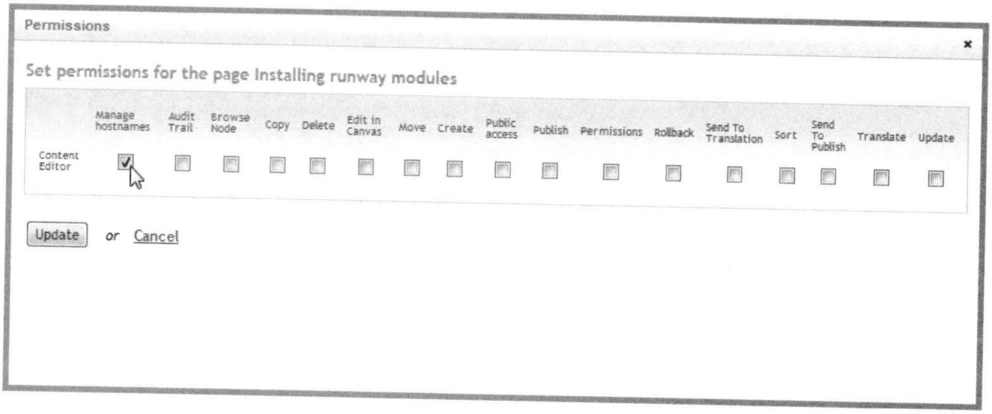

Permissions

Set permissions for the page Installing runway modules

	Manage hostnames	Audit Trail	Browse Node	Copy	Delete	Edit in Canvas	Move	Create	Public access	Publish	Permissions	Rollback	Send To Translation	Sort	Send To Publish	Translate	Update
Content Editor	☑	☐	☐	☐	☐	☐	☐	☐	☐	☐	☐	☐	☐	☐	☐	☐	☐

Update or Cancel

FIGURE 2-8

Users

Before reading the general discussion of what the Users section provides you, you should know the difference between users and members — a common question, to say the least. It's quite simple actually; a *user* is an account that has access to the Umbraco backoffice and all that this entails, whereas a *member* is an account that has access to restricted content on the front end, like a client login or extranet (see the "Members" section later in the chapter).

Having said that, read on to find out what the Users section does.

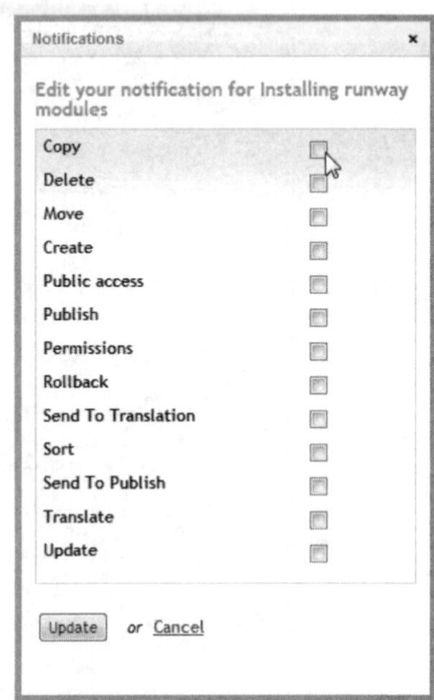

FIGURE 2-9

Functions and Properties

The Users section manages the administrators, editors, writers, translators, and whatever other custom user types you may have defined. This section is where you add and edit users that have access to the Umbraco backoffice. As shown in Figure 2-10 and Table 2-1, a number of properties exist for each user in the system.

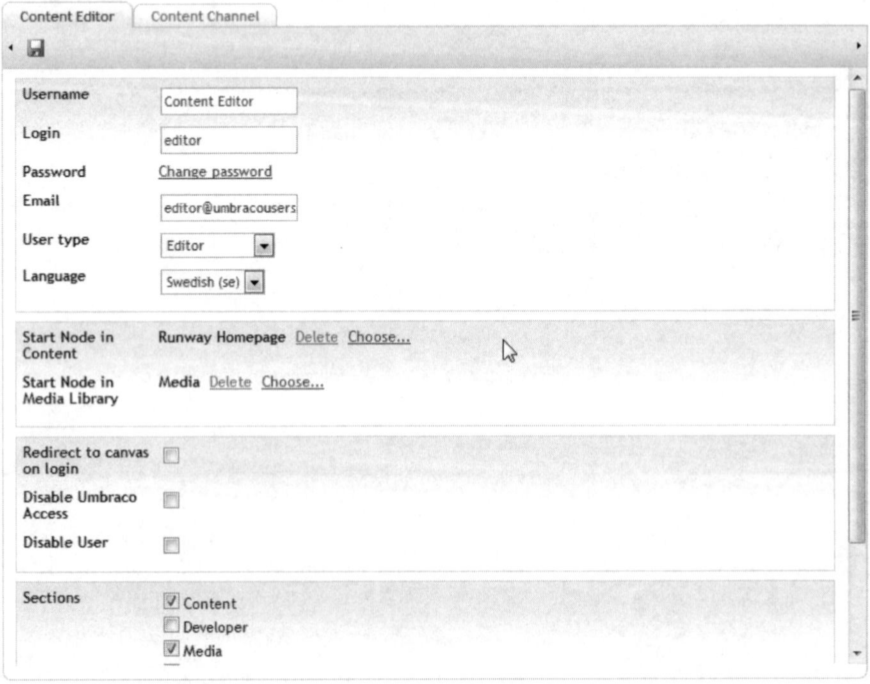

FIGURE 2-10

TABLE 2-1: User Account Properties

FIELD GROUP	FIELD	DESCRIPTION
User Properties	Username	The full name of the user.
	Login	The username that will be used to log in to Umbraco.
	Password	The user's password. Passwords are encrypted in Umbraco and can therefore not be retrieved from the system. If a user has lost his password, you must perform a reset.
	Email	The user's email address, used for system notifications if configured.
	User Type	This designation is important. Make sure to classify your user correctly. All user types have access to their designated sections. The type determines what they have access to in said sections based on pre-set permissions. ➤ **Administrator:** As the name suggests, the user has full access to all features in the Umbraco backoffice and receives system notifications, such as updates and critical patches, via the notification *bubble*, which appears in the lower-right corner of the backoffice interface. ➤ **Editor:** Has access to both the Save and Publish functions in the Content section, as well as other content features (discussed later this chapter). ➤ **Writer:** Has access only to the Save function in the Content section and cannot publish content to the end user. ➤ **Translator:** Has access only to Save and Send for review to the original author. The preceding settings are the default out-of-the-box settings in Umbraco. You can edit each of these sets of default permissions in the User Types section and also add your own custom user types.
	Language	Sets the language of the backoffice. It is set and controlled by standard .NET localizations features and is controlled in various setting files (discussed in Chapter 7).
Content Access	Start Node in Content	Determines which node in the Content tree the user should start in. That is, the user will have access to the selected node and all the children below that node.

continues

TABLE 2-1 *(continued)*

FIELD GROUP	FIELD	DESCRIPTION
	Start Node in Media Library	Determines which node in the Media tree the user should start in. That is the user will have access to the selected node and all the children below that node.
Status and Edit Mode	Redirect to canvas on login	This option places the editor in Canvas mode instead of the Umbraco backoffice. Canvas mode allows an editor to work with content in the context of the page that renders this content so that the editor sees the changes in real-time rather than in the admin backoffice.
	Disable Umbraco Access	Prevents the user from accessing the Umbraco backoffice, but the user account is still active.
	Disable User	Disables the user and prevents login.
Section Access	Sections	Determines which sections (including custom sections) the user should see when logging in.

After a user account has been created you cannot delete it. You must use the Disable User option to prevent future logins.

User Types

As discussed earlier, user types allow you to assign user accounts with predefined sets of permissions on the content tree. If one of the predefined user types does not fit your needs, you can create your own custom types. As shown in Figure 2-11, you will notice that the label for this user is kind of whacky — it has braces around the name. The braces mean this value is pulled from the localization files so that if the language is set to something other than English, the name is translated.

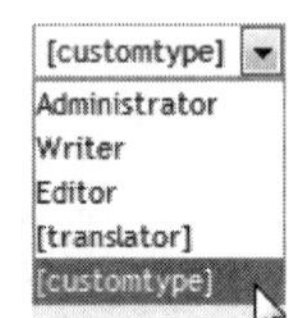

FIGURE 2-11

Setting Up a New Dictionary Label

In this exercise, you will set up a label for a new user type so that it can be read correctly in various languages.

1. In the left pane, under the Users node, right-click User Type and click the Create menu item.
2. In the User type Name field, type in the name of the new user type (without spaces).
3. Select the various default permissions, as shown in Figure 2-12, for the new user type. Click the Save icon.

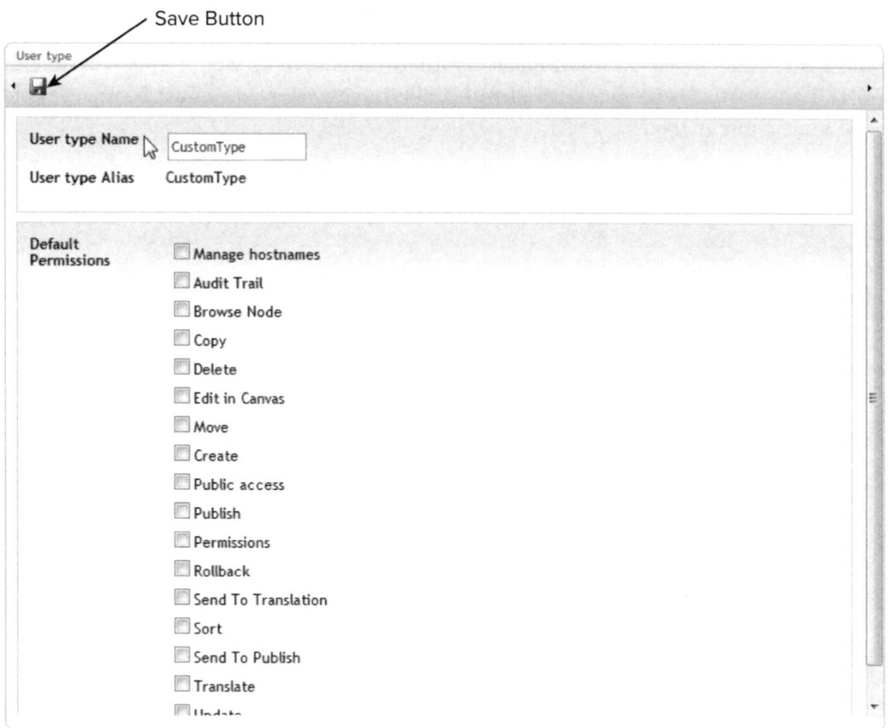

FIGURE 2-12

If you navigate to the details of Content Editor, you will see that the value in the drop-down list is surrounded by braces "[ ]." To change that value, follow these steps:

1. Navigate to your language settings folder: `<install root>\umbraco\config\lang`.
2. Open the associated language file to which you want to add the key and value (in this example, `en.xml`).
3. Find the section that begins with `<area alias="user">` and add the following to this section: **`<key alias="yourAliasHere">Your User Type Name Here</key>`**.
4. Repeat steps 1–3 for the other languages that you need (and know the translation for). That's it!

Permissions

In addition to the flexibility of the aforementioned user settings, Umbraco also comes equipped to handle more granular permissions on a per-user basis. This capability might come in handy when you have individual users who have special permissions but do not warrant a custom user type.

User permissions and access only apply to the content tree and nothing else.

Setting Up a User for Access to Multiple Start Nodes

As shown in Figure 2-13, you can set permissions at another dimension as well, namely by one or more content nodes. This feature is particularly useful if you have a user who must have access to multiple sections of your content tree.

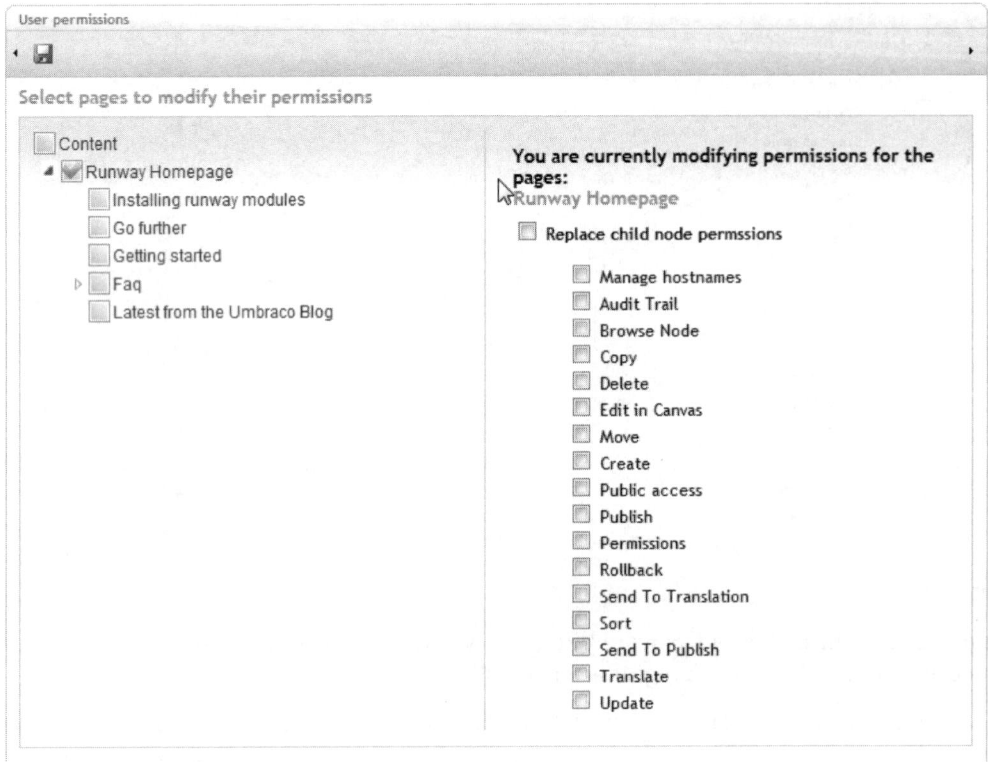

FIGURE 2-13

The following steps show you how to set up a user to have multiple start nodes in the content tree, effectively bypassing the settings of the user's account.

1. Set your user's start node (see the Content Access item in Table 2-1) under Content Access to the home node, Runway Homepage.
2. Expand the User permissions node in the left pane and select the name of your user from the resulting nodes.
3. Select the Runway Homepage check box, as shown in Figure 2-14.
4. Deselect all the boxes in the right pane.
5. Make sure to select the Replace child node permissions check box and then click Save, as shown in Figure 2-15.

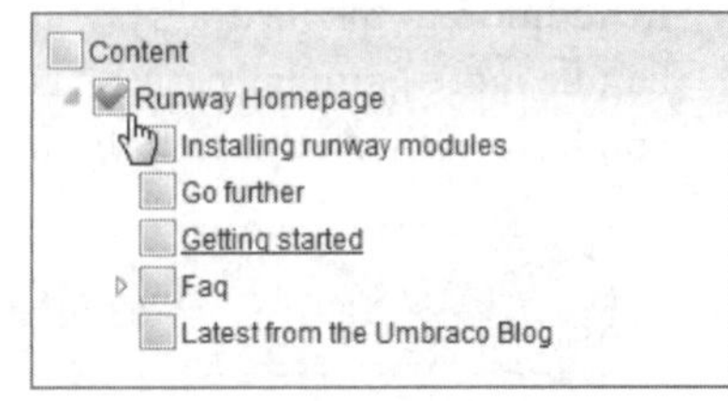

FIGURE 2-14

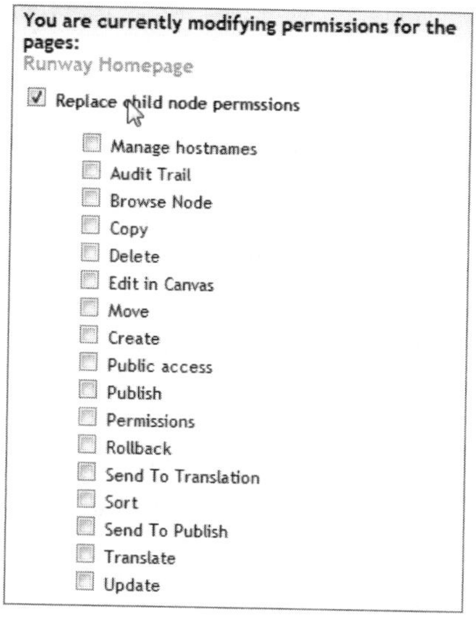

You are currently modifying permissions for the pages:
Runway Homepage

- [x] Replace child node permssions
  - [ ] Manage hostnames
  - [ ] Audit Trail
  - [ ] Browse Node
  - [ ] Copy
  - [ ] Delete
  - [ ] Edit in Canvas
  - [ ] Move
  - [ ] Create
  - [ ] Public access
  - [ ] Publish
  - [ ] Permissions
  - [ ] Rollback
  - [ ] Send To Translation
  - [ ] Sort
  - [ ] Send To Publish
  - [ ] Translate
  - [ ] Update

FIGURE 2-15

6. Deselect the Runway Homepage node and expand the rest of the tree.
7. Select at least two nodes in the children of Runway Homepage and apply the necessary permissions (be sure to include the Browse permission or the user won't see any of the nodes).
8. Again, select the Replace child node permissions check box to cascade the settings to any child nodes.

You can also set permissions on a page-by-page basis in the Content section. Reference Chapter 8 for more details on how this approach works.

Media

The Media section is fairly short and sweet because it simply deals with asset management such as images, files, and folder structure. Umbraco is not a document management system, and it doesn't claim to be. It provides just enough functionality to provide a content editor with a way to easily manage website assets and organize them.

If you are looking for advanced features, such as image cropping, resizing, text overlay, batch uploads, and more, be sure to check out the Umbraco community projects page on `http://our.umbraco.org`*. See Chapter 10 for more details about packages.*

Three different types of media are supported out of the box in Umbraco, as shown in Table 2-2 and Figure 2-16.

TABLE 2-2: Media Types and Properties

MEDIA TYPE	DESCRIPTION	AVAILABLE PROPERTIES
File	Use this type with any non-image assets such as PDF files, Word documents, or any file type that you need to upload.	➤ **umbracoFile:** This field holds the MediaId. This ID can be targeted to retrieve the full file path using built-in methods provided as part of the Umbraco API. Chapter 5 covers this property in detail. ➤ **umbracoExtension:** This field holds the type of file that was uploaded and returns the extension, such as .pdf, .doc, and so on. ➤ **umbracoBytes:** This field holds a string with the number of bytes of the file size that was uploaded.
Folder	Enables you to simply upload your images and files into an organized folder structure that you can set up to fit your needs.	➤ **contents:** This field is a folder browser that enables you to see what the contents of the folder is (if images, a thumbnail is shown).
Image	Images are treated a little differently than a standard file because they have different properties in the web landscape that you want to target. Notice that when you upload an image, additional fields display in the right pane to accommodate attributes specific to an image, such as height and width.	➤ **umbracoFile:** Holds the MediaId. You can target this ID to retrieve the full file path using built-in methods provided as part of the Umbraco API. Chapter 5 covers this property in detail. ➤ **umbracoWidth:** Holds a string value representing the width of the image in pixels. ➤ **umbracoHeight:** Holds a string value representing the height of the image in pixels. ➤ **umbracoExtension:** Holds the type of file that was uploaded and returns the extension, such as .gif, .png, and so on. ➤ **umbracoBytes:** Holds a string with the number of bytes of the file size that was uploaded.

Folders are useful for providing access to specific areas of your Media section. The process of setting up a user's start node in the Media section is discussed in the Content Access item in Table 2-1.

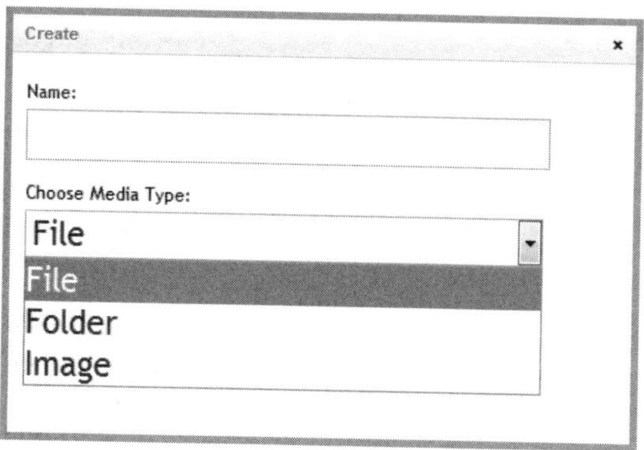

FIGURE 2-16

Settings

As the name suggests, the Settings section provides access to all the Umbraco-specific settings. Most of the nodes in this section have their own chapters in this book (as noted in the following list):

- **Stylesheets:** This is where you add new stylesheets and manage individual styles for inclusion in the rich-text editor (RTE). Chapter 4 provides the details of how to work with styles and the rich-text editor.
- **Templates:** Create and manage the website's .NET MasterPages (see Chapter 4 for details).
- **Scripts:** This node allows you to manage JavaScript and XML files for use in the CMS. See Chapter 4 for additional details.
- **Dictionary:** Manage labels and other values used to set dynamic content based on the user's locale and language settings (see Chapter 6).
- **Languages:** Manage the languages that should be set up for the end users of the website and also for the backoffice users.
- **Media Types:** Allows you to add additional media types for use in the Media section.

You can add media type properties in the Settings section, but for now the Umbraco backoffice will not display those properties in the media details. As of this writing, that feature is still unimplemented.

- **Document Types:** This is where you will manage and set up the entire structure of your website. Each node that is created in the Content section will be based on one or more of the document types that you define in this section. Chapter 5 covers document types in great detail.

Developer

The Developer section provides controls that enable you to extend Umbraco with custom functionality and extend it using the rich API. Many of the nodes in this section are covered in other chapters, but here's an overview of what they are:

- **Cache Browser:** This allows you to see what is in the Umbraco application memory cache. It is useful for troubleshooting or reviewing site performance.
- **Data Types:** The items under this node make up the fields that are on the content editor's user interface for any given document type. So, when you put a rich-text editor on a document type (covered in Chapter 3), you are essentially pulling it from here. You can configure the settings for the various data types for each one in this node.

Check out Chapter 12 for some examples on how to create your very own data types!

- **Macros:** Chapter 5 discusses what macros are and what they do in detail, but for now suffice it to say that they provide the gateway for a developer to embed custom functionality in the CMS-generated content.
- **Packages:** Packages provide a way for developers and webmasters to install custom functionality that others have developed. Chapter 10 covers a couple of classifications of packages in more detail and also shows you how to install them and even create your own.
- **Scripting Files:** If you are a fan of Ruby, LOLCode, or Python, you can use it to extend Umbraco just like you would with a .NET user control. Chapter 5 covers this topic further and also provides some examples.
- **XSLT Files:** As you probably know by now, Umbraco is operated largely on its XML cache. As a developer, you can gain access to this cache via XSLT stylesheets and transform the data to fit your needs. Chapters 5 and 11 cover XSLT macros.

Members

The Members section is where you manage accounts with access to the public website. As an administrator you can use this interface to add member accounts, groups, and types. With this interface, you can now set access restrictions on nodes within your content tree.

Some configuration changes are required in the `Web.config` *to make member types functional. Because access restrictions are so specific to your particular implementation, creating a member type and defining it as the default in* `Web.config` *is necessary. This process is discussed as part of the examples in Chapter 12.*

The Members section is broken down into three separate main nodes. As mentioned earlier, the member groups and member types will be specific to your implementation and are therefore left blank by default.

- **Members:** This is where all of the members are grouped into alphabetical folders to make finding individual members easy. As shown in Figure 2-17, when an individual letter is clicked a list of all the members appear in the right-hand pane.

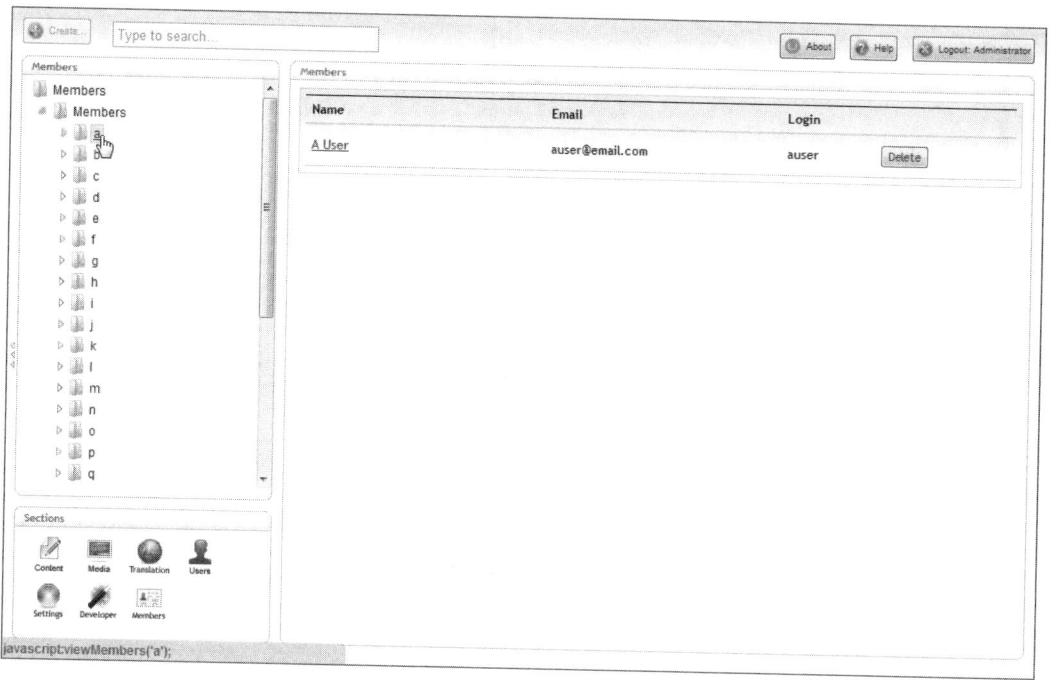

FIGURE 2-17

- **Member Groups:** This is used to provide role-based access to content nodes where public access is restricted. Each member must belong to one or more member groups.
- **Member Types:** This is used to define member profiles and associated properties. Chapter 12 provides examples and the details of how member types affect the login process.

Creating a Member Group

Creating a member group is the first thing you want to do. Members must belong to a member group to be able to log in. Follow these steps:

1. Log in to your Umbraco website.
2. Navigate to the Members section.
3. Right-click Member Groups and click the Create menu item.
4. Enter a name in the Create dialog that appears. Click the Create button, as shown in Figure 2-18.

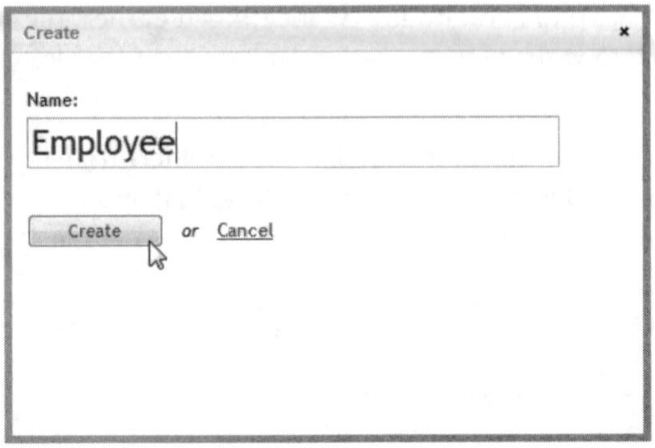

FIGURE 2-18

Creating a Member Type

Member types define the properties of a member account. As such, it is the second item that you should define in a blank Umbraco installation.

1. In the left pane under the Members node, right-click Member Types and click the Create menu item.
2. Enter a name for the member type in the Create dialog that appears and click the Create button.
3. In the Generic Properties tab, listed at the top of the right pane, set the required properties for this member type, such as address, shoe size, or whatever else is needed for your particular implementation, as shown in Figure 2-19.

Email address, name, and password are all captured as part of the standard member properties. In addition to these standard fields, you can add fields specific to your needs.

4. Save the new member type by clicking the Save icon, as shown in Figure 2-20.

Translation

The Translation section provides users with a way to access the translation workflow that comes standard with your Umbraco installation. If you choose to use this workflow, make sure that you designate users in the Users section with the Translation user type so that content editors and writers can assign content to those users for translation.

Have a look at Appendix D for a full overview of how to implement the translation workflow.

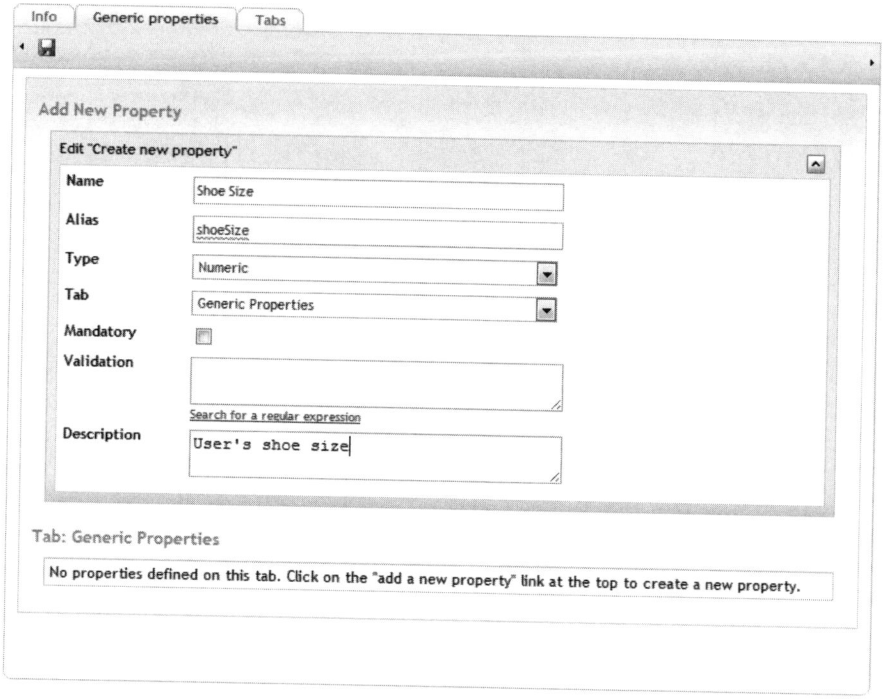

FIGURE 2-19

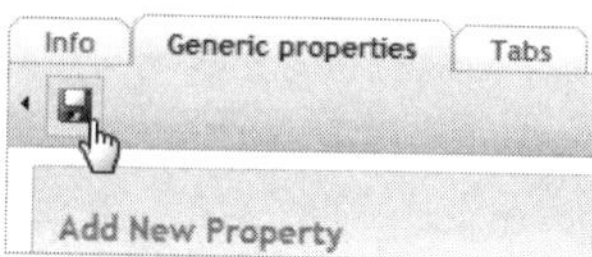

FIGURE 2-20

TAKE HOME POINTS

At the end of this chapter you should feel comfortable navigating the Umbraco backoffice. In addition, you should have a deeper understanding of how Umbraco implements the concepts of user management, settings management, and the general process of working with content. At a high-level this is what you should be "taking home."

- How to configure the backoffice and public website view for your particular needs.
- How to add and manage Umbraco users.
- How to support members for the public website.
- An understanding of what each section of the Umbraco backoffice does.

3

Document Types

- What are document types?
- How do you organize your site using document types?
- How do you work with document types outside of Umbraco?
- What are document type properties and which ones have special meaning?

This chapter covers all you need to know about the backbone of the content tree in Umbraco, which is made up of various document types. The simplest way to think about a document type is to visualize it as an object with various fields that hold data, similar to how a database table is set up in a relational database. The fields that you define for these document types determine how the data is stored in the database — that is, `Nvarchar`, `Ntext`, `Date`, and `Integers` — as well as how the user will interact with that data, in the form of the chosen Umbraco data type (covered more in Chapter 12). For the purposes of this chapter, it's sufficient to know that a data type is equivalent to an HTML input field that is used to enter content into the CMS.

See Appendix D for a comprehensive list of descriptions of each data type that come standard with your Umbraco installation.

In addition, this chapter covers the benefits of nesting document types and how to best design your site structure from the start to provide support for a flexible content structure.

THE DATA MODEL

As mentioned in Chapter 2, Umbraco persists all of its data to whatever installed database you chose to use as part of the installation process. This also includes storing all the document type properties in a key-value format. As you can see in Figure 3-1, quite a few tables make the document type "wheel" spin.

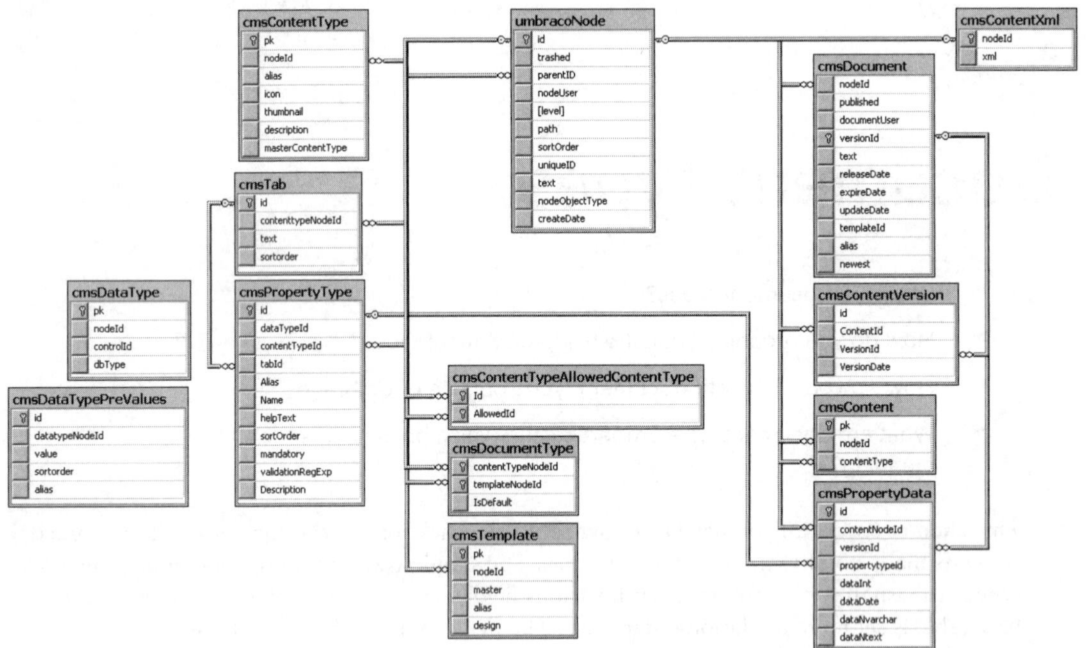

FIGURE USED WITH PERMISSION FROM HENDY RACHER

FIGURE 3-1

So, for every document type you create, you can also create a virtually endless number of properties, also known as fields. The structure you create here is going to dictate what the editor is allowed to create in the content tree and, in effect, how the final website will be structured.

Using Figure 3-1, you can tell the relationship between the various tables that make up the document type as a whole. At the end of the day, you don't have to worry too much about these relationships, but at least you have an overview of how the database(s) is made up.

This chapter covers more about the importance of designing your content structure before you start to build out your site. In a way, creating your document types forces you to think about how to organize your content. At this stage, you'll want to carefully structure your document types to keep the content input short and concise for your editors.

FLEXIBLE CONTENT STRUCTURE

Because Umbraco is built on such a loosely coupled design, you, as the administrator and developer, are provided with an endless combination of variations for structuring your site. As a result, thinking about what your sitemap should look like before you dig in is extra important. As a general rule, try to design the first two to three levels of your site before you start building out your document types.

It's recommended that you use a sitemap, mindmap diagram, or similar tool when you're in the analysis phase of your project. Doing so enables you to relatively quickly create a hierarchical structure and start to visualize what your site will ultimately look like. A quick Google search can yield all sorts of options for you.

Although the flexibility of Umbraco is great, knowing what level of control you should provide to the site's editors is important. The following sections describe how you can limit and control this structure intimately, providing a user-friendly experience for the end user and a proper setup for search engine optimization (SEO) purposes.

Creating a Document Type

To start, go over the interface used to maintain your document types. Navigate to the Settings section and click the Document Types node in the left pane. If you followed the installation steps outlined in Chapter 1, you should see several document types listed already, as shown in Figure 3-2.

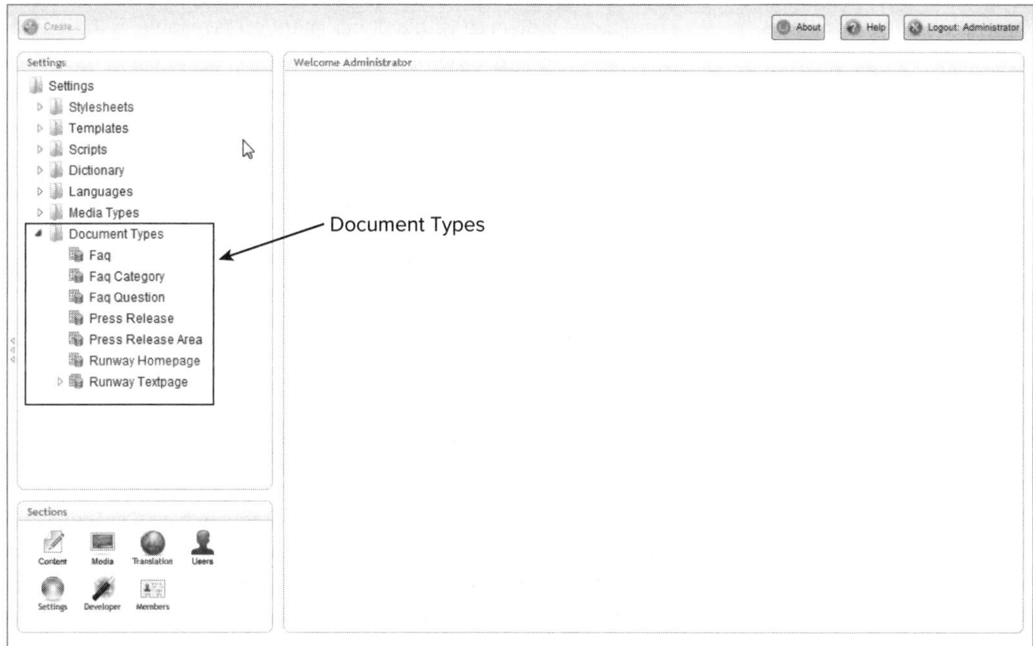

FIGURE 3-2

Figure 3-3 shows how the document type management section is made up of four tabs. These tabs are located in the right pane when you click a document type under the Document Types node. Table 3-1 provides a description of each tab and field.

FIGURE 3-3

TABLE 3-1: Document Type Tabs and Fields

TAB	FIELD	DESCRIPTION
Info	Name	The name of the document type as it is identified in the backoffice user interface (UI).
	Alias	Important for macros, especially XSLT macros, where you will want to target certain document types. The value in this field is used to drive the node names in the XSLT cache file in Umbraco 4.5 as well as what is found in the `documentTypeAlias` attribute in Umbraco 4.0.x.
	Icon	The icon that is displayed in the content tree next to the node that is created using this particular document type.
	Thumbnail	The image selected here is shown when you're creating a new content node in the pop-up dialog.
	Description	A short description shown in the pop-up dialog when you're creating a new content node.
	Allowed Templates	A list of all available templates, as found in the Templates node. Templates indicated with a check mark are available in the content properties after a content node has been created using this particular document type.
	Default Template	Indicates which template should be the default template when you're creating a content node from this particular document type. Not changeable if only one template is marked as allowed.
Structure	Allowed Child Nodetypes	Lists all the document types and restricts which document type(s) you can create as children of the selected document type.
Generic Properties		Use this to add new properties, otherwise known as fields, to your document type. This can include a wide variety of built-in data types as well as custom ones you create (covered in Chapter 10). You'll want to split up your properties across one or more tabs to render the editor's user interface well organized and intuitive.
Tabs	New Tab	Allows you to enter the name of a new tab, such as Content, Description, or whatever fits your document type. Below this field is a listing of all the existing tabs. In the examples used in this chapter, the Description tab has already been created. Also notice that you can set the sort order of the tabs.

To make your content tree look richer and more specific to your implementation, consider installing the FamFamFam icon set from the package repository (covered in Chapter 10). This set extends the basic list of icons provided as part of the installation and are made available to you in the Icon list mentioned in Table 3-1.

Creating a new document type takes just a few steps:

When creating your document type, start by creating the required tabs under the Tabs tab so that you can associate the properties to the correct tab under the Generic Properties tab later.

1. Right-click Document Types, and then click the Create menu item.
2. In the Create pop-up dialog that appears, as shown in Figure 3-4, leave the Master Document Type value as None and type in **Press Release** as the name of your new document type. Leave the Create matching template check box selected, because you use this template in the next chapter to output the content from this document type. This selection simply creates a new blank template in the Templates node, also located in the Settings section.

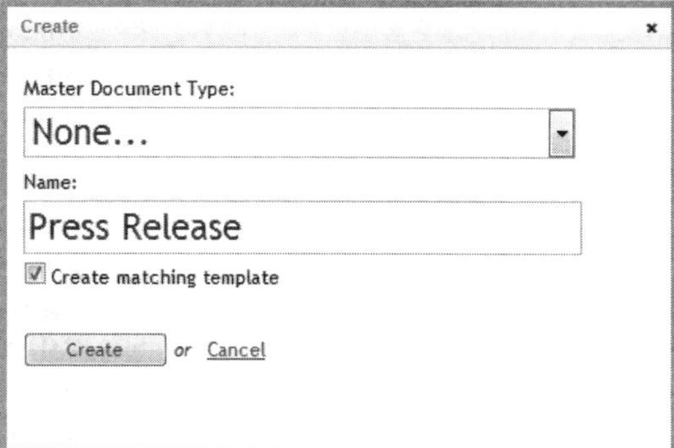

FIGURE 3-4

3. Click the Create button. The right-hand pane refreshes and you will now see, as described in Table 3-1, the Info tab selected.

See how the Alias value was automatically concatenated to remove any spaces from the name? This is intentional, because it will be the value used to name these nodes in the XML cache and also how you will target the newly created document type later on in your XSLT and .NET macros.

4. Select the Doc Pic icon in the Icon drop-down menu and choose `docWithImage.png` as the Thumbnail. Provide a short overview of what this document type does in the Description field.

Because you elected to create the matching template automatically in step 2, Umbraco pre-selects the Press Release template and sets it up as the default for you.

5. Navigate to the Tabs tab and create a tab called **Press Release Details.**
6. Save the document type to avoid losing changes.
7. Navigate to the Generic Properties tab and create the properties listed in Table 3-2, as shown in Figure 3-5, clicking the Save icon after creating each property.

TABLE 3-2: Properties for the Press Release Content Type

PROPERTY NAME	PROPERTY DETAILS
`Press Release Content`	➤ **Name:** Press Release Content ➤ **Alias:** `pressReleaseContent` ➤ **Type:** Rich-text Editor ➤ **Tab:** Press Release Details ➤ **Mandatory:** Yes (select) ➤ **Validation:** Leave this value blank for this field. ➤ **Description:** Content area for text and images
`Press Contact Name`	➤ **Name:** Press Contact Name ➤ **Alias:** `pressContactName` ➤ **Type:** Textstring ➤ **Tab:** Press Release Details ➤ **Mandatory:** Yes (select) ➤ **Validation:** Leave this value blank for this field. ➤ **Description:** Name of press contact
`Press Contact Phone`	➤ **Name:** Press Contact Phone ➤ **Alias:** `pressContactPhone` ➤ **Type:** Textstring ➤ **Tab:** Press Release Details ➤ **Mandatory:** Yes (select) ➤ **Validation:** `^[2-9]\d{2}-\d{3}-\d{4}$` ➤ **Description:** Phone number of press contact
`Hide from menus?`	➤ **Name:** Hide from menus? ➤ **Alias:** `umbracoNaviHide` ➤ **Type:** True/False ➤ **Tab:** Generic Properties ➤ **Mandatory:** No (unselected) ➤ **Validation:** Leave this value blank for this field. ➤ **Description:** Hide item from menus and macro output

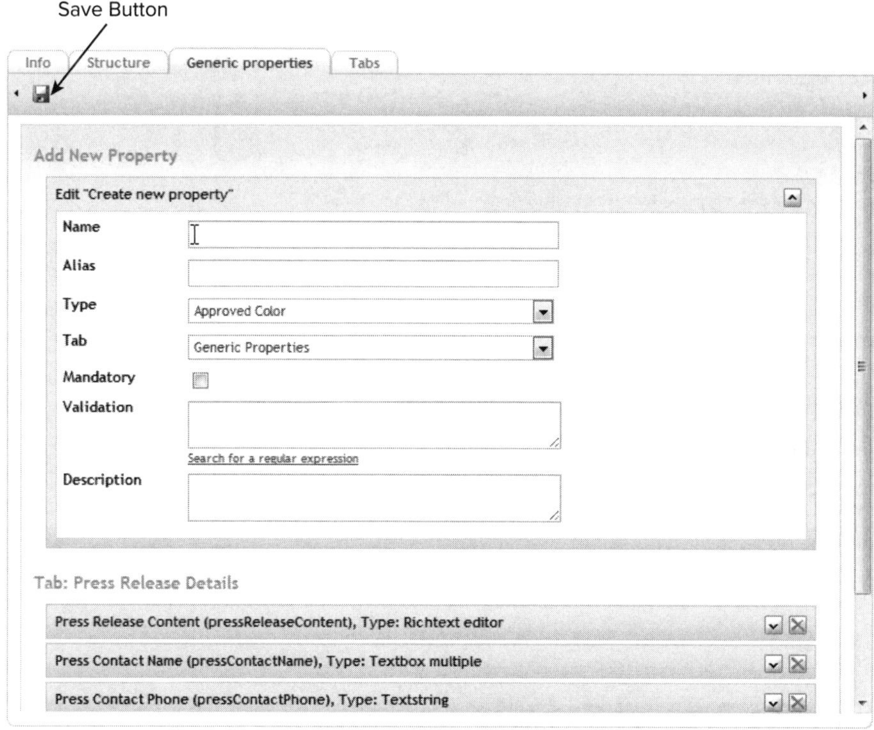

FIGURE 3-5

Several notes concerning these properties:

- **Alias:** Umbraco automatically fills in the Alias for you, removing special characters and creating a *camel-cased* value. If you want your alias to be different than the autogenerated value, feel free to change it.
- **Validation:** What's with the validation value for the Press Contact Phone? It's a *regular expression*, and yes, it looks cryptic to say the least. Regular expressions allow you to check strings against a defined pattern. Luckily, Umbraco has a built-in regular expression library for common validations like phone numbers, e-mail addresses, numeric values, currency, and much more. To utilize this feature, simply click on Search for a regular expression. As shown in Figure 3-6, simply use keywords to search for a matching expression and select the one that you need by clicking on the title. Search results are retrieved from `www.regexlib.com`.
- **Hide from Menus?:** The alias of the Hide from Menus field is a bit of a special Umbraco property. The name of this property has become a standard in the community and is used in XSLT templates as well.

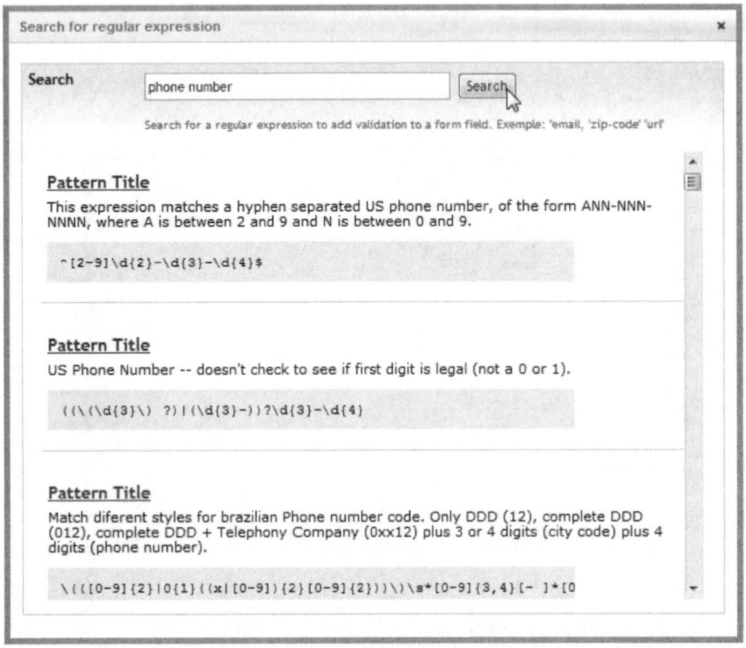

FIGURE 3-6

Restricting the Type of Content

You have now created a document type with the necessary settings and properties. However, if you tried to add a press release to your site you would see no option to do so yet — other than adding the press release as a new root node to the content tree. Umbraco is set up this way so that various types of content can be restricted as to where it lives within the content tree. This feature is helpful for a number of reasons. The most notable and clear example is in the case of a press release. Chances are that the website you're working on will have different authors for different types of content. In the example here, a PR person may be dedicated to writing press releases. Wouldn't it be nice if you could restrict the type of content that he or she can create? Well now you can.

To complete the example, create a press release container where your PR person can post all the press releases as shown in these steps:

1. Repeat steps 1–3 from the Creating a Document Type section earlier in the chapter to create a new document type, and name it **Press Release Area.**
2. Leave `folder.gif` selected for the Icon. Similarly, leave `folder.png` selected for the Thumbnail.
3. In the Structure tab, select Press Release in the Allowed child nodetypes list.
4. In the Tabs tab, create a tab called **Press Contact.**
5. In the Generic Properties tab, add the properties in Table 3-3, clicking the Save icon after creating each property.

TABLE 3-3: Press Release Container Document Type

PROPERTY NAME	PROPERTY DETAILS
`Press Contact Name`	➤ **Name:** Press Contact Name ➤ **Alias:** `pressContactName` ➤ **Type:** Textstring ➤ **Tab:** Press Release Details ➤ **Mandatory:** Yes (select) ➤ **Validation:** Leave this value blank for this field. ➤ **Description:** Name of press contact
`Press Contact Phone`	➤ **Name:** Press Contact Phone ➤ **Alias:** `pressContactPhone` ➤ **Type:** Textstring ➤ **Tab:** Press Release Details ➤ **Mandatory:** Yes (select) ➤ **Validation:** `^[2-9]\d{2}-\d{3}-\d{4}$` ➤ **Description:** Phone number of press contact

The reason you're recreating the same fields for this document type is because later on, when you work with templates in Chapter 4, you learn to recursively display the press contact name and phone number if none are entered for an individual press release.

Now you have a contained structure where only the Press Release document type nodes can be created under the Press Release Area, and nothing else. So, when your PR person logs in and sees the Press Releases node in the content tree, all he or she can add are press releases. To finish this setup, you must do one last thing, which is to allow the Press Release Area document type to be created under the Runway Homepage document type (so you can create the container for the PR person to access later). The steps involved in finishing up this setup are as follows:

1. Navigate to the Settings section in the Umbraco backoffice.
2. Expand the Document Types node and click the Runway Homepage document type.
3. Select the Structure tab by clicking it in the top of the right-hand pane.
4. Select Press Release Area document type as shown in Figure 3-7.
5. Save the Runway Homepage document type.

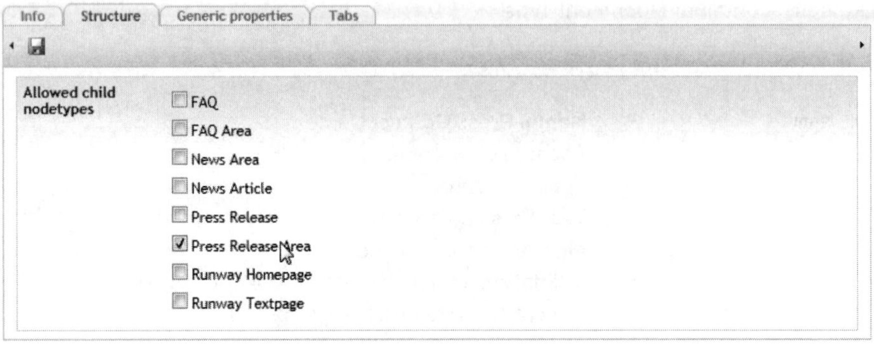

FIGURE 3-7

Using Parent Document Types

Parent document types allow you to share fields among multiple different document types. In fact, the previous exercise could have been structured in this fashion to share the Press Contact Name and Press Contact Phone fields among the Press Release Area and Press Release document types, removing the requirement to re-add the same properties to multiple document types. In that case, however, doing it for two separate document types isn't too difficult. However, this section looks at another case where this functionality makes more sense.

You want to add additional content to your site in the form of events, news, and clients. All of these would have at the very least some page content, and as with other content nodes, you may also want to be able to hide them from the navigation. The Runway Textpage document type already contains these fields, so why not use that as your base?

The structure you create using parent document types has no bearing on the Allowed child nodetypes' functionality, which means that even though, for example, an Event document type is created under Runway Textpage, you still must allow the Event type under Runway Textpage, or whatever type Events can be added under, for it to work.

In the following exercise, you can see how leveraging the power of master document types to create additional ones saves you from duplicating common properties such as the ones covered earlier. Events can consist of many properties, but for the purposes of this example the properties in Table 3-4 will suffice.

Another prime example of using master document types is to add commonly used properties such as META tags, which can then be recursively displayed through the use of Umbraco tags (covered in Chapter 4).

TABLE 3-4: Master Document Types

PROPERTY NAME	PROPERTY DETAILS
`Event Summary`	A short version of the full description of the event
`Body Text`	The detailed description of the event
`Event Start Date/Time`	The start date and time of the event
`Event End Date/Time`	The end date and time of the event
`Hide from menu`	The ability to hide the event from menus and other output through macros (covered in Chapter 5)

Here are the steps for using master document types:

1. Right-click the Document Types node, and then click the Create menu item.
2. In the resulting Create pop-up dialog, select Runway Textpage in the Master Document Type.

You cannot change the designation of master document types after the document type has been created. You must delete the document type and start over if you did not mean to assign a master. This is due to the enforced relationship of parent/child properties in the database.

3. Type in **Event** as the name of your new document type and leave the Create matching template check box selected.
4. Click the Create button to continue. Notice that the tree in the left pane refreshes, and the Runway Textpage has an arrow next to it, indicating that the Event document type was created as a child node, as illustrated in Figure 3-8.
5. Create a new tab called **Event Details.**
6. Add the properties shown in Table 3-5 to the Event document type, clicking the Save icon after you create each property.

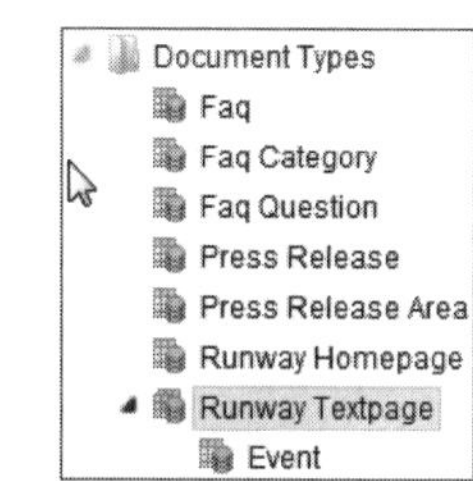

FIGURE 3-8

The Generic Properties and Tabs tabs provide a reminder saying that you must edit master document type properties on the related master document type itself, as shown in Figure 3-9.

TABLE 3-5: Properties to add to the Event Document Type

PROPERTY NAME	PROPERTY DETAILS
`Event Title`	➤ **Name:** Event Title ➤ **Alias:** `eventTitle` ➤ **Type:** Textstring ➤ **Tab:** Event Details ➤ **Mandatory:** Yes (select) ➤ **Validation:** Leave this value blank for this field. ➤ **Description:** Leave this value blank, as it is obvious what it's for.
`Event Summary`	➤ **Name:** Event Summary ➤ **Alias:** `eventSummary` ➤ **Type:** Simple Editor ➤ **Tab:** Event Details ➤ **Mandatory:** Yes (select) ➤ **Validation:** Leave this value blank for this field. ➤ **Description:** Leave this value blank, as it is obvious what it's for.
`Event Start Date/Time`	➤ **Name:** Event Start Date/Time ➤ **Alias:** `eventStartDateTime` ➤ **Type:** Date Picker with Time ➤ **Tab:** Event Details ➤ **Mandatory:** Yes (select) ➤ **Validation:** Leave this value blank for this field. ➤ **Description:** Leave this value blank, as it is obvious what it's for.
`Event End Date/Time`	➤ **Name:** Event End Date/Time ➤ **Alias:** `eventEndDateTime` ➤ **Type:** Date Picker with Time ➤ **Tab:** Event Details ➤ **Mandatory:** Yes (select) ➤ **Validation:** Leave this value blank for this field. ➤ **Description:** Leave this value blank, as it is obvious what it's for.

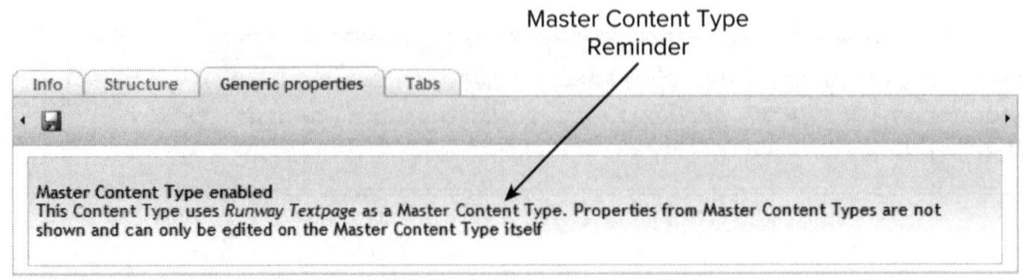
Master Content Type Reminder
Info
Structure
Generic properties
Tabs
Master Content Type enabled
This Content Type uses Runway Textpage as a Master Content Type. Properties from Master Content Types are not shown and can only be edited on the Master Content Type itself

FIGURE 3-9

7. Allow the new Event document type as a child node of the Runway Homepage, just like you did with the Press Release Area earlier in this chapter, by navigating to the Runway Homepage document type, clicking the Structure tab, selecting Event, and clicking the Save icon.

So far, this is all theoretical as you have not seen the results of your careful planning and labor. Chapter 8 deals with creating content where all this work will come together. For now, Figure 3-10 shows a preview of what the content editing UI looks like. You can see the Content tab, just like in a Runway Textpage node, and the addition of the Event Details tab and associated fields.

FIGURE 3-10

WORKING WITH DOCUMENT TYPES OUTSIDE OF UMBRACO

Adding document types can sometimes be time consuming and cumbersome, especially if the document type has a lot of tabs and fields. So, instead of forcing you to re-enter all this information time and time again, Umbraco provides the ability to export existing document types and import them into another installation.

Exporting a Document Type

As shown in Figure 3-11, exporting is an easy three-step process:

1. Right-click the document type you want to export.
2. Click Export Document Type.
3. Save the generated XML file on your computer.

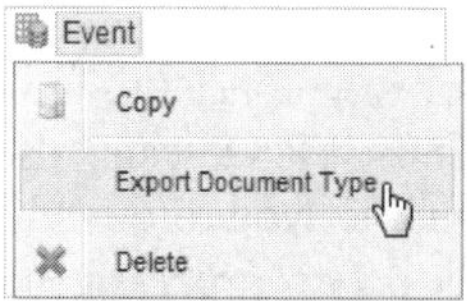

FIGURE 3-11

The file type that Umbraco generates is saved with an extension of `.udt`. You can open this using any text editor like Notepad. You can manually edit the document type by altering the XML in the exported `.udt` file. However, doing this is not advised because system-generated IDs can get out of sync and duplicated if you are not careful.

You can do a couple of things with your shiny new exported document type. The most obvious is importing it to another installation (see the next section in this chapter) to avoid starting from scratch and retyping all your properties and tabs.

If you have custom data types defined in a given Umbraco installation and you export your document type for use with another Umbraco installation, you end up with data type IDs that do not exist in the new system. This means that you must select the appropriate data type for those properties that do not utilize standard data types.

The other benefit to exporting document types is the ability to add them to your existing source control and versioning system (such as Subversion, which is an open-source source control system available at `http://subversion.tigris.org/`). This feature allows you to easily revert to older versions and, more importantly, have an offsite backup in case of a disaster.

Importing a Document Type

You can import a document type from an existing `.udt` file in a few simple steps, as shown in Figure 3-12.

1. Right-click the Document Types node, and click the Import Document Type menu item.
2. In the Import Document Type pop-up dialog, select the file from your computer, as shown in Figure 3-13.
3. Click the Import button.
4. In the confirmation dialog, double check that the correct document type was selected from your computer, and click the Import button.

FIGURE 3-12

The document type is now ready for you to use and alter as needed.

Exporting Document Types as Plain Old CLR Objects

Exporting document types as Plain Old *CLR* (common language runtime) Objects is a great feature when you need to interact with content nodes from .NET user controls. Umbraco generates Plain Old CLR Objects, also known as *POCOs*, with or without abstractions. Exporting document types enables you to quickly bring in this code to your project and start working with the content properties. This process generates objects for all of your document types.

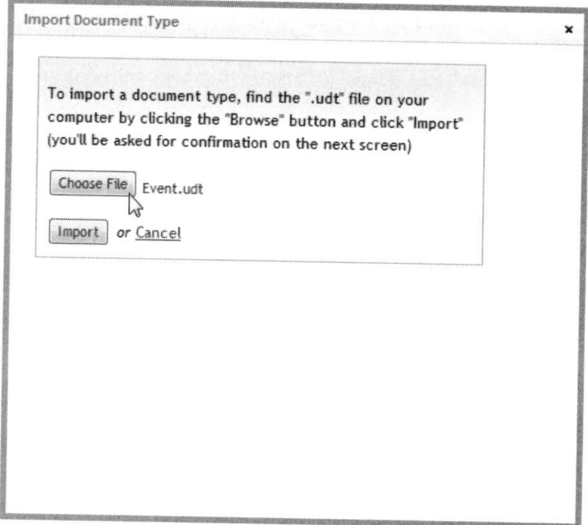

FIGURE 3-13

To generate the POCO stub files, follow these instructions:

1. Rick-click Document Types, and click the Export to .NET menu item.
2. In the Export to .NET dialog, shown in Figure 3-14, select the Generation Mode you desire.

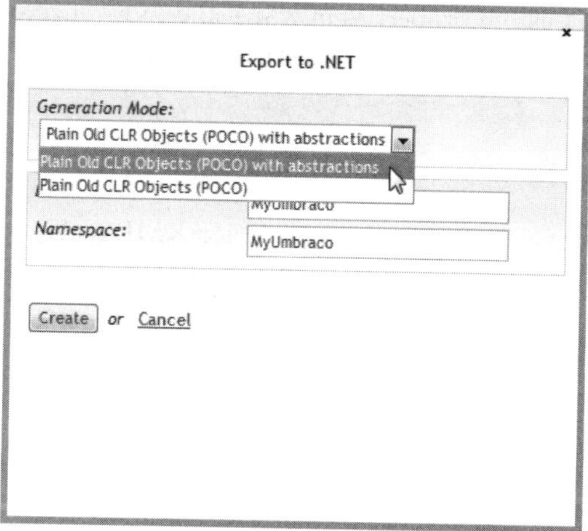

FIGURE 3-14

3. Enter the DataContext value desired. This value is used to create the name of your class followed by DataContext. For example, if you type in **Test**, the name of your class will be `TestDataContext`.
4. Enter the Namespace value desired. The namespace you choose here should match that of your Visual Studio project.

5. As shown in Figure 3-15, click the POCO download link to save the generated file to your computer. Remember to change the file extension to `.cs`.

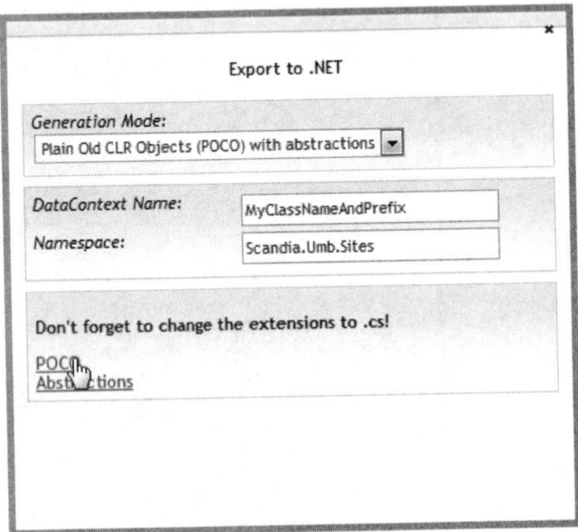

FIGURE 3-15

USING DOCUMENT TYPE PROPERTIES

Umbraco has a number of properties that are standard to all installations. You can reference these properties much like you do with your own custom properties in XSLT and .NET macros as well as in any templates. You can find examples of how to use these properties, along with your own custom ones, in Chapters 4 and 5.

Built-in Properties

The following properties are available for any given node in the Umbraco XML cache and .NET `Node` object. Table 3-6 provides a detailed description of each property. For examples on how to use the .NET `Node` object, see Chapter 12.

TABLE 3-6: Built-in Properties

PROPERTY NAME	DESCRIPTION
`id`	The unique sequential autogenerated node ID.
`parentId`	The ID of the parent node.
`level`	The level at which this node is currently on. Note here that the first level is the root, which is effectively 0. So, in the Runway installation, as used in Chapter 1, the Runway Homepage is at level 1.
`nodeType`	The ID of the document type that the current node is created from.
`template`	The ID of the template that the node is currently using.

PROPERTY NAME	DESCRIPTION
`sortOrder`	The order of the node within the current parent. `sortOrder` restarts with each parent level.
`urlName`	The name of the page in URL-friendly format. For example, the Runway Homepage has a `urlName` of **runway-homepage**. The `urlName` does not have the full path or an extension on it. This is all compiled based on the `path` property and is done at runtime.
`nodeName`	The name of the node as it was created — for example, Runway Homepage. This property affects the `urlName`, so if this is changed, the URL of the page is updated as well.
`creatorId`	The ID of the user who created the node.
`creatorName`	The given name associated with the user account that created the node.
`writerId`	The ID of the person who last edited the node.
`writerName`	The given name associated with the user account that last edited the node.
`createDate`	The date and time stamp when the node was created.
`updateDate`	The date and time stamp when the node was last updated.
`path`	A comma-delimited list of the hierarchical path of the node as it relates to the root node. For example, the Runway Homepage has a path of -1,1048.

The root node in the content tree always has an ID of -1.

Properties with Special Meaning

In addition to these built-in properties, Umbraco also has some properties with special features. This means that Umbraco will react to the values of these properties automatically when they exist on a given document type. Table 3-7 provides details on what all of these do.

TABLE 3-7: Umbraco Special Properties

PROPERTY NAME	DESCRIPTION
`umbracoRedirect`	Add this property to your document type, with a data type of Content Picker, if you want to have an editor select an internal page to redirect the end user to.
`umbracoInternalRedirectId`	This has the same end result as `umbracoRedirect`, except in this case Umbraco will load the content of the selected internal page transparently without redirecting to the new URL. Choose Content Picker as the data type, allowing the editor to select the target page using the content tree.

continues

TABLE 3-7 *(continued)*

PROPERTY NAME	DESCRIPTION
`umbracoUrlName`	This property allows you to alter the `urlName` of the page without changing the `nodeName`. For example, if you created a page with the title **This Is A Test Page**, the resulting `url-Name` would be `this-is-a-test-page.aspx`. With this property, you can change the URL to `test-page.aspx` instead. Note, don't add a trailing .aspx to this property because it is added automatically if you have not set your installation to `umbracoUseDirectoryUrls=true`, as discussed in Chapter 1.
`umbracoUrlAlias`	Add this property to your document type if you need multiple URLs to match a single node. For example, if you add **test-home,test/home** on the Runway Homepage node, the following URLs would be valid: `http://yoursiteurl.com/` `http://yoursiteurl.com/`**`test-home.aspx`** `http://yoursiteurl.com/`**`test/home.aspx`** This is particularly useful for marketing URLs and other tracking mechanisms. Keep in mind here that from a search engine optimization standpoint, having multiple URLs pointing to the same content reduces your score with many popular search engines such as Google and Yahoo.

TAKE HOME POINTS

By the time you finish this chapter you should have a good handle on how to configure and design the structure of your content. To summarize, you should now be comfortable with the following:

- How Umbraco stores your content
- Creating and editing document types
- Working with parent document types
- Exporting and importing document types for transferring document type definitions to other Umbraco installations
- Working with document types outside of Umbraco via code
- Knowing what document type properties are special in Umbraco and their associated features

Templates, Markup, and Master Pages

- How does Umbraco implement templates?
- How do you best separate and create your HTML markup for use in Umbraco templates?
- How do you inject content using special Umbraco tags?
- How do you use styles and scripts to create the base of your application?

Now that you've defined the document types and content structure for the site, you must create some way to display the content that the document types will hold. As Chapter 2 discusses, Umbraco is excellent at maintaining .NET standards. This chapter talks about .NET master pages. They are the foundation of how to structure and design the templates and markup needed for the output of content.

Master pages were introduced to developers as of .NET 2.0. They help developers create moldable, maintainable, and flexible layouts while separating content from structure. In addition, they provide you with a way to apply one or many styles consistently across multiple pages and child pages. Master pages are one of the many building blocks of Umbraco, so although you're going to see how this particular block works, you won't see the complete picture until later chapters. However, by the end of this chapter you will be able to create master pages and child master pages to mold and display your content to the end user.

BUILDING WEBSITE STRUCTURE USING TEMPLATES

Templates are the vehicle in which Umbraco delivers content from pre-defined document types (see Chapter 3) to the end user. The templates render not only the content that you save in Umbraco, but also the design elements and markup that you provide for the browser to display. The three major concerns when it comes to templates are

- **Effective separation:** One of the most common goals among developers is to develop applications that are easy to maintain and deploy. An important consideration in achieving this goal is the separation of business logic from presentation (the design and output). You accomplish this goal in Umbraco by leveraging .NET master pages and the features they present. This includes nesting and inheritance, covered later in this chapter.
- **Flexible presentation:** You should design any web application or website with maximum flexibility in mind. Users demand changes constantly, so the more flexible your layouts are, the easier you can overhaul or make your designs "fresh" while keeping disruptions of the underlying infrastructure to a minimum.
- **Reusability:** Finally, as a developer you are constantly striving to be more efficient in how you work. Creating templates that are reusable for multiple scenarios is key.

With these points in mind, let's start looking at how this all applies to Umbraco.

How Templates Build Layout and Structure

When defining the structure of your website, it is important to keep in mind how that structure will map to your templates. This is especially important when it comes to making your master pages as reusable as possible and avoiding code duplication.

Umbraco ships with a base template in the rendering engine. You can find it in the `~/umbraco/masterpages` directory in your installation. The following code snippet shows the contents of this file as it is shipped with your Umbraco installation.

```
<%@ Master Language="C#" AutoEventWireup="true" CodeBehind="default.master.cs"
inherits="umbraco.presentation.masterpages._default" %>
<asp:ContentPlaceHolder ID="ContentPlaceHolderDefault" runat="server">
</asp:ContentPlaceHolder>
```

To avoid the disadvantages of using absolute file and resource paths in controls and master pages, you can implement the paths using the web application root operator (~). .NET uses this operator to resolve the root of the application as it is configured in IIS and the application `Web.config`.

The default Umbraco master page has but one content placeholder, which is designated to render everything that your templates contain. A `ContentPlaceHolder` control defines a region for content in a master page, which will render all text, markup, and server controls from a related `Content` control found in a content page. The `Content` element is assigned to a `ContentPlaceHolder` using its `ContentPlaceHolderID` property. To populate a `ContentPlaceHolder` of a master page, simply create a `Content` element and point the `ContentPlaceHolderID` to the ID of the associated `ContentPlaceHolder` of the parent master page.

You can now start to think about how to structure and design your templates specific to this installation. The first rule is to always have one "base" template that contains the standard markup and tags of any HTML page. Listing 4-1 shows an example.

LISTING 4-1: SampleBase.htm

Available for download on Wrox.com

```
<!DOCTYPE html PUBLIC "-//W3C//DTD XHTML 1.0 Strict//EN"
      "http://www.w3.org/TR/xhtml1/DTD/xhtml1-strict.dtd">
<html xmlns="http://www.w3.org/1999/xhtml">
<head>
    <title>Site and Page Title</title>

    <!-- styles -->
    <link rel="stylesheet" type="text/css" href="~/css/styles.css"
       media="screen" />

    <!-- scripts -->
    <script language="JavaScript" type="text/javascript" src="~/scripts/bll.js">
    </script>
</head>
<body>
    <!-- markup, controls, and content of site -->
</body>
</html>
```

A couple of important considerations before proceeding are that in order to render .NET user controls, covered in Chapter 12, the `ContentPlaceHolders` that will render the controls must be surrounded by a `<form id="form1" runat="server"></form>` tag. If this tag is not present, .NET user controls will not be rendered at runtime. Also, consider the following content areas as standard for your templates.

- **Head:** For manipulating and overriding stylesheet and script files (as well as other custom code).
- **Header:** Houses site name, logo, search, and navigation elements.
- **Body:** Houses the meat of the rendered page, such as content images and so on.
- **Footer:** Houses standard footer information such as copyright, site owner, and so on.

The templates created in Umbraco could match the structure of the document types (refer to Chapter 3). However, in most cases you will find that the structure is not a one-to-one relationship and that some document types don't require templates (like repeatable content items such as news or events). In most cases, you will want to create your templates independent of the document type creation process. However, this is not always the case, as discussed in Chapter 3.

Figure 4-1 illustrates what the most common master page structure will look like. Here you can see how all the child templates of Master.master inherit the markup defined in the topmost template. The standard HTML tags and structure from Listing 4-1 would be added to Master.master and then be available to the lowest child template automatically.

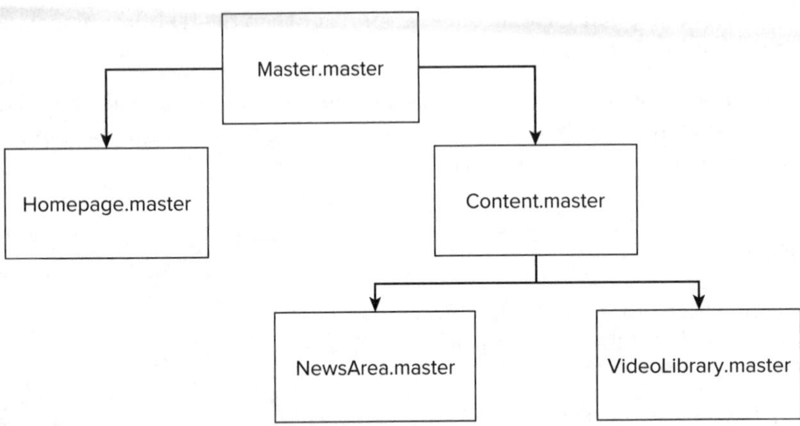

FIGURE 4-1

Creating Templates With Umbraco

To create the template structure as described in the previous section, you must log in to the Umbraco user interface (UI) and use the interface to create the templates and associated hierarchies. As a developer, you have the option to work on the templates in a development environment, such as Visual Studio 2010 or Notepad++, after the templates have been generated by Umbraco. This includes creating the database records and associated template IDs, which are referenced later when you save content for use with a particular template.

After logging in, navigate to the Settings section and find Templates in the left-hand tree. To create a new template, follow these simple steps:

1. Right-click Templates and select the Create menu item, as shown in Figure 4-2.

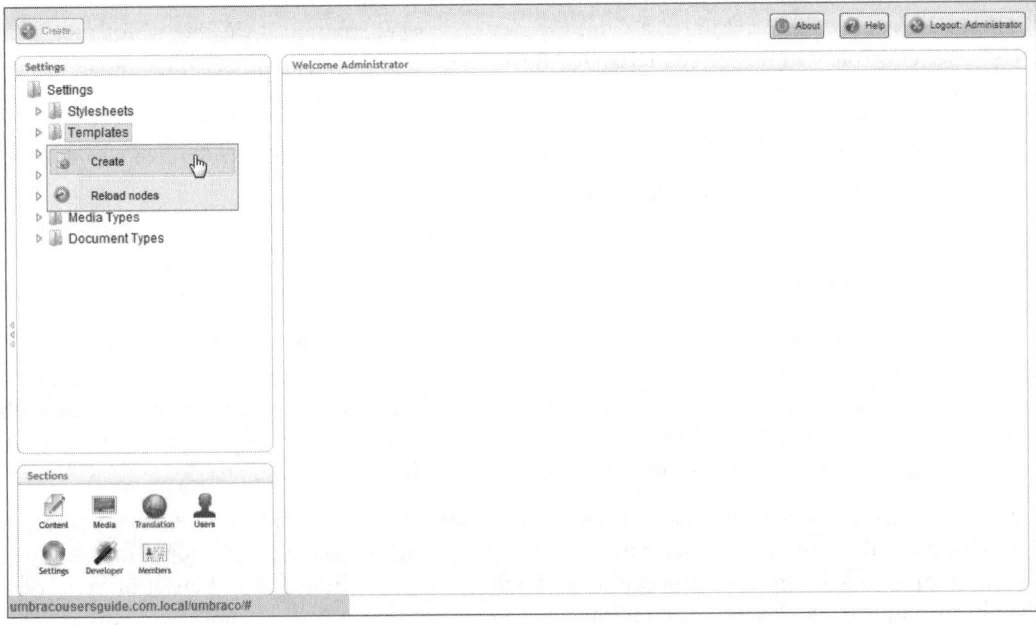

FIGURE 4-2

2. In the Create dialog, type the name of your template (without the `.master` extension) — in this case **`Master`**.

3. Click Create.

The page now reloads and the code editor displays with the bare-bones `Master.master` templates loaded, as shown in Figure 4-3. The template properties you see are

- **Name:** This is the name of the template as it is saved in the database and on the file system.
- **Alias:** The name used to reference the template when working with the Umbraco API.
- **Master Template:** Allows you to choose the master template from which to inherit.

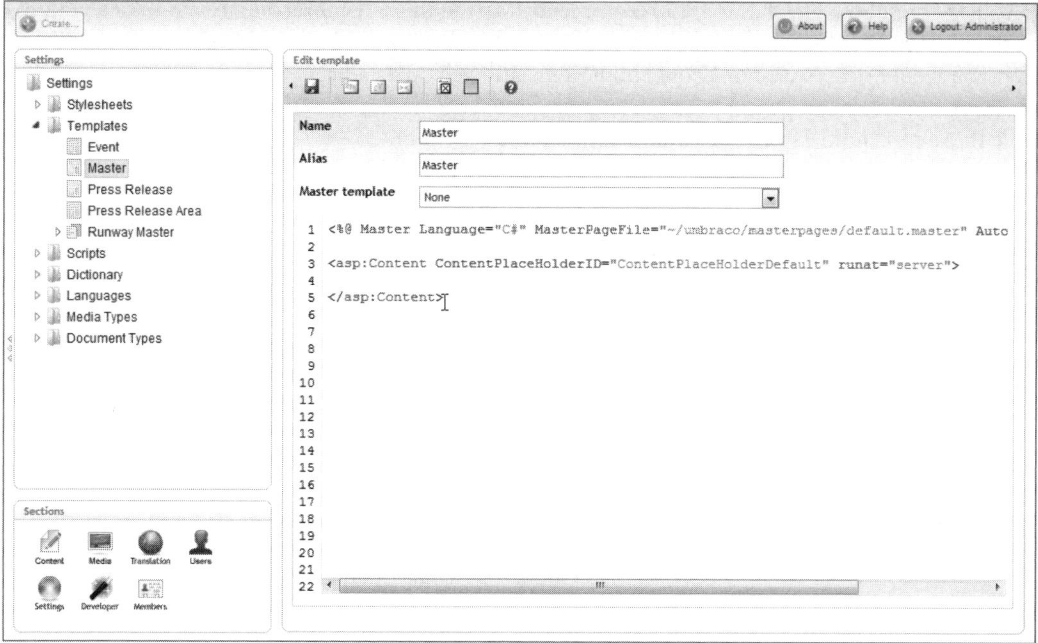

FIGURE 4-3

As you can tell from Figure 4-1, you have no reason to specify a master template because the one you're creating now is the *root* master page from which all or at least most other templates will inherit.

For subsequent templates, the process is much the same, the difference being that instead of right-clicking Templates, you might right-click the template that you want to create a child template in. However, before you do that, you must create the `ContentPlaceHolder` controls so that your inherited template knows which `ContentPlaceHolderIDs` to target.

DEFINING MARKUP

It's time to do some coding! Theory is great, but practice makes perfect.

Listing 4-2 and subsequent code listings in this section all build on one another to the final, complete solution at the end of the section. For the time being, you'll write your code using the Umbraco in-browser code editor.

Creating Markup Using the Umbraco UI

A few approaches exist for working with the master page files. As a programmer you might prefer working on the files in Visual Studio, especially if you're interested in leveraging tools such as IntelliSense and Source Control integration. You can also do it all via the Umbraco UI code editor. If you are brand new to the CMS, I recommend starting in the Umbraco editor to take advantage of the provided toolbar, as shown in Figure 4-4, which helps you insert code snippets and functions that you would otherwise not know about. This allows you as a user to insert `<asp:ContentPlaceHolder>` tags and label them, reference those placeholders in your child template, and let Umbraco show you the IDs of those placeholders to avoid typos and other mistakes.

FIGURE 4-4

So, in the Master, follow these steps:

1. Click the Insert content area placeholder icon, as shown in Figure 4-5.

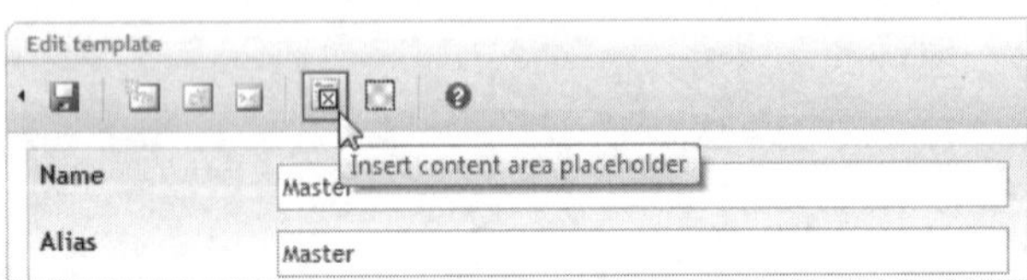

FIGURE 4-5

2. Name the container and click the Insert button, as shown in Figure 4-6.

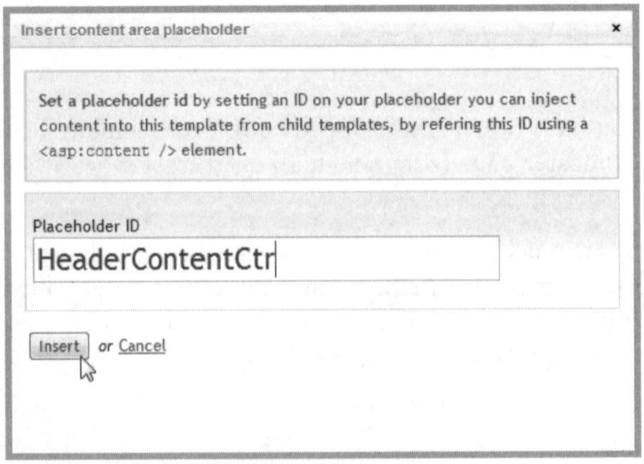

FIGURE 4-6

3. Repeat steps 1 and 2 for all the required content placeholders that you want to define. In this example, you add three additional placeholders before moving on to the next step: targeting the placeholders with content from child template(s).

Creating the Master Base Template

Starting at the top, you'll add some `ContentPlaceHolder` controls to the Master base template.

To work with your code outside of the Umbraco backoffice UI, please refer to Appendix B, which goes through a detailed setup of an Umbraco development environment in Visual Studio 2010.

LISTING 4-2: Master.master

Available for download on Wrox.com

```
<%@ Master Language="C#" MasterPageFile="~/umbraco/masterpages/default.master"
AutoEventWireup="true" %>

<asp:Content ContentPlaceHolderID="ContentPlaceHolderDefault" runat="server">
<!DOCTYPE html PUBLIC "-//W3C//DTD XHTML 1.0 Strict//EN"
      "http://www.w3.org/TR/xhtml1/DTD/xhtml1-strict.dtd">
<html xmlns="http://www.w3.org/1999/xhtml">
<head>
    <title>Umbraco User's Guide</title>

    <!-- styles -->
    <link rel="stylesheet" type="text/css" href="~/css/styles.css"
         media="screen" />

    <!-- scripts -->
    <script language="JavaScript" type="text/javascript" src="~/scripts/bll.js">
    </script>

    <!-- ContentPlaceHolder: Head -->
    <asp:ContentPlaceHolder ID="HeadContentCtr" runat="server" />
</head>
<body>
    <div id="header">
        <img src="~/images/log_uug.png" alt="Umbraco User's Guide" />

        <!-- ContentPlaceHolder: Header -->
        <asp:ContentPlaceHolder ID="HeaderContentCtr" runat="server" />
    </div>
    <div id="body">
        <!-- ContentPlaceHolder: Body -->
        <asp:ContentPlaceHolder ID="BodyContentCtr" runat="server" />
    </div>
    <div id="footer">
        <!-- print the year dynamically -->
```

continues

LISTING 4-2 *(continued)*

```
            &copy; <%= DateTime.Now.Year %>

            <!-- ContentPlaceHolder: Footer -->
            <asp:ContentPlaceHolder ID="FooterContentCtr" runat="server" />
        </div>
    </body>
    </html>
    </asp:Content>
```

Notice the following about this code:

- You're using the aforementioned Umbraco Master page `default.master` as the master page.
- Both the `<asp:Content />` and the `<asp:ContentPlaceHolder />` controls are introduced here to populate the placeholder defined in `default.master` as well as to define regions that you'll populate from the child templates later on.

Depending on the configuration settings of your Umbraco installation you may notice syntax highlighting and line numbers displayed as in standard editors. You can turn this option on or off depending on your preferences. You can find this setting in `<install root>/config/umbracoSettings.config`.

Creating the Textpage Template

The "master" template is now done and contains the underlying markup and layout code that is needed to produce the website design. However, at this point, you're still not showing any content. Even if you applied this template to a document type and ran the page, you would see nothing. The reason for this is that so far all you have done is create the general structure of the website. What are missing are the Umbraco content tags and macros that will ultimately render the content from the CMS.

Now take it one step further and create the Textpage template. This template will be a nested master page within the Master (see the section "Nesting and Inheritance with ASP.NET Master Pages" later in this chapter for further clarification) that you just created. Furthermore, the content specified in this master page will fill the `ContentPlaceHolders` that were defined in the `Master.master` and `TextPage.master`. Creating the Textpage involves the following steps:

1. Once again, while logged into the Umbraco backoffice, navigate to the Settings section.
2. Expand the Templates node and right-click on the Master template to create a new child template called Textpage.

   After the right-hand pane reloads, you will see that you now have the Master template set to "Master" and the template itself is rather empty, with the exception of the following:

   ```
   <%@ Master Language="C#" MasterPageFile="~/masterpages/Master.master"
       AutoEventWireup="true" %>
   ```

3. To build on this template and make it usable, that is, display something, you must populate the `ContentPlaceHolders` and reference content from your Umbraco document types. Now it's time to add some `<asp:Content>` tags that you can later fill with dynamic content from the CMS (see Listing 4-3).

LISTING 4-3: Textpage.master

Available for download on Wrox.com

```
<%@ Master Language="C#" MasterPageFile="~/masterpages/Master.master"
AutoEventWireup="true" %>

<%-- Populate the header container --%>
<asp:Content ID="HeaderContent" ContentPlaceHolderID="HeaderContentCtr"
runat="server">
    <h1>Umbraco User's Guide - The Friendly CMS</h1>
</asp:Content>

<%-- Populate the body container --%>
<asp:Content ID="BodyContent" ContentPlaceHolderID="BodyContentCtr"
runat="server">
    <h2>The Page Title</h2>

    <p>Some page content here.</p>
</asp:Content>
```

Any and all `ContentPlaceHolders` *are optional. As Listing 4-3 shows, the text page templates only utilize the* `HeaderContent` *and* `BodyContent` `ContentPlaceHolders`*. You can set default content for these placeholders by adding to them in the template. For example, the footer of the website may contain a copyright notice. If this is standard on 90 percent of your pages, just add that to the tag. Then, on pages where this changes, simply set the value where needed.*

```
<asp:ContentPlaceHolder ID="FooterContentCtr" runat="server">
    &copy; <%= DateTime.Now.Year %>
</asp:ContentPlaceHolder>
```

Populating the Placeholder for the Textpage.Master File

Follow these steps to populate the content placeholders from the `Textpage.Master` file that you just defined in the Master:

1. Navigate to the `Textpage.Master` file, located in the Templates node.
2. Click the Insert content area icon, as shown in Figure 4-7.

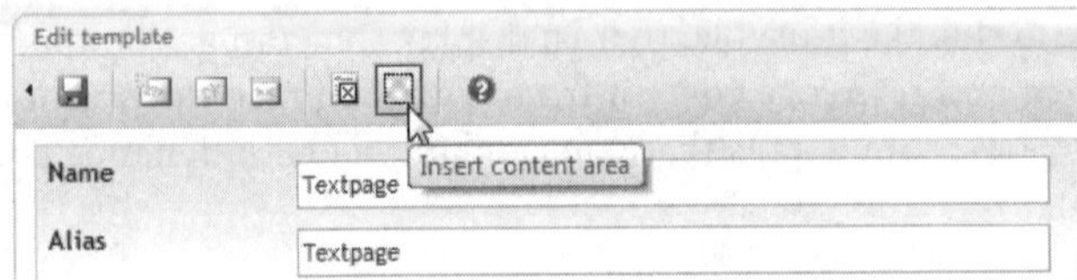

FIGURE 4-7

3. In the Insert content area dialog, choose the content placeholder that you want to add content to in the current child template, as shown in Figure 4-8.

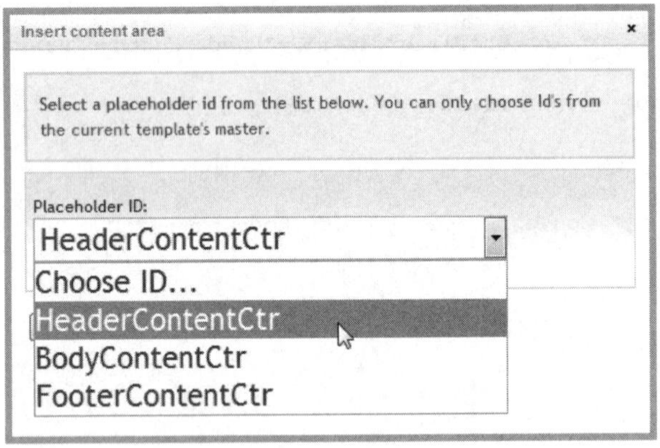

FIGURE 4-8

Even though a content placeholder exists in a parent master page, it's not mandatory to populate it from all child templates. A perfect scenario where you may have completely optional placeholders is the `HeadContentCtr` that you specified earlier in this chapter. You can use it to inject things such as page- or template-specific JavaScript or CSS file references or anything else that may belong in the head tag, but not on a global level.

USING SPECIAL UMBRACO TAGS

Like most CMSs, Umbraco utilizes special tags to render any content that is entered by a user in the backoffice. If you're at all familiar with .NET syntax for including user controls or custom tags, this should make you feel right at home. Here's what a basic tag looks like:

```
<umbraco:Item field="pageName" runat="server"></umbraco:Item>
```

This is the tag in its simplest form. It can get more complex than this — in fact, a lot more complex. The Umbraco backoffice UI has a widget to insert these Umbraco items in your templates, so you don't have to do the heavy lifting. This includes built-in fields, like the one field reference in the previous code snippet, as well as custom document type properties. You can launch the Insert Umbraco page field dialog (shown in Figure 4-9) by clicking the insert Umbraco page field button located toward the top of the right-hand pane next to the Save button.

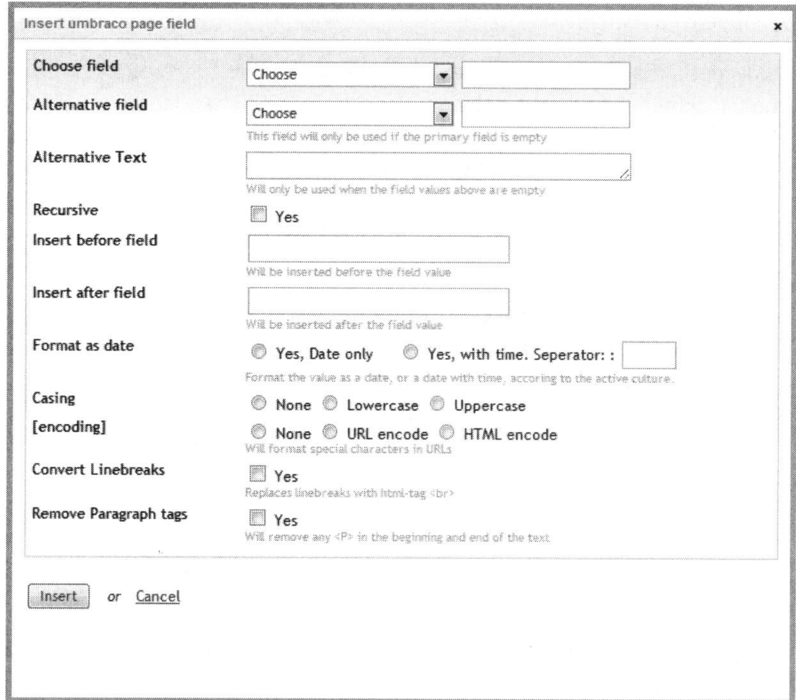

FIGURE 4-9

The Insert Umbraco page field dialog contains the fields presented in Table 4-1.

TABLE 4-1: Umbraco Page Fields

FIELD	DESCRIPTION
Choose field	Allows you to pick from any of the built-in properties provided by Umbraco or any of the custom properties that you defined in your document types.
Alternative field	Offers the same list of properties as available in the Choose Field, only the Alternative Field option is used if the Choose Field value is null or empty. For example, you may have specified a property called `contentPageTitle` that is optional for the user to fill in. Because it is optional, and it is the heading of the page, you must ensure that some value is in place. So, if the user leaves this field blank, you can tell Umbraco to use an alternate field instead (such as `@pageName`, which is always available as a built-in property).

continues

TABLE 4-1 *(continued)*

FIELD	DESCRIPTION
Alternative Text	You can specify this static string if, for some reason, both of the preceding properties are empty.
Recursive	Indicates if the selected page field is recursive and tells Umbraco to traverse up the content tree hierarchy to look for a value in parent nodes if one is not available on the page where this field is being rendered. This is especially useful for something like meta keywords that you can add to the homepage node and then only specify on a page-by-page basis where the keywords may differ from the overall website. See Chapter 3 and master document types for more information on this.
Insert before field/ Insert after field	Comes in handy when you want to concatenate strings with Umbraco property values. To piggy-back on the previous example, you can use this when implementing meta tags in your header. <umbraco:Item field="metaKeyWords" **insertTextBefore="<meta** **name="keywords" content="" ** **insertTextAfter=""/>"** runat="server"></umbraco:Item>
Format as date	If your field is a date, Umbraco can automatically format the date for you. This is also locale or culture specific.
Casing	Umbraco can output the value of your field by converting it to either uppercase of lowercase.
[encoding]	Encodes the string into either HTML or URL structured formats.
Convert Linebreaks	If the displayed property is of type Textbox Multiple, Umbraco can automatically convert any newline characters with HTML-friendly tags.
Remove Paragraph tags	Conveniently removes the paragraph tags from single paragraph text (created in either the Textbox Multiple or Rich Text Editor data types).

As of Umbraco version 4.x, you can include what is referred to as Inline XSLT statements. This provides you with far greater capabilities to manipulate the output of any given field. For example, if you wanted to format the date of a field in a particular way, different from the standard format that Umbraco field attributes provide, you could add the optional XSLT attribute to the umbraco:Item tag, like so:

```
<umbraco:Item field="dateField"
xslt="umbraco.library:FormatDateTime({0},'MMM dd, yyyy')"
    runat="server">
```

Now that you know what all of these attributes mean and do, take a look at the Textpage.master template again, but this time populated with document type properties and the <umbraco:Item...> tag.

Fields that are prefixed by the `@` *(at) symbol in the list are built-in Umbraco properties and are populated automatically by Umbraco, as covered in Chapter 3. The properties that do not have this prefix are custom properties defined for each individual installation.*

Available for download on Wrox.com

LISTING 4-3: Textpage.master *(continued)*

```
<%@ Master Language="C#" MasterPageFile="~/masterpages/Master.master"
AutoEventWireup="true" %>

<%-- Populate the header container --%>
<asp:Content ID="HeaderContent" ContentPlaceHolderID="HeaderContentCtr"
runat="server">
    <h1><umbraco:Item field="siteName" recursive="true"
runat="server"></umbraco:Item></h1>
</asp:Content>

<%-- Populate the body container --%>
<asp:Content ID="BodyContent" ContentPlaceHolderID="BodyContentCtr"
runat="server">
    <h2><umbraco:Item field="pageTitle" useIfEmpty="pageName"
runat="server"></umbraco:Item><umbraco:Item field="pageTitle"
useIfEmpty="pageName" runat="server"></umbraco:Item></h2>

    <umbraco:Item field="bodyText" runat="server"></umbraco:Item>
</asp:Content>

<%-- Populate the footer container --%>
<asp:Content ID="FooterContent" runat="server"
ContentPlaceHolderID="FooterContentCtr">
    <p>Last Published: <umbraco:Item field="updateDate"
formatAsDateWithTime="true" formatAsDateWithTimeSeparator=" "
runat="server"></umbraco:Item></p>
</asp:Content>
```

You may be wondering where the navigation and all the fun stuff is. Chapter 5 covers this in the discussion about macros. Macros bring endless power and flexibility to the table via .NET user controls, XSLT stylesheets to render cached content, and even IronPython and Ruby, as well as other supported languages on the .NET DLR (dynamic language runtime).

Applying the Template

You've worked very hard on making the templates look great, but so far you really have no way to display them. The next step is to apply them to the content; that is, associate the template(s) with applicable document types. You accomplish this task, too, in the backoffice UI.

1. Navigate to the desired document type in the Settings section.
2. Make sure the Info tab is selected.
3. As shown in Figure 4-10, select which template(s) you want to allow for this document type. If you want to allow more than one, choose the default template.

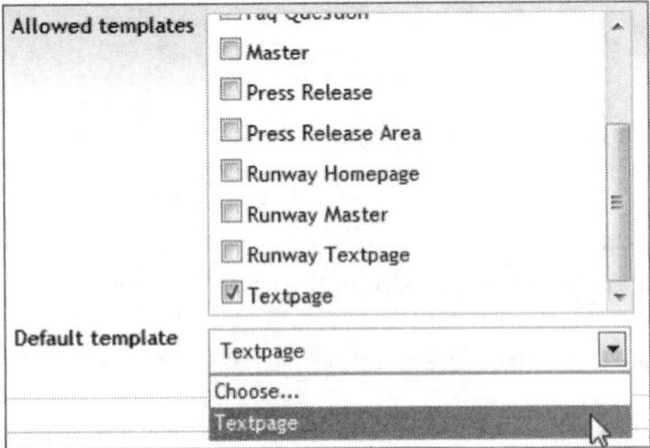

FIGURE 4-10

Nesting and Inheritance with ASP.NET Master Pages

As you can see from the earlier examples and descriptions, Umbraco's leveraging of the .NET master page implementation natively is an immense benefit to you as a developer. Thus far, this chapter has covered how to use nesting and how children fill in content regions in parent templates. So, how does this all work? Take a look at Figure 4-11, and see how it starts.

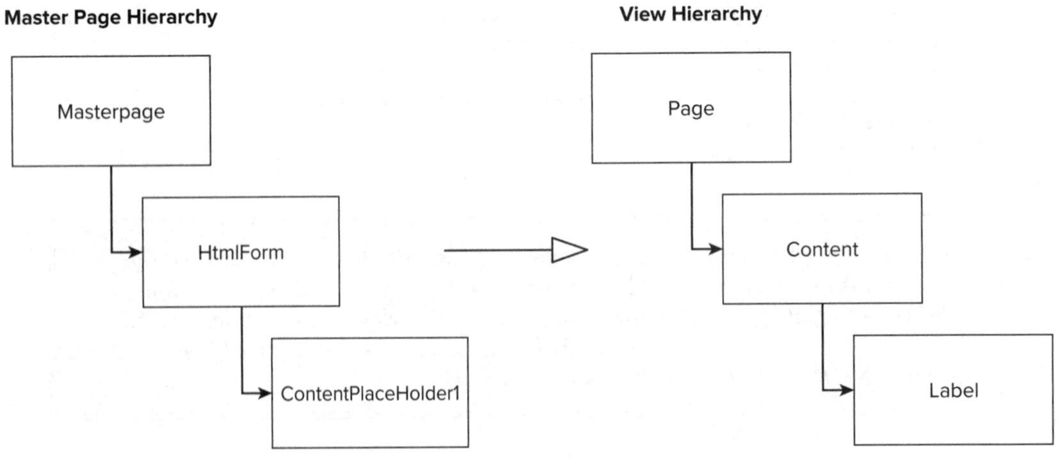

FIGURE 4-11

.NET compiles the view that is presented to the user from the bottom up. Figure 4-11 illustrates what it would look like at this juncture.

Up until now, view and master page were two separate objects, each with its own hierarchy. Figure 4-12 illustrates this hierarchy. The master page applies itself during runtime — it replaces the page's children with itself.

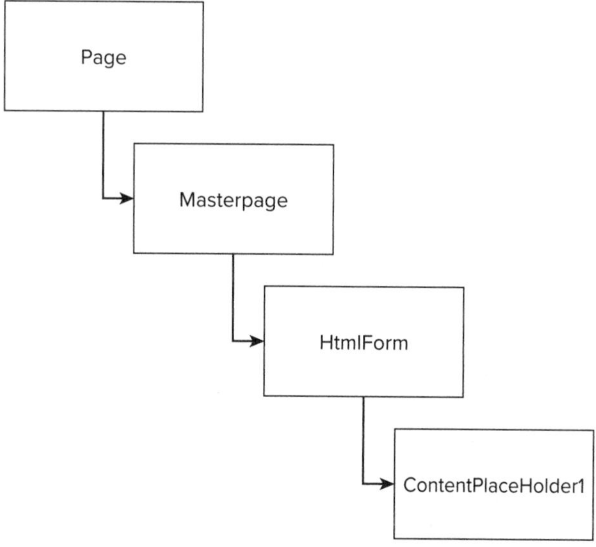

FIGURE 4-12

Now the master page looks for `<asp:Content>` controls associated with the view. When it finds an `<asp:Content>` control that matches an `<asp:ContentPlaceHolder>`, it moves the controls into the matched `<asp:ContentPlaceHolder>`. In your simple setup, the master page will find a match for `ContentPlaceHolder1` and copy over the Label. You wind up with what is shown in Figure 4-13.

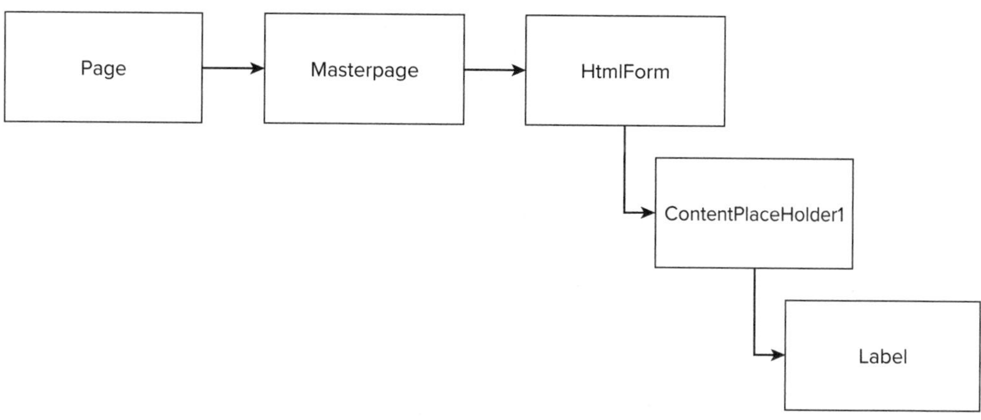

FIGURE 4-13

All of this work occurs after the content page's `PreInit` event, but before the content page's `Init` event. During this brief slice of time, the master page is deserving of its name. The master page is in control, giving orders and rearranging controls. However, by the time the `Init` event fires, the master page becomes just another child control inside the page. In fact, the `MasterPage` class derives from the `UserControl` class. Think of master pages as masters during design time. However, when the application is executing, treating the master page as just another child control is more accurate.

UMBRACO AND YOUR MARKUP

Through the various examples that you've seen, you may have noticed the use of XHTML for markup. At this time, this is the latest approved and widely used W3C standard, with HTML5 right around the corner. By default, Umbraco is configured to validate and recognize XHTML 1.0 Strict with the option to turn this off. This means that the Rich Text Editor data type, which uses Tidy for HTML cleanup, validates against that W3C specification. You can turn off this validation in the Umbraco settings, but for best practices it is recommended that you leave it intact and write standards-based HTML and Cascading Style Sheets (CSS).

You Get What You Put In — A Good Thing

You'll be glad to know that Umbraco is one of the few CMSs that does not alter your markup in any way at runtime. No extraneous tags or comments are inserted into the view; no automatic stripping of tags occurs, or other modifications of *your* code. There are two exception to this rule (but no, it's not a catch, I promise):

- **TinyMCE:** This is the open source Rich Text Editor (RTE) that ships with Umbraco. As a developer and owner of an Umbraco site, you can edit how this control behaves by configuring the settings in `<install root>/config/umbraco.settings`. By default, the RTE will "clean up" empty tags (like empty `TD`s, `DIV`s, and so on). But, you can change all these settings to your preference in the config file(s).

If you prefer to use another editor, Umbraco allows you to do just that by rolling your own Data Type. That is one of the strong sides of the system, it's API.

- **Empty tags:** When writing XSTL files, the .NET XSLT 1.0 engine will *not* allow empty tags unless you change the content type from XML to HTML. Unfortunately, XSLT 1.0 does not produce XHTML Strict, but rather HTML 4.0, so some conflict exists between standards here. This is a limitation of the .NET engine and not Umbraco. For example, the following `<div class="clear"></div>` renders as `<div class="clear" />` if the output method is set to XML as opposed to HTML.

```
<xsl:output method="html" omit-xml-declaration="yes"/>
```

USING ALTTEMPLATE

Often times the same content may need to take on different shapes to serve a different purpose. One very common, and timely, example of this is switching the layout of your content for a mobile device. Traditionally, the developer must create a different document type with the same properties, create a duplicate page for the same content, and apply the alternate template to serve up the alternate view.

There are cases when you need to present certain content in multiple formats. In this section, you'll see how data that is presented in one way can be repurposed by using something in Umbraco called *AltTemplate*.

Umbraco enables you to create and assign multiple templates to a particular document type. Make sure that you're targeting at least one of the same document type properties across the multiple templates; otherwise none of your content will be displayed. You can allow multiple templates for one document type by selecting them in the Info tab of a selected document type, as show in Figure 4-14.

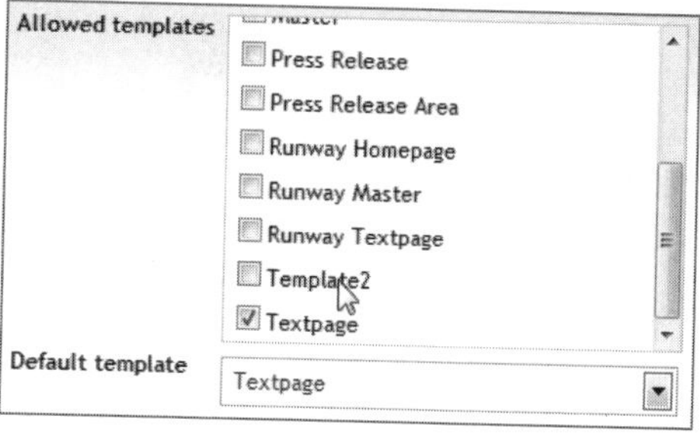

FIGURE 4-14

Now that you've assigned all the templates for the document type — your content container — you can dynamically load this template by appending the following to the current URL:

```
?altTemplate=template2
```

This causes the current page to reload with the alternate template applied. The beauty of this is that the content author didn't have to create two separate pages and maintain duplicate copies of the content.

A second method to calling up an alternate template is to simply append the template alias to the end of the current URL. For example, if the URL of your page is `http://localhost/somepage.aspx` you can apply the alternate template by changing the URL to `http://localhost/somepage/template2.aspx`.

The value in the key/value pair, `template2`*, is the alias of the template as opposed to the name. Most of the time, these two values are the same — but not always. For example, if you save a template using special characters (space, +, -, and so on), Umbraco truncates the alias by removing the special characters.*

Changing the Document Type using AltTemplate

One of the many common uses of `AltTemplate` is to be able to take content and serve it to the browser as a different content type, thus altering how the user can interact with and use the output from the CMS. Take an example where you want to serve up a table of data in an Excel document as opposed to standard plain HTML. For example:

```
<table class="data-table" border="1">
    <tr>
        <th>First Name</th>
        <th>Last Name</th>
        <th>Title</th>
        <th>Currently Employed</th>
    </tr>
    <tr>
        <td>John</td>
        <td>Doe</td>
        <td>Director Of Professional Services</td>
        <td>Yes</td>
    </tr>
    <tr>
        <td>Jane</td>
        <td>Plane</td>
        <td>Vice President</td>
        <td>Yes</td>
    </tr>
    <tr>
        <td>Mike</td>
        <td>Vick</td>
        <td>Sr. Engineer</td>
        <td>No</td>
    </tr>
    <tr>
        <td>Roland</td>
        <td>Wolters</td>
        <td>Engineer</td>
        <td>Yes</td>
    </tr>
</table>
```

Displayed in the browser, this would simply render a table with the data in various columns, decorated with table borders. However, let's make this same data table available as a downloadable Excel file that users can manipulate by sorting, pivoting, or using any of the other standard operations provided by Excel.

Listings 4-4 and 4-5 demonstrate the switching of content type using the `altTemplate` attribute.

I've jumped ahead a little here by introducing the concept of macros (covered in Chapter 5). For now, you can assume that this will all work.

LISTING 4-4: ExcelDownload.master

Available for download on Wrox.com

```
<%@ Master Language="C#" MasterPageFile="/umbraco/masterpages/default.master"
 AutoEventWireup="true" %>
<asp:Content ContentPlaceHolderID="ContentPlaceHolderDefault"
 runat="server">
<umbraco:Macro Alias="ExportTableDataToExcel"
 runat="server"></umbraco:Macro>
</asp:Content>
```

LISTING 4-5: ExportTableDataToExcel.xslt

Available for download on Wrox.com

```
<?xml version="1.0" encoding="UTF-8"?>
<!DOCTYPE xsl:stylesheet [
  <!ENTITY nbsp " ">
]>
<xsl:stylesheet
        version="1.0"
        xmlns:xsl="http://www.w3.org/1999/XSL/Transform"
        xmlns:msxml="urn:schemas-microsoft-com:xslt"
        xmlns:usg="urn:usg-com:xslt"
        xmlns:umbraco.library="urn:umbraco.library"
xmlns:Exslt.ExsltCommon="urn:Exslt.ExsltCommon"
xmlns:Exslt.ExsltDatesAndTimes="urn:Exslt.ExsltDatesAndTimes"
xmlns:Exslt.ExsltMath="urn:Exslt.ExsltMath"
xmlns:Exslt.ExsltRegularExpressions="urn:Exslt.ExsltRegularExpressions"
xmlns:Exslt.ExsltStrings="urn:Exslt.ExsltStrings"
xmlns:Exslt.ExsltSets="urn:Exslt.ExsltSets"
        exclude-result-prefixes="msxml umbraco.library Exslt.ExsltCommon
Exslt.ExsltDatesAndTimes Exslt.ExsltMath Exslt.ExsltRegularExpressions
Exslt.ExsltStrings Exslt.ExsltSets usg">
  <xsl:output method="xml" omit-xml-declaration="yes"/>


  <msxml:script language="CSharp" implements-prefix="usg">
    <msxml:assembly name="System.Web" />
    <msxml:using namespace="System.Web" />

    <![CDATA[
public void changeOutPut(String ContentType, String FileName) {
        HttpContext.Current.Response.ContentType = ContentType;
        HttpContext.Current.Response.AddHeader("content-disposition",
                        "attachment;filename=" + FileName);
}
]]>

  </msxml:script>
```

continues

LISTING 4-5 *(continued)*

```
  <xsl:param name="currentPage"/>

  <xsl:template match="/">
    <xsl:variable name="fileName" select="concat('name-data-',@nodeName,'.xls')"
/>
    <xsl:value-of select="usg:changeOutPut('application/msexcel',$fileName)" />
    <table cellpadding="0" cellspacing="0" border="0">
        <tr>
            <th>First Name</th>
            <th>Last Name</th>
            <th>Title</th>
            <th>Currently Employed</th>
        </tr>
        <tr>
            <td>John</td>
            <td>Doe</td>
            <td>Director Of Professional Services</td>
            <td>Yes</td>
        </tr>
        <tr>
            <td>Jane</td>
            <td>Plane</td>
            <td>Vice President</td>
            <td>Yes</td>
        </tr>
        <tr>
            <td>Mike</td>
            <td>Vick</td>
            <td>Sr. Engineer</td>
            <td>No</td>
        </tr>
        <tr>
            <td>Roland</td>
            <td>Wolters</td>
            <td>Engineer</td>
            <td>Yes</td>
        </tr>
    </table>
  </xsl:template>

</xsl:stylesheet>
```

The No Template Effect

If no template is selected, the effect will be a blank white page with no output at all. This is because Umbraco relies solely on the use of master pages to render the content. So, if no template is selected, then effectively no way exists to output content to the browser.

Checking the template ID of nodes/pages in the XML cache is also possible, as discussed in Chapter 2 and shown in Listings 4-6 and 4-7.

LISTING 4-6: Checking the templateId in Umbraco v 4.x

Available for download on Wrox.com

```
<node id="1049" parentID="1048" level="2" writerID="0" creatorID="0"
nodeType="1046" template="0" sortOrder="1" createDate="2008-06-
01T23:12:54" updateDate="2010-08-01T08:20:16" nodeName="Installing runway
modules" urlName="installing-runway-modules" writerName="Administrator"
creatorName="Administrator" nodeTypeAlias="RunwayTextpage" path="-
1,1048,1049">…</>
```

LISTING 4-7: Checking the templateId in Umbraco v 4.5

Available for download on Wrox.com

```
<Textpage id="1049" parentID="1048" level="2" writerID="0" creatorID="0"
nodeType="1046" template="0" sortOrder="1" createDate="2008-06-01T23:12:54"
updateDate="2010-08-06T07:55:42" nodeName="Installing runway modules"
urlName="installing-runway-modules" writerName="Administrator"
creatorName="Administrator" path="-1,1048,1049" isDoc="">…</>
```

When the `templateId` is `0` or blank, it's a good indication that a template has not been selected for the node/page in question. The possibility also exists that Umbraco may need to rebuild the cache (if you have it configured to be `on`, which is the default value). As shown in Figure 4-15, simply right-click on the top Content node in the content tree and select Republish entire site.

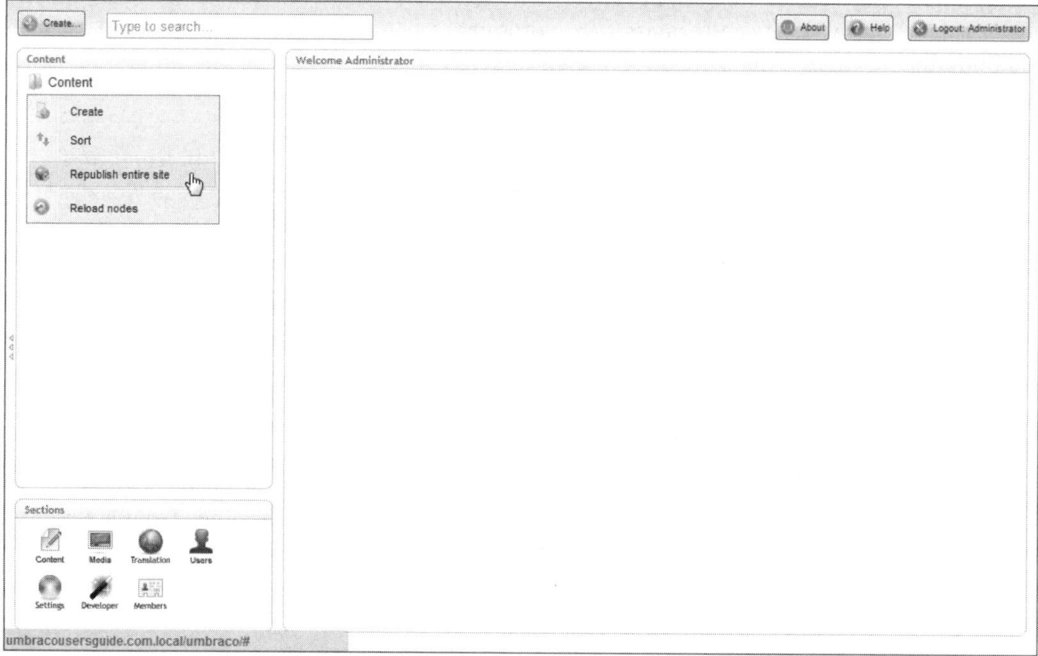

FIGURE 4-15

STYLES AND SCRIPTS

Styles and scripts are what bring a website to life. They are a critical part of today's website architecture and Umbraco has made them a large part of the backoffice UI. Like with all the other coding functionality, both CSS and JavaScript files are edited in a syntax highlighter that also includes row numbers. As a developer, you can maintain and code all of your styles and scripts within the Umbraco UI, but best practice dictates that you work on such assets outside of the web UI to maintain processes such as code versioning and multi-developer environments.

As mentioned earlier, please see Appendix B for working with files outside of Umbraco and for best practice advice on how to set up your development environment in Visual Studio 2010.

Defining Your Styles

The CMS allows you to expose your styles to the Rich Text Editor data type in order for authors to truly get a WYSIWYG (What You See Is What You Get) environment in which to edit content. Best practice suggests that as a developer, you plan your styles in at least two different physical files — one for the layouts of your site and one that dictates aspects such as paragraph styles, floating images, headings, bulleted lists, and so on. The idea is that applying the "content" styles to the editor data type without the baggage of all the layout styles as well is then possible.

This can have an effect on the TinyMCE Rich Text Editor, specifically when dealing with body background. If you choose to go with a single CSS file for all your styles, you can override individual classes of the TinyMCE editor to avoid having, for example, a black background in the editor frame. You do this by targeting selectors like `.mceContentBody` *and* `.mceEditorIframe`*. You can inspect the output HTML of the TinyMCE data type by using FireBug in Mozilla Firefox.*

Layout and Organization

Now it's time to create some CSS stylesheets and associated styles. As mentioned earlier you will have a total of two stylesheets for this implementation — one that houses the layout styles (and standard resets), and one that you'll apply to the Rich Text Editor data type:

- `runway.css`
- `rte-content.css`

Follow these steps:

1. Navigate to the Settings section of the backoffice.
2. Right-click the Stylesheets node, and select the Create menu item.
3. In the Create dialog that appears, shown in Figure 4-16, name your stylesheet **`rte-content`**.

Make sure to exclude the .css extension *here because it is automatically created by Umbraco when you save the file.*

4. Click the Create button.

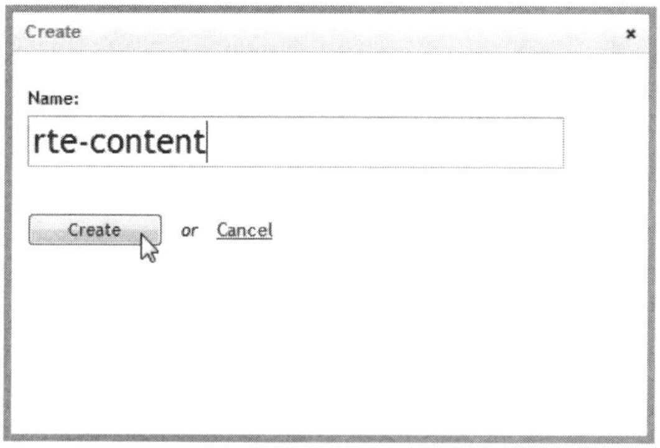

FIGURE 4-16

These steps create a file called `rte-content.css` in the `/css/` directory of your installation (for example, `c:/Inetpub/wwwroot/umbusersguide.com/css/rte-content.css`), as also indicated in the `Path` property of the stylesheet, shown in Figure 4-17. This figure also shows the result after you create the initial stylesheet.

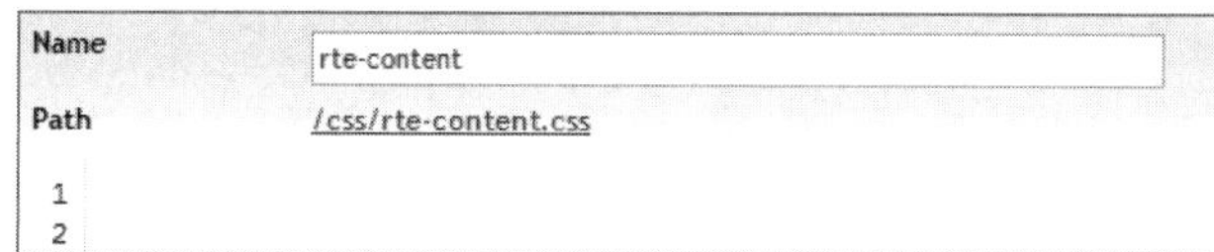

FIGURE 4-17

Use Listings 4-8 and 4-9 when populating your stylesheets.

`Runway.css` *is already installed if you followed the installation steps outlined in Chapter 1. If you did not elect to install Runway and modules, simply create your own stylesheets as needed for your website.*

Available for download on Wrox.com

LISTING 4-8: runway.css

```
/*LAYOUT*/

body{text-align: center; padding: 0px; margin: 0px; background: #F6F7F9;}

#main{margin: auto; margin-top: 20px; text-align: center; width: 870px;}

#top{border-bottom: 1px solid #CED7DE;}

#top ul{list-style: none; padding: 0px 0px 15px 0px; margin: 0px;}
#top ul li{display: inline; margin: 0px; padding: 0xp;}
#top ul li a{padding: 10px;}

#body{margin: auto; padding: 2em 0em 2em 0em;}
#footer{padding-top: 5px; clear: both;}

/* Subpages layout */
#content{text-align: left;}

#subNavigation{width: 20em; float: right;}
#subNavigation ul{list-style: none; border: 1px solid #FFE8CD; background: #FFF9D8;}

/* FONTS standards */
body {font-size: 14px; background:#fff; font-family: "Lucida Grande", Arial,
 sans-serif;}

h1, h2, h3, h4, h5, h6 {color: #426FC8; font-weight: 500;}
h1 {font-size:60px; line-height: 1; margin-bottom:0.5em; font-weight: bold;
text-align: center; letter-spacing: -1px; width: auto; color: #666;}
h2 {font-size:25px; margin-bottom:0.75em;}

h3 {font-size: 18px;line-height:1;margin-bottom:1em;}
h4 {font-size:1.2em;line-height:1.25;margin-bottom:1.25em;height:1.25em;}
h5 {font-size:1em;font-weight:bold;margin-bottom:1.5em;}
h6 {font-size:1em;font-weight:bold;}
h1 img, h2 img, h3 img, h4 img, h5 img, h6 img {margin:0;}

p {margin:0 0 1.5em; color: #666; font-size: 16px;}
p img {float:left;margin:1.5em 1.5em 1.5em 0;padding:0;}
p img.right {float:right;margin:1.5em 0 1.5em 1.5em;}

/* LINKS standards */
a:focus, a:hover {color:#000;}
a {color: #14223E;text-decoration:underline;}
h1 a{color: #666; text-decoration: none;}

/* ELEMENTS standards */
blockquote {margin:1.5em;color:#666;font-style:italic;}
strong {font-weight:bold;}
em, dfn {font-style:italic;}
dfn {font-weight:bold;}
```

```
sup, sub {line-height:0;}
abbr, acronym {border-bottom:1px dotted #666;}
address {margin:0 0 1.5em;font-style:italic;}
del {color:#666;}
pre, code {margin:1.5em 0;white-space:pre;}
pre, code, tt {font:1em "andale mono", "lucida console",
monospace;line-height:1.5;}
li ul, li ol {margin:0 1.5em;}
ul, ol {margin:0 1.5em 1.5em 1.5em;}
ul {list-style-type:disc;}
ol {list-style-type:decimal;}
dl {margin:0 0 1.5em 0;}
dl dt {font-weight:bold;}
dd {margin-left:1.5em;}
table {margin-bottom:1.4em;width:100%;}
th {font-weight:bold;background:#C3D9FF;}
th, td {padding:4px 10px 4px 5px;}
tr.even td {background:#E5ECF9;}
tfoot {font-style:italic;}
caption {background:#eee;}

/* FORM ELEMENTS */
label {font-weight:bold;}
fieldset {padding:1.4em;margin:0 0 1.5em 0;border:1px solid #ccc;}
legend {font-weight:bold;font-size:1.2em;}
input.text, input.title, textarea, select {margin:0.5em 0;border:1px solid #bbb;}
input.text:focus, input.title:focus, textarea:focus, select:focus
{border:1px solid #666;}
input.text, input.title {width:300px;padding:5px;}
input.title {font-size:1.5em;}
textarea {width:300px;height:250px;padding:5px;}
.error, .notice, .success {padding:.8em;margin-bottom:1em;border:2px solid #ddd;}
.error {background:#FBE3E4;color:#8a1f11;border-color:#FBC2C4;}
.notice {background:#FFF6BF;color:#514721;border-color:#FFD324;}
.success {background:#E6EFC2;color:#264409;border-color:#C6D880;}
.error a {color:#8a1f11;}
.notice a {color:#514721;}
.success a {color:#264409;}

.error ul{margin-bottom: 0; padding-bottom: 0;}
```

LISTING 4-9: rte-content.css

Available for download on Wrox.com

```
p {
    font-size: 13px;
    line-height: 18px;
    margin: 10px 0;
}
img {
    background: #dff0f9;
    padding: 8px;
```

continues

LISTING 4-9 *(continued)*

```
    border: 1px solid #7f7f7f;
    margin: 0 10px 10px 10px;
}
.left {
    float: left;
    margin-left: 0;
}
.right {
    float: right;
    margin-right: 0;
}
ul {
    margin: 15px 25px;
}
ul li {
    background: url(images/ico_arrow_more.gif) no-repeat 0 3px;
    padding-left: 10px;
    margin-bottom: 10px;
}

h2, h3 {
    font-size: 16px;
    font-weight: 600;
    margin-top: 25px;
}

h3 {
    font-size: 13px;
}

<!-- Styles to override TinyMCE defaults -->
.mceItemTable
{
    margin: 10px;
    border-collapse: collapse;
    border: 1px solid #000;
    width: 95%;
}

.mceItemTable td
{
    padding: 5px;
    border: 1px solid #000;
}

.mceItemTable td.heading
{
    background: #ececec;
    color: #333;
    font-weight: 600;
}
```

Handling Images

A point of contention exists in the community about how to handle images for a website within Umbraco (and in general). Everyone has a twist on the "standards" and for Umbraco there seems to be two main schools of thought. One is to utilize Umbraco's media storage capabilities to maintain any and all website image assets. The argument is that now the images are easily editable by content editors and writers. The other is to create a non-editable folder inside your website root and reference the images from there. Both are valid, but one is preferable. Best practice suggests that you maintain and manage your website assets outside of Umbraco's media library. Here's why:

- Website assets that make up the layout and design of a website should not be editable and easily changed by non-technical users. Even in a template-based system, such assets should be regionalized and strictly controlled so that the integrity and layout of the website is not hampered.
- Although Umbraco 4.5 (and later versions) cache media items, loading media assets by requesting them directly from the CMS for each reload of a given page still causes a performance hit.
- Maintaining the files within the Umbraco media library can be cumbersome and unpredictable because the default storage of such items is in randomly generated folder names. This means that for each file that is saved, you, as a developer, have to go and find the ID of the generated folder and reference the file by something like `/media/2345/`*`filename`*`.tif`. This is not ideal and can make for messy image references in your stylesheet.
- If you choose to store the files under `<install root>/css/images`, the paths in your CSS file are also simplified because all you need to do is use the relative path `images/*.tif|.gif|.png` to reference an asset.

So, it's really a question of what you and your team are used to and how much access you are willing to give to the editors and writers of the content. Use the preceding criteria as a guideline to make your decision.

Styles and the Rich Text Editor

The Rich Text Editor (RTE) data type provides a way to associate CSS classes and other selectors to the content that is entered and rendered by the RTE. This feature is very useful, because if it didn't exist, then users would not be able to get a feel for how the various elements will look after they are rendered as part of the overall template. I guess you could say that without this feature, the result would be WYSIWYDG (What You See Is What You Don't Get).

Fortunately for you as a developer, associating CSS classes to the content editor is made super simple and flexible by the styles backoffice UI, which allows you to hand-pick the selectors you want to expose to the authors of the content. The following exercise walks you through this process step by step.

1. Navigate to Settings ➪ Stylesheets.
2. Expand the node and right-click on the `rte-content.css` file that you created earlier.
3. Click Create as shown in Figure 4-18.

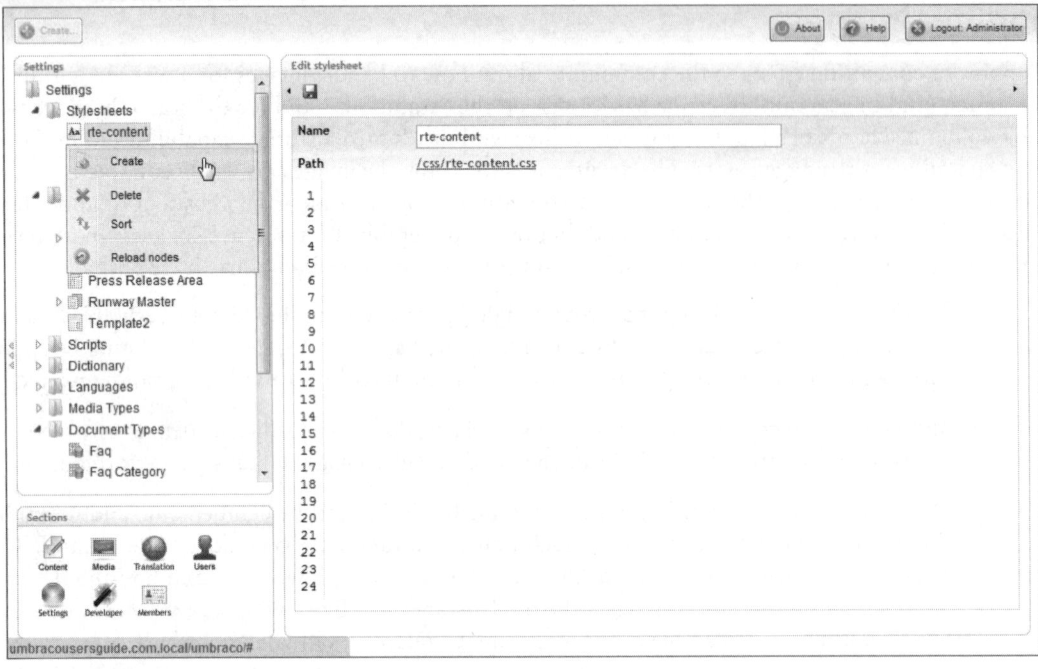

FIGURE 4-18

4. In the Create dialog, name your style, as shown in Figure 4-19.

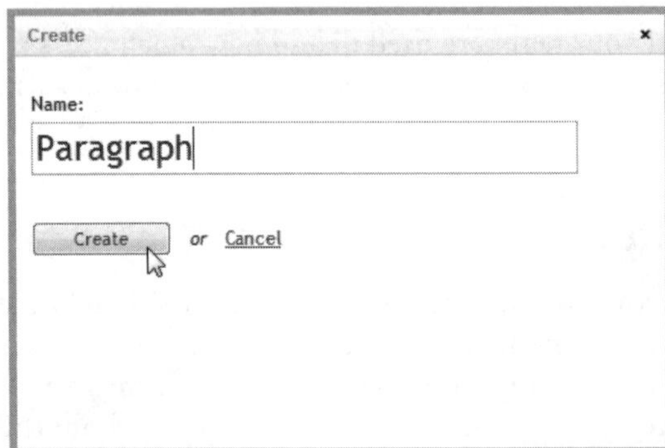

FIGURE 4-19

5. After creating the style you must assign an Alias to the style that will be used to actually apply the selector in your HTML. As shown in Figure 4-20, set your Alias to the `p` tag.

Aliases must be simple class names or full selectors. For example, `.headline`, `h1`, `h2`, `hr`, `td`, `.text`, *are all valid class and selector aliases, although this example,* `div.text`, *would not be valid. Adding this selector results in the RTE not applying a class to the selected element.*

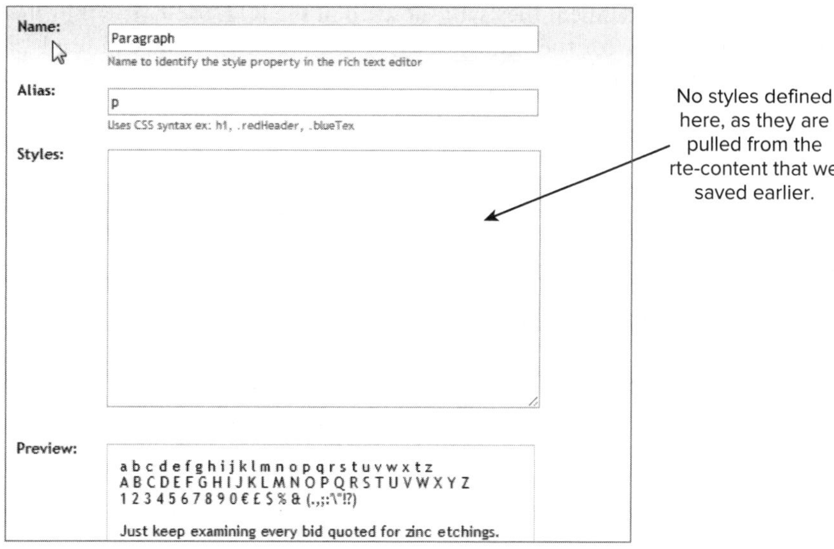

FIGURE 4-20

6. Repeat steps 1-5 for all the styles that you want to expose for the author to use.
7. You must do one more thing before exposing the styles to the end user: Assign the `rte-content.css` stylesheet as an available stylesheet to the RTE and make sure the Style dropdown is turned on for the data type. You do so by choosing Developer ➪ Data Types ➪ Rich Text Editor in the backoffice, as shown in Figure 4-21.

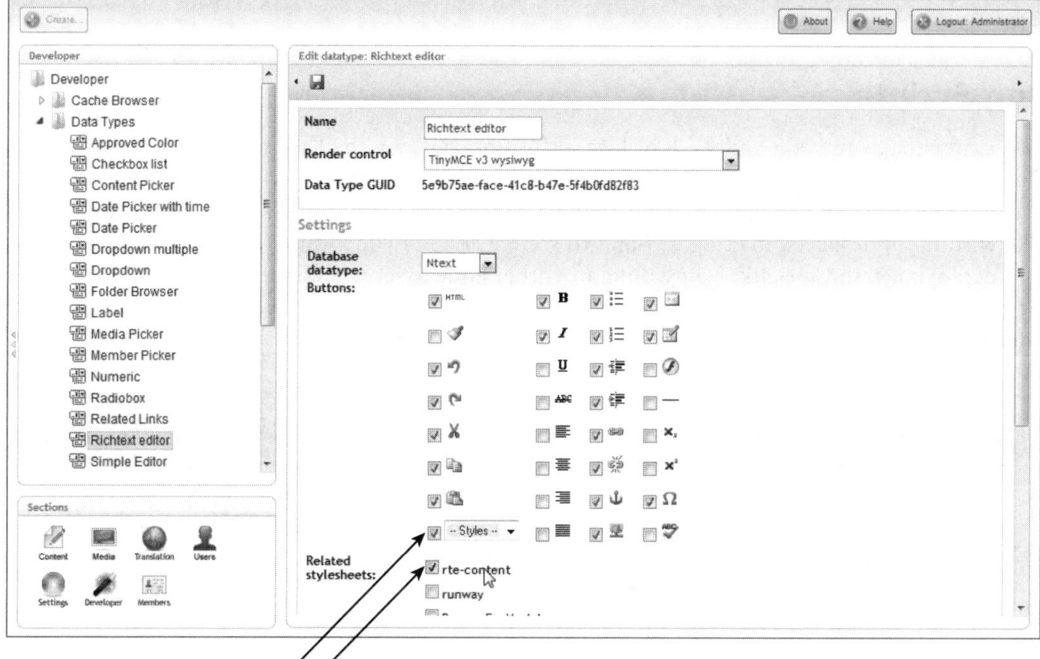

FIGURE 4-21

After all the styles have been defined, they will show up in the RTE toolbar within the Styles drop-down menu and be ready for the author to apply to the content. The end result should be similar to what you see in Figure 4-22.

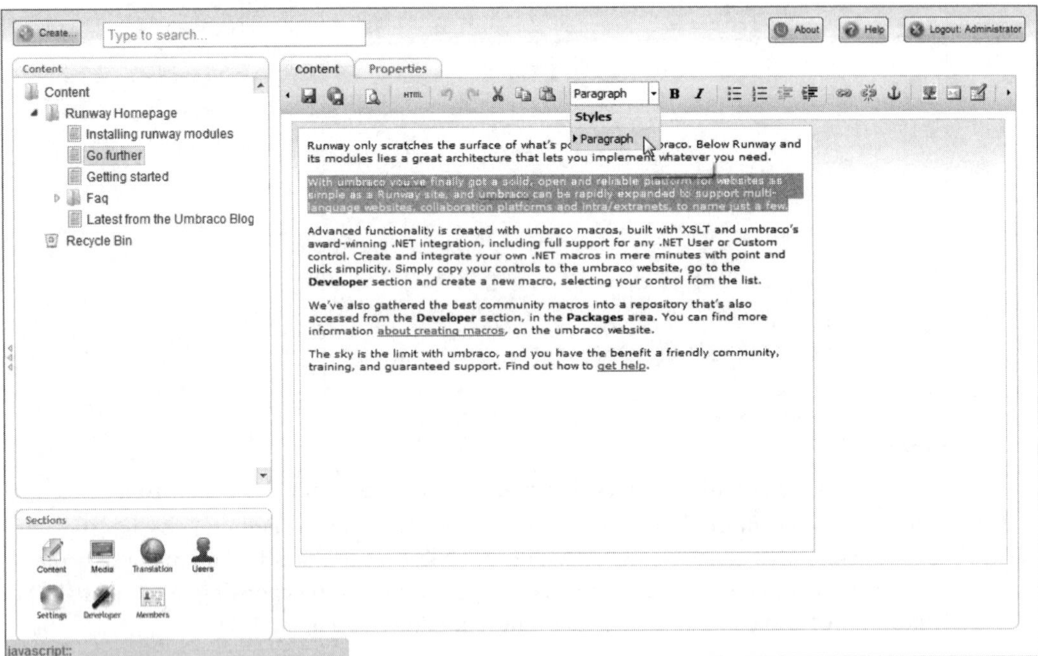

FIGURE 4-22

Using Scripts

You can manage and edit scripts, like JavaScript libraries, via the Umbraco backoffice as well. The functionality of script management is more limited than stylesheets, but you do the coding in the same interface. Being able to make changes quickly to a script file is useful for developers, but like with the stylesheets, making changes to source code in your source controlled environment and deploying script files like you would any other code asset is recommended. Again, please see Appendix B for further instructions on how to set up your external Visual Studio development environment.

When working with XSLT files or .NET macros, a developer can leverage the extension method for registering a JavaScript library in the page without cluttering up your code. To do this, use `umbraco.library:RegisterJavaScriptFile ('String key', 'String url')`*, which takes care of outputting the proper HTML syntax for including a JavaScript file in your page.*

TAKE HOME POINTS

You should now be prepared to tackle the layouts and rendering of all the content that you want to add to your Umbraco website. In particular, you should be well aware of the following concepts:

- Working with .NET master pages and child master pages to render the content from your content tree
- Being confident that the HTML markup you put in is what comes out when your website is rendered by Umbraco
- Using Umbraco specific tags to output content values and manipulating the way the values are rendered
- Knowing how to best work with images as assets to your layouts versus images needed for content creation
- Incorporating your own styles to impose stylistic rules on content editors via the Rich Text Editor

5

Using Macros

- What are macros in Umbraco?
- How do you build custom functionality into your Umbraco pages?
- How do you use XSLT to output content from the content tree?
- How do you extend the backoffice using .NET user controls?
- What other supported DLR languages can you use?

So far in this book, you've created the underlying structure for a site. But in this chapter, you'll add meat to this structure using the core of Umbraco's flexibility and extensibility — macros. Umbraco can easily be extended using custom functionality from .NET User Controls and XSLT templates. This is especially crucial when you are converting an existing application to the Umbraco CMS or when you're creating output of content nodes outside of the standard templates you created in Chapter 4.

So, coming out of this chapter you'll be able to generate lists of content nodes, add your own custom fields for use in your document types, and parse content in a .NET User Control. Let the fun begin!

INTRODUCTION TO UMBRACO MACROS

In order to introduce custom functionality and specialty output to your Umbraco site, you will need to know about macros. A *macro* is essentially a callable action that executes a predefined chunk of code. This code can be made up of the following technologies/languages:

- .NET C# and VB User Controls
- .NET Custom Control (Server Control)
- XSLT Template
- IronPython, LOL Code, Ruby, and more

Macros are created in the Developer section ➪ Macros node. You can create one using the following steps:

1. Navigate to the Developer section in the backoffice, found at `http://<install domain>/umbraco`.
2. Right-click Macros, then click the Create menu option, as shown in Figure 5-1.

FIGURE 5-1

3. Select the .NET User Control, XSLT template, or other code source and save your Macro.

Figure 5-2 shows a "bird's-eye-view" of how to create macros in Umbraco, giving an overview of the fields and functions, which are described in Table 5-1.

Umbraco will create the Alias automatically by concatenating the Name value, stripping out spaces and special characters.

In addition to creating the macro manually, you can specify that your XSLT file automatically generate the macro and preselect the newly create XSLT file as the source for this macro. This is the best practice way of creating your XSLT macros.

In a typical site there is little concern about caching your macros. The Cache Period option is mostly for high-traffic sites and should be used with care because it may impact the rendering of certain content. For example, if you are using a .NET user control to pull in stock quotes, the caching set here can impact the information if it is presented in real-time.

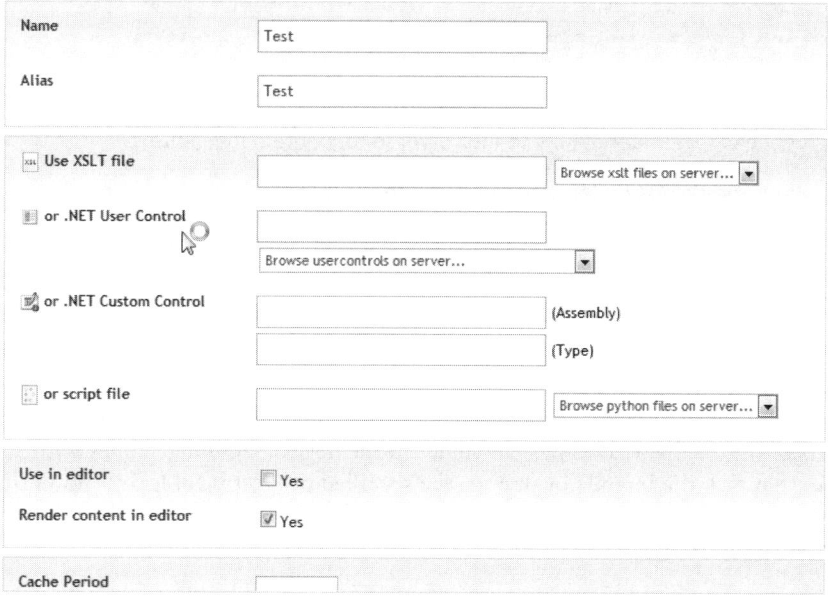

FIGURE 5-2

TABLE 5-1: Macro Functions

FIELD/FUNCTION	DESCRIPTION
Name	The human readable name/description of your macro.
Alias	This targets the macro in templates and within content when it's later used.
Use XSLT file	Select the XSLT file that you want to use. XSLT files are stored in the `xslt` folder in your Umbraco installation.
or .NET User Control	Select the `.ascx` file that you want like to use. The User Control files must be placed in the `usercontrols` folder in your Umbraco installation in order to appear in the drop-down list.
or .NET Custom Control	Specify the assembly and type for the custom control that you have placed in the site's `/bin` folder.
or script file	Select the script file that you want to use.
Use in editor	Selecting this option allows you to select this macro for insertion in the Rich Text Editor data type.
Render content in editor	This option renders the contents of your .NET user control within the Rich Text Editor data type in the backoffice.

continues

TABLE 5-1 *(continued)*

FIELD/FUNCTION	DESCRIPTION
Cache Period	The number of seconds you want the macro to be cached on the client. This reduces the number of trips to the server to regenerate the content.
Cache By Page	This is the default option, used to cache the output by URL.
Cache Personalized	If selected, the macro caches content by member login. This is useful for personalization features like names, etc.

Macro Parameters

You've surely noticed that we have two tabs for editing a macro. The Parameters tab allows you to specify public properties that can be used to pass in values to the macro. Umbraco comes with a set of predefined types that pick the intended value for the specified property. Table 5-2 shows the details of the various types, while Figure 5-3 shows the output of the various types and how they are presented to the user when inserting your macro.

TABLE 5-2: Macro Parameter Types

MACRO PARAMETER TYPE	DESCRIPTION	CODE OUTPUT
`bool`	Allows the user to specify true or false by toggling a check box.	A 1 (one) or 0 (zero) is rendered as the value.
`contentAll`	A content node picker is provided as the control for picking the desired start node.	A list of node ID's encapsulated in the `<contentAll />` XML element.
`contentPicker`	A content node picker is provided as the control for picking the desired node.	The selected node's ID is returned encapsulated in the `<contentPicker />` XML element.
`contentRandom`	A content node picker is provided as the control for picking the desired start node.	The random node's ID is returned encapsulated in the `<contentRandom />` XML element.
`contentSubs`	A content node picker is provided as the control for picking the desired start node.	An XML nodeset is returned with the complete Umbraco XML representation of the content below and including the start node chosen.
`contentTree`	A content node picker is provided as the control for picking the desired start node.	An XML nodeset is returned with the complete Umbraco XML representation of the content below and including the start node chosen.

MACRO PARAMETER TYPE	DESCRIPTION	CODE OUTPUT
`contentType`	A drop-down list of the document types in the Settings section.	ID of the selected document type.
`contentTypeMultiple`	A multi-select list box of all available document types from the Settings section.	A comma-separated list of document type IDs.
`mediaCurrent`	A media picker control is provided allowing the user to select a folder, file, or image from the media tree.	The ID of the selected media item.
`number`	A small input text field for entering a numeric value.	The value entered.
`propertyTypePicker`	A drop-down list of the various document type properties from all document types that you created.	The name of the document type property.
`propertyTypePickerMultiple`	A multi-select list box of all available document type properties from the Settings section.	A comma-separated list of document type property names.
`tabPicker`	A drop-down list with all available tabs as they were created for your document types in the Settings section.	The selected tab name.
`tabPickerMultiple`	A multi-select list box of all available document type tabs from the Settings section.	A comma-separated list of tab names.
`text`	A single-line text box input control for entering a text string.	The entered text string.
`textMultiLine`	A multi-line text box input control for entering a text string.	The entered text string.

Naming your macro parameters with reserve .NET tag property names will not work. For example, do not create a macro parameter named Id or CssClass as those are reserved for use in standard .NET tags.

Insert Macro ×

Boolean	☐ Yes
Content All	Choose...
Content Picker	Choose...
Content Random	Choose...
Content Subs	Choose...
Content Tree	Choose...
Content Type	
Content Type Multiple	FAQ FAQ Area Runway Homepage Runway Textpage
Media	Choose...
Number	
Property Type Picker	
Property Type Picker Multiple	answer author

OK or Cancel

FIGURE 5-3

Rendering Macros In Your Site

You have two ways of displaying the results of your created macros independent of how they are sourced (XSLT, .NET, or other). Depending on how you configured the macro in the settings, as described earlier in this chapter in Table 5-2, you can add the macro tag in a Rich Text Editor data type control within your content, as shown in Figure 5-4, or you can add the macro tag directly in your master page templates, as shown in Figure 5-5.

FIGURE 5-4

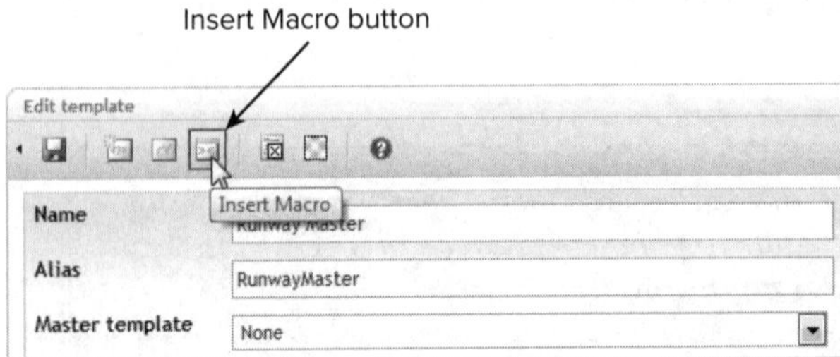

FIGURE 5-5

A macro inserted in your template will have the following format:

```
<umbraco:Macro Alias="NameOfMacroHere" parameter1="" parameter2=""
runat="server"></umbraco:Macro>
```

This example shows that parameters, as we discussed in the previous section, are added as simple tag attributes. The result in the Rich Text Editor is slightly different and is not meant to be edited by hand: you use the Macro button shown in Figure 5-4 to edit and control your macro.

XSLT POWERED MACROS

Using XSLT can be rather daunting if it's a new language for you. But, once you have a grasp of how to use it, you can whip up custom navigation, RSS feeds, depicted calendars, product lists, and much more with great ease. The good news is that Umbraco comes with a set of predefined templates that you can use to generate standard output such as navigation and sitemaps. What's more is that they serve as a powerful learning tool to get you started on creating more advanced output and tailoring the stylesheets to your needs.

About XSLT

If you're an avid XSL developer you can skip this section because it covers the bare-bone basics of what XSLT is and how it applies to Umbraco. XSLT stands for Extensible Stylesheet Language Transformation and is made up of XSL. XSL is basically a way to render structured data, in the form of XML elements, to the browser. There are a number of other ways to parse XML elements but we won't get into those here; however, you can find out how to parse these elements in *Beginning XSLT and XPath: Transforming XML Documents and Data* (Wiley, 2009).

Microsoft .NET uses the XSL 1.0 specification. This means that you cannot take advantage of more advanced functions and methods presented in XSL 2.0.

The most important part of learning and using XSLT with Umbraco is understanding how you traverse the cached XML content tree using the XML Path Language, aka XPath. Inspecting and learning the structure of the XML cache will allow you to drill down and specify exactly what parts of the content structure you are looking for. The XML cache file can be found in `~/App_Data/umbraco.config`.

In addition, Umbraco uses a parameter, `currentPage`, that is always available to you. This parameter holds the entire nodeset of the current node where the template is going to be executed, which in turn also includes all child nodes and grandchild nodes. From a performance standpoint this is great because you are not constantly querying the entire XML nodeset from memory.

Finally, you should know that Umbraco comes with something called an XSLT Extension Library, which allows you to easily do things like formatting dates, split strings, truncate strings, and a whole lot more. Of course, on top of that you can also leverage the EXSLT extensions that are part of the XSL parsing libraries in .NET.

All these important XSLT features — XPath, `currentPage`, and the XSLT Extension Library — are thoroughly examined through various examples, both in the remaining portions of this chapter, as well as throughout the rest of the book.

For more details on XSL and the W3C specification, please visit `http://www.w3c.org/TR/xsl`.

XSLT macros can ONLY access published content because it looks at the in-memory XML cache found in `~/App_Data/umbraco.config`. *This XML structure does not include unpublished nodes. To access unpublished content, you have to use either .NET driven macros, DLR (Python and Ruby) driven macros, or add XSLT extensions to access the data from the database.*

Using the Built-in XSLT Templates

As mentioned earlier, Umbraco ships with a number of XSLT templates to get you going. When creating a new XSLT file, as shown in Figure 5-6, you can choose to base your new file on one of the templates listed in Table 5-3.

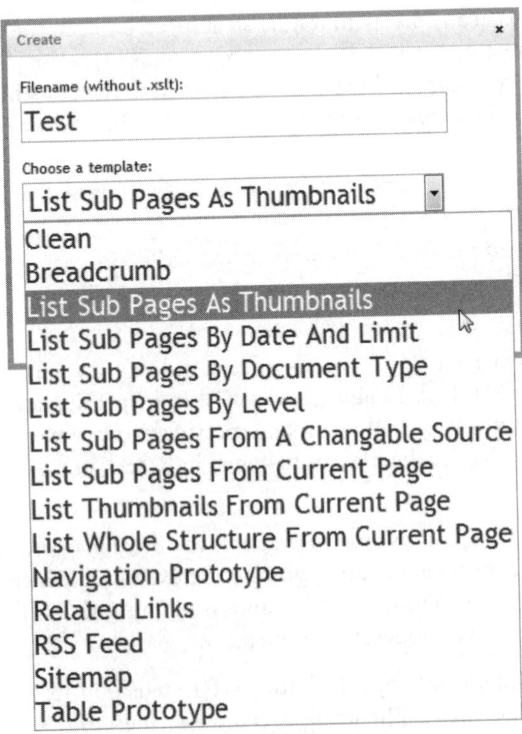

FIGURE 5-6

TABLE 5-3: Built-in XSLT Templates

TEMPLATE NAME	DESCRIPTION	RESULT EXAMPLE
Breadcrumb	Used to indicate the path of the current page that the user is on. Typically used at the top of each page within your website.	Home ⇨ Subpage ⇨ Sub-sub page
List Sub Pages As Thumbnails	Pages listed using this template will render a provided media picker field by targeting the "_thumb" version of the image.	
List Sub Pages By Date And Limit	Lists x number of pages, specified in the variable named `numberOfItems`, and sorted by the last updated date in descending order.	Unordered list of pages
List Sub Pages By Document Type	Outputs a list of pages that are filtered by the specified document type.	Unordered list of pages
List Sub Pages By Level	Only pages that are at the given level in the content tree are rendered. Specify the number of levels by changing the variable named "level".	Unordered list of pages
List Sub Pages From A Changeable Source	This template allows you to specify where to start in the content tree by providing a `nodeId`. The `nodeId` of the page can be found in the Properties tab on the content node from within the content tree.	Unordered list of pages
List Sub Pages From Current Page	Lists all of the direct child pages from the current page that the user is viewing.	Unordered list of pages
List Whole Structure From Current Page	Lists the entire content structure recursively.	Unordered list of pages
Navigation Prototype	Outputs pages by level to render a list with built-in logic to select the current page that the user is viewing.	Unordered list of pages
Related Links	Related links is different that the standard page output. It renders items added using the Related Links data type. This data type is discussed in greater detail in Appendix D.	Unordered list of pages that are chosen using the Related Links data type
RSS Feed	Outputs pages from the current page in valid RSS version 2.0 format. This includes changing the content type so that the browser streams the content in the correct format.	Valid RSS feed

continues

TABLE 5-3 *(continued)*

TEMPLATE NAME	DESCRIPTION	RESULT EXAMPLE
Sitemap	Recursively outputs all of the pages in your content tree.	Unordered list of pages
Table Prototype	Renders pages from the current page in an HTML table with various options for alternate row color and more.	HTML table

To get an idea of what a template looks like, see Listing 5-1, which shows how the Breadcrumb template is created. Bolded portions of the template show the critical parts of the XSLT file that specify what pages to select and also shows the use of an XSLT extension method from the `umbraco.library` extensions method library, covered in detail in "Using XSLT Extensions" later in this chapter.

LISTING 5-1: Breadcrumb.xslt

Available for download on Wrox.com

```
<?xml version="1.0" encoding="UTF-8"?>
<!DOCTYPE xsl:stylesheet [  <!ENTITY nbsp " ">]>
<xsl:stylesheet
  version="1.0"
  xmlns:xsl="http://www.w3.org/1999/XSL/Transform"
  xmlns:msxml="urn:schemas-microsoft-com:xslt"
  xmlns:umbraco.library="urn:umbraco.library"
xmlns:Exslt.ExsltCommon="urn:Exslt.ExsltCommon"
xmlns:Exslt.ExsltDatesAndTimes="urn:Exslt.ExsltDatesAndTimes"
xmlns:Exslt.ExsltMath="urn:Exslt.ExsltMath"
xmlns:Exslt.ExsltRegularExpressions="urn:Exslt.ExsltRegularExpressions"
xmlns:Exslt.ExsltStrings="urn:Exslt.ExsltStrings"
xmlns:Exslt.ExsltSets="urn:Exslt.ExsltSets"
  exclude-result-prefixes="msxml umbraco.library Exslt.ExsltCommon
Exslt.ExsltDatesAndTimes Exslt.ExsltMath Exslt.ExsltRegularExpressions
Exslt.ExsltStrings Exslt.ExsltSets ">

  <xsl:output method="xml" omit-xml-declaration="yes"/>

  <xsl:param name="currentPage"/>

  <xsl:variable name="minLevel" select="1"/>

  <xsl:template match="/">

    <xsl:if test="$currentPage/@level &gt; $minLevel">
      <ul>
        <xsl:for-each select="$currentPage/ancestor::* [@level &gt; $minLevel
 and string(umbracoNaviHide) != '1']">
          <li>
            <a href="{umbraco.library:NiceUrl(@id)}">
              <xsl:value-of select="@nodeName"/>
            </a>
```

```
          </li>
        </xsl:for-each>
        <!-- print currentpage -->
        <li>
          <xsl:value-of select="$currentPage/@nodeName"/>
        </li>
      </ul>
    </xsl:if>
  </xsl:template>
</xsl:stylesheet>
```

To save an XSLT file in the Umbraco backoffice you can use the commonly used keyboard combination, Ctrl+S.

The following steps provide a step-by-step walkthrough of Listing 5-1.

1. The template starts at the current node by referencing the `currentPage` parameter and traverses up the tree using the `ancestor` *axes* to start at the top most parent of this node.
2. The XPath statement is further refined by filtering with the `@level` attribute, which tells the loop where to start in the hierarchy.
3. The XPath statement makes sure to only include nodes where the `umbracoNaviHide` property is not set to a value of 1 (or true as it is meant in this case).
4. Inside the loop you output an HTML list item, and inside that is a bit of magic, namely a call to one of the afore mentioned XSLT extension methods. See the next section for details on how to insert and use extension methods.
5. The output that the user will see is set to be the `@nodeName`, which is an attribute of the current node and represents the Name that you give the node when it is first created, as seen in Figure 5-7.

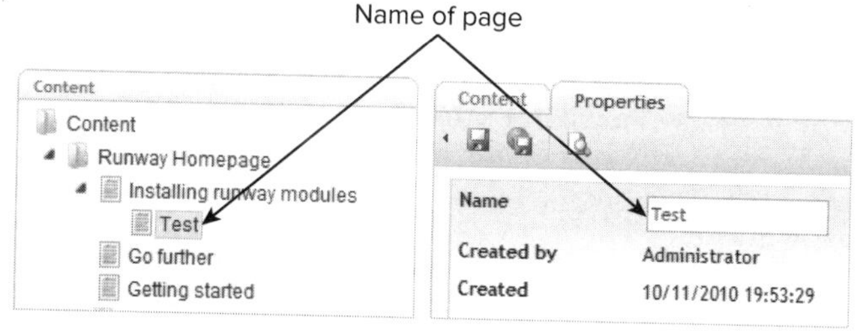

FIGURE 5-7

6. Finally, and outside of the `<xsl:for-each />` loop, you output the current node to indicate the page that the user is presently viewing.

Creating an XSLT Macro

Now that you know the inner workings of this template, let's see how to create this from scratch.

1. Navigate to the Developer section.
2. Right-click XSLT Files and click the Create menu option.
3. Enter **SiteBreadcrumb** in the Filename field and choose Breadcrumb as the template in the dropdown, as shown in Figure 5-8. Leave the Create Macro option selected (not shown here, but easily visible on your screen).

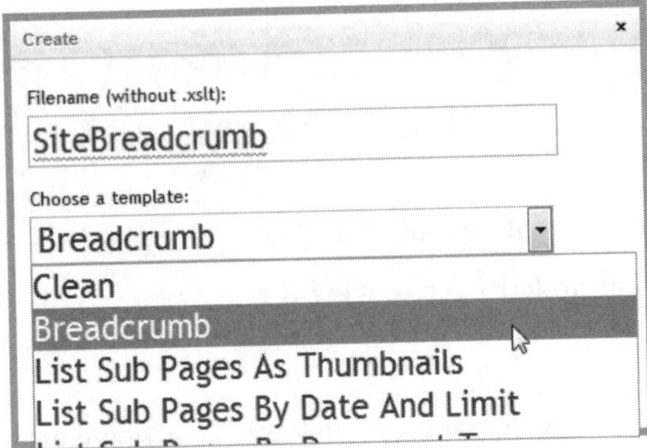

FIGURE 5-8

6. Click the Create button.

You can now reload the Macros node in the Developers section and see that a Macro was added named Site Breadcrumb, with the newly created XSLT file pre-selected.

So, now what? You have a terrific little macro but need somewhere to put it. The appropriate location to include this macro is in one of your templates, seeing as you want this displayed on all your internal pages and it is context sensitive. The bolded code in Listing 5-2 shows the syntax for including a macro in your template. If you installed Runway during installation in Chapter 1, the best template to place this macro in is Runway Textpage, as shown in Listing 5-2.

LISTING 5-2: RunwayTextpage.master

Available for download on Wrox.com

```
<%@ Master Language="C#" MasterPageFile="~/masterpages/RunwayMaster.master"
AutoEventWireup="true" %>
<asp:Content ContentPlaceHolderID="RunwayMasterContentPlaceHolder"
runat="server">
    <div id="content">
        <umbraco:Macro Alias="SiteBreadcrumb"
runat="server"></umbraco:Macro>
```

```
                <div id="contentHeader">
               <h2><umbraco:Item runat="server" field="pageName"/></h2>
           </div>
           <umbraco:Item runat="server" field="bodyText" />
       </div>
       <div id="subNavigation"></div>
   </asp:Content>
```

There's an easier way to insert the macro tag than typing it in there. To use the built-in Insert Macro tool, follow these steps.

1. Navigate to the Runway Textpage template in the Settings section.
2. Place the cursor where you want to insert the macro.
3. Click the Insert Macro button as shown in Figure 5-9.

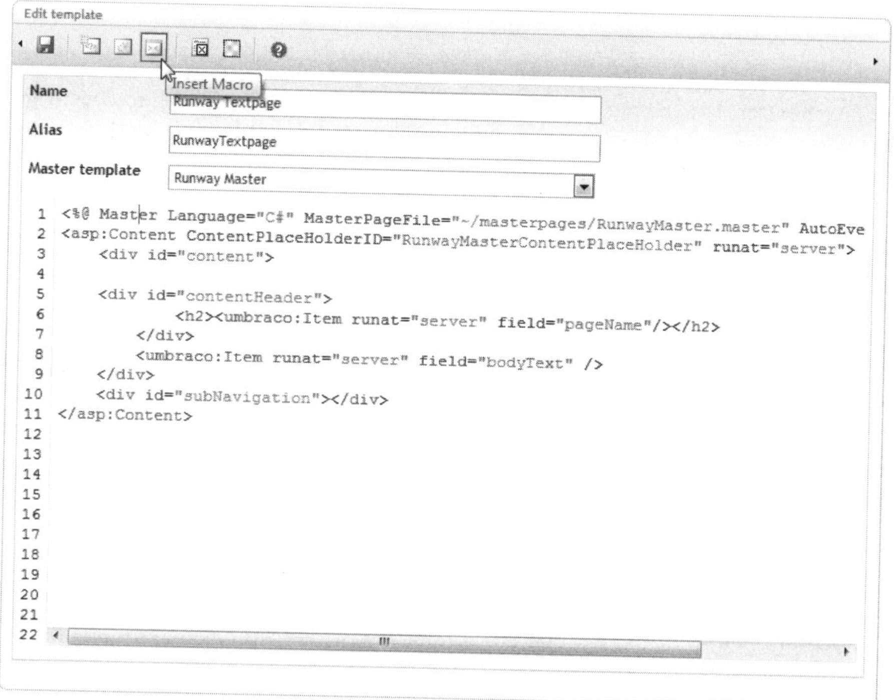

FIGURE 5-9

4. Select the macro to insert it and then click the OK button.

If you've specified macro parameters, clicking the OK button reveals a properties screen asking you to fill in the various fields associated with the macro parameters before the tag is inserted into the template.

Using XSLT Extensions to Make Macros Richer

Using XSLT extensions will provide you with a whole new set of tools to render and work with content nodes, custom data, and other standard features of .NET. Umbraco ships with the following libraries:

- `Exslt.ExsltCommon`
- `Exslt.ExsltDatesAndTimes`
- `Exslt.ExsltMath`
- `Exslt.ExsltRegularExpressions`
- `Exslt.ExsltSets`
- `Exslt.ExsltStrings`
- `umbraco.library`

The combination of all these libraries gives you access to hundreds of extension methods to make output of data easier. For the purposes of this book, however, we are going to cover the methods provided in the `umbraco.library` method library. The Umbraco library contains methods that allow you to access Umbraco data and functions specific to working with Umbraco pages, data types, and document types. It's beyond the scope of this book to describe each and every method in the `umbraco.library` library, so in Table 5-4 you get an overview of what the most widely used methods can do for you.

You can easily generate your own XSLT extensions library by creating a public class with public static methods in it. For an example of this, please refer to Chapter 12.

TABLE 5-4: Most Popular XSLT Extension Methods

METHOD NAME	DESCRIPTION	OUTPUT
`AddJquery()`	Umbraco uses jQuery for the back-office. So, instead of adding your own copy of jQuery you can rely on this convenient method to add a reference to the Umbraco UI copy. This inserts a script tag with the appropriate path in your HTML `<head>` section.	`<script id="ContentPlaceHolderDefault_jQuery" type="text/javascript" src="/umbraco_client/ui/jquery.js"></script>`
`CurrentDate()`	Retrieves the current date and time from the server.	Date

METHOD NAME	DESCRIPTION	OUTPUT
`DateAdd('String Date', 'String AddType', 'Int32 add')`	Adds a number of units to a given date object. `AddType` is the units, (day, hour, etc.) `Int32` is the number of units to add.	Date
`FormatDateTime ('String Date', 'String Format')`	Outputs the date in the format that you specify (MM/dd/yyyy, ddd MMM hh:mm:sss, etc.).	String
`GetMedia ('Int32 MediaId', 'Boolean Deep')`	Returns the nodeset for a media object. To see how to render an image from the media section, see the section "Going Further with XSLT" in this chapter.	XML nodeset
`GetXmlAll()`	Returns the entire XML document representing the content tree from the cache.	XML nodeset
`GetXmlNodeById ('String id')`	Returns a nodeset made up of the content structure starting at the supplied node ID.	XML nodeset
`IsLoggedOn()`	Determines if a member is currently logged on.	Boolean
`NiceUrl ('Int32 nodeID')`	Returns the absolute URL of the specified node ID. Used to link to internal pages.	String
`RequestQueryString ('String key')`	Retrieves the value of the supplied key from the request object query string.	String
`Split ('String StringToSplit', 'String Separator')`	Returns enumerable nodeset of the tokens in a string that are separated by the specified separator.	XML nodeset, for example: `<values>` `<value>1</value>` `<value>2</value>` `<value>3</value>` `</values>`
`TruncateString ('String Text', 'Int32 MaxLength', 'String AddString')`	Returns the first `MaxLength` number of characters from the input string and appends the specified string to the end. Useful when displaying things like search results with an appended "..." if the string is above a certain number of characters.	String

To utilize any of the methods in Table 5-4, and the rest of the available methods, simply follow these steps:

1. Open your XSLT file in the backoffice editor by navigating to the Developer section and expanding the XSLT Files node by clicking the arrow.
2. Place the cursor in the template where you want to insert the library method.
3. Click the Insert xsl:value-of button as shown in Figure 5-10.

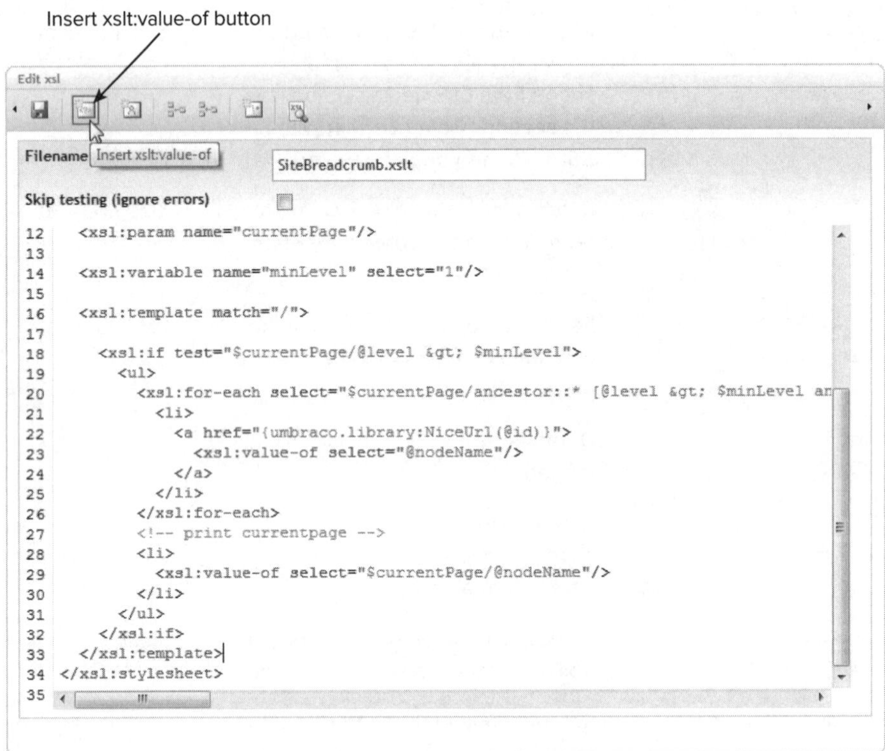

FIGURE 5-10

4. Click the Get Extension button.
5. Select `umbraco.library` in the first drop-down list.
6. Select the method to use in the second drop-down list.
7. If the method takes arguments, you are asked to enter them after selecting the method to use, as shown in Figure 5-11.

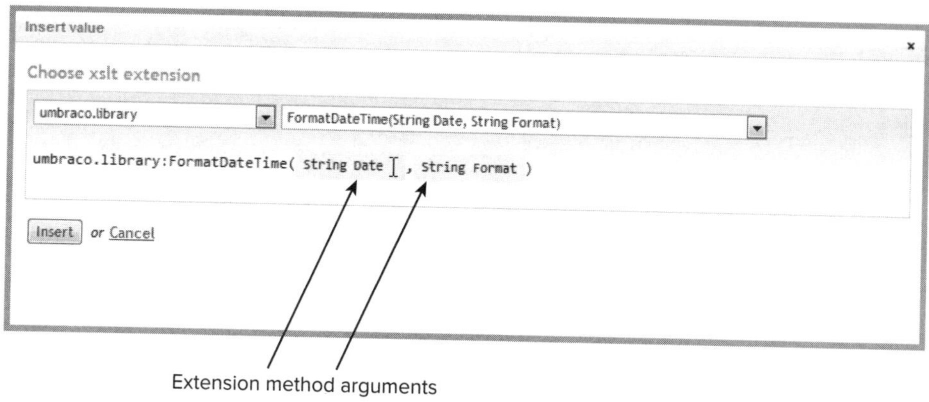

FIGURE 5-11

Going Further with XSLT

Believe it or not, what you've seen so far are the basics. XSLT can get a lot more advanced and complicated. Again, it is not the job of this book to teach you all there is to know about XSLT, but to make your journey a tad more useful, the examples in Listings 5-3 and 5-5 take you through some more common usages of XSLT within Umbraco.

Output an Image from the Media Library

Media items, such as images, files, and folders, can be retrieved using the `GetMedia` XSLT extension that you were introduced to in the previous section. However, `GetMedia` returns a nodeset so it's not as simple as just calling the method. In addition, you also need to specify what information you want out of the nodeset. Listing 5-3 shows you how this is done. The steps that follow walk you through the process.

To select a media item to display, simply add the Media Picker data type to one of your document types and you can target a file, folder, or image using that data type when editing a node.

The Media Picker data type stores the chosen media item using the associated node Id for the media item.

1. In the Developer section, create a new XSLT file and name it **MediaOutput**, based on the Clean template, and select the Create Macro check box, as shown in Figure 5-12.
2. Navigate to the macro details and add a new parameter in the Parameter tab:
   - **Alias:** `PropertyAlias`
   - **Name:** Field Name
   - **Type:** Text

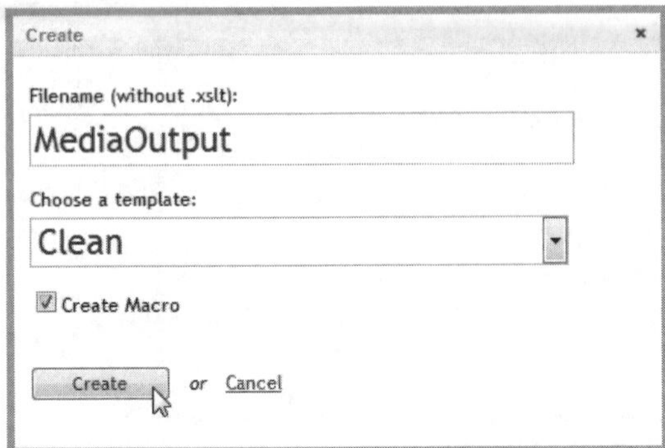

FIGURE 5-12

3. Add the code in Listing 5-3, or 5-4 if you are running Umbraco 4.0.x, to your XSLT file.

LISTING 5-3: MediaOutput-4.5.xslt

Available for download on Wrox.com

```
<?xml version="1.0" encoding="UTF-8"?>
<!DOCTYPE xsl:stylesheet [ <!ENTITY nbsp " "> ]>
<xsl:stylesheet
  version="1.0"
  xmlns:xsl="http://www.w3.org/1999/XSL/Transform"
  xmlns:msxml="urn:schemas-microsoft-com:xslt"
  xmlns:umbraco.library="urn:umbraco.library"
xmlns:Exslt.ExsltCommon="urn:Exslt.ExsltCommon"
xmlns:Exslt.ExsltDatesAndTimes="urn:Exslt.ExsltDatesAndTimes"
xmlns:Exslt.ExsltMath="urn:Exslt.ExsltMath"
xmlns:Exslt.ExsltRegularExpressions="urn:Exslt.ExsltRegularExpressions"
xmlns:Exslt.ExsltStrings="urn:Exslt.ExsltStrings"
xmlns:Exslt.ExsltSets="urn:Exslt.ExsltSets"
  exclude-result-prefixes="msxml umbraco.library Exslt.ExsltCommon
Exslt.ExsltDatesAndTimes Exslt.ExsltMath Exslt.ExsltRegularExpressions
Exslt.ExsltStrings Exslt.ExsltSets ">


    <xsl:output method="xml" omit-xml-declaration="yes"/>

    <xsl:param name="currentPage"/>
    <xsl:variable name="propertyAlias" select="/macro/propertyAlias"/>
    <xsl:variable name="propertyValue" select="$currentPage/*
              [name()=$propertyAlias]"/>

    <xsl:template match="/">
        <!-- check to make sure the property value that we pass in
             is not empty -->
        <xsl:if test="$propertyValue!=''">
            <!-- localize the media nodeset into a shorter variable
                 name for readability -->
            <xsl:variable name="mediaItem"
select="umbraco.library:GetMedia($propertyValue, 'false')"/>
```

```
                <xsl:if test="$mediaItem!=''">
                    <img>
                        <xsl:attribute name="src">
                            <xsl:value-of select="$mediaItem/umbracoFile" />
                        </xsl:attribute>
                        <xsl:attribute name="width">
                            <xsl:value-of select="$mediaItem/umbracoWidth" />
                        </xsl:attribute>
                        <xsl:attribute name="height">
                            <xsl:value-of select="$mediaItem/umbracoHeight" />
                        </xsl:attribute>
                        <xsl:attribute name="alt">
                            <xsl:value-of select="$mediaItem/@nodeName" />
                        </xsl:attribute>
                    </img>
                </xsl:if>
            </xsl:if>
        </xsl:template>
    </xsl:stylesheet>
```

LISTING 5-4: MediaOutput-4.0.x.xslt

Available for download on Wrox.com

```
<?xml version="1.0" encoding="UTF-8"?>
<!DOCTYPE xsl:stylesheet [ <!ENTITY nbsp " "> ]>
<xsl:stylesheet
  version="1.0"
  xmlns:xsl="http://www.w3.org/1999/XSL/Transform"
  xmlns:msxml="urn:schemas-microsoft-com:xslt"
  xmlns:umbraco.library="urn:umbraco.library"
xmlns:Exslt.ExsltCommon="urn:Exslt.ExsltCommon"
xmlns:Exslt.ExsltDatesAndTimes="urn:Exslt.ExsltDatesAndTimes"
xmlns:Exslt.ExsltMath="urn:Exslt.ExsltMath"
xmlns:Exslt.ExsltRegularExpressions="urn:Exslt.ExsltRegularExpressions"
xmlns:Exslt.ExsltStrings="urn:Exslt.ExsltStrings"
xmlns:Exslt.ExsltSets="urn:Exslt.ExsltSets"
  exclude-result-prefixes="msxml umbraco.library Exslt.ExsltCommon
Exslt.ExsltDatesAndTimes Exslt.ExsltMath Exslt.ExsltRegularExpressions
Exslt.ExsltStrings Exslt.ExsltSets ">


    <xsl:output method="xml" omit-xml-declaration="yes"/>

    <xsl:param name="currentPage"/>
    <xsl:variable name="propertyAlias" select="/macro/propertyAlias"/>

    <xsl:template match="/">
        <!-- check to make sure the property value that we
             pass in is not empty -->
        <xsl:if test="$propertyAlias!=''">
            <!-- localize the media nodeset into a shorter variable
                 name for readability -->
            <xsl:variable name="mediaItem"
```

continues

LISTING 5-4 *(continued)*

```
select="umbraco.library:GetMedia($currentPage/data [@alias=$propertyAlias],
 'false')"/>
            <xsl:if test="$mediaItem!=''">
                <img>
                    <xsl:attribute name="src">
                        <xsl:value-of select="$mediaItem/data
[@alias='umbracoFile']" />
                    </xsl:attribute>
                    <xsl:attribute name="width">
                        <xsl:value-of select="$mediaItem/data
[@alias='umbracoWidth']" />
                    </xsl:attribute>
                    <xsl:attribute name="height">
                        <xsl:value-of select="$mediaItem/data
[@alias='umbracoHeight']" />
                    </xsl:attribute>
                    <xsl:attribute name="alt">
                        <xsl:value-of select="$mediaItem/@nodeName" />
                    </xsl:attribute>
                </img>
            </xsl:if>
        </xsl:if>
    </xsl:template>
</xsl:stylesheet>
```

Grouping Output by Date

Often times you will want to output lists of information in a certain order and/or grouping. One great example of this is the Event document type that you added in Chapter 3. On the event details page, you may want to output all of the events grouped by month, as shown in the following steps:

1. In the Developer section, create a new XSLT file and name it **EventOutputGroupedByMonth**, based on the Clean template, and select the Create Macro check box.

See "Creating an XSLT Macro" earlier in this chapter for detailed steps on how to create an XSLT file and associated macro.

2. Add the code in Listing 5-5, or 5-6 if you are running Umbraco 4.0.x, to your XSLT file.

LISTING 5-5: EventOutputGroupedByMonth-4.5.xslt

Available for download on Wrox.com

```
<?xml version="1.0" encoding="UTF-8"?>
<!DOCTYPE xsl:stylesheet [
  <!ENTITY nbsp " ">
]>
<xsl:stylesheet
  version="1.0"
  xmlns:xsl="http://www.w3.org/1999/XSL/Transform"
```

```
    xmlns:msxml="urn:schemas-microsoft-com:xslt"
    xmlns:umbraco.library="urn:umbraco.library"
  xmlns:Exslt.ExsltCommon="urn:Exslt.ExsltCommon"
  xmlns:Exslt.ExsltDatesAndTimes="urn:Exslt.ExsltDatesAndTimes"
  xmlns:Exslt.ExsltMath="urn:Exslt.ExsltMath"
  xmlns:Exslt.ExsltRegularExpressions="urn:Exslt.ExsltRegularExpressions"
  xmlns:Exslt.ExsltStrings="urn:Exslt.ExsltStrings"
  xmlns:Exslt.ExsltSets="urn:Exslt.ExsltSets"
  xmlns:scandia.library="urn:scandia.library"
    exclude-result-prefixes="msxml umbraco.library Exslt.ExsltCommon
  Exslt.ExsltDatesAndTimes Exslt.ExsltMath Exslt.ExsltRegularExpressions
  Exslt.ExsltStrings Exslt.ExsltSets scandia.library ">

    <xsl:output method="html" omit-xml-declaration="yes"/>

    <xsl:param name="currentPage"/>

    <!-- Local variables -->
    <xsl:variable name="documentTypeAlias" select="string('Event')"/> <!-- the
  specific document type that we're are looking for -->
    <!-- store the nodes into a localized and sorted nodeset -->
    <xsl:variable name="data">
      <xsl:for-each select="$currentPage/descendant-or-self::* [name() =
  $documentTypeAlias and string(umbracoNaviHide) != '1']">
        <xsl:sort select="." data-type="text" />
        <xsl:copy-of select="."/>
      </xsl:for-each>
    </xsl:variable>
    <!-- create a key that we can use to "look up" data based on in our
          loop below and match only the Event document type -->
    <xsl:key name="nodes-by-MMMM" match="Event"
  use="umbraco.library:FormatDateTime(eventStartDateTime,'MMMM')"/>

    <xsl:template match="/">
      <!-- create a nodeset of the data we stored earlier and pick out
            the 'Event' nodes, then group them by the full month string -->
      <xsl:for-each select="msxml:node-set($data)/Event [count(. | key('nodes-
  by-MMMM', umbraco.library:FormatDateTime(eventStartDateTime,'MMMM'))[1]) =
  1]">
        <xsl:sort select="eventStartDateTime" order="descending" />

        <div class="news-month">
          <div class="heading">
            <xsl:value-of
  select="umbraco.library:FormatDateTime(eventStartDateTime,'MMM yyyy')"/>
          </div>
          <ul class="ctr-events">
          <!-- This inner loop simply outputs the nodes that match the selected
                key we specified outside of this template -->
            <xsl:for-each select="key('nodes-by-MMMM',
  umbraco.library:FormatDateTime(eventStartDateTime,'MMMM'))">
                <li>
                  <!-- create an anchor element so we can link to the
                        event details -->
```

continues

LISTING 5-5 *(continued)*

```
                <xsl:element name="a">
                  <xsl:attribute name="href">
                    <xsl:value-of select="umbraco.library:NiceUrl(@id)"/>
                  </xsl:attribute>
                  <xsl:value-of select="eventTitle"/>
                </xsl:element>
                <div class="fulldate">
                  <xsl:value-of
select="umbraco.library:FormatDateTime(eventStartDateTime,'MMM dd, yyyy')"/>
                </div>
              </li>
          </xsl:for-each>
        </ul>
      </div>
    </xsl:for-each>
  </xsl:template>
</xsl:stylesheet>
```

LISTING 5-6: EventOutputGroupedByMonth-4.0.x.xslt

Available for download on Wrox.com

```
<?xml version="1.0" encoding="UTF-8"?>
<!DOCTYPE xsl:stylesheet [
  <!ENTITY nbsp " ">
]>
<xsl:stylesheet
  version="1.0"
  xmlns:xsl="http://www.w3.org/1999/XSL/Transform"
  xmlns:msxml="urn:schemas-microsoft-com:xslt"
  xmlns:umbraco.library="urn:umbraco.library"
xmlns:Exslt.ExsltCommon="urn:Exslt.ExsltCommon"
xmlns:Exslt.ExsltDatesAndTimes="urn:Exslt.ExsltDatesAndTimes"
xmlns:Exslt.ExsltMath="urn:Exslt.ExsltMath"
xmlns:Exslt.ExsltRegularExpressions="urn:Exslt.ExsltRegularExpressions"
xmlns:Exslt.ExsltStrings="urn:Exslt.ExsltStrings"
xmlns:Exslt.ExsltSets="urn:Exslt.ExsltSets"
xmlns:scandia.library="urn:scandia.library"
  exclude-result-prefixes="msxml umbraco.library Exslt.ExsltCommon
Exslt.ExsltDatesAndTimes Exslt.ExsltMath Exslt.ExsltRegularExpressions
Exslt.ExsltStrings Exslt.ExsltSets scandia.library ">

  <xsl:output method="html" omit-xml-declaration="yes"/>

  <xsl:param name="currentPage"/>

  <!-- Local variables -->
  <xsl:variable name="documentTypeAlias" select="string('Event')"/>
  <!-- the specific document type that we're are looking for -->
```

```
  <!-- store the nodes into a localized and sorted nodeset -->
  <xsl:variable name="data">
    <xsl:for-each select="$currentPage/descendant-or-self::node [string(data
 [@alias='umbracoNaviHide']) != '1' and @nodeTypeAlias=$documentTypeAlias]">
      <xsl:sort select="." data-type="text" />
      <xsl:copy-of select="."/>
    </xsl:for-each>
  </xsl:variable>
  <!-- create a key that we can use to "look up" data based on in our
        loop below and match only the Event document type -->
  <xsl:key name="nodes-by-MMMM" match="node"
 use="umbraco.library:FormatDateTime(data
 [@alias='eventStartDateTime'],'MMMM')"/>

  <xsl:template match="/">
    <!-- create a nodeset of the data we stored earlier and pick out
          the 'Event' nodes, then group them by the full month string -->
    <xsl:for-each select="msxml:node-set($data)[count(. | key('nodes-by-MMMM',
 umbraco.library:FormatDateTime(data [@alias='eventStartDateTime'],'MMMM'))[1])
 = 1]">
      <xsl:sort select="string(data [@alias='eventStartDateTime'])"
 order="descending" />

      <div class="news-month">
        <div class="heading">
          <xsl:value-of select="umbraco.library:FormatDateTime(data
 [@alias='eventStartDateTime'],'MMM yyyy')"/>
        </div>
        <ul class="ctr-events">
          <!-- This inner loop simply outputs the nodes that match the
                selected key we specified outside of this template -->
          <xsl:for-each select="key('nodes-by-MMMM',
 umbraco.library:FormatDateTime(data [@alias='eventStartDateTime'],'MMMM'))">
            <li>
              <!-- create an anchor element so we can link to the
                    event details -->
              <xsl:element name="a">
                <xsl:attribute name="href">
                  <xsl:value-of select="umbraco.library:NiceUrl(@id)"/>
                </xsl:attribute>
                <xsl:value-of select="data [@alias='eventTitle']"/>
              </xsl:element>
              <div class="fulldate">
                <xsl:value-of select="umbraco.library:FormatDateTime(data
 [@alias='eventStartDateTime'],'MMM dd, yyyy')"/>
              </div>
            </li>
          </xsl:for-each>
        </ul>
      </div>
    </xsl:for-each>
  </xsl:template>
</xsl:stylesheet>
```

The above grouping method is known as the Muenchian Method. More on that topic can be found at, `http://en.wikipedia.org/wiki/Muenchian_grouping`.

For more examples and utilizations of XSLT macros take a look at Chapter 11. In addition to this book, take a look at `http://our.umbraco.org`, *specifically the Projects section, where developers continuously share their solutions with the community.*

.NET USER CONTROLS

.NET user controls provide an endless number of possibilities for your Umbraco installation. With user controls you can harness the power of .NET code inside your templates and content pages. If you can create something in a custom .NET application inside a user control, it's also possible to render/function it in an Umbraco rendered page.

Remember to have a `<form runat="server"/>` *tag in your template that encapsulates the user control. If you don't, the user control will not work.*

This section shows how to extend the user experience by adding dynamic form functionality, as well as how to create custom data types for user input in the backoffice.

For detailed information on how to tap into the Umbraco Event Model, go to Chapter 12.

Using the built-in wrapper makes deploying custom code a real breeze. The simplest and most straightforward way to work with Umbraco and custom code is to create a standalone Visual Studio project in — basically — 6 steps.

1. Add your user controls (`.ascx` files).
2. Write the code as needed.
3. Build your solution and/or project.
4. Copy the `.ascx` file(s) to the `<install root>/usercontrols` folder and copy the project DLL and any other dependency libraries used to the `<install root>/bin` folder.
5. Create a macro, just like you did in the "Introduction to Umbraco Macros" section in the beginning of this chapter, and browse to the required user control in the dropdown.
6. Add the macro to your template or page, and that's it!

If you don't see your newly created user control in the edit macro details view, simply touch the `web.config` *file in your installation and the application will restart manually. Touching the* `web.config` *means that you make a change to the file by adding a space and saving the file to update its last updated timestamp. This should clear any potential caching and you should see the file(s) listed.*

If you do not have direct access to the root of your Umbraco website, installing the Config Tree package, found at `http://our.umbraco.org/projects/developer-tools/config-tree`*, allows you edit access to the* `web.config` *and other configuration files in your Umbraco installation.*

To make the backoffice as flexible as possible, Umbraco introduced the `UserControlWrapper`, which allows you to develop various input fields and add them as data types in the Developer section. See Chapter 12 for further information and examples on this topic.

In addition to allowing you to do everything in XSLT, .NET user controls provide you with methods for working with unpublished content.

SUPPORT FOR THE .NET DLR

One of the most versatile aspects of Umbraco is its support for additional languages through the .NET Dynamic Language Runtime (DLR) text. Out of the box, you can create macros that are based on IronPython and IronRuby, simply by using the backoffice interface. This is a great alternative to XSLT and .NET driven macros for those who prefer working with a different language.

This section simply provides you with syntactical examples of how to render the content using these alternate languages. The author suggests the following online resources for further reading about the DLR languages mentioned in the following sections.

- **`http://ironruby.codeplex.com/`**: This is an IronRuby open source project.
- **`http://ironpython.codeplex.com/`**: This is an IronPython open source project.

For those of you who prefer working with IronPython or IronRuby, the examples in Listings 5-7, 5-8, and 5-9 should provide you with a good introduction on how to tap into the Umbraco content using one of these languages.

IronPython

Here are some examples of what you can do using IronPython as your language of choice in your Umbraco macros. The options are virtually endless, just like when you work with .NET.

Listing Pages from Current Page

In Listing 5-7, you can see how few lines of code it takes to generate an unordered list of pages using IronPython.

LISTING 5-7: PagesFromCurentNode.py

```
from umbraco.presentation.nodeFactory import Node
from umbraco import library

#list all of the subpages from the 'currentPage'

result = "<ul>"

for childNode in currentPage.Children:
  result += "<li><a href='" + library.NiceUrl(childNode.Id) +  "'>" +
childNode.Name + "</a></li>"

result += "</ul>"

print result
```

Subpages from Changeable Source

As discussed earlier, DLR driven macros can also take parameters. Listing 5-8 shows an example of this.

LISTING 5-8: SubpagesFromSource.py

```
from umbraco.presentation.nodeFactory import Node
from umbraco import library

#set the node id you would like to fetch pages from here
#you can also set it as a macro property with the alias 'nodeId' instead

rootNodeId = int(nodeId)

result = "<ul>"

for childNode in Node(rootNodeId).Children:
  result += "<li><a href='" + library.NiceUrl(childNode.Id) +  "'>" +
childNode.Name + "</a></li>"

result += "</ul>"

print result
```

Notice the extreme similarities between the two code listings. The simple difference is that in Listing 5-8 you are taking the nodeId as an argument through a macro parameter, which makes the macro much more flexible and reusable for other potential sections of the site.

IronRuby

To illustrate its versatility, here is an example of what the Ruby solution looks like as well.

LISTING 5-9: ChangeSourceRuby.rb

```
result = "<ul>";

currentPage.Children.each do |this_item|
  result += "<li><a href='" + this_item.NiceUrl + "'>"
            + this_item.Name + "</a></li>"
end

result += "</ul>"

puts result
```

As with previous examples, these are just the tip of the iceberg so to speak. The point was to show you that if you prefer any of these languages, Umbraco isn't about to stand in your way.

USER GENERATED FORMS USING UMBRACO CONTOUR

Umbraco HQ has a suite of PRO products that they sell outside of the MIT license. They provide these products at a very reasonable cost and the benefits of the added features far outweigh the costs in terms of the time it would take to develop.

Contour is one of those products that developers and site administrators agree is a terrific and priceless add-on. It allows non-technical editors and administrators to easily create and publish interactive data collection forms with a few simple clicks. Installing and purchasing a license for this product produces a separate section in the Umbraco backoffice called Contour, as shown in Figure 5-13.

Contour can easily be installed by navigating to the Developer section, expanding the Packages node, expanding the Umbraco Package Repository node, and clicking on the Umbraco PRO node. Contour will be available in the resulting right-hand pane.

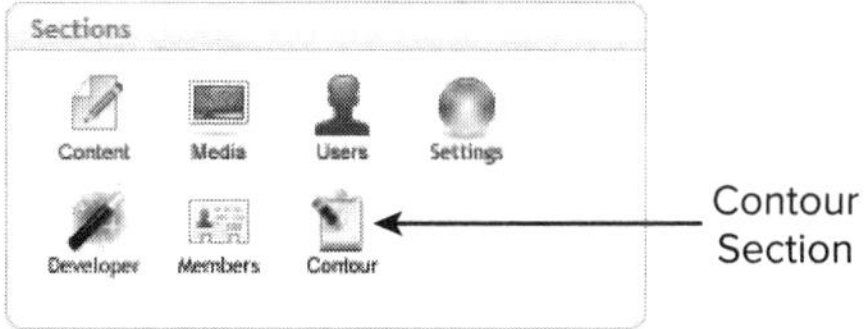

FIGURE 5-13

To create a Contour form, follow these steps:

1. Navigate to the Contour section.
2. Right-click the Forms node and click the Create menu option as shown in Figure 5-14.

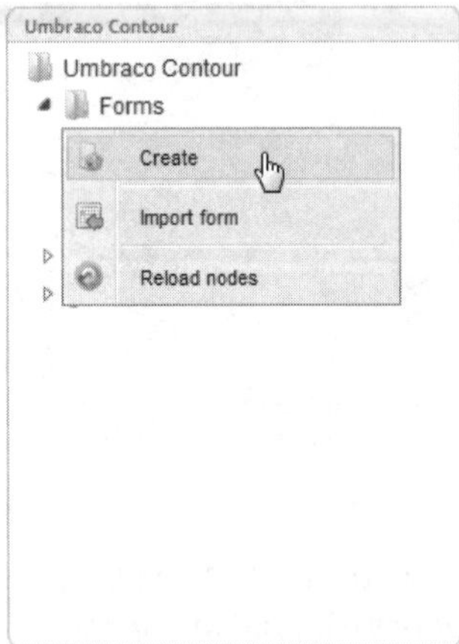

FIGURE 5-14

3. Start by editing the Form Name and Fieldset Title by clicking the fields as shown in Figure 5-15.

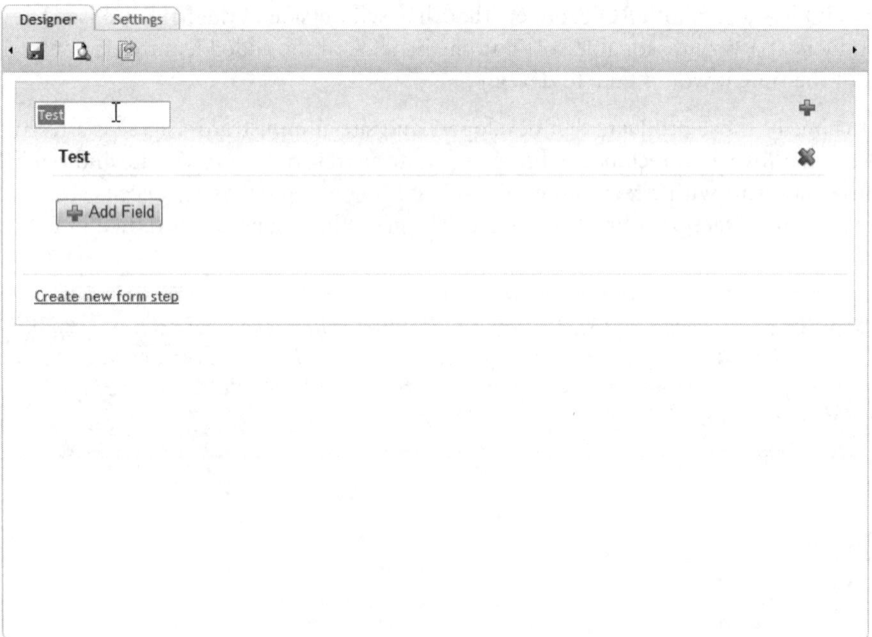

FIGURE 5-15

4. Now, simply add fields to your form by clicking the Add Field button.

5. You can easily edit the field type and other attributes (including select list, check boxes, hidden fields, data pickers, and other cool form field types) by setting them in the Add Field dialog, as shown in Figure 5-16.

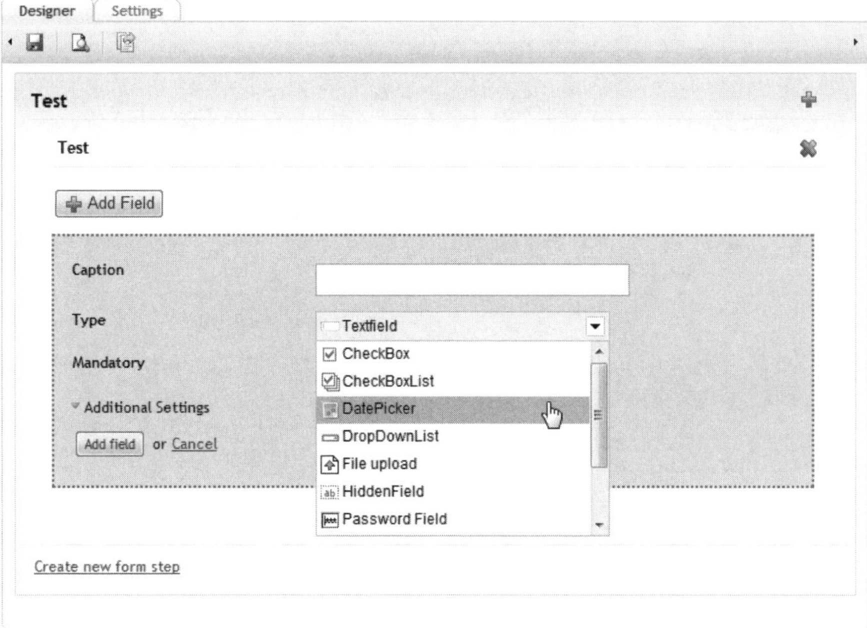

FIGURE 5-16

6. Keep adding fields as needed and Save your form.

If you expand the form, you'll find additional features for any given form. The Entries node gives you a detailed view of the submissions with various filters and sorting capabilities. This includes the ability to export the submitted data in CSV, XML, and HTML formats, as shown in Figure 5-17.

What's more is that you can also specify a number of predefined workflow actions based on the status of the form lifecycle. The following events are captured:

- **Opened:** A user has opened the form to start working with the data.
- **Resumed:** A saved but un-submitted form is resumed.
- **Partially Submitted:** An incomplete form was submitted.
- **Submitted:** The form was completed and submitted.
- **Approved:** An action was performed on the form entry within the Entries section of the form by an admin.
- **Deleted:** The form entry was deleted.

Each of the previous events come with a predefined list of event hooks that you can tap into. The even cooler part is that you can combine any and all of these actions into a single step, giving you virtually endless combinations of actions (as shown in Table 5-5).

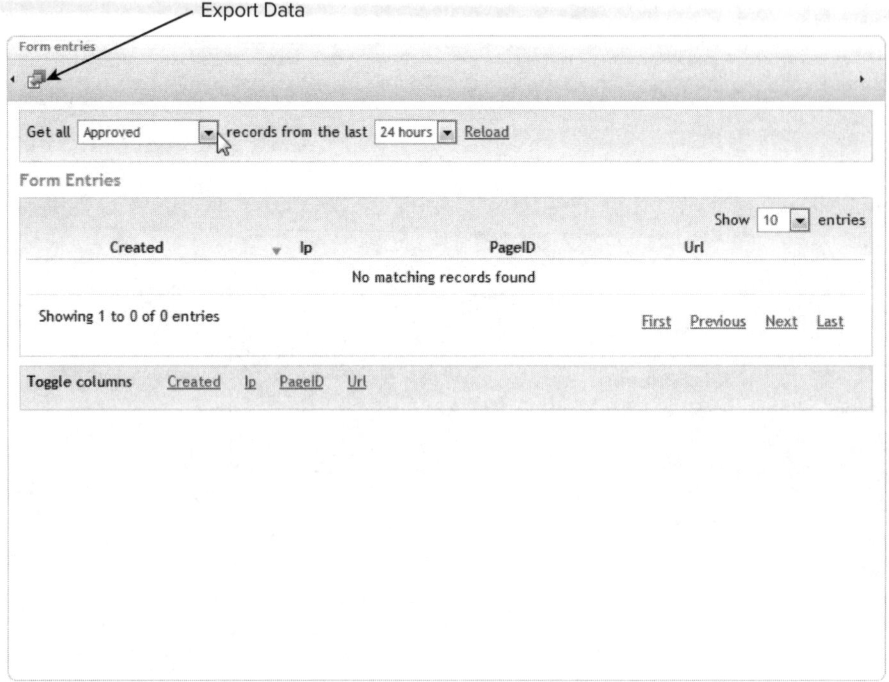

FIGURE 5-17

TABLE 5-5: Combinations of Actions

ACTION	DESCRIPTION
Perform Filtering	This is useful to, for example, detect if offensive language is entered in the form. You can then choose whether to Approve or Delete the entry.
Post as XML	Allows you to post the results of the entry as an XML object to a given URL. You can alternatively choose to transform the XML before posting it to the URL.
Post form to URL	Allows you to post the data in a POST of GET to a provided URL.
Save as File	Allows you to save the results as a file to the server by specifying file type, location, and format via XSLT.
Save as Umbraco Document	This feature gives you the option to create a node in the content tree. Very useful in the case where people are submitting FAQs, comments, or other dynamic data that may belong to a specific section of the site. Select whether to publish the submissions or not and where the submission should be entered.

ACTION	DESCRIPTION
Send Email	As expected this will send an email notification to a specified user notifying them of a submission. In addition you can use inline tags to add the values of the form submission including in the TO field for email confirmations of signup, purchases, and other applications.
Send XSLT Transformed Email	Similar to above except this provides you with the flexibility of formatting the email using an XSLT file for more advanced HTML emails, etc.

As you can see, developing something this complex would be a project all on its own. The opportunity cost for you and/or your client is tremendous with the value this provides in a short timeframe.

Additional Umbraco PRO products are covered in Chapter 13.

TAKE HOME POINTS

This is a big chapter and an important one for the success of your work with Umbraco. It's the foundation of what makes Umbraco such an impressive CMS and a development framework. Here's what you should be taking away from Chapter 5:

- Using macros to extend the functionality of your Umbraco pages and content.
- Using XSLT to render content in various formats, including menus, content snippets like news lists, etc.
- Leveraging the power of .NET user controls to include extended functionality, anything you can think of!
- An understanding of IronPython and IronRuby as macro languages.
- Tapping into Umbraco Contour to provide interactive forms to the end users of your website.

Languages and Dictionaries

- How do you set up a new language for the admin user interface?
- How do you use dictionaries to translate labels and buttons?
- How do you set the locale for date formats?
- How do you add a new language?

This chapter is all about customizing Umbraco to your needs, especially as it relates to languages, locales, and cultures. Umbraco was built with internationalization in mind and is therefore relatively easy to customize with any of the pre-existing languages or one custom to your implementation. You can even set the language for each individual user, and Umbraco is smart enough to translate labels, dates, and other specific strings to that person's settings.

LANGUAGES

Table 6-1 lists the pre-installed language packs for the backoffice user interface.

A difference exists between adding and working with languages for the backoffice user interface and localizing your public website. To support multi-lingual sites, please refer to Chapter 7.

As you can see from Table 6-1, Umbraco offers a lot of flexibility out of the box. A later section covers in detail how to add a language and configure a user for that new language. You can find all the language files in the `<install root>/umbraco/config/lang` directory.

Do you need more information on .NET and cultures? Take a look at the following article on the MSDN knowledge base site: `http://msdn.microsoft.com/en-us/library/system.globalization.cultureinfo.aspx`.

TABLE 6-1: Pre-installed Language Packs

LANGUAGE	CULTURE	LOCATION
Danish	da-DK	da.xml
German	de-DE	de.xml
English (uk)	en-UK	en.xml
Spanish	es-ES	es.xml
French	fr-FR	fr.xml
Italian	it-IT	it.xml
Dutch	nl-NL	nl.xml
Norwegian	nb-NO	no.xml
Swedish (se)	sv-SE	se.xml

Changing the Default Language

Eventually, you may get a client located somewhere in the world where one of the pre-installed languages doesn't do the job. Right now, you can find the languages listed in Table 6-1 as a drop-down form control within the user details form. Figure 6-1 shows the interface. The next section describes in detail how to add another language to this drop-down form control.

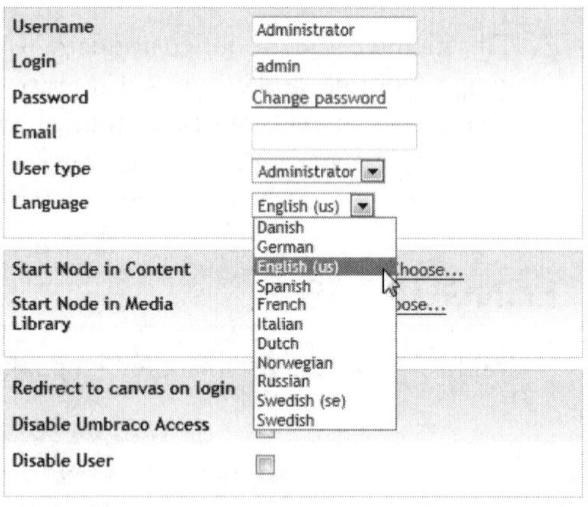

FIGURE 6-1

In the `Web.config` file for your Umbraco installation you can change the default backoffice user interface language by setting the alias of the language in the `umbracoDefaultUILanguage` `appSettings` key. See Listing 6-1 for an example of changing the default language.

LISTING 6-1: Web.config (partial)

```
<appSettings>
    ...
    <add key="umbracoDisableXsltExtensions" value="true" />
    <add key="umbracoDefaultUILanguage" value="fr" />
    <add key="umbracoProfileUrl" value="profiler" />
    ...
</appSettings>
```

Adding and Updating Language Files

Adding a language that is not already pre-installed is a simple task. The bulk of the work is adding all the translations, and not the actual installation of the language pack. The first and foremost requirement is that you need FTP or some other form of remote access to the server where your Umbraco application is hosted. As pointed out earlier, you configure languages using an XML file that contains all the defined and configurable keys that make up the backoffice user interface. Take a look at Listing 6-2 for an extract of the English language file. As you can see, a language file is made up of several different components. Starting at the top, you see:

- **`<language />` node:** This defines the language to which you want this file to apply. For a listing of all the available languages and cultures in .NET, see Table 6-2.
- **`<creator />` element:** You can use this to define who wrote the translation. This element is helpful and necessary if you intend to share your translation with the community by making it available on `http://our.umbraco.org/projects`.
- **`<area />` node:** This specifies where the individual key is going to be applied. Areas are predefined and cannot be added or changed because they cross-reference with the underlying Umbraco architecture.
- **`<key />` node:** This defines the actual translatable label that is used throughout the Umbraco backoffice.

LISTING 6-2: SampleLanguageFile.xml

```
<language alias="en" intName="English (us)" localName="English" lcid=""
culture="en-US">
  <creator>
    <name>umbraco</name>
    <link>http://umbraco.org</link>
  </creator>
  <area alias="main">
    <key alias="sections">Sections</key>
    ...
  </area>
  <area alias="defaultdialogs">
    <key alias="link">Link</key>
    <key alias="macroDoesNotHaveProperties" version="4.0">
      <![CDATA[This macro does not contain any properties you can edit]]>
    </key>
    ...
  </area>
  ...
</language>
```

Notice also that the `CDATA` section is used in one of the keys in Listing 6-2, which avoids parsing problems if characters such as <, &, or > were used in the description. A `CDATA` section tells the XML parser to avoid anything within its start and end tags. Table 6-2 provides a list of all the available languages and associated culture codes.

TABLE 6-2: Available Cultures in .NET

CULTURE CODE	LANGUAGE
af	Afrikaans
af-ZA	Afrikaans – South Africa
sq	Albanian
is-IS	Icelandic – Iceland
sq-AL	Albanian – Albania
ar	Arabic
ar-DZ	Arabic – Algeria
ar-BH	Arabic – Bahrain
ar-EG	Arabic – Egypt
ar-IQ	Arabic – Iraq
ar-JO	Arabic – Jordan
ar-KW	Arabic – Kuwait
ar-LB	Arabic – Lebanon
ar-LY	Arabic – Libya
ar-MA	Arabic – Morocco
ar-OM	Arabic – Oman
ar-QA	Arabic – Qatar
ar-SA	Arabic – Saudi Arabia
ar-SY	Arabic – Syria
ar-TN	Arabic – Tunisia
ar-AE	Arabic – United Arab Emirates
ar-YE	Arabic – Yemen
hy	Armenian
hy-AM	Armenian – Armenia
az	Azeri
az-AZ-Cyrl	Azeri (Cyrillic) – Azerbaijan

CULTURE CODE	LANGUAGE
az-AZ-Latn	Azeri (Latin) – Azerbaijan
eu	Basque
eu-ES	Basque – Basque
be	Belarusian
be-BY	Belarusian – Belarus
bg	Bulgarian
bg-BG	Bulgarian – Bulgaria
ca	Catalan
ca-ES	Catalan – Catalan
zh-HK	Chinese – Hong Kong SAR
zh-MO	Chinese – Macao SAR
nn-NO	Norwegian (Nynorsk) – Norway
zh-CN	Chinese – China
zh-CHS	Chinese (Simplified)
zh-SG	Chinese – Singapore
zh-TW	Chinese – Taiwan
zh-CHT	Chinese (Traditional)
hr	Croatian
hr-HR	Croatian – Croatia
cs	Czech
cs-CZ	Czech – Czech Republic
da	Danish
da-DK	Danish – Denmark
div	Dhivehi
div-MV	Dhivehi – Maldives
nl	Dutch

continues

TABLE 6-2 *(continued)*

CULTURE CODE	LANGUAGE
nl-BE	Dutch – Belgium
nl-NL	Dutch – The Netherlands
en	English
en-AU	English – Australia
en-BZ	English – Belize
en-CA	English – Canada
en-CB	English – Caribbean
en-IE	English – Ireland
es-BO	Spanish – Bolivia
en-JM	English – Jamaica
en-NZ	English – New Zealand
en-PH	English – Philippines
en-ZA	English – South Africa
en-TT	English – Trinidad and Tobago
en-GB	English – United Kingdom
en-US	English – United States
en-ZW	English – Zimbabwe
et	Estonian
et-EE	Estonian – Estonia
fo	Faroese
fo-FO	Faroese – Faroe Islands
fa	Farsi
fa-IR	Farsi – Iran
fi	Finnish
fi-FI	Finnish – Finland
fr	French

CULTURE CODE	LANGUAGE
fr-BE	French – Belgium
fr-CA	French – Canada
fr-FR	French – France
fr-LU	French – Luxembourg
fr-MC	French – Monaco
fr-CH	French – Switzerland
gl	Galician
gl-ES	Galician – Galician
ka	Georgian
ka-GE	Georgian – Georgia
de	German
de-AT	German – Austria
de-DE	German – Germany
de-LI	German – Liechtenstein
de-LU	German – Luxembourg
de-CH	German – Switzerland
el	Greek
el-GR	Greek – Greece
gu	Gujarati
gu-IN	Gujarati – India
he	Hebrew
he-IL	Hebrew – Israel
hi	Hindi
hi-IN	Hindi – India
hu	Hungarian
hu-HU	Hungarian – Hungary
is	Icelandic

continues

TABLE 6-2 *(continued)*

CULTURE CODE	LANGUAGE
id	Indonesian
id-ID	Indonesian – Indonesia
it	Italian
it-IT	Italian – Italy
it-CH	Italian – Switzerland
ja	Japanese
ja-JP	Japanese – Japan
kn	Kannada
kn-IN	Kannada – India
kk	Kazakh
kk-KZ	Kazakh – Kazakhstan
kok	Konkani
kok-IN	Konkani – India
ko	Korean
ko-KR	Korean – Korea
ky	Kyrgyz
ky-KG	Kyrgyz – Kyrgyzstan
lv	Latvian
lv-LV	Latvian – Latvia
lt	Lithuanian
lt-LT	Lithuanian – Lithuania
mk	Macedonian
mk-MK	Macedonian – Former Yugoslav Republic of Macedonia
ms	Malay
ms-BN	Malay – Brunei

CULTURE CODE	LANGUAGE
ms-MY	Malay – Malaysia
mr	Marathi
mr-IN	Marathi – India
mn	Mongolian
mn-MN	Mongolian – Mongolia
no	Norwegian
nb-NO	Norwegian (Bokmal) – Norway
pl	Polish
pl-PL	Polish – Poland
pt	Portuguese
pt-BR	Portuguese – Brazil
pt-PT	Portuguese – Portugal
pa	Punjabi
pa-IN	Punjabi – India
ro	Romanian
ro-RO	Romanian – Romania
ru	Russian
ru-RU	Russian – Russia
sa	Sanskrit
sa-IN	Sanskrit – India
sr-SP-Cyrl	Serbian (Cyrillic) – Serbia
sr-SP-Latn	Serbian (Latin) – Serbia
sk	Slovak
sk-SK	Slovak – Slovakia
sl	Slovenian
sl-SI	Slovenian – Slovenia
es	Spanish

continues

TABLE 6-2 *(continued)*

CULTURE CODE	LANGUAGE
es-AR	Spanish – Argentina
es-CL	Spanish – Chile
es-CO	Spanish – Colombia
es-CR	Spanish – Costa Rica
es-DO	Spanish – Dominican Republic
es-EC	Spanish – Ecuador
es-SV	Spanish – El Salvador
es-GT	Spanish – Guatemala
es-HN	Spanish – Honduras
es-MX	Spanish – Mexico
es-NI	Spanish – Nicaragua
es-PA	Spanish – Panama
es-PY	Spanish – Paraguay
es-PE	Spanish – Peru
es-PR	Spanish – Puerto Rico
es-ES	Spanish – Spain
es-UY	Spanish – Uruguay
es-VE	Spanish – Venezuela
sw	Swahili
sw-KE	Swahili – Kenya
sv	Swedish
sv-FI	Swedish – Finland
sv-SE	Swedish – Sweden
syr	Syriac
syr-SY	Syriac – Syria
ta	Tamil

CULTURE CODE	LANGUAGE
ta-IN	Tamil – India
tt	Tatar
tt-RU	Tatar – Russia
te	Telugu
te-IN	Telugu – India
th	Thai
th-TH	Thai – Thailand
tr	Turkish
tr-TR	Turkish – Turkey
uk	Ukrainian
uk-UA	Ukrainian – Ukraine
ur	Urdu
ur-PK	Urdu – Pakistan
uz	Uzbek
uz-UZ-Cyrl	Uzbek (Cyrillic) – Uzbekistan
uz-UZ-Latn	Uzbek (Latin) – Uzbekistan
vi	Vietnamese

Changing the Backoffice UI Language

Not all your administrators or editors will be comfortable working with the default English language that is set in the Umbraco backoffice. In order to support languages that are not shipped with Umbraco, you must add the language file and name it according to the associated culture code, as listed in Table 6-2. The instructions that follow detail how to do this.

1. Copy an existing language file in the `<install root>/umbraco/config/lang` folder by right-clicking the file (for example en.xml) and selecting the Copy menu item. Paste the copied file by right-clicking in the same folder pane and selecting Copy menu item.
2. Rename the copied file using the culture code associated with your selected language.
3. Open the file and set the appropriate language and culture using the values shown in Table 6-2.
4. Translate all the `<key .../>` elements as needed for the new language.

5. Save the new language file.
6. Navigate to the Users section in the Umbraco backoffice.
7. Select the user that requires the new language by clicking the user node and changing the language designation, as shown in Figure 6-1.

If the user whom you are updating to use the new language is logged in while you make the change, he or she must log out and log in to the backoffice again for the language to update.

DICTIONARIES

By definition, a dictionary is "a reference book containing an alphabetical list of words with information about them," as defined by the Princeton Wordnet dictionary. This holds true even in the world of Umbraco. The following sections describe how to work with dictionaries and why you would want to use them in the first place.

A dictionary in the context of Umbraco is a way for you to support multi-lingual labels and portions of text while maintaining these values in a common place. For example, if you needed to translate all the items in your top website navigation, you can use Umbraco dictionary entries to define how each item displays depending on the user's chosen language. The sections that follow show you how to implement this flexibility using the Umbraco backoffice.

The Umbraco Approach

The use of dictionaries has two distinct applications in the realm of Umbraco:

- For translations in a multi-lingual website
- To implement acronyms or other items that may be constants throughout the content of your site

The former is probably the most common use for an Umbraco dictionary. What does using one do for you as an author, editor, or administrator? It enables you to set a dictionary key and apply values to this key on a per-language basis. Figure 6-2 shows an example of this usage. In this case, you can see a dictionary item called *SiteName*, which is translated in both English (United States) and French.

Similarly, as described in the second bullet, if you use a term in several places throughout your site you can define it once in one place. If you must make a change to this term, you can simply make that change in one place, and that change is instantaneously propagated wherever the dictionary item is used!

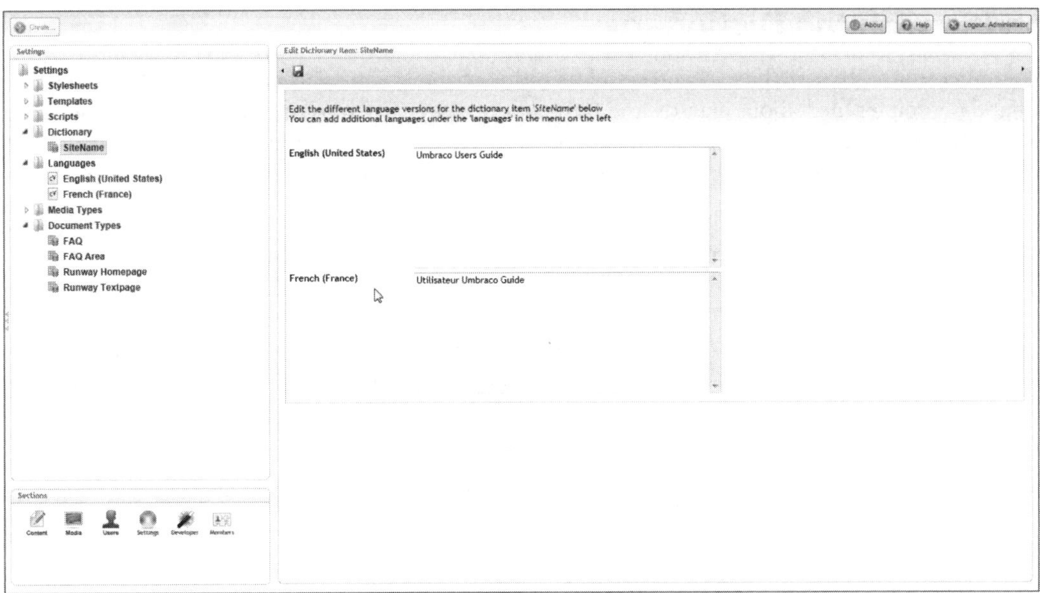

FIGURE 6-2

Adding a Language

To leverage multiple languages with Umbraco, both for use in the dictionary and to support localization (discussed in Chapter 7), you must add languages in the backoffice. To add a language in Umbraco, follow these simple steps:

1. Navigate to the Settings section in the Umbraco backoffice.
2. Right-click the Languages node and click the Create menu option.
3. Choose the language that you want to add from the Choose Language drop-down list, as shown in Figure 6-3.
4. Click the Create button.

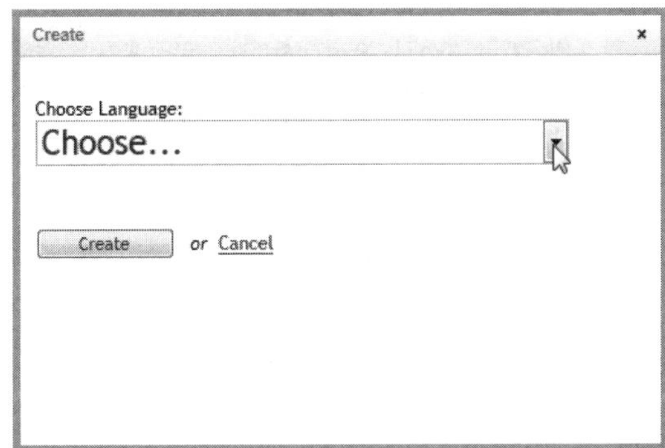

FIGURE 6-3

Now you can add dictionary items and translations for the added language(s) as well as specify the language as default for a given host, as discussed in Chapter 7.

Working with the Dictionary

To implement all that we have covered so far in this chapter, you must put on your XSLT hat. In Chapter 5 you learned about macros and how to leverage XSLT to output content. Umbraco ships with a library function called `GetDictionaryItem`. This library method takes a single argument, which is the key of the dictionary item that you are outputting to the page via your macro.

Listing 6-3 provides an example of how you can translate the name of your site by outputting the `SiteName` key as part of a macro that you can then include in your topmost template.

For examples on how to include an XSLT extension method, like the one used in Listing 6-3, refer to Chapter 5, specifically the "Using XSLT Extensions" section.

Available for download on Wrox.com

LISTING 6-3: OutputDictionaryItems.xslt

```
<?xml version="1.0" encoding="UTF-8"?>
<!DOCTYPE xsl:stylesheet [ <!ENTITY nbsp " "> ]>
<xsl:stylesheet
       version="1.0"
       xmlns:xsl="http://www.w3.org/1999/XSL/Transform"
       xmlns:msxml="urn:schemas-microsoft-com:xslt"
       xmlns:umbraco.library="urn:umbraco.library"
xmlns:Exslt.ExsltCommon="urn:Exslt.ExsltCommon"
xmlns:Exslt.ExsltDatesAndTimes="urn:Exslt.ExsltDatesAndTimes"
xmlns:Exslt.ExsltMath="urn:Exslt.ExsltMath"
xmlns:Exslt.ExsltRegularExpressions="urn:Exslt.ExsltRegularExpressions"
xmlns:Exslt.ExsltStrings="urn:Exslt.ExsltStrings"
xmlns:Exslt.ExsltSets="urn:Exslt.ExsltSets"
xmlns:umbusersguide.library="urn:umbusersguide.library"
       exclude-result-prefixes="msxml umbraco.library Exslt.ExsltCommon
Exslt.ExsltDatesAndTimes Exslt.ExsltMath Exslt.ExsltRegularExpressions
Exslt.ExsltStrings Exslt.ExsltSets umbusersguide.library ">

    <xsl:output method="xml" omit-xml-declaration="yes"/>

    <xsl:param name="currentPage"/>

    <xsl:template match="/">
        <!-- start writing XSLT -->
        <xsl:value-of select="umbraco.library:GetDictionaryItem('SiteName')"/>
    </xsl:template>
</xsl:stylesheet>
```

Create a macro based on the preceding XSLT and include it in your Runway Master template by using the `umbraco:Macro` tag, as shown in Listing 6-4.

LISTING 6-4: Umbraco Macro Tag for Dictionary Item

```
<umbraco:Macro Alias="OutputDictionaryItems" runat="server"></umbraco:Macro>
```

The other approach to inserting and referencing dictionary items is by adding them directly to your template, as opposed to working with the dictionary item in an XSLT macro. The example in Listing 6-3 is overly verbose for outputting a single value. So, to output single values from the dictionary, you can simply leverage the `<umbraco:Item />` tag using the following steps:

1. Navigate to the Runway Master template.
2. Click the Insert umbraco page field icon, as shown in Figure 6-4.

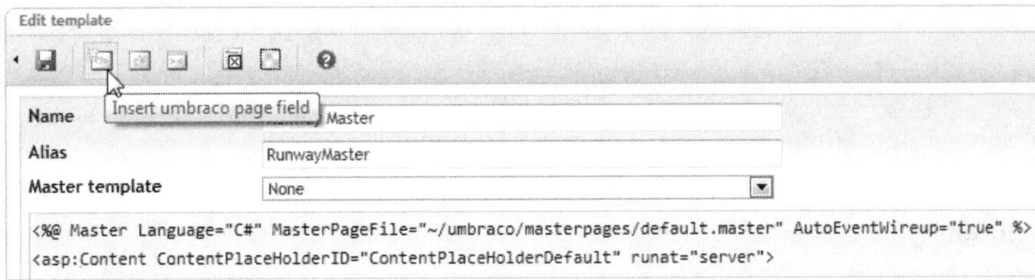

FIGURE 6-4

3. In the dialog that appears, instead of choosing a field in the drop-down list, in the empty text box type the name of the dictionary item that you need, prefixed with a hash sign (#), as shown in Figure 6-5.

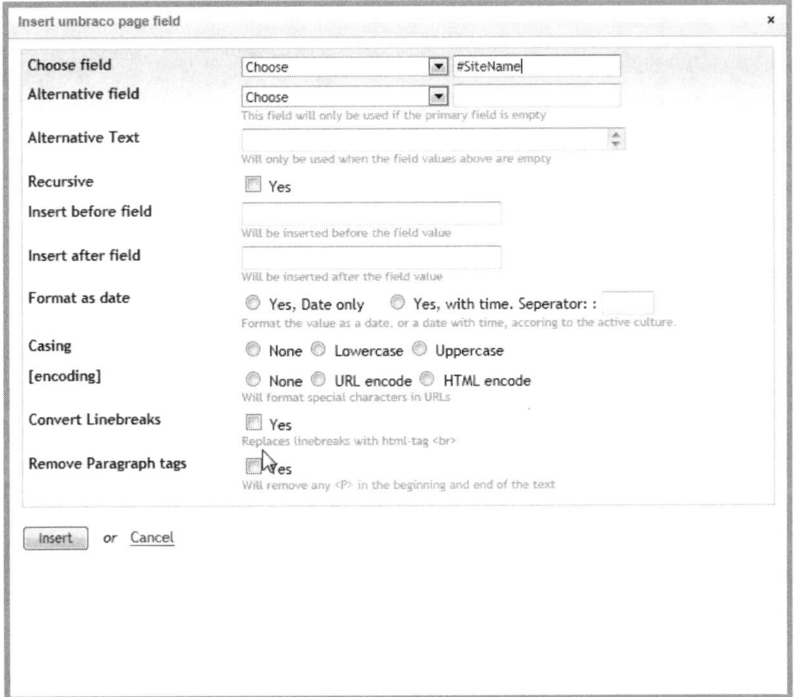

FIGURE 6-5

4. Click the Insert button to finish. The tag is added to your template and looks like `<umbraco:Item field="#SiteName" runat="server"></umbraco:Item>`.

Dictionary item names are case-sensitive.

TAKE HOME POINTS

Now that you're done with this chapter, you should have a firm grasp on how to accomplish the following:

- Changing the backoffice user interface language for individual users
- Adding a new language pack to support additional languages
- Utilizing the Umbraco dictionary to support multi-lingual labels or for defining site-wide phrases
- Outputting dictionary items using XSLT macros

7

Multiple Sites, Hostnames, and Localization

- How do you manage multiple sites in one Umbraco installation?
- How do you set up hostnames as entry points for multiple sites, localization and multiple languages?
- How do you configure the Umbraco translation workflow?

For various reasons you may need to host multiple sites within one Umbraco installation. Example usages include:

- Multiple versions of the same site in different languages.
- Sub-domains for function-specific areas of the site. For example, you may want to have your product catalog accessible at `catalog.yoursite.com` to have a separate entry point and structure.
- You could host multiple small sites that are completely unrelated and segregate user access to individual sites. This saves money in a hosting scenario.

There are other example multiple hostnames usage within one Umbraco installation, but these are a few that will be covered in this book.

Be careful when using the multiple site approach for completely unrelated sites because the number of nodes that Umbraco supports is shared across multiple sites in this case. Generally speaking, Umbraco can support up to 300,000 nodes without any performance issues.

SETTING UP MULTIPLE SITES

To have Umbraco route incoming requests to the appropriate sites in the installation, you must set up hostnames for Umbraco to "listen" for. The examples throughout this chapter have the Runway site set up to be translated into two languages: English and Swedish.

To support multiple sites and entry points for your Umbraco installation, you must leave the default setting of `umbracoHideTopLevelNodeFromPath` as `true`. This tells Umbraco to exclude the Content node from the path, thus pointing to the first second-level node as the homepage. In the following examples, you will instruct Umbraco to map a configured hostname to the correct second-level node in the content tree.

Next you must set up your Umbraco installation to have at least two second-level (in the context of the content tree) nodes so that you can set up the necessary hostnames. Because this example is a multi-lingual setup, the steps show how to add another language, Swedish, to the installation as well as how to copy the Runway site that was installed in Chapter 1 and paste it under the Content node:

1. Navigate to the Settings section of your installation.
2. Right-click the Languages node and click the Create menu item.
3. Select Swedish (Sweden) from the drop-down list, and click the Create button.
4. Navigate to the Content section in the Umbraco backoffice.
5. Right-click the Runway Homepage node and click the Copy menu item, as shown in Figure 7-1.
6. In the resulting dialog, select Content by clicking the Content node, as shown in Figure 7-2.

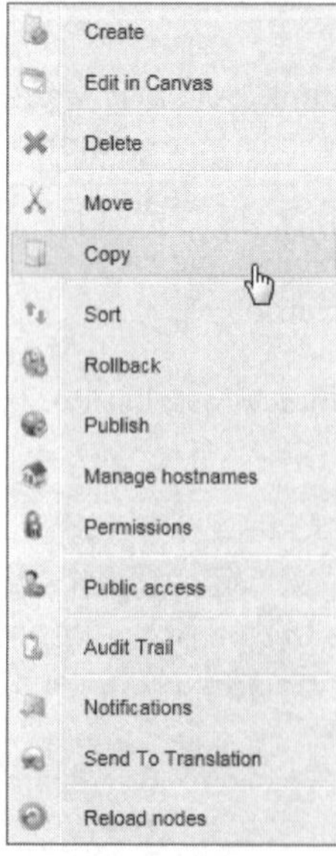

FIGURE 7-1

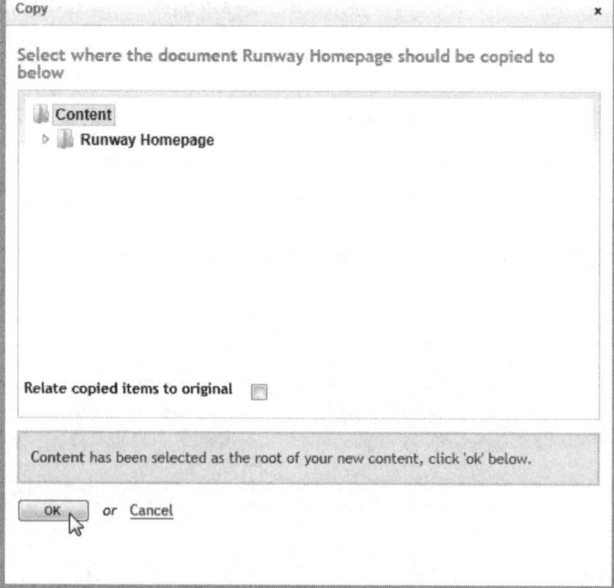

FIGURE 7-2

7. Click the OK button to proceed.
8. Click the Close this window link in the resulting confirmation dialog.

You now have an identical copy of the original Runway site in unpublished status, as shown in Figure 7-3.

To differentiate the two sites, you should rename the homepage nodes for each site to something more identifiable. For example, Runway Website (en) and Runway Website (se) would be viable candidates. What you name your sites is not relevant as you will see shortly when you apply the hostnames that you created in the preceding steps.

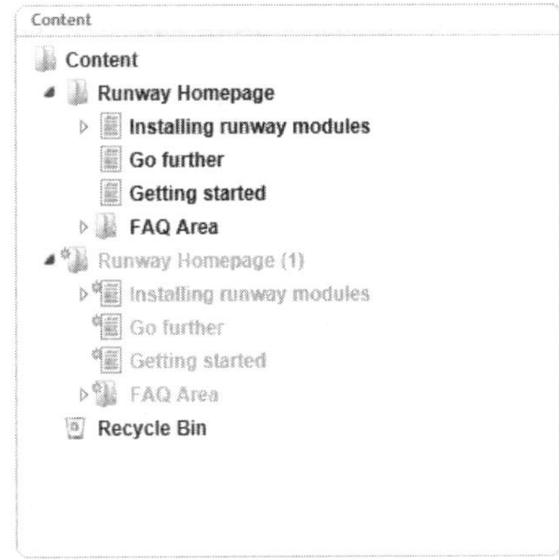

FIGURE 7-3

You rename a node simply by changing the Name value in the Properties tab.

You can now publish the Swedish website so that you have something to work with:

1. Right-click the Runway Website (se) node and click Publish.
2. Select Publish Runway Website (se) and all its subpages as well as Include unpublished child pages, as shown in Figure 7-4.
3. Click the Publish button to finish.

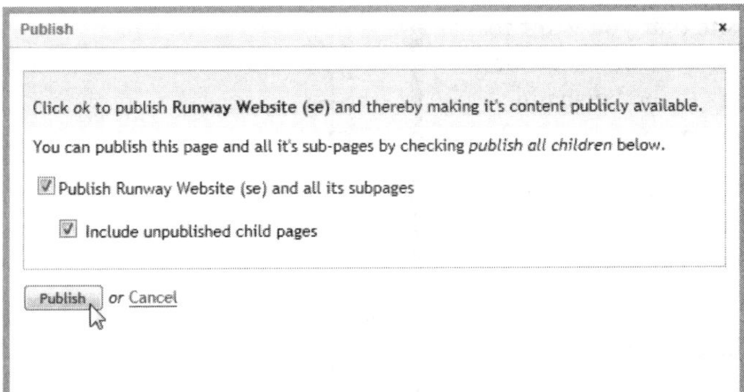

FIGURE 7-4

One last configuration change is necessary to ensure that multiple sites within your installation will work. Locate your `umbracoSettings.config` file. This file is located in `<installation path>/config/umbracoSettings.config`. Locate the `<requestHandler />` settings section in this file and set the `<useDomainPrefixes />` value to `true`, as shown in Listing 7-1. This ensures that all URLs are unique so page links do not cross from one website to another.

LISTING 7-1: Setting URLs to use domain prefixes

```
<requestHandler>
  <!-- this will ensure that urls are unique when running with multiple
    root nodes -->
  <useDomainPrefixes>true</useDomainPrefixes>
  ...
</requestHandler>
```

So far, you haven't made any real changes to the public site. If you tried to access your site at this point (in this example, by pointing your browser to `http://umbracousersguide.com.local`), you'll notice that the same site keeps popping up. That's because it's the default homepage node at the moment. You may also notice that the Link to document in the Properties tab for each of the homepage nodes links to the start of the corresponding content structure. In other words, the English version has `runway-homepage-(en).aspx` and the Swedish version has `runway-homepage-(se).aspx`.

WORKING WITH HOSTNAMES

Two steps are necessary in setting up multiple hostnames within one Umbraco installation. You must instruct the Web server to listen to the required hostnames, and then you must tell Umbraco where to redirect the request. IIS (Internet Information Services) is the Web server that Umbraco uses because it is based on .NET.

To set up your IIS website to bind to one or more hostnames, follow these instructions:

1. Open your IIS server console by searching for Internet Information in your Start menu search box, as shown in Figure 7-5.
2. Navigate to the website that you want to change by expanding the {Your Computer Name} and Sites nodes in the left-hand pane, as shown in Figure 7-6.
3. Locate the website to change and right-click to open the context menu, and then click the Edit Bindings menu item.
4. In the resulting dialog, click the Add button. The Add Site Binding dialog appears.
5. Enter the hostname that you want to add; in this case **umbracousersguide.se.local,** as shown in Figure 7-7. You can leave all other fields with their default values.
6. Click the OK button in the Add Site Binding dialog.

FIGURE 7-5

7. Click the Close button in the Site Bindings dialog.

FIGURE 7-6

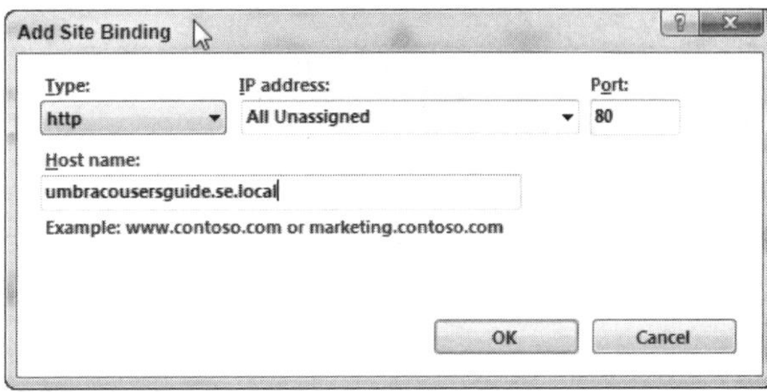

FIGURE 7-7

For local development and testing, you can use your Windows `hosts` *file to set up pointers to the newly created hostnames so that they will resolve to the websites when you type them in to the browser. To do this, simply open your* `hosts` *file, located in* `C:\Windows\System32\drivers\etc`*, in a text editor like Notepad and add a tab-delimited entry with the IP address of your development computer and the hostname you selected in the preceding steps.*

Now that IIS knows where to send the incoming requests, it's time to configure Umbraco to route those requests to the correct site as you set it up in the previous section:

1. Right-click Runway Homepage (en) in the Content section.
2. Click Manage Hostnames in the resulting context menu.
3. In the Manage hostnames dialog, enter the domain that you want to use for the English version, **umbracousersguide.com.local**, and choose English (United States) in the Language drop-down list, as shown in Figure 7-8.
4. Click the Add new domain button.
5. Click the Close this window link that appears under the newly created domain, as shown in Figure 7-9.
6. Repeat steps 2–5 on the Runway Homepage (se) node and select Swedish (Sweden) for the language there.

If you were to take a look at the Properties tab for either homepage node now, you will find a new item called Alternative Links. This reflects the domain that you added for each of the homepage nodes, which means that the two separate sites are now available on individual domains. To illustrate that this really works, change the Site Description to see the label change between the domains, as shown in Figure 7-10.

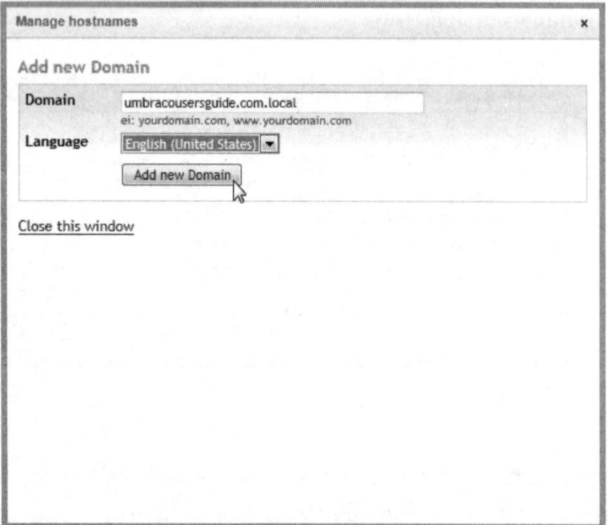

FIGURE 7-8

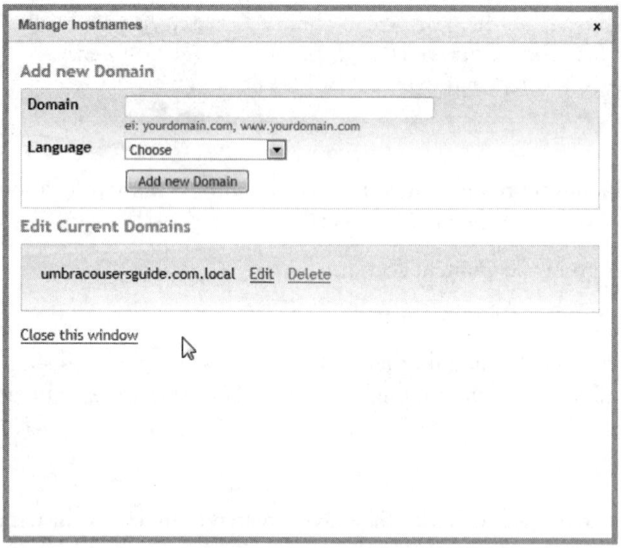

Manage hostnames ×

Add new Domain

Domain

ei: yourdomain.com, www.yourdomain.com

Language Choose

Add new Domain

Edit Current Domains

umbracousersguide.com.local Edit Delete

Close this window

FIGURE 7-9

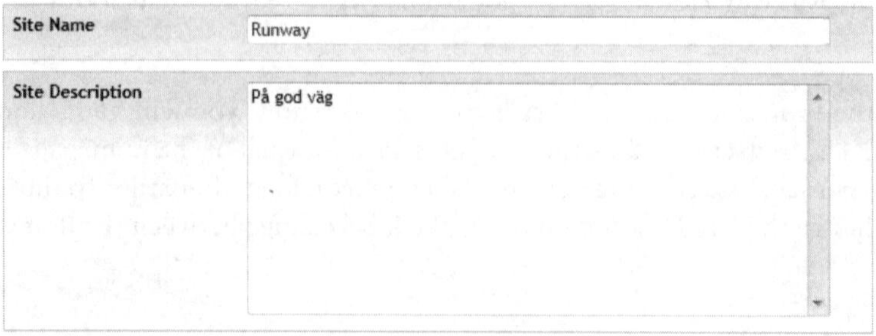

Site Name Runway

Site Description På god väg

FIGURE 7-10

Not only has the language changed for the two domains, but you will also notice that the culture changed so that dates, currencies, and other regionally specific values are now correct for the chosen language.

As you can see, you now have two separately accessible domains for which to serve up content in different languages. Each page needs to be translated individually and you can now assign editors and translators to each site. The next section provides an overview of the translation workflow that is built into Umbraco.

TRANSLATION WORKFLOW

Umbraco's translation features are not unlike those in many other CMSs' implementations. Umbraco employs an industry standard workflow that allows translation agencies to be part of the mix without having full access to the content or permission to publish anything to the public site. Umbraco generates a translation file in XML format that the translator user logs in to pick up. The translator user edits the file or uses an industry standard translation program to parse the XML file, makes the necessary translations, saves the file, and finally uploads the translated content back to Umbraco.

Chapter 2 covers in detail how to set up a user with restricted access, delves into granular permissions, and discusses setting multiple start nodes for content access.

To start a Workflow, you need to register a user (as was covered in Chapter 2, in the section "Umbraco Building Blocks"), give him access to the Translation section, and tell Umbraco where he should start in the content tree (in this case the start node is Runway Website (se). The complete user details should look like those shown in Figure 7-11.

A translation user has access to a restricted version of the Umbraco backoffice. In the example in the "Working with Hostnames" section, you set the start node for the translation user, but in a translation workflow that is a fruitless exercise because the user will only see the Translation section when he logs in. Of course, the user could have access to both the Content and Translation sections, in which case the restricted content access still applies.

Username	Translator
Login	Translator
Password	Change password
Email	niksfiles@gmail.com
User type	[translator]
Language	English (us)
Start Node in Content	Runway Website (se) Delete Choose...
Start Node in Media Library	Media Delete Choose...
Redirect to canvas on login	☐
Disable Umbraco Access	☐
Disable User	☐
Sections	☐ Content ☐ Developer ☐ Media ☐ Members ☐ Settings ☑ Translation ☐ Users

FIGURE 7-11

Sending content to translation is a breeze after you've added at least one translation user to the backoffice. The following steps take you through the process:

1. While logged in as an administrator (or editor), navigate to the Content section in Umbraco.
2. Expand the Runway Website (se) node and right-click the Installing runway modules node.
3. Click the Send To Translation menu item, as shown in Figure 7-12.
4. In the resulting dialog, select the translation user to whom you want to send this request (in this example only one is available and selected by default).
5. Select which language to translate the content to. This value is also preselected because you are in the Swedish version of the site already.
6. Optionally, you can specify whether or not to include all subpages and whether you want to add a comment, as shown in Figure 7-13.

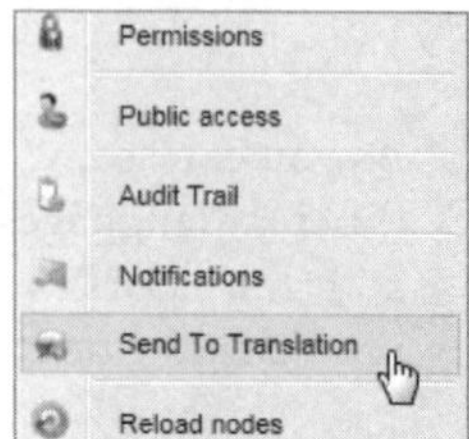

FIGURE 7-12

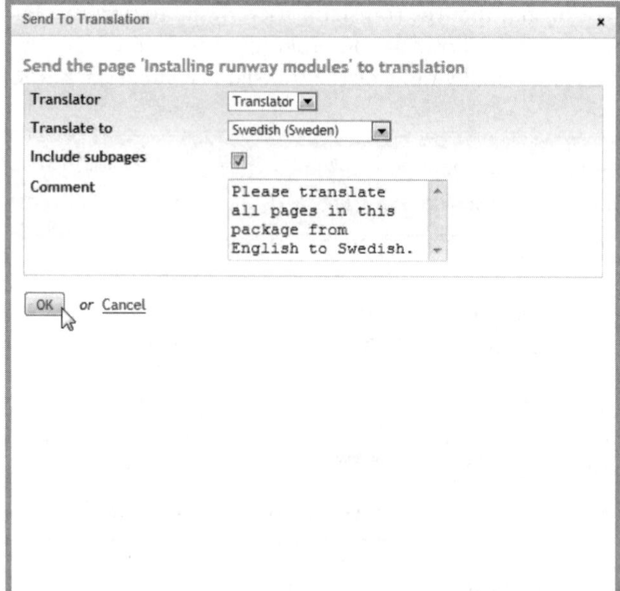

FIGURE 7-13

7. Close the confirmation dialog by clicking the Close this window link.

If a valid e-mail server is configured for your installation, an e-mail is sent to the translators at this point, notifying them that a translation task has been assigned to them. In older versions of Umbraco, this was the only way of accessing an assigned task. Since version 4.0.5.2, the backoffice tools and access were added for convenience and accessibility.

This part of the workflow is now done. You can repeat the process for any and all sections of the website that you want translated. Alternatively, you can send the entire site for translation by starting at the Homepage node. This gives you the flexibility to use multiple translators for individual sections of the site. From this point on, the translator process takes over.

1. If you are logged in with your administrator role, log out of Umbraco before proceeding.
2. Log in to Umbraco using the Translator account that you set up in the "Setting Up Multiple Sites" section earlier in this chapter. All you should see is the translation section with two nodes: "Tasks assigned to you" and "Tasks created by you."
3. Expand the Tasks assigned to you node to reveal all the outstanding translations that have been assigned. Similarly, click the node itself to list the outstanding translations in more detail, as shown in Figure 7-14.

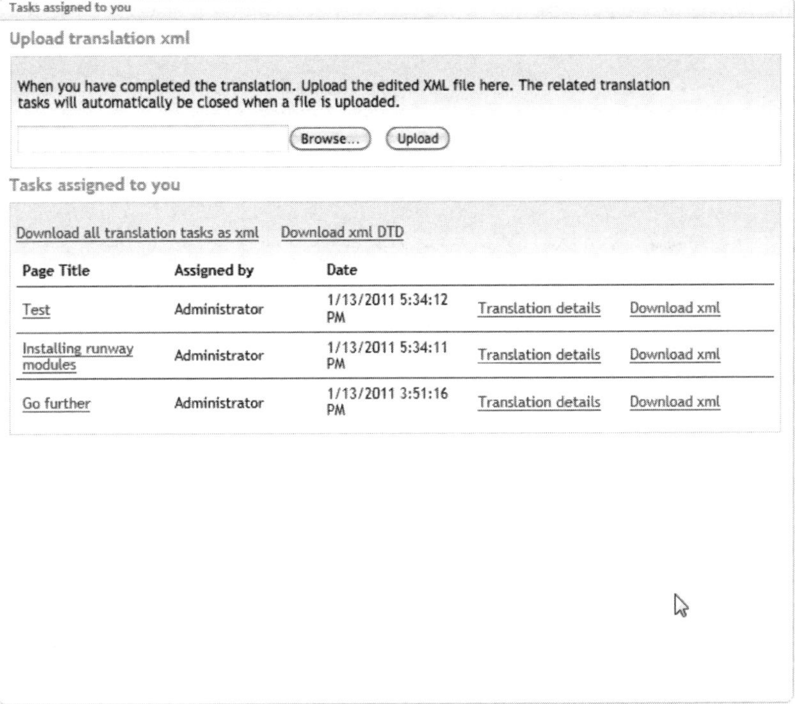

FIGURE 7-14

4. Click the Translation Details of the Installing runway modules content node to see the details of the content that needs translation. In this case, two fields need translation: Page Title and Body Text. Also, notice how the comment that you filled in earlier shows up for the translator to receive special instructions (see Figure 7-15).
5. Download the XML translation file by clicking the Download link next to the Download xml option. This prompts you to save the file on your local hard drive.
6. Locate the saved XML file and open it. For the purposes of this book, you can edit the content directly in the XML file. As mentioned in this section's introduction, the typical scenario

is such that a translator user would import the XML into a translation parsing program and perform the actual translation in there.

7. In the XML file, update `nodeName` attributes to Installation av Runway moduler, as shown in Figure 7-16.

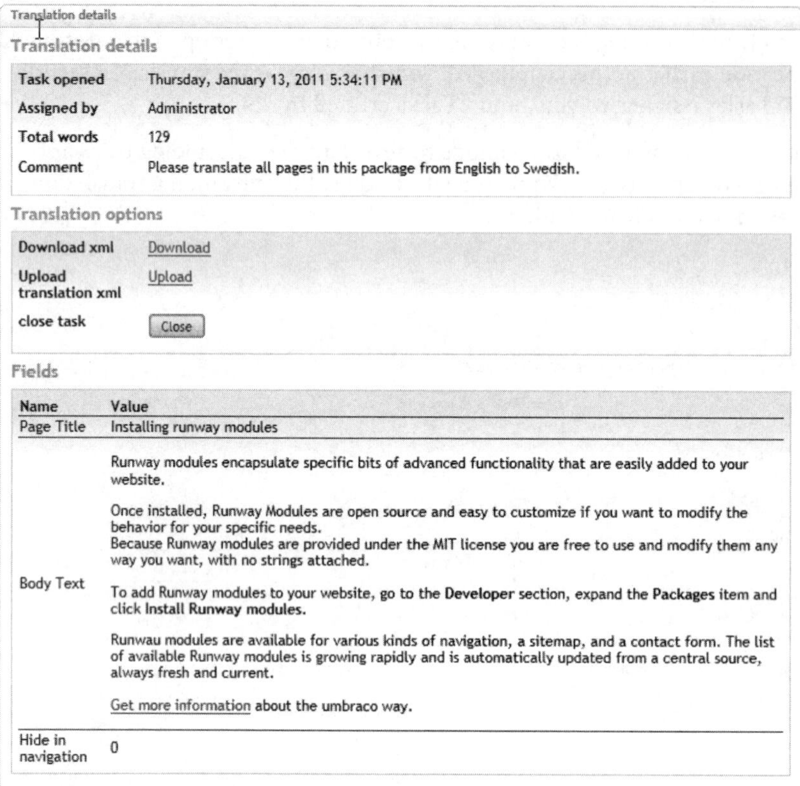

FIGURE 7-15

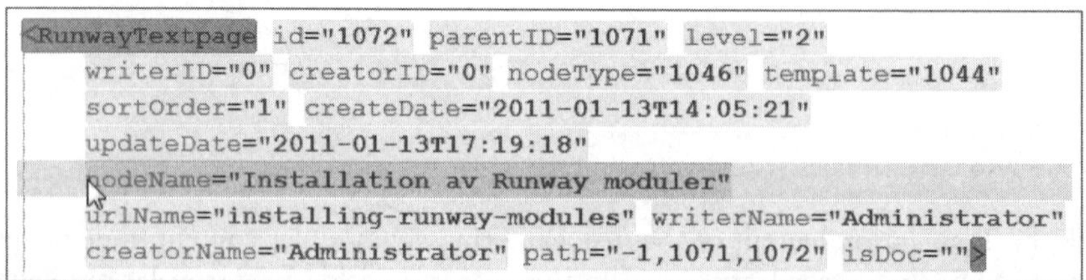

FIGURE 7-16

8. Save the file to persist the changes you made.

9. Go back to the Umbraco backoffice and log in using the Translator account, unless you are still logged in.

10. Click the Tasks assigned to you node and locate the Upload translation xml section in the right-hand pane, as shown in Figure 7-17.

Upload translation xml

When you have completed the translation. Upload the edited XML file here. The related translation tasks will automatically be closed when a file is uploaded.

Browse... Upload

FIGURE 7-17

11. Click the Browse button to locate the saved XML file on your local hard drive, as shown in Figure 7-18.

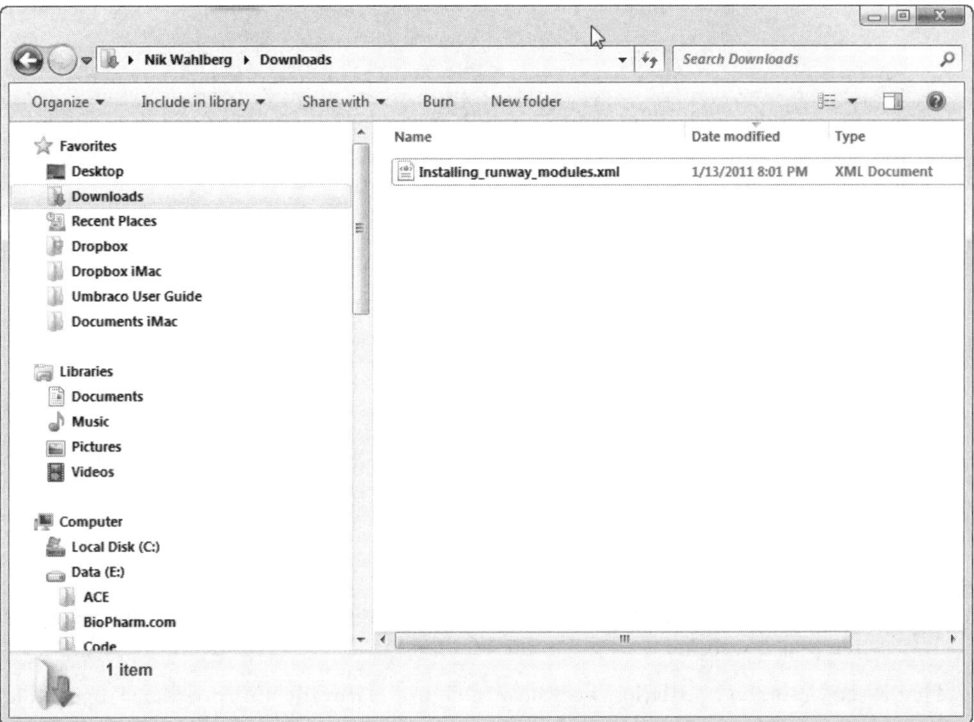

FIGURE 7-18

12. Click the Upload button to submit the translation for the given page; in this case, the Installing runway modules translation.

When you click the Upload button Umbraco saves a new version of the page with the applicable translations. This action does not publish these changes because that decision is still up to the original author of the page.

Umbraco processes the translation and presents you with a confirmation that the page has been updated and saved. In addition, you get the opportunity to preview the page here in the context of the site, as shown in Figure 7-19. Also, the page that was just translated no longer appears in the tasks assigned to you.

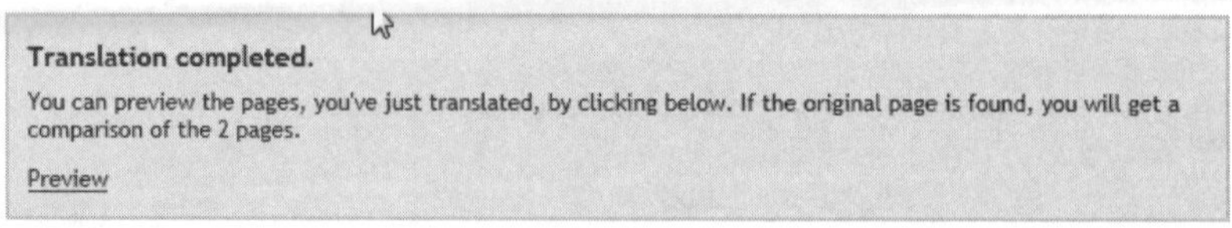

FIGURE 7-19

Now that the translation is done, the ball is back in the original creator's court. The next step in the workflow is to review the translation and publish the changes. To do these tasks, follow these steps:

1. Log out of the Umbraco backoffice and log in using your administrator account.

As shown in Figure 7-20, the page that was just translated is marked as having been changed but not published, indicated by the orange asterisk next to the page name.

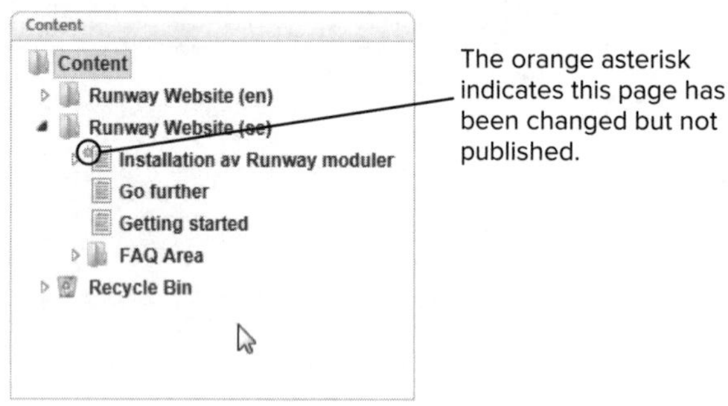

FIGURE 7-20

2. After reviewing the changes, click the Save & Publish icon to make the changes viewable on the public website.

That is the Umbraco translation workflow in detail. Naturally, this process is repeatable for any number of pages or any size website.

TAKE HOME POINTS

At the end of this chapter you should be able to create multi-lingual sites and work with world-class translation agencies to get it just right! Here's what you've learned:

- How to set up IIS to bind multiple domains to your website
- How to copy the original site to create a duplicate for translation
- How to add hostnames and assign languages to sites so Umbraco can route requests appropriately
- How to set up a translator user
- How to use the translation workflow to translate a page in a multi-lingual site
- And maybe a bit of Swedish!

PART II
Content Production

Creating Content

- How do you best organize your content?
- What are Smart template structures?
- Why work with document types?
- What are the ins and outs of the Rich Text Editor?

It's time for the good stuff and the real reason you're working with a CMS in the first place. Content is king! Okay, that phrase works better if you replace *content* with *cash*, but you get the point. You should walk away from this chapter knowing how to work with your content in Umbraco, not only adding and editing it, but more important how to plan for and organize your content.

CONTENT MANAGEMENT BEST PRACTICES

Many content management systems force a proprietary content structure on the authors and editors. Umbraco is different in this aspect because deciding how to set up the structure is up to you as the owner of the system. This applies both to content as well as presentation, and is referred to as the *template structure*.

As you know by now, Umbraco is entirely web-based, which means that all you need is an active Internet connection and a (relatively) modern browser, and you're in business. As easy as that sounds, there are some high-level tasks you should consider before diving into creating your first website using Umbraco:

- **Create a sitemap.** In Chapter 3 you read about document types, the importance of organizing them, and the impact that this organization has on your content tree. Planning the structure of your content tree is equally important. From past experience, the author can recommend creating a visual hierarchy of the content before you right-click and create that first node. This can help you visualize the structure of your website, and creating the content will go that much smoother.

- **Consider required media.** The media tree is best organized to reflect the structure of your content. This is especially true when you are working in a multi-editor environment where restricted access and start nodes come into play.
- **User-friendliness and readability of your content.** As important as it is for you to have a nice backoffice environment in which to work, ensuring that the end result is usable and user friendly for the website visitor is even more important. The structure of the content you create in the backoffice should allow your visitor not only to read the content, but also to search engines and other indexers.

To learn more about how to search engines, read your content, and about other SEO *techniques, take a look at Google's Webmaster Tools at* `www.google.com/webmasters/`.

CREATING A STRUCTURE

The basis of all created content is rooted in the document types that you create. Without any defined document types, no way would exist to create the content. Chapter 3 covers the details of creating a document type and how they are constructed. This chapter discusses what it means to structure the document types to create the content tree that you designed in your planning phase, as suggested earlier in this chapter.

Think about how you want the users of the Umbraco backoffice to work with the content tree. Some questions you might ask are:

- Will I need to have different roles accessing only parts of the content structure?
- Will restricting the types of content that can be created in certain parts of the content tree be necessary?
- Should editors have access to the Media library? If so, only parts of it? Should they simply have the ability to upload a file/document on a per-page basis?

The answers to these questions (and more) will determine how you build out your document types. For the purposes of this example, assume that the requirements dictate that you create two different editors — one for standard page content (who will have access to all the content) and one for editing news articles only. This means that the news editor should not be able to add standard content pages to the site. To control this access, you set the allowed child types as appropriate when creating the document type for news articles (covered in Chapter 3).

For the news articles, you want to create two distinct document types that you can add to the content tree (see Figure 8-1 for an illustration of the content tree):

- **News Area:** This acts as a container for all the news articles.
- **News Article:** This is the actual news article that will be added to the site. This is the document type that holds all the news properties (such as article date, summary, and so on).

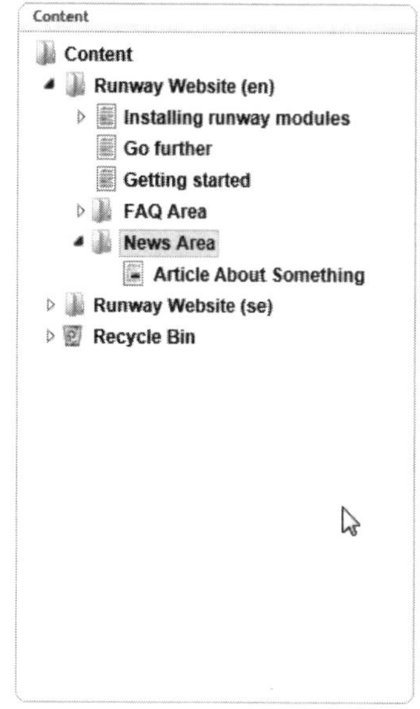

FIGURE 8-1

Because you planned your content, you know that News Article will be a child node of the News Area, so creating the News Article first makes sense. Also, in this case, News Article will not have any child nodes allowed, so it's the perfect place to start:

1. Create the News Article document type. Note that you can create the News Area document type and the associated template in one swift move. If you need a refresher on how to work with Document Types, see Chapter 3.
2. Set the News Article as an allowed child type of the News Area, as shown in Figure 8-2.
3. Allow the News Area to be a child type of the Runway Homepage document type.

Creating the News Article as a child document type of the News Area is not necessary because the two of them will not share any common properties. Setting the News Article as an allowed child type is not synonymous with its being a child of the News Area document type. The allowed child node type designation refers to the relationship between the two document types in the context of the content tree only.

Remember, too, that creating parent document types to share common properties, such as meta tags, is a good idea to avoid document property duplication. For more information on how to work with parent document types, see Chapter 3.

You can apply the same approach to many other types of content, of course, such as events, profiles, staff records, and so on. The next section discusses how templates fit into the content creation scheme.

The other noteworthy feature of Umbraco is its flexible node-sorting capabilities. You can easily sort nodes at all levels of the content tree by right-clicking a container node and clicking the Sort menu item. You have two ways to sort your nodes from the resulting Sort dialog:

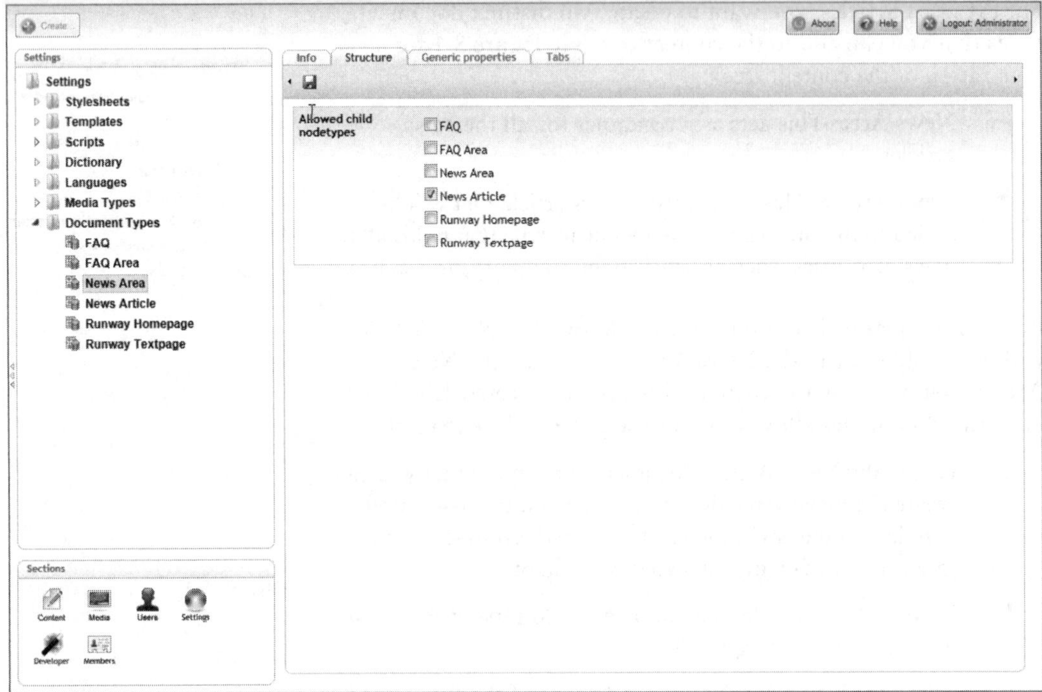

FIGURE 8-2

- Simply drag the nodes.
- Click the headers in the columns to sort by either name or creation date, as shown in Figure 8-3.

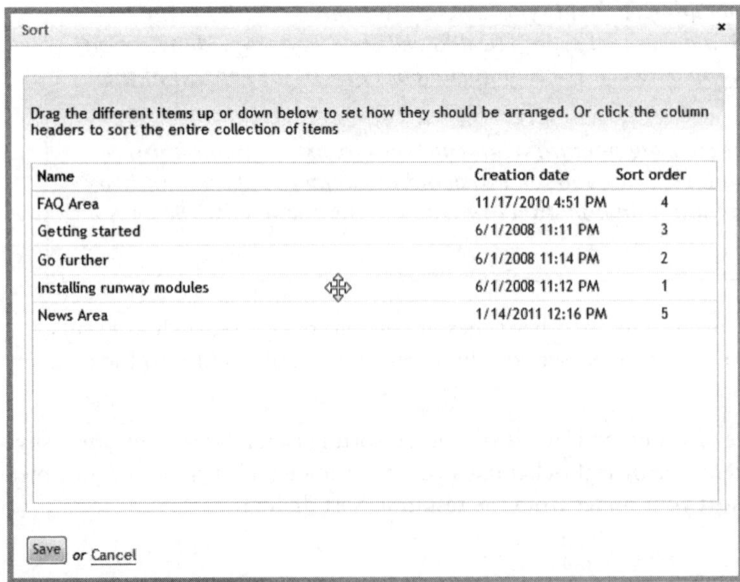

FIGURE 8-3

ORGANIZING TEMPLATES FOR REUSE

Chapter 4 focuses on the creation and management of the templates themselves. This section discusses the practical application of those templates and how managing templates correctly can make for a very flexible presentation engine.

In most cases a document type has a one-to-one relationship with a template. By default, this is the case when you create a document type and elect to have a template created as part of the process. What you may not know is that any given document type can have any number of associated templates, as shown in Figure 8-4.

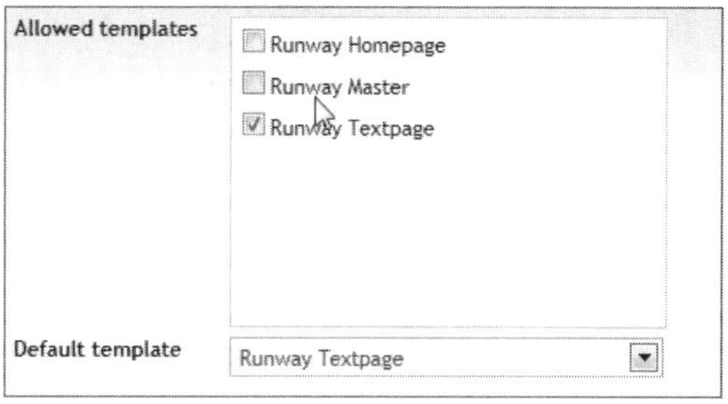

FIGURE 8-4

Several reasons exist for this feature:

- A document type may support different types of output based on media type or device type.
- A node's content may need to have the flexibility to be presented differently without having to recreate the content using a different document type.
- Features of a page may need to be toggled by an editor, such as the inclusion of second-level navigation, a sidebar, or other content.
- A multi-site environment, as in Chapter 6, needs to have different templates based on the site that is being rendered.

So, when you create your templates, make sure to take into account the various page types that they need to support. One example of when to share a document type with two templates is for toggling a feature of a page. To illustrate the point, follow these steps:

1. Log in to your Umbraco installation and click the Settings section.
2. Expand Templates ➪ Runway Master to reveal the two child templates, Runway Homepage and Runway Textpage.
3. Right-click Runway Master and click the Create menu option.
4. In the name field, type in **Runway Textpage + Sidebar**, as shown in Figure 8-5, and click Create.
5. Copy the template contents from Listing 8-1 into the newly created templates, replacing what appears there by default. What this does is utilize the `sideNavigation` container that is already defined, and populates it with the `sidebarContent` field.

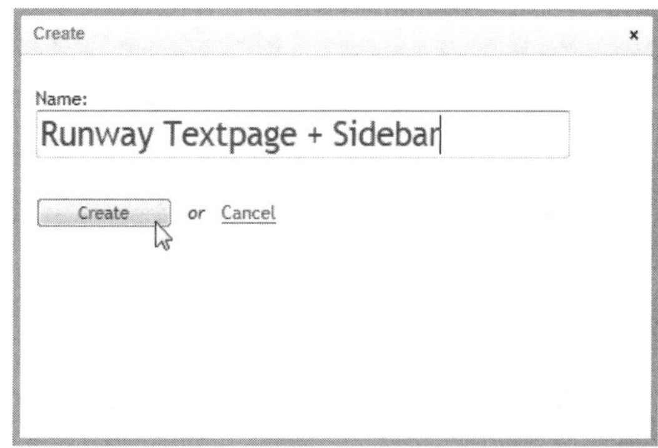

FIGURE 8-5

Available for download on Wrox.com

LISTING 8-1: RunwayTextpage+Sidebar.master

```
<%@ Master Language="C#" MasterPageFile="~/masterpages/RunwayMaster.master"
 AutoEventWireup="true" %>
<asp:Content ContentPlaceHolderID="RunwayMasterContentPlaceHolder"
     runat="server">
    <div id="content">
        <umbraco:Macro Alias="SiteBreadcrumb" runat="server"></umbraco:Macro>
            <div id="contentHeader">
            <h2><umbraco:Item runat="server" field="pageName"/></h2>
        </div>
        <umbraco:Item runat="server" field="bodyText" />
    </div>
    <div id="subNavigation">
            <umbraco:Item runat="server" field="sidebarContent" />
        </div>
</asp:Content>
```

6. While still in the Settings section of Umbraco, expand the Document Types node and click the Runway Textpage document type to open the details in the right-hand pane.

7. As shown in Figure 8-6, select the newly created template in the Allowed templates field.

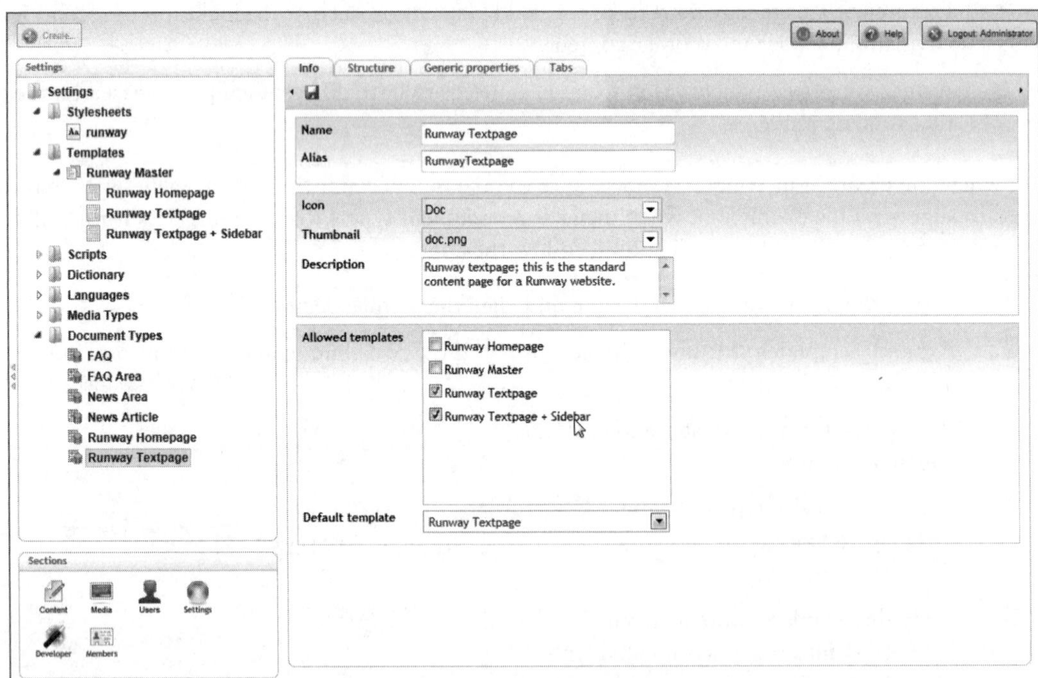

FIGURE 8-6

8. Click the Generic Properties tab toward the top of the screen.

9. Click the Click here to add a new property option, and fill in the fields as illustrated in Figure 8-7 (Description is optional).

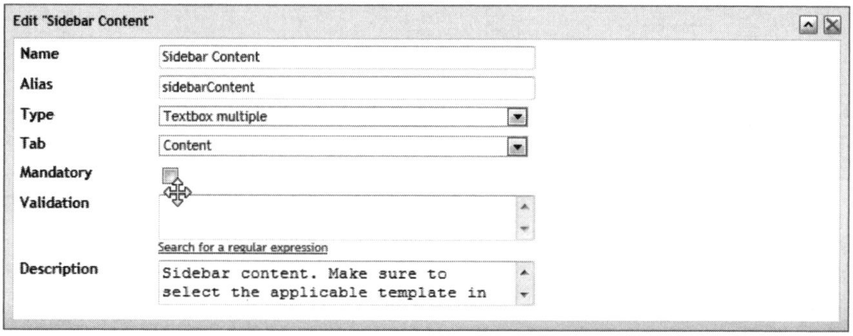

Edit "Sidebar Content"

Name	Sidebar Content
Alias	sidebarContent
Type	Textbox multiple
Tab	Content
Mandatory	
Validation	
	Search for a regular expression
Description	Sidebar content. Make sure to select the applicable template in

FIGURE 8-7

10. Save the document type.

What you have done so far is to extend the functionality of the text page document type and add a template to support the new sidebar feature. To see this feature in action, you can change one of the pages in the content tree and check out the result as described in the following steps. When you view the details of any content page in the content tree, you can now see the added Sidebar Content field, as shown in Figure 8-8.

FIGURE 8-8

1. Click the Content section in Umbraco.
2. Expand the Runway Homepage node and click the Installing runway modules node.
3. Enter some content in the Sidebar Content field.

A tip text snippet was added in this example to remind editors that they must select the appropriate template when utilizing the Sidebar Content field.

4. Click the Properties tab and select the new template, as shown in Figure 8-9.

FIGURE 8-9

5. Save and publish the page and view the results.

You can programmatically achieve similar results with a single template by inserting a macro that checks the length of the `sidebarContent` *field and injects some strategically placed CSS to remove the sidebar container when no content exists. These methods are outside the scope of this book.*

UNDERSTANDING THE RICH TEXT EDITOR

Any person with moderate word processing skills can operate the Umbraco Rich Text Editor (RTE) data type. Built with ease of use in mind, the *TinyMCE* editing control provides the user with a very familiar and standardized set of tools for managing content. The standard tools with which Umbraco ships are shown in Figure 8-10 and described in Table 8-1.

TABLE 8-1: Umbraco's Rich Text Editor Tools

ICON	TOOL NAME	DESCRIPTION
	Save	Saves the current state of the node to the database but does not publish the change to make it viewable on your website.
	Save and Publish	Saves the changes to the node that you're working on and publishes the content to the XML cache. This makes the changes available to the public-facing website.
	Preview	Previews a saved page without publishing to see it in the context of the template that is chosen.
HTML	HTML View	Edits the HTML that the RTE generates from pasting or typing content. To enable or disable individual tags and attributes that the RTE allows, change the `<validElements />` section in the `<install root>/config/tinyMceConfig.config`.
	Undo	Undoes changes.
	Redo	Redo changes.
	Cut	Cuts selected text and elements within the RTE.
	Copy	Copies selected text and element within the RTE.
	Paste	Pastes content from external programs such as Notepad or Word.
Styles	Text Styles	By default, this list is blank because styles are specific to the website that you are implementing. This means that defining the styles is up to you (refer to Chapter 4).
B	Bold	Makes selected text bold.
I	Italic	Makes selected text italic.
	Unordered List	Creates a bulleted list.
	Ordered List	Creates a numbered list.

continues

TABLE 8-1 *(continued)*

ICON	TOOL NAME	DESCRIPTION
	Outdent	If a block of text or other elements has been indented, this button is active for you to remove indentation.
	Indent	Indents blocks of content by 30 *pixels*.
	Insert/Edit Link	Links selected text or elements to internal or external pages, or to media items (such as files).
	Unlink	Removes the link from the selected text or elements.
	Insert/Edit Anchor	Inserts "jump-to" points within a long page. You use this in conjunction with Insert/edit link to enable a user to jump to a section by clicking a link in the page.
	Insert/Edit Image	Insert an image from the media library or upload a new one. Figure 8-11 shows the associated dialog box for this feature.
	Insert Macro	Inserts custom-coded functionality in your RTE. The particular macro needs to have the Use in editor feature selected in order for it to appear in this list.
	Insert Table	Inserts an HTML <table /> for formatting or tabular data. Figure 8-12 shows the associated dialog box for this feature.
	Insert Custom Character	Inserts non-standard characters from a character table.

Any content that you need to publish on your website that has formatting (bold, italicize, bulleted lists, images, paragraphs, etc.), should be entered using the Umbraco RTE data type. The meat of your page is a valid candidate for this data type because the probability of needing to format the content using styles and images is very likely. The contradiction to this case might be the output of a simple summary paragraph that needs no author-injected styling, but would be rendered as part of your templates (ex. news article listing). In this case, you want to retain the control of the output and therefore you might use the Textstring Multiple data type instead.

For a detailed description of the standard Umbraco data types, please see Appendix D.

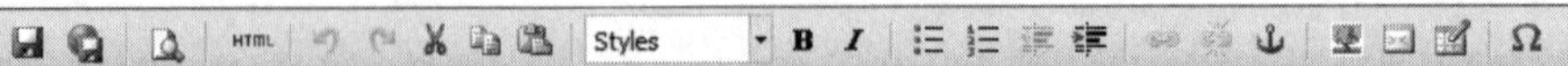

FIGURE 8-10

Insert picture
Url
/media/157/top_logo.gif
Name
Umbraco
Dimensions
Width: 123 Height: 38
Constrain proportions
umbraco
Choose
Create New
Media
Corporate Logos
Umbraco
IBM
Apple
Microsoft
Insert
or Cancel

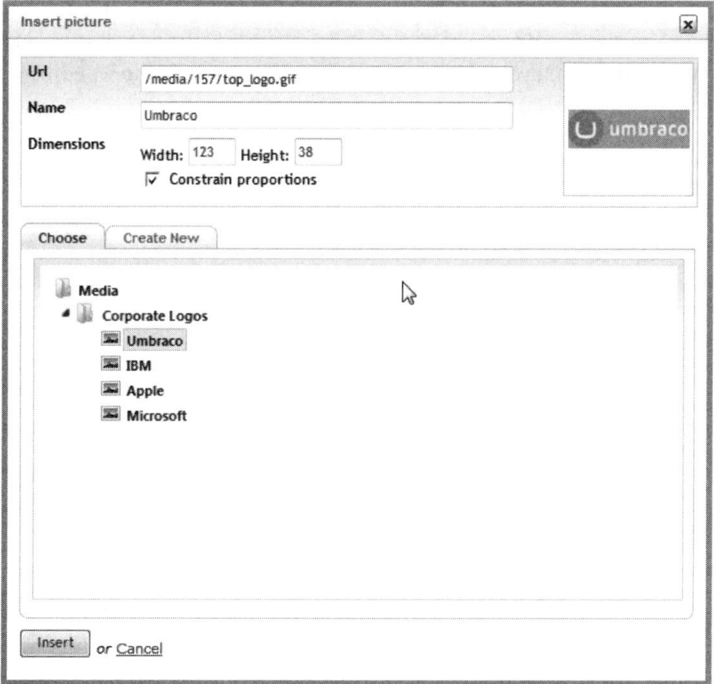

FIGURE 8-11

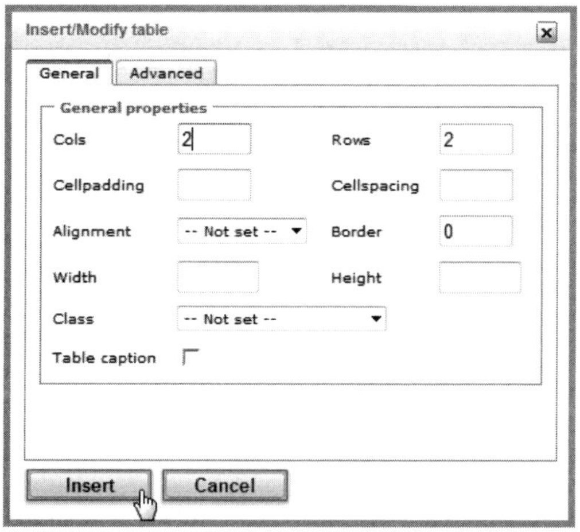

Insert/Modify table
General
Advanced
General properties
Cols 2
Rows 2
Cellpadding
Cellspacing
Alignment -- Not set --
Border 0
Width
Height
Class -- Not set --
Table caption
Insert
Cancel

FIGURE 8-12

Using the standard toolbar should feel familiar if you have ever used Microsoft Word or other word processing software. If editors need access to additional tools, such as for inserting videos or flash movies, you can enable those features in the Developer section ➪ Data Types ➪ Richtext editor, as shown in Figure 8-13.

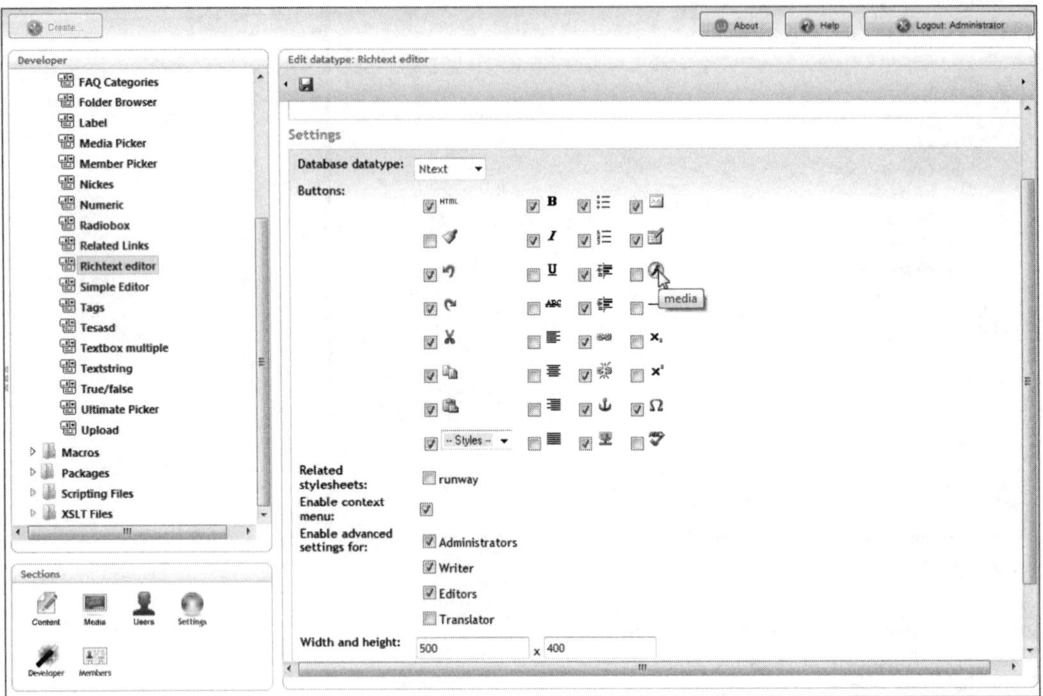

FIGURE 8-13

If you need different options for the Rich Text Editor for different document types, you can easily generate a new version of the default Rich Text Editor by creating a new data type and choosing TinyMCE v3 WYSIWYG as the render control, as shown in Figure 8-14.

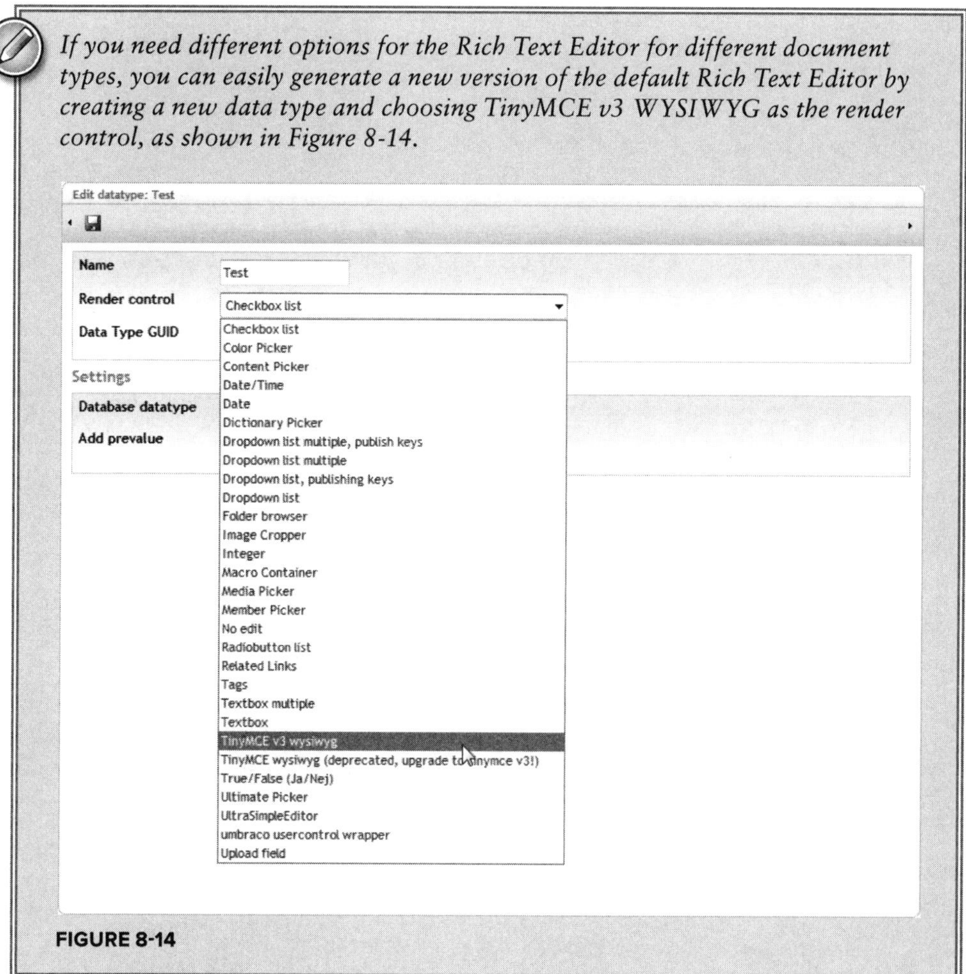

FIGURE 8-14

TAKE HOME POINTS

By now you should have enough knowledge about the right tools to create and publish content, including the following:

- A solid understanding of how to plan your content before you start building a website in Umbraco.
- Understanding why planning before you start is important.
- Creating a structure both for document types and content and how they relate.
- Organizing your templates for greatest reuse.
- A working knowledge of how the Rich Text Editor works.

Adding Functionality

- What are Umbraco tags all about?
- How do you generate content programmatically?
- How do you set up search using Examine?
- What are the steps for deploying custom functionality?

Umbraco is great at allowing you to add, edit, and work with content. It has a flexible template engine and great tools for creating content structures and managing resources and users. But what really makes it powerful is that you can extend and customize it to your particular needs. This chapter offers you a look at how to do that and what tools are at your disposal, such as Razor and Examine. Also, you'll see further examples of how to leverage XSLT-, .NET-, and Umbraco-specific tags (the not-so-well-known attributes).

For a detailed look at the power of XSLT and .NET macros, see Chapters 11 and 12.

USING THE UMBRACO TAGS

Chapter 4 introduced you to the special tags that Umbraco utilizes for outputting content to templates. These tags are referenced in templates as .NET custom tags and take on the format you see in the following code:

```
<umbraco:item field="" someOtherAttribute="" runat="server" .../>
```

If you have ever registered a user control (`.ascx`) in a .NET project, this code should look strikingly familiar to you. In its most basic form, the tag takes the field attribute and returns a value for the specified field name, assuming it exists in the context of the page that the template is rendering. For a summary of the various available attributes and what they do, see Table 9-1.

TABLE 9-1: Umbraco Tag Attributes

ATTRIBUTE NAME	DESCRIPTION	EXAMPLE USAGE
`field`	The field from which you are trying to get data.	See previous code snippet for an example.
`insertTextBefore`	Allows you to insert text before the output of the field value.	`<umbraco:item field="bodyText"` **`insertTextBefore="We have had: "`** `runat="server"/>`
`insertTextAfter`	Allows you to insert text after the output of the field value.	`<umbraco:item field="bodyText"` **`insertTextAfter=" inches of snow this year."`** `runat="server"/>`
`recursive`	Tells Umbraco to continue looking at any parents of the current page for a value if the value is null or empty at the current page.	`<umbraco:item field="bodyText"` **`recursive="true"`** `runat="server"/>`
`formatAsDate`	Indicates that Umbraco should format the output as a standard date.	`<umbraco:item field="bodyText"` **`formatAsDate="true"`** `runat="server"/>`
`formatAsDateWithTime`	Just like `formatAsDate`, this outputs a date but appends the time stamp as well. When using this attribute you must also specify `formatAsDateWithTimeSeparator`.	`<umbraco:item field="bodyText"` **`formatAsDateWithTime="true"`** **`formatAsDateWithTimeSeparator=" "`** `runat="server"/>`
`useIfEmpty`	Allows you to specify an alternate field to output if the value from the `field` attribute is null or empty.	`<umbraco:item field="bodyText"` **`useIfEmpty="anotherFieldAlias"`** `runat="server"/>`
`textIfEmpty`	Allows you to specify a static string value to use if the `field` attribute is null or empty.	`<umbraco:item field="bodyText"` **`textIfEmpty="No value was specified for this field."`** `runat="server"/>`
`convertLineBreaks`	When you're using the Textbox Multiple or Simple Editor data types, this attribute will force Umbraco to replace the newline character (`\r\n`) with the HTML equivalent ` `.	`<umbraco:item field="bodyText"` **`convertLineBreaks="true"`** `runat="server"/>`

ATTRIBUTE NAME	DESCRIPTION	EXAMPLE USAGE
`stripParagraph`	Tells Umbraco to remove the first paragraph (`<p>`) tag and the last paragraph (`</p>`) tag from the field value.	`<umbraco:item field="bodyText"` **`stripParagraph="true"`** `runat="server"/>`
`case`	Converts the field value into either `lower` or `upper` case.	`<umbraco:item field="bodyText"` **`case="lower|upper"`** `runat="server"/>`
`urlEncode`	Allows you to URL-encode the field value; for example, you can replace the space character with `%20`. For a full list of URL-friendly character replacements and what they are, see `http://legalxhtml.org/xhtml/HTML+URL-encoded+Hex+Entities`.	`<umbraco:item field="bodyText"` **`urlEncode="true"`** `runat="server"/>`
`htmlEncode`	Converts special (non-alphanumeric) characters into their HTML entity equivalent. For example, `&` (ampersand) will render as `&`.	`<umbraco:item field="bodyText"` **`htmlEncode="true"`** `runat="server"/>`
`xslt`	Allows you to access the extensive XSLT helper libraries to format the field value. For example, instead of using `formatAsDate`, the value can be passed to a helper function with greater format control — `umbraco.library:FormatDateTime()`. Notice that the brace notation (`{0}`) is used to inject the field value as needed.	`<umbraco:Item field="dateField"` **`xslt="umbraco.library:FormatDateTime({0},'MMM dd, yyyy')"`** `runat="server">`

In many cases you can use a combination of the preceding attributes. For example, if you are trying to insert an HTML tag with attribute values (like a meta tag), you can accomplish this by using the `insertBefore` and `insertAfter` attributes simultaneously. See Listing 9-1 for an example. To see how you can access these attributes via the Umbraco backoffice UI, see Chapter 4.

LISTING 9-1: OutputMetaTag.master

Available for download on Wrox.com

```
<%@ Master Language="C#"
MasterPageFile="~/umbraco/masterpages/default.master"
AutoEventWireup="true"
 %>
<asp:Content ContentPlaceHolderID="ContentPlaceHolderDefault" runat="server">
    <!DOCTYPE html PUBLIC "-//W3C//DTD XHTML 1.0 Strict//EN"
"http://www.w3.org/TR/xhtml1/DTD/xhtml1-strict.dtd"[]>
    <html xmlns="http://www.w3.org/1999/xhtml">
        <head id="head" runat="server">
            <title>Email Output Template</title>
        </head>
        <body>
            <umbraco:Item field="siteName"
              insertTextBefore="&lt;meta property='og:site_name' content='"
              insertTextAfter="'/&gt;" recursive="true" runat="server">
            </umbraco:Item>
        </body>
    </html>
</asp:content>
```

GENERATING WEBSITE NAVIGATION MENUS

Umbraco ships with a whole list of templates for generating lists of nodes for navigation, breadcrumbs, and other usage. This section provides some additional examples of how to work with XSLT and *Razor* to generate menus from your content structure. Razor is a *view engine* and is new in .NET 4.0. Razor allows you to access dynamic objects and display their associated data structures and values in the view (WebForm or other standard ASP.NET template). A common occurrence in websites is to have a multi-level top navigation with second level pages listed in dropdown menus. Listing 9-2 shows you how to do this.

Because Umbraco renders exactly what you tell it to render, the output from Listing 9-2 can easily be styled using CSS and JavaScript to create an engaging and functional menu.

LISTING 9-2: TwoTierTopNav.xslt

Available for download on Wrox.com

```
<?xml version="1.0" encoding="UTF-8"?>
<!DOCTYPE xsl:stylesheet [
    <!ENTITY nbsp " ">
```

```
]>
<xsl:stylesheet
    version="1.0"
    xmlns:xsl="http://www.w3.org/1999/XSL/Transform"
    xmlns:msxml="urn:schemas-microsoft-com:xslt"
    xmlns:umbraco.library="urn:umbraco.library"
xmlns:Exslt.ExsltCommon="urn:Exslt.ExsltCommon"
xmlns:Exslt.ExsltDatesAndTimes="urn:Exslt.ExsltDatesAndTimes"
xmlns:Exslt.ExsltMath="urn:Exslt.ExsltMath"
xmlns:Exslt.ExsltRegularExpressions="urn:Exslt.ExsltRegularExpressions"
xmlns:Exslt.ExsltStrings="urn:Exslt.ExsltStrings"
xmlns:Exslt.ExsltSets="urn:Exslt.ExsltSets"
xmlns:umbusersguide.library="urn:umbusersguide.library"
    exclude-result-prefixes="msxml umbraco.library Exslt.ExsltCommon
Exslt.ExsltDatesAndTimes Exslt.ExsltMath Exslt.ExsltRegularExpressions
Exslt.ExsltStrings Exslt.ExsltSets umbusersguide.library ">

    <xsl:output method="xml" omit-xml-declaration="yes" />
    <xsl:param name="currentPage"/>

    <xsl:template match="/">
        <!-- Top level with an ID allowing you to style
             the navigation.
        -->
        <ul id="Navigation">
            <xsl:apply-templates select="$currentPage/*
               [@isDoc and string(umbracoNaviHide) != '1']"/>
        </ul>
    </xsl:template>

    <xsl:template match="*">
        <li>
            <a href="{umbraco.library:NiceUrl(@id)}">
                <xsl:value-of select="@nodeName"/>
            </a>

            <!-- check to see if the current page in the loop
                 has any direct children. If so, build the next
                 level here.
            -->
            <xsl:if test="./*
                 [@isDoc and string(umbracoNaviHide) != '1']">
                <ul>
                    <xsl:apply-templates select="./*
                        [@isDoc and string(umbracoNaviHide) != '1']"/>
                </ul>
            </xsl:if>
        </li>
    </xsl:template>
</xsl:stylesheet>
```

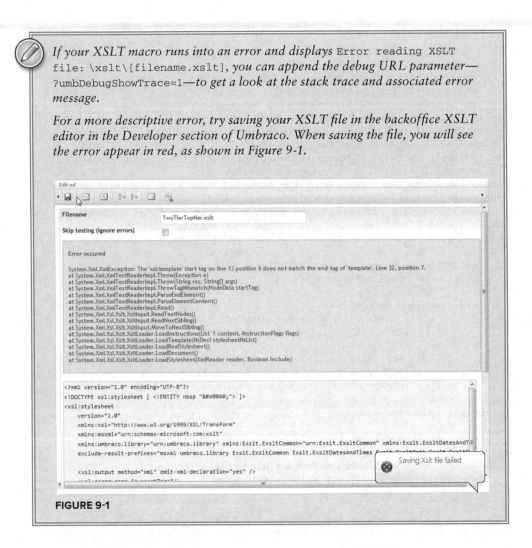

> *If your XSLT macro runs into an error and displays* `Error reading XSLT file: \xslt\[filename.xslt]`*, you can append the debug URL parameter—*`?umbDebugShowTrace=1`*—to get a look at the stack trace and associated error message.*
>
> *For a more descriptive error, try saving your XSLT file in the backoffice XSLT editor in the Developer section of Umbraco. When saving the file, you will see the error appear in red, as shown in Figure 9-1.* 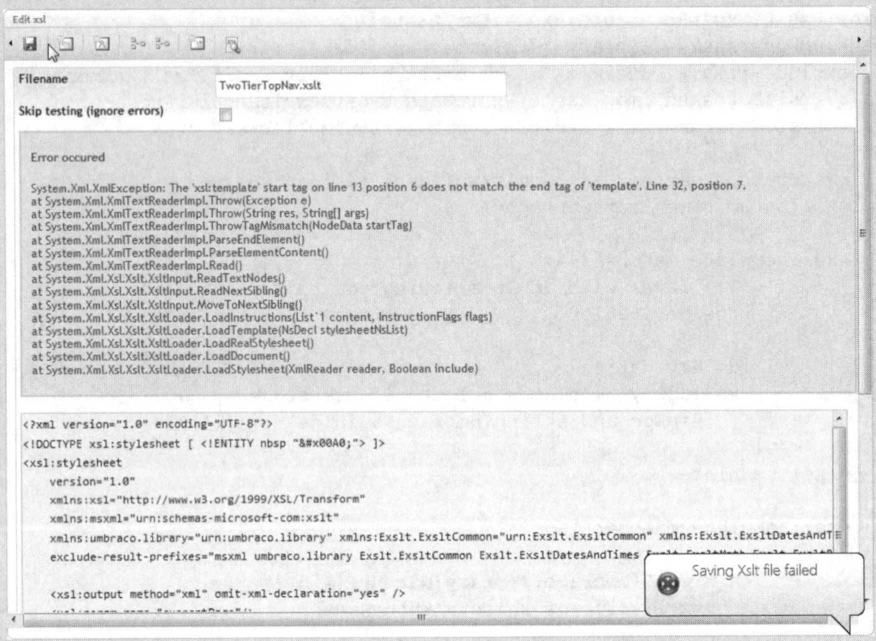
>
> **FIGURE 9-1**

Umbraco 4.6, the latest stable version at the time of this writing, has added Razor (CSHTML) support. This means that you can now leverage a third dynamic language runtime language for macro functionality (covered in Chapter 5). Listing 9-3 contains a sample Razor-driven macro. Razor provides you with access to the equivalent of `currentPage` in XSLT (covered in Chapter 11), something called the *Model*. Model contains all the properties that you have saved for any given document type.

Available for download on Wrox.com

LISTING 9-3: SecondLevelNav.razor

```
<ul>
    @foreach(var page in Model.Children) {
        <li><a href="@page.Url">@page.Name</li>
    }
</ul>
```

The preceding is a very simple example of Razor. It can certainly get more complex, and for some people Razor will become a replacement for the use of XSLT as a rendering engine.

PROVIDING THE LATEST NEWS, EVENTS, AND POSTS

One recurring requirement when you are building custom websites is to provide the ability to autogenerate lists of pages or particular items (outside of standard navigation). For example, most corporate websites have something like Latest News, Upcoming Events, and so on. Obviously, it would be great if you didn't have to manually create those lists and standard content. If you did them manually, you would have to update the content in several places every time you added a news article or event to the site. Enter macros and document types (again). Building on previous examples in Chapter 5 and the use of Runway, Listing 9-4 outputs a listing of FAQs entered in your Runway website.

The XSLT template in Listing 9-4 is originally based on the List Subpages by Document Type template that you can find in the Create new XSLT dialog (covered in Chapter 5).

Available for download on Wrox.com

LISTING 9-4: ListFaqs.xslt

```
<?xml version="1.0" encoding="UTF-8"?>
<!DOCTYPE xsl:stylesheet [ <!ENTITY nbsp " "> ]>
<xsl:stylesheet
    version="1.0"
    xmlns:xsl="http://www.w3.org/1999/XSL/Transform"
    xmlns:msxml="urn:schemas-microsoft-com:xslt"
    xmlns:umbraco.library="urn:umbraco.library"
xmlns:Exslt.ExsltCommon="urn:Exslt.ExsltCommon"
xmlns:Exslt.ExsltDatesAndTimes="urn:Exslt.ExsltDatesAndTimes"
xmlns:Exslt.ExsltMath="urn:Exslt.ExsltMath"
xmlns:Exslt.ExsltRegularExpressions="urn:Exslt.ExsltRegularExpressions"
xmlns:Exslt.ExsltStrings="urn:Exslt.ExsltStrings"
xmlns:Exslt.ExsltSets="urn:Exslt.ExsltSets"
xmlns:umbusersguide.library="urn:umbusersguide.library"
    exclude-result-prefixes="msxml umbraco.library Exslt.ExsltCommon
Exslt.ExsltDatesAndTimes Exslt.ExsltMath Exslt.ExsltRegularExpressions
Exslt.ExsltStrings Exslt.ExsltSets umbusersguide.library ">

    <xsl:output method="xml" omit-xml-declaration="yes" />

    <xsl:param name="currentPage"/>

    <!-- Input the documenttype you want here -->
    <xsl:variable name="documentTypeAlias" select="string('FAQ')"/>
```

continues

LISTING 9-4 *(continued)*

```
    <xsl:template match="/">
        <!-- The fun starts here -->
        <div class="faq-list">
            <xsl:for-each select="$currentPage/*
              [name() = $documentTypeAlias and
              string(umbracoNaviHide) != '1']">
                <div class="faq">
                    <a href="{umbraco.library:NiceUrl(@id)}">
                        <xsl:value-of select="@nodeName"/>
                    </a><br />
                    <span class="label">Q:</span>
                    <xsl:value-of select="question"
                       disable-output-escaping="yes"/>
                </div>
            </xsl:for-each>
        </div>
    </xsl:template>
</xsl:stylesheet>
```

The document type alias variable that is defined in the beginning of Listing 9-4 is case sensitive. Make sure you check the casing of your document type alias if no content is being rendered from XSLT or other macros.

Similarly, rendering could certainly be done using Razor as your rendering engine, or .NET user control, or any of the other methods discussed in Chapter 5. Hopefully, you can see how you can apply the same concept to just about any content type that you need to output.

For more examples on outputting autogenerated lists, visit `http://our.umbraco.org` *and take a look at the wiki entries.*

USING EXAMINE TO SEARCH CONTENT

As of Umbraco 4.5, *Examine*, which is a custom search engine built on Lucene.NET, comes standard as part of the backoffice search feature. Because of that, setting up indexers that you can use to search the content that is published on your website is relatively easy.

To setup Examine for your website, follow these simple steps.

1. **Configure a new index set in `<install root>/config/ExamineIndex.config`.** To make this task easy, copy the `InternalIndexSet` that is already defined. For your reference, this is the one that is used to support the Umbraco backoffice searching. To set Examine up in your Runway site, copy the code in Listing 9-5.

2. **Create a *searcher* that you can attach to in your .NET code.** This searcher specifies a number of settings, such as whether indexing should be handled asynchronously, the binaries to run the search, and which index set should be used when executing a search. All these settings appear in the `<install root>/config/ExamineSettings.config`. See Listing 9-6 for an example of a searcher for your Runway site. Add the bolded code in Listing 9-6 to your `ExamineSettings.config` file.
3. **Gain access to the indexes that are created when you publish a node.** You do this by creating a .NET macro with the contents in Listings 9-7 and 9-8. For information on creating macros, see Chapter 5.
4. **Add the Search Results macro to a page or template so that you can call the URL in a browser.** For example, add it to `http://umbracousersguide.local/search-results.aspx`.
5. **Add a search field to your master template that simply redirects to your newly created search macro and appends the search term in the URL query string `s`.** Listing 9-9 shows an example of this. Copy the code in Listing 9-9 into your `Runway.Master` template.
6. **Restart the application.** You do this by simply resaving the `web.config` file in the `<install root>web.config`.

LISTING 9-5: ExamineIndex-partial.config

Available for download on Wrox.com

```
<IndexSet SetName="RunwayIndexSet"
   IndexPath="~/App_Data/ExamineIndexes/Runway/">
      <!-- fields specific to Umbraco -->
    <IndexAttributeFields>
      <add Name="id" /> <!-- required -->
      <add Name="nodeName" /> <!-- required -->
      <add Name="updateDate" />
      <add Name="writerName" />
      <add Name="path" />
      <add Name="nodeTypeAlias" /> <!-- required -->
    </IndexAttributeFields>
      <!-- fields that you have defined in your various document types -->
    <IndexUserFields>
      <add Name="bodyText" />
      <add Name="sidebarContent" />
    </IndexUserFields>
    <IncludeNodeTypes />
      <!-- specify any document types that you do NOT want to be indexed -->
    <ExcludeNodeTypes>
      <add Name="FAQArea" />
    </ExcludeNodeTypes>
</IndexSet>
```

The `IndexPath` *that you specify must be writable by IIS. If IIS does not have write privileges on this folder, the index won't be created and therefore cannot be searched.*

Available for download on Wrox.com

LISTING 9-6: ExamineSettings-partial.config

```
<Examine>
  <ExamineIndexProviders>
    <providers>
      ...
        <add name="RunwayIndexer"
type="UmbracoExamine.MemberLuceneExamineIndexer, UmbracoExamine"
             runAsync="true"
             supportUnpublished="true"
             supportProtected="true"
             interval="10"
             analyzer="Lucene.Net.Analysis.Standard.StandardAnalyzer,
Lucene.Net"/>
      ...
    </providers>
  </ExamineIndexProviders>
  <ExamineSearchProviders defaultProvider="InternalSearcher">
    <providers>
      ...
        <add name="RunwaySearcher"
          type="UmbracoExamine.LuceneExamineSearcher, UmbracoExamine"
             analyzer="Lucene.Net.Analysis.Standard.StandardAnalyzer,
Lucene.Net"
             indexSet="RunwayIndexSet"/>
      ...
    </providers>
  </ExamineSearchProviders>
</Examine>
```

Available for download on Wrox.com

LISTING 9-7: SearchResults.ascx

```
<%@ Control Language="C#" AutoEventWireup="true" CodeBehind="SearchResults.ascx.cs"
Inherits="UmbracoUsersGuide.usercontrols.SearchResults" %>
<%@ Import Namespace="UmbracoUsersGuide.usercontrols" %>

<%-- provide some stats of the search here --%>
<p>
    Your search for : <b><u><%=SearchTerm%></u></b> returned 
    <i><b><%=this.SearchResultsCollection.Count()%></b>  result(s)</i>
</p>

<%-- Create a simple repeater template to use for output --%>
<asp:Repeater ID="SearchResultListing" runat="server" >
    <HeaderTemplate>
        <ul class="search-results">
    </HeaderTemplate>
    <ItemTemplate>
        <li>
            <a class="title"
href="<%#((Examine.SearchResult)Container.DataItem).FullUrl()%>">
                <%#
```

```
((Examine.SearchResult)Container.DataItem).Fields["nodeName"]%>
            </a>
            <div class="details">
              <p>
    <%#((Examine.SearchResult)Container.DataItem).GetDetails(300)%></p>
            </div>
            <div class="url">
                <a
href="<%#((Examine.SearchResult)Container.DataItem).FullUrl()%>"><%#((Examine.
SearchResult)Container.DataItem).FullUrl()%></a>
            </div>
        </li>
    </ItemTemplate>
    <FooterTemplate>
        </ul>
    </FooterTemplate>
</asp:Repeater>
```

LISTING 9-8: SearchResults.ascx.cs

Available for download on Wrox.com

```
using System;
using System.Collections.Generic;
using System.Linq;
using System.Web;
using System.Web.UI;
using System.Web.UI.WebControls;
using Examine;
using UmbracoExamine;
using UmbracoExamine.SearchCriteria;

namespace UmbracoUsersGuide.usercontrols
{
    public static class SearchResultExtensions
    {
        // Create a set of helper methods to make output
        // cleaner.
        public static string FullUrl(this SearchResult sr)
        {
            // Generate the URL for the returned node using
            // the umbraco library method NiceUrl.
            var urlStr = umbraco.library.NiceUrl(sr.Id);
            return urlStr;
        }

        public static string GetDetails (this SearchResult sr, int length)
        {
            var contentStr = "";
            var truncateStr = "...";
            if (sr.Fields.ContainsKey("bodyText"))
            {
                contentStr = sr.Fields["bodyText"];
            }
            else if (sr.Fields.ContainsKey("question"))
```

continues

LISTING 9-8 *(continued)*

```
            {
                contentStr = sr.Fields["question"];
            }
            else if (sr.Fields.ContainsKey("answer"))
            {
                contentStr = sr.Fields["answer"];
            }

            // Only show the first 300 characters of the node
            // contents and use that as the preview of the
            // page content in the repeater.
            if (contentStr.Length > length)
              contentStr=contentStr.Substring(0, length) + truncateStr;
            return contentStr;
        }
    }
    public partial class SearchResults : System.Web.UI.UserControl
    {
        /// <summary>
        /// The term being searched on
        /// </summary>
        protected string SearchTerm { get; private set; }

        /// <summary>
        /// The search results list
        /// </summary>
        protected IEnumerable<SearchResult> SearchResultsCollection
                { get; private set; }

        public SearchResults()
        {
            // Initialize the class with some default values
            SearchTerm = string.Empty;
            SearchResultsCollection = new List<SearchResult>();
        }

        protected void Page_Load(object sender, EventArgs e)
        {
            // Grab the search term from the URL query string
            // 's', if it's null or empty break out of this load
            // event.
            SearchTerm = Request.QueryString["s"];
            if (string.IsNullOrEmpty(SearchTerm)) return;

            // Setup the search criteria by pointing to the searcher
            // that you created in ExamineSettings.config
            var criteria = ExamineManager.Instance
                    .SearchProviderCollection["RunwaySearcher"]
                    .CreateSearchCriteria(IndexTypes.Content);

            // Configure a filter that will query all of the fields
            // that you have specified below and that you can feed to
```

```
                // searcher below.
                var filter = criteria
                   .GroupedOr(new string[] { "nodeName", "bodyText", "question",
                       "answer" }, SearchTerm)
                   .Not()
                   .Field("umbracoNaviHide", "1") // filter out the hidden pages
                   .Compile();

                // Execute the actual search, again pointing to
                // the searcher that was configured in
                // ExamineSettings.config.
                SearchResultsCollection =
                 ExamineManager.Instance
                   .SearchProviderCollection["RunwaySearcher"]
                   .Search(filter);

                // Bind the results to the repeater that's in the view
                SearchResultListing.DataSource = SearchResultsCollection;
                SearchResultListing.DataBind();
            }
        }
    }
```

Available for download on Wrox.com

LISTING 9-9: SearchFieldForTemplate.txt

```
<input type="text" id="search-term" name="search" value="" />
<input type="button" name="searchBtn" value="Search" onclick="runSearch();" />
<script type="text/javascript">
    function runSearch(){
         var searchResultsUrl =
        "http://umbracousersguide.local/search-results.aspx";
        document.location.href = searchResultsUrl + "?s=" +
           document.getElementById("search-term").value;
    }
</script>
```

TAKE HOME POINTS

You should now be comfortable adding some more advanced functionality to your Umbraco-powered website. In particular, you should know how to do the following:

- Use Umbraco tags to output content and manipulate it to your needs.
- Generate site navigation menus using XSLT and the Razor view engine.
- Work with repeatable content in multiple locations throughout your site.
- Add a search mechanism to your Umbraco site using Examine and Lucene.NET.

10

Packages—Whatever You Can Imagine

- What are packages?
- How do you use existing community packages?
- What's the purpose of the Umbraco package repository?
- How do you use Commercial packages?
- How do you create your own packages?

In virtually all open source projects, especially within the content management system (CMS) space, add-on modules are available that developers and editors alike can install to enrich the functionality of the system. You've probably seen them referred to as apps, modules, add-ons, plugins, extensions, and so on. In Umbraco, these extensions are officially referred to as *packages*. As of the writing of this book, a new version of Umbraco is in Beta, referred to as Juno. This upcoming version will also support skins, or themes, which will provide even greater flexibility and ease in deploying new websites using Umbraco.

Through this chapter you will learn how to install and use existing packages and also how to create your very own Umbraco package.

UNDERSTANDING PACKAGES

Packages are made up of a collection of elements from within an Umbraco website. You can find them in the Developer section, as shown in Figure 10-1. You can install and use packages in Umbraco in a few different ways:

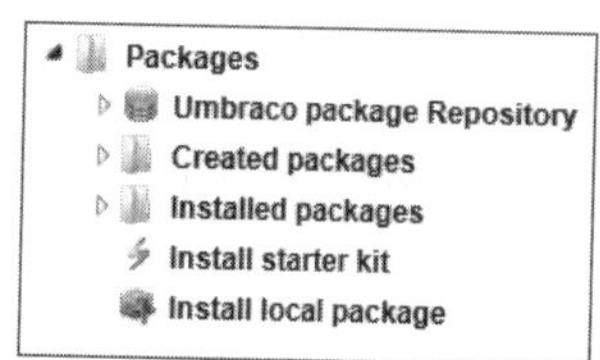

FIGURE 10-1

- **Umbraco Repository:** Packages in this repository are put out by Umbraco HQ (like Courier, Contour, and other PRO packages), but also include packages from the community where the Karma of the package is higher than 15.

WHAT IS KARMA?

Karma is a rating system that is used within the Umbraco community developer's site, found at `http://our.umbraco.org`. Karma points are handed out for contributions within the community and apply to community members, packages, and forum posts across the site. Members of the community site are awarded points for participating in the forums, sharing packages, adding to the wiki, and reviewing other developers' work.

Packages have the same rating where other developers will award Karma points to projects they find useful or just think are cool additions to the CMS.

- **Created packages:** This lists all the packages that you have created within this particular installation of Umbraco. From here you can download an already-created package or edit the package.
- **Installed packages:** As the name suggests, this lists all currently installed packages and provides you with an overview of the packages, the package contents, and an option to uninstall the selected package, as shown in Figure 10-2.

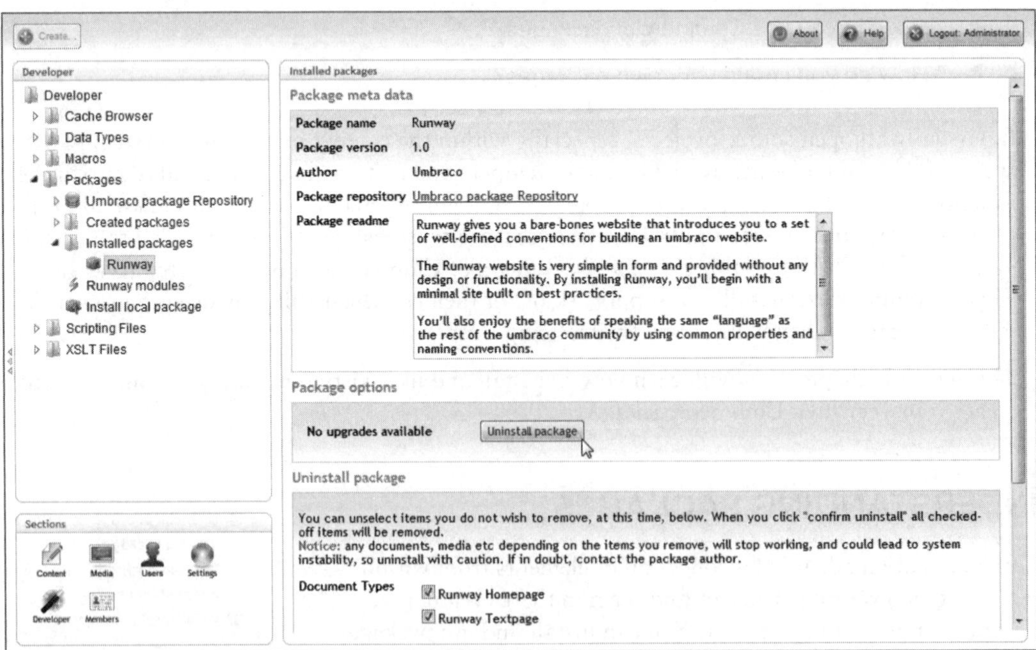

FIGURE 10-2

- **Install starter kit:** This option will allow you to install one of the available starter kits that come with Umbraco as of version 4.6. These are the same options that are presented during installation, covered in Chapter 1.
- **Install local package:** This option allows you to install a downloaded package from the community site, or perhaps a package that you created from another installation. Downloaded packages are in Zip archive format (you find out the details of this archive later in this chapter).

USING COMMUNITY PACKAGES

The most versatile collection of packages is created by hundreds of contributors within the community. If you need the functionality, there's a good chance someone else did before you and released a package for it. This section talks about your alternatives to finding great packages.

Be aware that some projects are certainly of lesser quality and reliability than others. The packages that are released on `http://our.umbraco.org` *and CodePlex are not moderated in any way. So, use caution when deploying things in a production environment. Deploying packages in a local development environment before pushing to a live website is strongly recommended.*

Our.umbraco.org/projects

As mentioned earlier, you can find packages by going to `http://our.umbraco.org/projects`, where you can download all the available packages. Several views of the packages list are available. The default view is a grouping of projects based on the selected categories and tags that the package creator chooses when uploading a new package. You can also find a short list of the latest added projects on the homepage, as well as the best rated projects further down on the projects page. If that isn't enough, you can also get a view of the projects by looking at the extensive tag cloud, as shown in Figure 10-3.

Each developer chooses what to release with an uploaded package. Some include the source code and some do not. It depends on the nature of the functionality and whether or not the package is available as a commercial, licensed product as well. Most projects on the community site include the installer archive, some form of documentation, and a set of forums where users can post bugs and ask questions as necessary.

The single most important thing to check when deciding on a package to install is the `Compatible with:` *attribute. This tells you whether or not the package is going to work with your installation.*

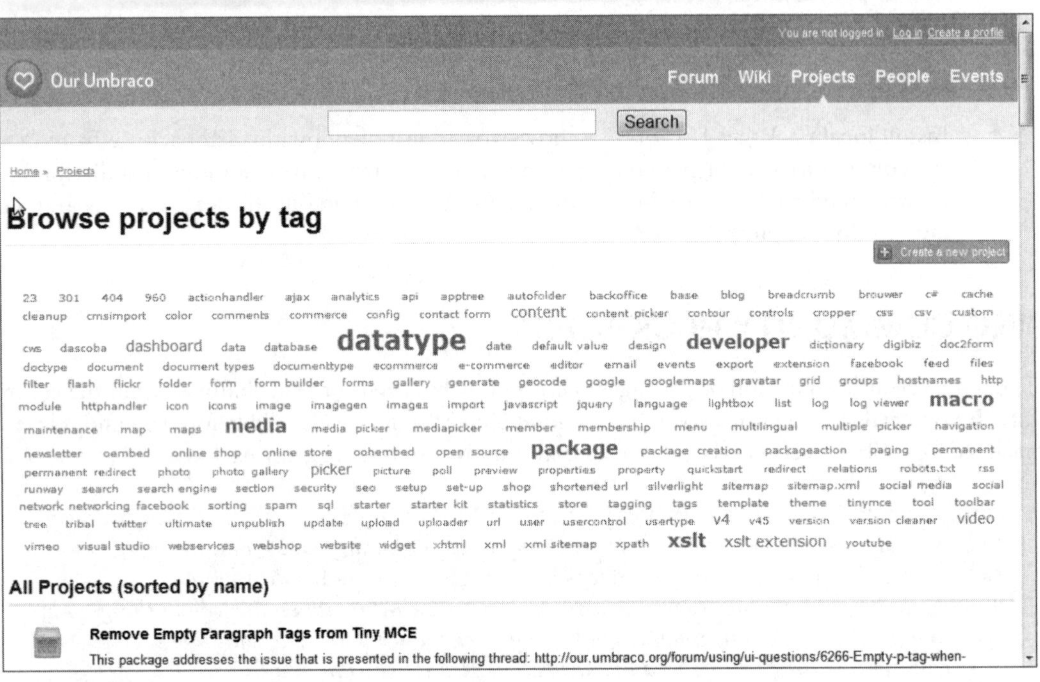

FIGURE 10-3

CodePlex.com

Umbraco as an open source product uses CodePlex for its releases, source code (including beta and other builds), bug tracking, documentation, and a list of the official Umbraco core team. The direct URL for the Umbraco source repository is `http://umbraco.codeplex.com/`. More importantly, the community members have also chosen, in many cases, to use CodePlex for releasing open source packages. Some of the most noteworthy packages and projects include the following:

- **uComponents** (`http://ucomponents.codeplex.com/`): A relative newcomer to the package scene, uComponents provides a whole slew of data types and XSLT extensions (covered in Chapter 12). Some of the data types include multi-node tree picker, drag and drop in the content tree, dynamic widgets like a slider, and other industry-leading user interface (UI) widgets.
- **Examine** (`http://examine.codeplex.com/`): Examine is a search provider using Lucene.net as its search engine. This project is now part of the core when you install Umbraco and is even used in the backoffice for searching. The corresponding CodePlex site is a great resource for creating your own search providers and how to execute searches on your document types.
- **Blog 4 Umbraco** (`http://blog4umbraco.codeplex.com/`): Blog 4 Umbraco is the official blog package for Umbraco and was a teaser project put out by Umbraco HQ. It's fully open source and has all the expected standard features of a blog, including tag cloud, blog comments, spam filtering, ping services, and a skinning engine.

UNDERSTANDING THE PACKAGE REPOSITORY

The Umbraco repository is made up of six major groupings, as shown in Figure 10-4. Because the packages are broken down into categorical groupings, users can more easily find the tools they require in this continuously expanding list of packages. As noted earlier, not all packages qualify for the package repository, so in a sense this is a list of packages that have been used and reviewed enough by the community or Umbraco HQ to qualify and be deemed a potentially good addition to your website.

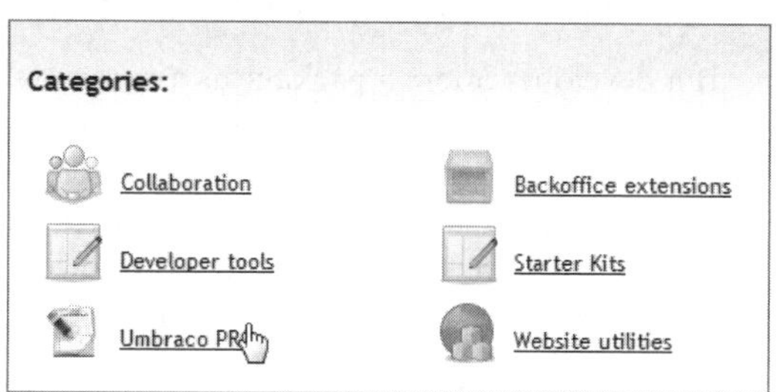

FIGURE 10-4

The repository categories are as follow:

- **Collaboration:** You can find packages such as Blog 4 Umbraco and other communication based packages in this category.
- **Backoffice extensions:** This category houses packages such as custom data types, bulk editing of content, browser extensions, and custom trees.
- **Developer tools:** As developers work with the system, they build tools to make their lives easier. Some of the tools are shared for others to make use of, too, such as a log viewer, config file editing from the backoffice, document type icons, and so on.
- **Starter Kits:** The packages in this category are great for beginners who want to see best practices on how to implement a basic website using Umbraco. Installing any of these can give you an idea of how to structure document types and manage XSLT files, as well as a view of what works in general.
- **Umbraco PRO:** As the name suggests, this category is where Umbraco HQ make the PRO tools available for download. To get a license for these tools you must visit `http://umbraco.org` and purchase the license from there.
- **Website utilities:** The most versatile of the categories, this grouping provides extensions for content editors with tools such as uTube (chromeless YouTube plugin), multi-file uploads to the media library, Twitter feeds, and so on.

As you can see, the repository strives to be an easy-to-use installer platform from which developers and site administrators can gain access to well-functioning and reliable packages to extend site functionality without any coding or heavy customizations.

USING COMMERCIAL PACKAGES

Clearly, there is a gap to fill and business to be made for developing and marketing commercial packages. A few developers outside of Umbraco HQ have done well, most notably those for CMSImport, which allows you to import data from other data sources as Umbraco content; and uCommerce, which offers eCommerce capabilities and management within Umbraco. Other successes exist as well, and the list is constantly growing.

If a developer offers a package as a commercial product, it will also (at least most of the time) be available in a limited version that's free, and in most cases is listed on `http://our.umbraco.org/projects`. In addition, the package will have a Purchase button next to it, as shown in Figure 10-5. Currently, this button takes you to the developer's site or means of selling his or her package.

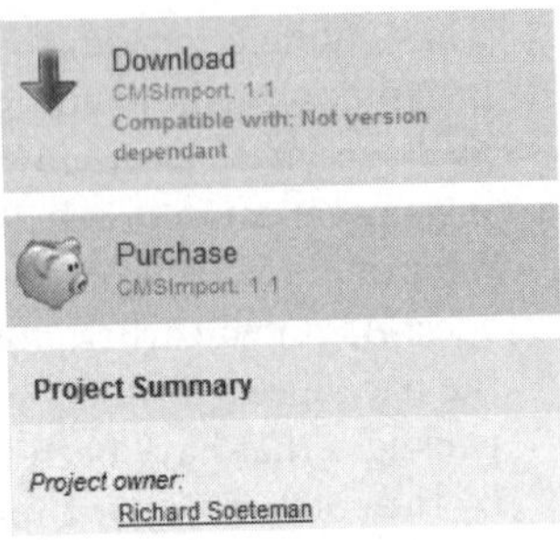

FIGURE 10-5

At the time of this writing no official place exists to sell commercial packages for Umbraco. In the works, however, is the Package Marketplace, which will allow developers the opportunity to add packages and themes for sale via the community site.

CREATING YOUR OWN PACKAGES

Creating your own package is not only easy using the backoffice tools, but it's also handy for modularizing functionality that can be shared across all of your projects. Plus, if you've developed something that you think others may benefit from, why not share the goods? To create a package, follow these steps:

1. Right-clicking the Packages node in the Developer section, as shown in Figure 10-6.
2. Name your new package **Site Breadcrumb** by filling in the name field in the resulting popup.
3. Fill in all the fields in the Package Properties tab, as shown in Figure 10-7.
   - **Package URL:** The URL of the site where this package is described/documented.
   - **Package Version:** That is, 1.0 or 0.1 and so on.
   - **Package file:** This field remains empty until you publish the package.
   - **Author Name:** Full name of the author of the project. Contributors can be added to the project details when uploading to the community site, but only one author should be listed as part of the package details.
   - **Author url:** Your blog or corporate site URL.

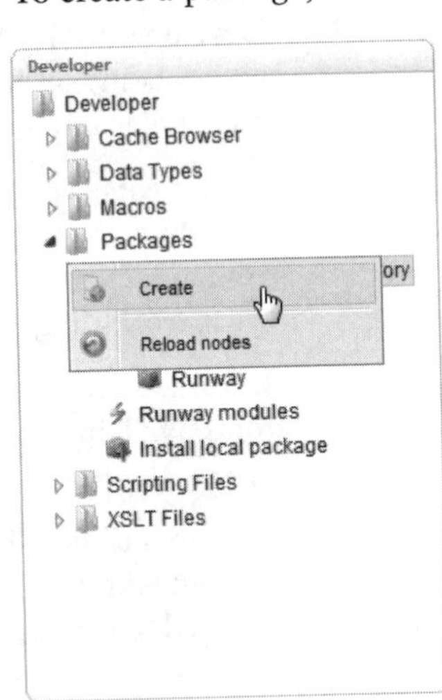

FIGURE 10-6

- **License Name:** Researching the license model for the package is up to you. The default is MIT, just like the Umbraco core.
- **License url:** This would be the URL for the details of your license.
- **Readme:** This field is your opportunity to educate the installer of what the package does and to include any special instructions.

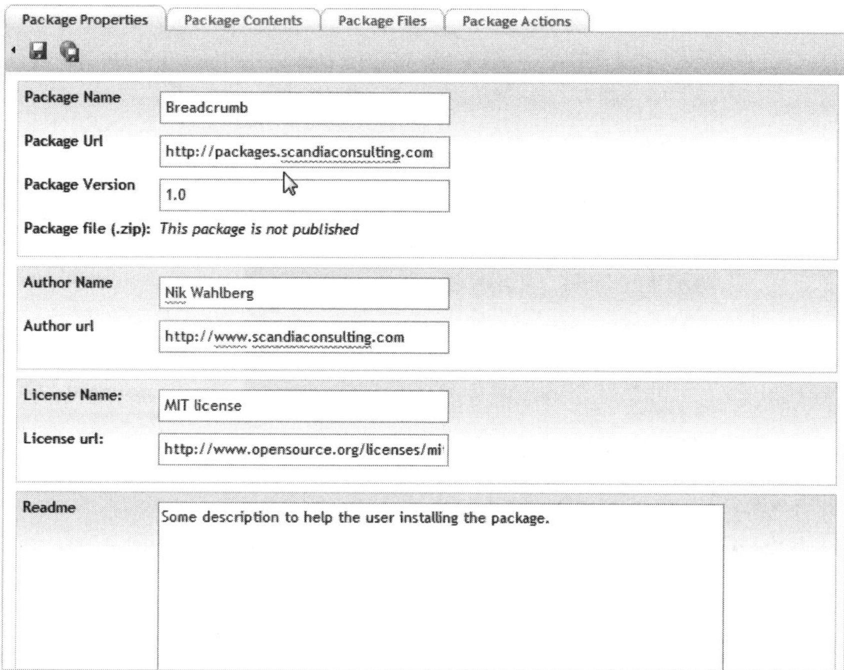

FIGURE 10-7

4. Click the Package Contents tab and select the applicable elements to include. For this example, select the Site Breadcrumb check box in the Macros section, as shown in Figure 10-8.

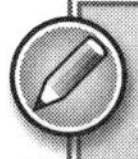

You do not have to select the associated XSLT file for this package as that will automatically be included when selecting the macro. Same thing goes for .NET macros which will automatically include the associated .ascx files.

If your package included .NET driven functionality, you would have to select the associated assemblies in the Package Files tab from the installation path of your website.

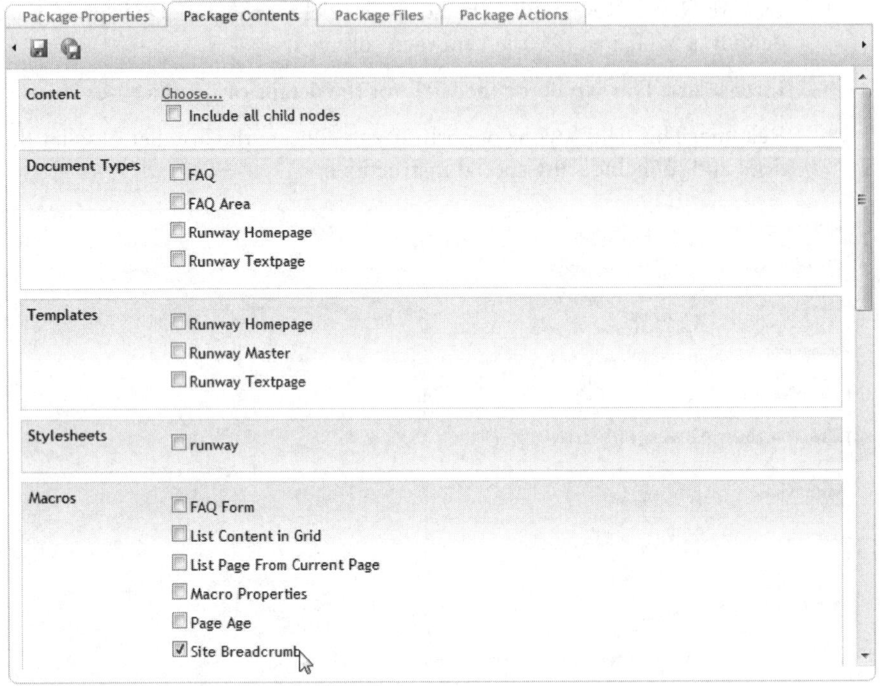

FIGURE 10-8

5. Publish the package by clicking the Publish button, as shown in Figure 10-9.

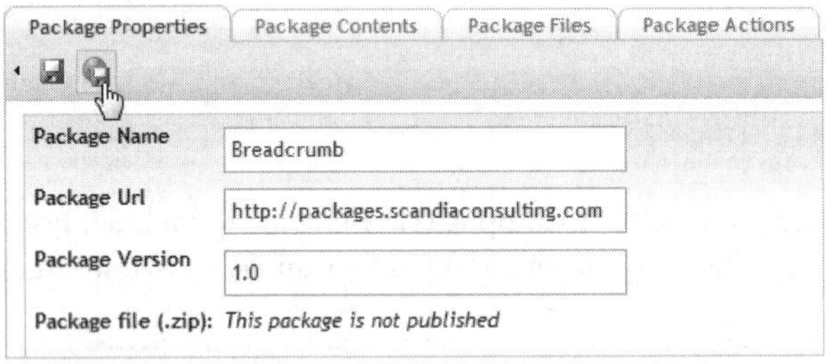

Package Properties | Package Contents | Package Files | Package Actions

Package Name: Breadcrumb
Package Url: http://packages.scandiaconsulting.com
Package Version: 1.0
Package file (.zip): *This package is not published*

FIGURE 10-9

6. Navigate back to the Package Properties tab and download your new package by clicking the Download link.

Now, clearly that wasn't very exciting. All you did was create a package with one file in it, essentially. In Chapter 12 you will create a more complex macro that includes additional functionality such as .NET assemblies.

In addition to using the built-in tools for creating packages, you can extend the functionality by using the Package Actions tab. Package Actions are a means for you as a developer to execute common tasks during and after the installation process of a package. The actions are configured as instructions using XML. Examples of usage for these actions include adding an `<umbraco:macro />` tag to an existing template, allowing a document type as a child element of another, or moving nodes in the content tree. Table 10-1 lists the available package actions.

TABLE 10-1: Package Actions

ACTION ALIAS	DESCRIPTION	SAMPLE CODE
`addApplication`	Creates a new application and adds it to the database.	`<Action runat="install" [undo="false"] alias="addApplication" appName="Application Name" appAlias="myApplication" appIcon="application.gif"/>`
`addApplicationTree`	Creates a new application tree and adds it to the database.	`<Action runat="install" [undo="false"] alias="addApplicationTree" silent="[true/false]" initialize="[true/false]" sortOrder="1" applicationAlias="appAlias" treeAlias="myTree" treeTitle="My Tree" iconOpened="folder_o.gif" iconClosed="folder.gif" assemblyName="umbraco" treeHandlerType="treeClass" action="alert('js called');"/>`
`addRestExtension`	Adds an extension in the `restExtensions .config file;` for use with `/base.`	`<Action runat="install" alias="addRestExtension" documentName="News"> <ext assembly="/bin/umbraco" type="umbracoBase.library " alias="currentMember"> <permission method="login" allowAll="true" /> </ext> <ext assembly="/bin/umbraco" type="umbracoBase.library " alias="currentPage"> <permission method="data" allowAll="true" /> </ext> </Action>`

continues

TABLE 10-1 *(continued)*

ACTION ALIAS	DESCRIPTION	SAMPLE CODE
addDashboardSection	Creates a new dashboard section. Uses the standard dashboard XML as a child node of the action itself.	<Action runat="install" [undo="false"] alias="addDashboardSection" dashboardAlias="MyDashboard Section"> <section> <areas> <area>default</area> <area>content</area> </areas> <tab caption="Last Edits"> <control>/usercontrols/latest Edits.ascx</control> <control>/usercontrols/ PostCreate.ascx</control> </tab> <tab caption="Create blog post"> <control>/usercontrols/new. ascx</control> </tab> </section> </Action>
addXsltExtension	Adds an extension to the xsltExtensions.config file, for use when a public class is being added with the macro.	<Action runat="install" alias="addXsltExtension" assembly="/assembly" type="your.library" extensionAlias="your.extension" />
allowDocumentType	Allows a document type to be created below another document type; for example, to allow Runway Textpage to be created under Runway Homepage.	<Action runat="install" alias="allowDocumenttype" documentTypeAlias="MyNewDocument Type" parentDocumentTypeAlias="Home Page"/>

ACTION ALIAS	DESCRIPTION	SAMPLE CODE
`moveRootDocument`	Moves a document located in the root of the website into a child of another root node. By default, all created content when installing a macro is placed under the root node.	`<Action runat="install" alias="moveRootDocument" documentName="News" parentDocumentType="Home" />`
`publishRootDocument`	Publishes a document located in the root of the website.	`<Action runat="install" alias="publishRootDocument" documentName="News" />`
`addStringToHtml Element`	Inserts a string into a specific HTML element in a specific template. The undo option makes sure that the string can be removed again at uninstall.	`<Action runat="install" alias="addStringToHtmlElement" templateAlias="news" htmlElementId="newsSection" position="[beginning/end"> <![CDATA[hello world!]]> </Action>`

`/base` *is a class that you can use as a developer to execute REST-driven data exchange via, for example, AJAX calls.*

In addition to the package actions that come with your Umbraco installation, you can find a community-driven repository at `http://packageactioncontrib.codeplex.com/`.

TAKE HOME POINTS

At this point you can share your custom code and implementations with the community by creating packages and releasing them for others to install. In addition, you should now be able to package up changes and new functionality and easily deploy the updates to other Umbraco installations. To summarize, you've learned the following:

- How to install other community released packages.
- Where to find and get the latest released packages for your Umbraco installation.
- How to create your own packages for distribution and deployment.

11

Using XSLT

- What is XSLT?
- How do you transform cached content?
- What is XPath all about?
- How do you work with media items in XSLT?
- What are some uses of XSLT for Umbraco?

Ask most developers and they will shudder at the thought of having to use *XSLT*, Extensible Stylesheet Language Transformation, in any environment. But the truth is that it's a very powerful rendering language and is a perfect fit for the Umbraco XML cache. For those of you who are new to this language, "XSLT is a declarative, XML-based language used for the transformation of XML documents into other XML documents." This is the short version of the definition on Wikipedia. In the case of Umbraco, the "other XML documents" refer in most cases to the output of HTML, and in some cases the output of other tag-based content. Because XSLT is, in essence, a flavor of XML, it requires that all output and logical markup have a matching start and close tag. You will see the practical application of this requirement in the examples throughout of this chapter.

In Umbraco you can leverage XSLT to access the content that is created in the content tree via macros, as discussed in Chapter 5. To access the XSLT repository, navigate to the Developer section, as shown in Figure 11-1. This chapter shows you the flexibility and versatility of using XSLT to generate content for menus, repeatable lists, and much more.

A lot of the discussion in this chapter has to do with XPath and XSLT. If you'd like more information or instruction on these languages, check out Beginning XSLT and XPath: Transforming XML Documents and Data *by Ian Williams (Wiley, 2009).*

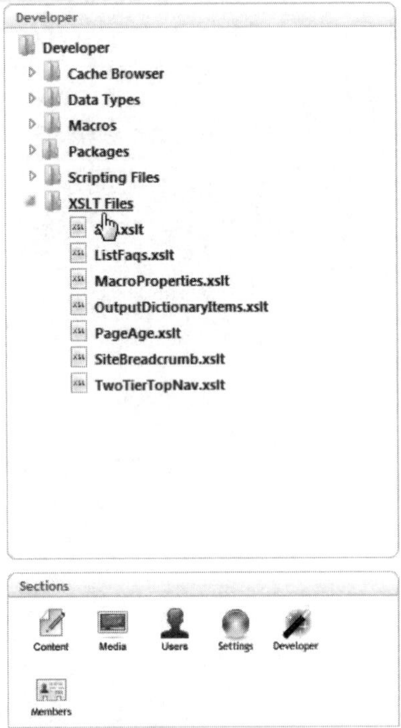

FIGURE 11-1

USING XSLT FOR PUBLISHED CONTENT

You must keep one important thing in mind when you are deciding whether to use .NET or XSLT to render your macros. Although .NET provides you with access to both published and unpublished content, XSLT-powered macros can only access published content that resides in the cache. This offers a couple of benefits:

- When requesting content, you can be sure that unpublished content will never be displayed.
- You'll have no roundtrips to the database to retrieve content. So, any operations on the content tree are very fast.

When accessing content in .NET you can use the `Document` *API to access all content. This makes requests to the database, so be sparse with your usage of the* `Document` *API in large installations. Umbraco also exposes the functionality of using the NodeFactory, discussed in Chapter 12. This factory allows you to run XSLT and XPath statements on published content from your .NET user controls.*

For more information, see Chapter 12.

To get a clear picture of what the XML cache looks like, you can open up the cache file. In Umbraco 4.5.x and later, you can find this file in `<install root>/App_Data/umbraco.config`. In earlier versions, you can find the file by going to `<install root>/data/umbraco.config`.

As with earlier demonstrations in this book, you will get output that differs from the examples for both Umbraco versions 4.5.x and 4.x. The most obvious difference that you'll see is that the old version of the schema used the same tag name for all nodes in the XML cache, namely `<node .../>`. In the new version, this is no longer the case and nodes are named after their respective document type alias, such as `<TextPage .../>`. What you'll also see in the examples in this chapter is that the new schema makes for less verbose XPath statements and an easier-to-read XML structure.

To set a newer version of Umbraco to use the old XML schema, simply change the `<UseLegacyXmlSchema />` *tag in* `<install root>/config/umbracoSettings.config` *to* `true`.

To exclude a node from the published XML cache, simply navigate to the Properties tab of the node in the content tree (located in the Content section), and click the Unpublish button, as shown in Figure 11-2.

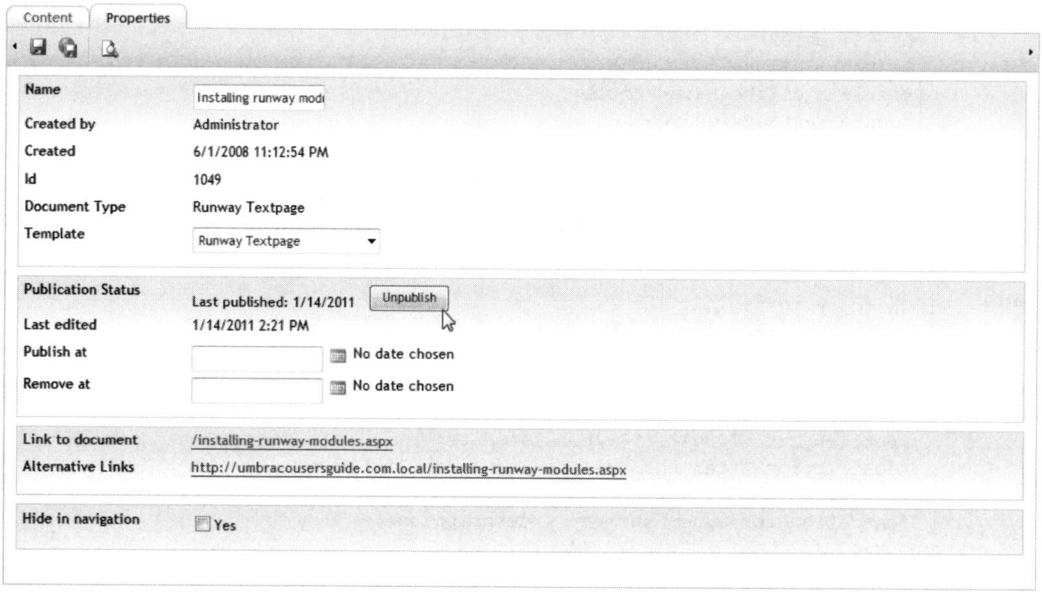

FIGURE 11-2

UNDERSTANDING XPATH

XPath, or XML Path Language, is one of those things that takes a while to grasp, at least for most developers. It's been compared to regular expressions, which in my opinion is a bit much because it's not nearly that complicated. XPath is a query language for selecting nodes from an XML document source. In the Umbraco scenario, you use XPath as part of the XSLT to target nodes from the `umbraco.config` (XML cache) mentioned earlier in this chapter. In a nutshell, XPath allows you to traverse any node structure by providing a set of steps that make up a path, or more complex instructions to programmatically manipulate the output from the source XML. To illustrate the concept, before you dig into the practicals of using XPath in Umbraco, take a look at Listing 11-1 as a basis for the following XPath examples. This is an abbreviation of the classic `book.xml` example that you see in most XSL/XPath examples on the Internet.

LISTING 11-1: books.xml

Available for download on Wrox.com

```
<?xml version="1.0"?>
<catalog>
   <book id="bk101">
      <author>Gambardella, Matthew</author>
      <title>XML Developer's Guide</title>
      <genre>Computer</genre>
      <price>44.95</price>
      <publish_date>2000-10-01</publish_date>
      <description>An in-depth look at creating applications
      with XML.</description>
   </book>
   <book id="bk102">
      <author>Ralls, Kim</author>
      <title>Midnight Rain</title>
      <genre>Fantasy</genre>
      <price>5.95</price>
      <publish_date>2000-12-16</publish_date>
      <description>A former architect battles corporate zombies,
      an evil sorceress, and her own childhood to become queen
      of the world.</description>
   </book>
   <book id="bk103">
      <author>Corets, Eva</author>
      <title>Maeve Ascendant</title>
      <genre>Fantasy</genre>
      <price>5.95</price>
      <publish_date>2000-11-17</publish_date>
      <description>After the collapse of a nanotechnology
      society in England, the young survivors lay the
      foundation for a new society.</description>
   </book>
</catalog>
```

The following example XPath statement queries the XML source for the book with an `Id` of `bk102`:

```
<xsl:variable name="theSecondBook" select="//catalog/book [@id='bk102']" />
```

This returns the entire book node and its children, as shown in the following code snippet.

```
<catalog>
   ...
   <book id="bk102">
      <author>Gambardella, Matthew</author>
      <title>XML Developer's Guide</title>
      <genre>Computer</genre>
      <price>44.95</price>
      <publish_date>2000-10-01</publish_date>
      <description>An in-depth look at creating applications
      with XML.</description>
   </book>
   ...
</catalog>
```

If you now wanted to get the title of the returned book, you could use the following:

```
<xsl:value-of select="$theSecondBook/title" />
```

The example of selecting a single book is practical only if you know the Id of the book that you're looking for. Instead, you can output all the books in the inventory by performing a standard for-each loop. The following example returns *all* the nodes whose name equals book.

```
<xsl:for-each select="//catalog/book">
  <h3><xsl:value-of select="current()/title" /></h3>
  <p><xsl:value-of select="current()/description" /></p>
  <hr />
</xsl:for-each>
```

Again, these are simple cases but should provide you with a basic idea of how paths can ultimately get you to the information that you seek. All the paths in the code are based on the notion that you know the structure of the XML that you are querying. If you don't know that, then you don't know what to ask for. This, of course, is true in other environments as well, such as using SQL to query database tables.

In addition to simply writing out paths as they are formed in the XML document, you can use something called an XPath axis. Axes allow you to step up, down, and sideways within the XML structure to grab data. You use them by name (see Table 11-1 for available axes), along with a node test (that is, the node name that you are looking for) and one or more *predicates*. A predicate is defined as [consisting] "of an expression, called a predicate expression, enclosed in square brackets. A predicate serves to filter a sequence, retaining some items and discarding others." The axis and node test are separated by ::, and the predicate/s are enclosed in [].

Speaking of structures, if you need to look at the structure of the XML that you are querying—for example, if you didn't know what the structure of the `<catalog />` *was—you could output the contents of the catalog node by writing* `<xsl:copy-of select="catalog" />`*. This lists the catalog node and all of its children, just like you see in Listing 11-1. Note that when viewing the results of an* `<xsl:copy-of />` *in a browser, you must view the source to see the output because the XML tags won't display.*

TABLE 11-1: XPath Axes

AXIS	DESCRIPTION
`ancestor`	Contains the ancestors of the context node. Ancestors include the parent, and its parent, and its parent, and so on, all the way back up to the root node.
`ancestor-or-self`	Contains the context node and its ancestors.
`attribute`	Contains the attributes of the context node.
`child`	Contains the children of the context node.
`descendant`	Contains the descendants of the context node. Descendants include the node's children, and that child's children, and its children, and so on (until there are no more children).
`descendant-or-self`	Contains the context node and its descendants.
`following`	Contains all nodes that come after the context node (that is, after its closing tag).
`following-sibling`	Contains the following siblings of the context node. Siblings are at the same level as the context node and share its parent.
`namespace`	Contains the namespace of the context node.
`parent`	Contains the parent of the context node.
`preceding`	Contains all nodes that come before the context node (that is, before its opening tag).
`self`	Contains the context node.

See the examples in the end of this chapter for more details on how to use XPath within Umbraco.

WORKING WITH MEDIA

Working with media and XSLT is a bit specialized. It relies heavily on the use of XSLT extensions because media is not cached or treated the same as standard content nodes are in Umbraco. A media item has several properties, as discussed in Chapter 2. Most commonly, you want to use XSLT to output a media item that someone selected as part of the content entry using the Media Picker data type, as shown in Figure 11-3.

If you queried the FAQ node in this case to get the selected media item, all you would get back is the media node `Id`. Listing 11-2 shows an extract of the FAQ node as it would come back to you when you query for it in Listing 11-3.

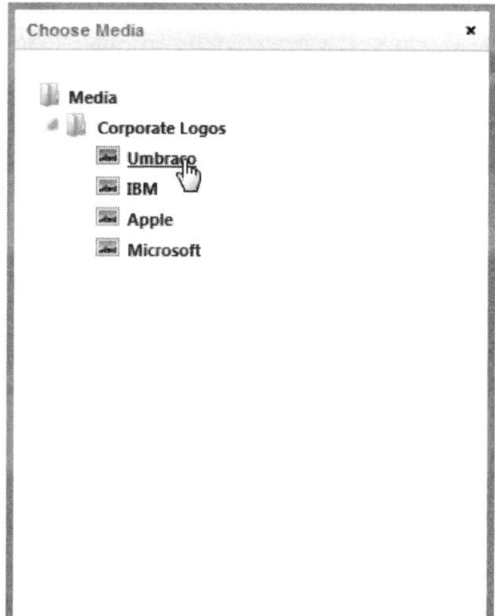

FIGURE 11-3

LISTING 11-2: FAQ Node from Cache

```
<FAQ id="1057" parentID="1055" level="3" writerID="0" creatorID="0"
nodeType="1053" template="0" sortOrder="2" createDate="2010-11-18T07:08:03"
updateDate="2011-01-21T17:03:17" nodeName="How do I add a page?" urlName="how-
do-i-add-a-page" writerName="Administrator" creatorName="Administrator"
path="-1,1048,1055,1057" isDoc="">
  <author>Nik</author>
  <category><![CDATA[2]]></category>
  <screenshot>1091</screenshot>
  <question><![CDATA[
    <p>I was just wondering how I might add a page to the backend?</p>
  ]]></question>
  <answer><![CDATA[
    <p>d</p>
  ]]></answer>
</FAQ>
```

LISTING 11-3: OutputMediaId.xslt

Available for download on Wrox.com

```
<?xml version="1.0" encoding="UTF-8"?>
<!DOCTYPE xsl:stylesheet [ <!ENTITY nbsp " "> ]>
<xsl:stylesheet
    version="1.0"
    xmlns:xsl="http://www.w3.org/1999/XSL/Transform"
    xmlns:msxml="urn:schemas-microsoft-com:xslt"
    xmlns:umbraco.library="urn:umbraco.library"
```

continues

LISTING 11-3 *(continued)*

```
xmlns:Exslt.ExsltCommon="urn:Exslt.ExsltCommon"
xmlns:Exslt.ExsltDatesAndTimes="urn:Exslt.ExsltDatesAndTimes"
xmlns:Exslt.ExsltMath="urn:Exslt.ExsltMath"
xmlns:Exslt.ExsltRegularExpressions="urn:Exslt.ExsltRegularExpressions"
xmlns:Exslt.ExsltStrings="urn:Exslt.ExsltStrings"
xmlns:Exslt.ExsltSets="urn:Exslt.ExsltSets"
xmlns:umbusersguide.library="urn:umbusersguide.library"
    exclude-result-prefixes="msxml umbraco.library Exslt.ExsltCommon
Exslt.ExsltDatesAndTimes Exslt.ExsltMath Exslt.ExsltRegularExpressions
Exslt.ExsltStrings Exslt.ExsltSets umbusersguide.library ">

  <xsl:output method="xml" omit-xml-declaration="yes"/>

  <xsl:param name="currentPage"/>

  <xsl:template match="/">
    Media: <xsl:value-of select="$currentPage/screenshot" />
  </xsl:template>

</xsl:stylesheet>
```

The result from Listing 11-3 is simply `1091`. In this case, what you want to do is return this output as an image to the page. Listing 11-4 shows you how to do this using `GetMedia()`, the XSLT extension method from the Umbraco library.

LISTING 11-4: OutputMediaAsImage.xslt

```
<?xml version="1.0" encoding="UTF-8"?>
<!DOCTYPE xsl:stylesheet [ <!ENTITY nbsp " "> ]>
<xsl:stylesheet
    version="1.0"
    xmlns:xsl="http://www.w3.org/1999/XSL/Transform"
    xmlns:msxml="urn:schemas-microsoft-com:xslt"
    xmlns:umbraco.library="urn:umbraco.library"
xmlns:Exslt.ExsltCommon="urn:Exslt.ExsltCommon"
xmlns:Exslt.ExsltDatesAndTimes="urn:Exslt.ExsltDatesAndTimes"
xmlns:Exslt.ExsltMath="urn:Exslt.ExsltMath"
xmlns:Exslt.ExsltRegularExpressions="urn:Exslt.ExsltRegularExpressions"
xmlns:Exslt.ExsltStrings="urn:Exslt.ExsltStrings"
xmlns:Exslt.ExsltSets="urn:Exslt.ExsltSets"
xmlns:umbusersguide.library="urn:umbusersguide.library"
    exclude-result-prefixes="msxml umbraco.library Exslt.ExsltCommon
Exslt.ExsltDatesAndTimes Exslt.ExsltMath Exslt.ExsltRegularExpressions
Exslt.ExsltStrings Exslt.ExsltSets umbusersguide.library ">

<xsl:output method="xml" omit-xml-declaration="yes"/>

<xsl:param name="currentPage"/>

<xsl:template match="/">
    <!-- save the media id into a local variable so it's
         easier to reference later -->
```

```
    <xsl:variable name="mediaId" select="$currentPage/screenshot" />

    <!-- output the image tag and get the source of the image using the ID -->
    <!-- first we need to check to make sure media ID is not empty -->
    <xsl:if test="$mediaId!=''">
        <img>
            <xsl:attribute name="src">
                <xsl:value-of select="
umbraco.library:GetMedia($mediaId,'false')/umbracoFile " />
            </xsl:attribute>
            <xsl:attribute name="width">
                <xsl:value-of select="
umbraco.library:GetMedia($mediaId,'false')/umbracoWidth " />
            </xsl:attribute>
            <xsl:attribute name="height">
                <xsl:value-of select="
umbraco.library:GetMedia($mediaId,'false')/umbracoHeight" />
            </xsl:attribute>
            <xsl:attribute name="alt">
                <xsl:value-of select="@nodeName" />
            </xsl:attribute>
        </img>
    </xsl:if>
</xsl:template>
</xsl:stylesheet>
```

To output values as attributes in an HTML tag within XSLT, you can also use the curly brace notation, like so:

```
<img src="{$imageSrc}" width="{$imageWidth}" height="{$imageHeight}"
    alt="{@nodeName}" />
```

LOOKING AT SOME XSLT EXAMPLES

To dig even further into how Umbraco implements XSLT, look at the examples that follow in the rest of the chapter.

When utilizing the Umbraco built-in editor for XSLT manipulation (in the backoffice), you can always refer to the Visualize XSLT tool to see how your XSLT macro will render. This tool allows you to select a target in the content tree and run your XSLT template as is without your having to add the macro to a template or node. Here's how that works:

1. While in the XSLT editor in the Developer section, click the Visualize XSLT button in the toolbar, as shown in Figure 11-4.

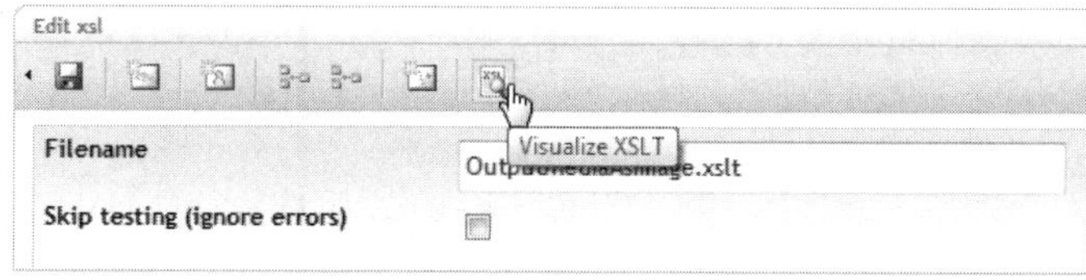

FIGURE 11-4

2. In the resulting Choose Content dialog, select the node from which you want to test your code. Using the example from the earlier "Working with Media" section, select the FAQ node that has the image you are trying to display, as shown in Figure 11-5.

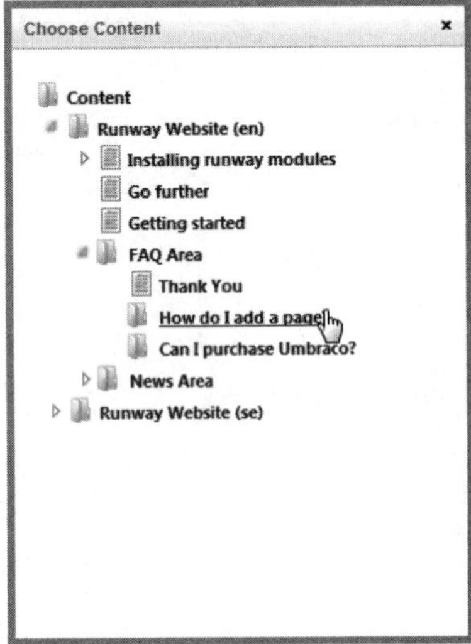

FIGURE 11-5

3. Click the Visualize XSLT button again. The corresponding image appears, as shown in Figure 11-6.

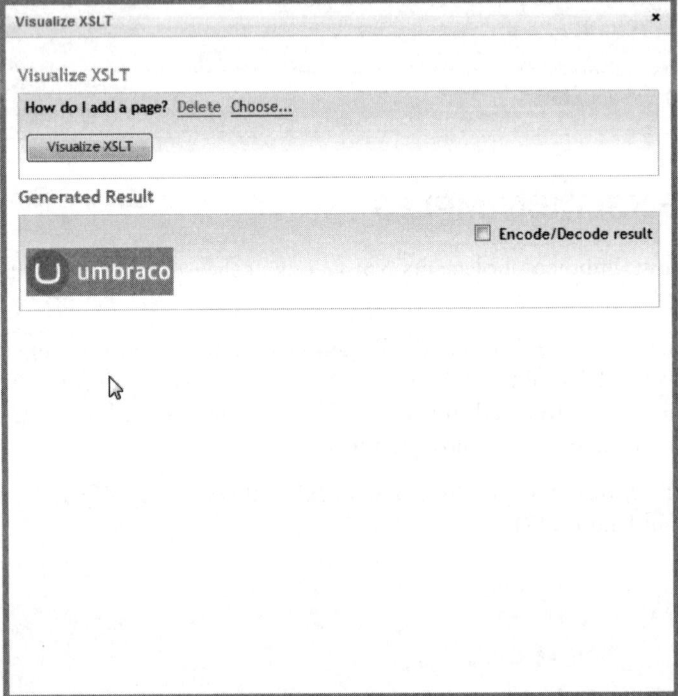

FIGURE 11-6

4. Close the dialog when you are done to return to the XSLT code editor.

List All Content

The script in Listing 11-5 enables you to list all the content starting at the root node. This example is easy because you can take advantage of one of the XSLT extension methods that come with Umbraco.

Available for download on Wrox.com

LISTING 11-5: ListAllContent.xslt

```
<?xml version="1.0" encoding="UTF-8"?>
<!DOCTYPE xsl:stylesheet [ <!ENTITY nbsp " "> ]>
<xsl:stylesheet
    version="1.0"
    xmlns:xsl="http://www.w3.org/1999/XSL/Transform"
    xmlns:msxml="urn:schemas-microsoft-com:xslt"
    xmlns:umbraco.library="urn:umbraco.library"
xmlns:Exslt.ExsltCommon="urn:Exslt.ExsltCommon"
xmlns:Exslt.ExsltDatesAndTimes="urn:Exslt.ExsltDatesAndTimes"
xmlns:Exslt.ExsltMath="urn:Exslt.ExsltMath"
xmlns:Exslt.ExsltRegularExpressions="urn:Exslt.ExsltRegularExpressions"
xmlns:Exslt.ExsltStrings="urn:Exslt.ExsltStrings"
xmlns:Exslt.ExsltSets="urn:Exslt.ExsltSets"
xmlns:umbusersguide.library="urn:umbusersguide.library"
    exclude-result-prefixes="msxml umbraco.library Exslt.ExsltCommon
Exslt.ExsltDatesAndTimes Exslt.ExsltMath Exslt.ExsltRegularExpressions
Exslt.ExsltStrings Exslt.ExsltSets umbusersguide.library ">

    <xsl:output method="xml" omit-xml-declaration="yes" />

    <xsl:param name="currentPage"/>

    <xsl:template match="/">
        <!-- The fun starts here -->
        <ul>
        <xsl:for-each select="umbraco.library:GetXmlAll()/descendant::*
[@isDoc and string(umbracoNaviHide) != '1']">
            <li class="level-{@level}"> <!-- create indentations
                                            using CSS class definitions -->
                <a href="{umbraco.library:NiceUrl(@id)}">
                    <xsl:value-of select="@nodeName"/>
                </a>
            </li>
        </xsl:for-each>
        </ul>
    </xsl:template>
</xsl:stylesheet>
```

The `select` statement in Listing 11-5 can be broken down as follows:

1. `umbraco.library:GetXmlAll()` retrieves the entire XML cache.
2. `descendants::*` tells the `select` statement to return all the children, children's children, and so on where the asterisk is a wildcard statement specifying that all node types are valid.
3. `@isDoc` is a boolean condition making sure that the `isDoc` attribute exists on the node. It also filters out any that don't.

The `isDoc` *attribute was introduced along with the new XML schema. This allows you to differentiate between a document node (or a node that represents a page with fields), from the field nodes themselves. In the old schema, field values were all contained in the* `<data />` *nodes and the pages in the* `<node />` *node.*

4. `string(umbracoNaviHide) != 1` checks to make sure that the document node does not contain an `<umbracoNaviHide />` node with a value of 1.

Now take a look at Listing 11-6 to see what this same script looks like in Umbraco 4.0.x and earlier. The difference here is that the script now specifies that it's looking for all nodes named `node`, as opposed to the wildcard in 4.5.x. Also, to check whether the field `umbracoNaviHide` equals 1, you must query for it by the node name `data` and checking its attribute value.

LISTING 11-6: ListAllPages-40x.xslt

Available for download on Wrox.com

```
<?xml version="1.0" encoding="UTF-8"?>
<!DOCTYPE xsl:stylesheet [ <!ENTITY nbsp " "> ]>
<xsl:stylesheet
       version="1.0"
       xmlns:xsl="http://www.w3.org/1999/XSL/Transform"
       xmlns:msxml="urn:schemas-microsoft-com:xslt"
       xmlns:umbraco.library="urn:umbraco.library"
xmlns:Exslt.ExsltCommon="urn:Exslt.ExsltCommon"
xmlns:Exslt.ExsltDatesAndTimes="urn:Exslt.ExsltDatesAndTimes"
xmlns:Exslt.ExsltMath="urn:Exslt.ExsltMath"
xmlns:Exslt.ExsltRegularExpressions="urn:Exslt.ExsltRegularExpressions"
xmlns:Exslt.ExsltStrings="urn:Exslt.ExsltStrings"
xmlns:Exslt.ExsltSets="urn:Exslt.ExsltSets"
xmlns:umbusersguide.library="urn:umbusersguide.library"
       exclude-result-prefixes="msxml umbraco.library Exslt.ExsltCommon
Exslt.ExsltDatesAndTimes Exslt.ExsltMath Exslt.ExsltRegularExpressions
Exslt.ExsltStrings Exslt.ExsltSets umbusersguide.library ">

    <xsl:output method="xml" omit-xml-declaration="yes" />

    <xsl:param name="currentPage"/>

    <xsl:template match="/">
          <!-- The fun starts here -->
          <ul>
          <xsl:for-each
              select="umbraco.library:GetXmlAll()/descendant::node
              [string(data[@alias='umbracoNaviHide'] != '1']">
                <li class="level-{@level}"> <!-- create indentations using
                                                 CSS class definitions -->
                       <a href="{umbraco.library:NiceUrl(@id)}">
                              <xsl:value-of select="@nodeName"/>
                       </a>
                </li>
```

```
            </xsl:for-each>
            </ul>
        </xsl:template>
    </xsl:stylesheet>
```

Counting, Looping, and Conditional Statements

Suppose you want to loop out some nodes, but want only the latest three of them, and they must have a value. Imagine that you want to apply this looping to the FAQs list on your homepage. Listing 11-7 does this task for Umbraco version 4.5.x and later.

Available for download on Wrox.com

LISTING 11-7: ListLatestFaqs.xslt

```
<?xml version="1.0" encoding="UTF-8"?>
<!DOCTYPE xsl:stylesheet [ <!ENTITY nbsp " "> ]>
<xsl:stylesheet
    version="1.0"
    xmlns:xsl="http://www.w3.org/1999/XSL/Transform"
    xmlns:msxml="urn:schemas-microsoft-com:xslt"
    xmlns:umbraco.library="urn:umbraco.library"
xmlns:Exslt.ExsltCommon="urn:Exslt.ExsltCommon"
xmlns:Exslt.ExsltDatesAndTimes="urn:Exslt.ExsltDatesAndTimes"
xmlns:Exslt.ExsltMath="urn:Exslt.ExsltMath"
xmlns:Exslt.ExsltRegularExpressions="urn:Exslt.ExsltRegularExpressions"
xmlns:Exslt.ExsltStrings="urn:Exslt.ExsltStrings"
xmlns:Exslt.ExsltSets="urn:Exslt.ExsltSets"
xmlns:umbusersguide.library="urn:umbusersguide.library"
    exclude-result-prefixes="msxml umbraco.library Exslt.ExsltCommon
Exslt.ExsltDatesAndTimes Exslt.ExsltMath Exslt.ExsltRegularExpressions
Exslt.ExsltStrings Exslt.ExsltSets umbusersguide.library ">

    <xsl:output method="xml" omit-xml-declaration="yes" />

    <xsl:param name="currentPage"/>

    <!-- Specify the document type -->
    <xsl:variable name="documentTypeAlias" select="string('FAQ')"/>

    <xsl:template match="/">
        <!-- Output latest FAQs list -->
        <h2>Latest FAQs</h2>
        <ul>
        <xsl:for-each select="$currentPage/* [name() = $documentTypeAlias and
string(umbracoNaviHide) != '1']">
            <!-- specify sort order so we get the latest
            updated FAQ first -->
            <xsl:sort select="@updateDate" order="descending" />

            <!-- Test to make sure that the current
            position in the loop is less than or equal
            to 3 -->
```

continues

LISTING 11-7 *(continued)*

```
            <xsl:if test="position()&lt;=3">
                <li>
                    [<xsl:value-of
select="umbraco.library:FormatDateTime(@updateDate,'MM/dd/yy hh:mm:ss')" />]
                    <a href="{umbraco.library:NiceUrl(@id)}">
                        <xsl:value-of select="@nodeName"/>
                    </a>
                </li>
            </xsl:if>
        </xsl:for-each>
        </ul>
    </xsl:template>
</xsl:stylesheet>
```

The following list breaks down what's going on in Listing 11-7:

- **`currentPage`:** This variable contains all the XML from the node where the XSLT is executed and its child elements. Remember that `currentPage` can always be used as a starting point even if you are traversing the content tree upwards using the ancestor axis. This is a much more efficient way to query content because you are not asking for the entire cache every time, like you would with `umbraco.library:GetXMLAll()`, for example.
- **`name()`:** This built-in function retrieves the name of the node; that is, `<TextPage .../>` will return `TextPage`.
- **`xsl:sort`:** This tells the parser to sort the returning records by the given `select` statement. The `select` statement can be any valid XPath statement.
- **`position()`:** This is another built-in node set function that provides you with the current position within the `for-each` loop. It's much like a manually incremented index in a standard .NET `for` loop.

For good measure, Listing 11-8 shows how to list the latest FAQs in Umbraco version 4.x.

Available for download on Wrox.com

LISTING 11-8: ListLatestFaqs-40x.xslt

```
<?xml version="1.0" encoding="UTF-8"?>
<!DOCTYPE xsl:stylesheet [ <!ENTITY nbsp " "> ]>
<xsl:stylesheet
    version="1.0"
    xmlns:xsl="http://www.w3.org/1999/XSL/Transform"
    xmlns:msxml="urn:schemas-microsoft-com:xslt"
```

```
    xmlns:umbraco.library="urn:umbraco.library"
xmlns:Exslt.ExsltCommon="urn:Exslt.ExsltCommon"
xmlns:Exslt.ExsltDatesAndTimes="urn:Exslt.ExsltDatesAndTimes"
xmlns:Exslt.ExsltMath="urn:Exslt.ExsltMath"
xmlns:Exslt.ExsltRegularExpressions="urn:Exslt.ExsltRegularExpressions"
xmlns:Exslt.ExsltStrings="urn:Exslt.ExsltStrings"
xmlns:Exslt.ExsltSets="urn:Exslt.ExsltSets"
xmlns:umbusersguide.library="urn:umbusersguide.library"
    exclude-result-prefixes="msxml umbraco.library Exslt.ExsltCommon
Exslt.ExsltDatesAndTimes Exslt.ExsltMath Exslt.ExsltRegularExpressions
Exslt.ExsltStrings Exslt.ExsltSets umbusersguide.library ">

    <xsl:output method="xml" omit-xml-declaration="yes" />

    <xsl:param name="currentPage"/>

    <!-- Specify the document type -->
    <xsl:variable name="documentTypeAlias" select="string('FAQ')"/>

    <xsl:template match="/">
        <!-- Output latest FAQs list -->
        <h2>Latest FAQs</h2>
        <ul>
        <xsl:for-each select="$currentPage/node
[@nodeTypeAlias=$documentTypeAlias and string(data [@alias='umbracoNaviHide'])
!= '1']">
            <!-- specify sort order so we get the latest
            updated FAQ first -->
            <xsl:sort select="@updateDate" order="descending" />

            <!-- Test to make sure that the current
            position in the loop is less than or equal
            to 3 -->
            <xsl:if test="position()&lt;=3">
                <li>
                    [<xsl:value-of
select="umbraco.library:FormatDateTime(@updateDate,'MM/dd/yy hh:mm:ss')" />]
                    <a href="{umbraco.library:NiceUrl(@id)}">
                        <xsl:value-of select="@nodeName"/>
                    </a>
                </li>
            </xsl:if>
        </xsl:for-each>
        </ul>
    </xsl:template>

</xsl:stylesheet>
```

For a list of available node set functions, see Table 11-2.

TABLE 11-2: Node Set Functions

FUNCTION	DESCRIPTION
`last()`	Returns the number of nodes in a node set.
`position()`	Returns the position of the context node (current node). The starting value is 1. As you loop through each node, the position increments.
`count(node1, node2, ...)`	Returns the total number of nodes in the node set as provided between the parentheses. If you leave the parentheses blank, it will use the context node.
`id((string1, string2, ...) node)`	Returns the nodes whose ID matches the string (s) passed to the function.
`local-name(node_set)`	Returns the local name of the first node in the node set. The local name is the name without the namespace prefix. To use the context node, simply leave `node_set` blank.
`name(node_set)`	Returns the full, qualified name of the first node in the node set. To use the context node, simply leave `node_set` blank.

TAKE HOME POINTS

This intense chapter contains lots of information. However, it touches only the tip of the iceberg as far as what is possible with XSLT. It should provide you with a functional understanding of how to implement macros using XSLT in Umbraco and more. You can now:

- Access published content using XSLT and XPath.
- Understand the makeup and structure of an XPath statement.
- Display images and file paths via XSLT and `GetMedia()`.
- Access Umbraco-specific content by using `for` loops and examining the content cache via `<xsl:copy-of .../>`.

12

Working with .NET Controls

- How do you create a macro?
- How do you use macro parameters to pass data?
- How do you create content programmatically?
- What's the best way to interact with unpublished content?
- Why are XSLT extensions so powerful?
- What is the Umbraco event model?
- How do you use LINQ to link to Umbraco?

Because Umbraco is so tightly integrated with standard .NET concepts extending it using .NET user controls, classes, and various configuration methods is easy. This chapter gives you a more detailed look at the power of extending Umbraco using custom .NET code. Plenty of examples should get you started creating custom Web applications in no time.

The assumption in this chapter, as well as the book, is that you have previous experience with and working knowledge of the following concepts:

- Working with *Microsoft Visual Studio* to create solutions and projects
- Creating and working with user controls (`.ascx`)
- Extending and working with .NET classes
- .NET events
- Deploying files to a website

For great examples of how other community developers have extended Umbraco, check out the projects repository at `http://our.umbraco.org/projects`.

One of the benefits of using .NET to interact with Umbraco content is that it allows you to retrieve content that is not published, as opposed to XSLT, where you only have access to the published content (from cache). The exception to this is using XSLT extensions, which are covered later in this chapter (and which are still powered by .NET code).

CREATING A MACRO

Chapter 5 discusses how to work with macros in detail, but for the purposes of this chapter, you will go through the motions one more time. To create a macro, follow these steps:

1. Navigate to the Developers section.
2. Right-click the Macros node and click the Create menu item.
3. In the dialog that appears, name your macro **List Sub Pages From Current Page** and click the Create button.

Okay, so now what? Well, you need some code to point to in order for this macro to actually do anything. Because this chapter talks strictly about .NET, you will create some code in a Visual Studio Project next.

If you do not own a license for Visual Studio, you have some options: Either download a trial version of the full version, download the Express version `www.microsoft.com/express/Downloads/`, *or take a look at Microsoft WebMatrix at* `www.microsoft.com/web/webmatrix/`.

.NET SAMPLES

This section is riddled with code examples and usages for extending the functionality of Umbraco. The examples include the following:

Remember to check out the download section of the Wrox website for all these code samples.

- Recreating an XSLT template in .NET to see how the languages compare (pros and cons of each)
- Rendering a node in a GridView and other standard .NET controls
- Creating an Umbraco document programmatically
- Creating a custom data type

- A simple contact form
- Hooking up a login form for use with Umbraco members

Clearly you can do a lot more in terms of making Umbraco a fully fledged custom application, but these samples should get you going.

The downloadable Visual Studio project accompanying this book named UmbUsersGuide.Samples is a solid representation of what your project template should look like. It includes the standard folder structure, all required references to Umbraco libraries, and sample build events to automatically deploy the project DLLs and other files to your website installation.

List Subpages from Current Page

The List Subpages from Current Page macro recreates the same output as one of the existing XSLT templates that you looked at in Chapter 5. See Figure 12-1 for a view of the expected output.

FIGURE 12-1

To create your new user control, simply follow these steps:

1. Right-click the `usercontrols` folder in your project, as shown in Figure 12-2.

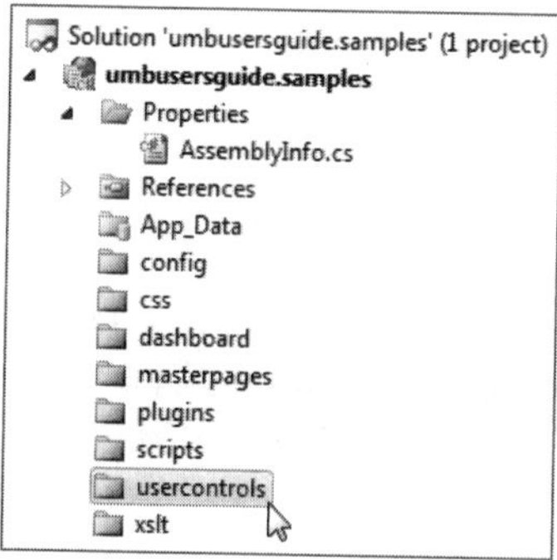

FIGURE 12-2

2. Click New Item in the Add submenu, as shown in Figure 12-3.

3. Select Web User Control, and name your new control **ListSubPagesFromCurrentPage.ascx**. Then click the Add button, as shown in Figure 12-4.

4. Add the code from Listing 12-1 to your newly created user control code-behind file.

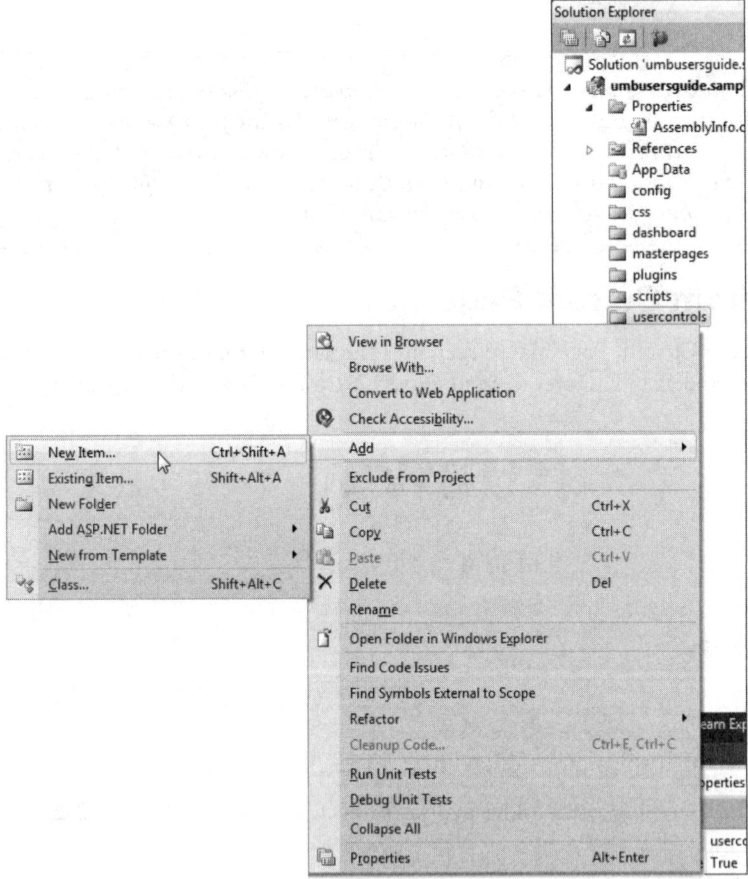

FIGURE 12-3

The code in Listing 12-1 uses the Umbraco `NodeFactory`*. This class allows you to programmatically query the XML cache, just like discussed in Chapter 11 using XSLT. It's fast, read-only, doesn't make any trips to the database, is ideal for this example, and should always be used when presenting data from the content tree in your .NET code. Later, this chapter covers the Document API, which allows for* CRUD *operations and interaction with the underlying database.*

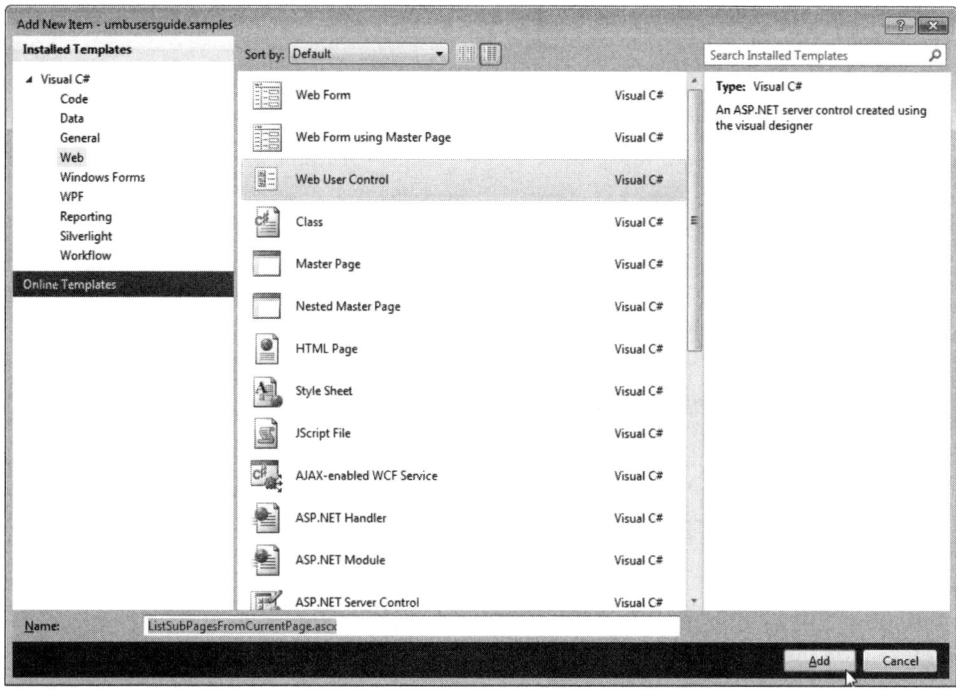

FIGURE 12-4

LISTING 12-1: ListSubPagesFromCurrentPage.ascx.cs

Available for download on Wrox.com

```
using System;
using System.Text;
using umbraco;
using umbraco.presentation.nodeFactory;

namespace UmbUsersGuide.Samples.UserControls
{
    public partial class ListSubPagesFromCurrentPage :
System.Web.UI.UserControl
    {
        protected void Page_Load(object sender, EventArgs e)
        {

            // Get the current node that we are on
            // reflects the node where this control is currently
            // included.
            var n = Node.GetCurrent();

            // start html string for output
            var htmlOut = new StringBuilder();
            htmlOut.Append("<ul>");
```

continues

LISTING 12-1 *(continued)*

```
                // Loop over the nodes children and generate
                // some HTML to present to the view
                var childNodes = n.Children;
                foreach (Node childNode in  childNodes)
                {
                    htmlOut.Append("<li>");
                        htmlOut.AppendFormat("<a href=\"{0}\">{1}</a>",
                            library.NiceUrl(childNode.Id),
                            childNode.Name);
                    htmlOut.Append("</li>");
                }

                // finish the html string builder
                htmlOut.Append("</ul>");

                // Render the HTML in our output panel.
                _outputPanel.Text = htmlOut.ToString();
            }
        }
    }
```

5. Add the code from Listing 12-2 to the ListSubPagesFromCurrentPage.ascx file.
6. Navigate to the macro that you created in the Creating a Macro section and select the newly added .ascx file as the macro file. For a refresher on working with macros see Chapter 5.

LISTING 12-2: ListSubPagesFromCurrentPage.ascx

Available for download on Wrox.com

```
<%@ Control Language="C#" AutoEventWireup="true"
CodeBehind="ListSubPagesFromCurrentPage.ascx.cs"
Inherits="UmbUsersGuide.Samples.UserControls.ListSubPagesFromCurrentPage" %>
<asp:Literal ID="_outputPanel" runat="server"></asp:Literal>
```

Insert the macro in the Runway master template, and you should see a standard unordered HTML list with the children of the current page nicely linked using the SEO-friendly URLs generated by the Umbraco library `NiceUrl` method.

Rendering Nodes in a Grid Control

So, you have created some document types that allow your users to work with products in the content tree. One of the requirements for displaying the products is to output all the products and their properties in a sortable table. If you have ever worked with a .NET GridView control you already know that it allows for automatic sorting and paging as long as you provide the data in one of the following *ADO.NET* formats:

- DataTable
- DataSet
- DataView

Umbraco allows you to render the nodes as a DataTable very easily. See Listing 12-3 for an example of returning nodes in a DataTable type. The corresponding view is shown in Listing 12-4.

LISTING 12-3: ListPagesAsGridView.ascx.cs

Available for download on Wrox.com

```
using System;
using umbraco.presentation.nodeFactory;

namespace UmbUsersGuide.Samples.UserControls
{
    public partial class ListPagesAsGridView : System.Web.UI.UserControl
    {
        protected void Page_Load(object sender, EventArgs e)
        {
            // Get the current node that we are on
            // reflects the node where this control is currently
            // included.
            var n = Node.GetCurrent();

            // Simply set the data source for the GridView
            // and data bind it.
            _nodeGrid.DataSource = n.ChildrenAsTable();
            _nodeGrid.DataBind();
        }
    }
}
```

LISTING 12-4: ListPagesAsGridView.ascx

Available for download on Wrox.com

```
<%@ Control Language="C#" AutoEventWireup="true"
CodeBehind="ListPagesAsGridView.ascx.cs"
Inherits="UmbUsersGuide.Samples.UserControls.ListPagesAsGridView" %>
<asp:GridView ID="_nodeGrid" runat="server">
</asp:GridView>
```

If you receive a system exception (`System.Web.HttpException`*) when running your newly created macro, the reason is most likely because you are missing the* `<form id="1" runat="server" />` *tag in your master page, or you have placed the macro outside of the existing form tag.*

Running this code renders all the properties of the returned nodes. You can, of course, further refine this output by working with all the features of the .NET GridView control (such as sorting, paging, DataColumns, and so on).

Creating a Page Programmatically

Programmatically adding content to the tree from user input will sometimes be necessary. A great example of this is if your site supports a knowledgebase or frequently asked questions (FAQ). So, you need to add a form to one of your pages that takes the user's input, maps the various fields to predefined document type properties, and saves the document. You build on this example over the next few sections.

You must first create a new document type (discussed in Chapter 3) so that you have something to work with, as shown in Figure 12-5 and in the following steps.

FIGURE 12-5

1. Right-click Document Types in the Settings section and then click the Create menu item.
2. In the dialog that appears, name your new document type **FAQ**, and deselect the Create matching template check box.
3. Add a new tab called **FAQ**.
4. Add the following properties to the new tab:
   - Author {type: Textstring}
   - Category {type: Textstring}
   - Question {type: Richtext Editor}
   - Answer {type: Richtext Editor, mandatory: true}
5. Save the document type.

6. Add another document type for the container of the submitted FAQs called **FAQ Area** with a Richtext Editor property named bodyText and no matching template, allowing FAQ as an allowed child nodetype on this document type.
7. Choose the Runway Textpage as an allowed template and set it as the default.
8. In the Structure tab add FAQ Area as an allowed child nodetype on the Runway Homepage document type.
9. Add FAQ Area as a content node in the content tree. Choose the Content Section and right-click Runway Homepage. Click the Create menu item and choose FAQ Area as the Document Type, as shown in Figure 12-6.

FIGURE 12-6

10. Publish the FAQ Area node by clicking the Save & Publish button in the toolbar in the top left-hand corner of the pane.
11. With that out of the way, create a new user control in the Visual Studio project called **CreateFAQ.ascx**, as shown in Listings 12-5 and 12-6. Basically, here's what's going on in the code:

    - You set the Umbraco user object that will be the creator of the document. You must reference the `umbraco.BusinessLogic` assembly to get the user object.
    - You create and save a new Umbraco node using the document API. You must reference the `umbraco.cms.businesslogic.web` assembly for this.
    - You set some of the FAQ document type properties for this new node based on user input.
    - You redirect user to a Thank You page that you created.

Available for download on Wrox.com

LISTING 12-5: CreateFAQ.ascx.cs

```
using System;
using umbraco.BusinessLogic;
using umbraco.cms.businesslogic.web;

namespace UmbUsersGuide.Samples.UserControls
{
    public partial class CreateFAQ : System.Web.UI.UserControl
    {
        protected void Page_Load(object sender, EventArgs e)
        {
        }

        protected void _save_Click(object sender, EventArgs e)
        {
            // need to register a user to associate the newly created
            // document with. Since this is an anonymous user, we'll
            // use the admin account which always has an ID of 0
            User adminUser = new User(0);

            // create a new document using the Umbraco Document API
            Document faq = Document.MakeNew(
                _questionTitle.Text, // this will be the nodeName
                DocumentType.GetByAlias("faq"), // get the document
                                    type ID by the alias we created
                adminUser,
                1055); // the parent ID where this new page
                          should live (the FAQ Area)

            // inject the user input into the document type properties
            // of the FAQ node that was just created above
            faq.getProperty("question").Value = _question.Text;
            faq.getProperty("author").Value = _yourName.Text;

            // We could optionally choose to publish the node here
            // In this case we're not going to as we don't want
            // unreviewd questions to appear on the site.
            //faq.Publish(adminUser);

            // This adds the created and published document to
            // the xml cache
            //umbraco.library.UpdateDocumentCache(faq.Id);

            // Redirect the user to a Thank You page that we created
            // in the content tree. We use Umbraco's NiceUrl helper
            // method to generate the URL by node id
            Response.Redirect(umbraco.library.NiceUrl(1056), true);
        }
    }
}
```

LISTING 12-6: CreateFAQ.ascx

Available for download on Wrox.com

```
<%@ Control Language="C#" AutoEventWireup="true"
CodeBehind="CreateFAQ.ascx.cs"
Inherits="UmbUsersGuide.Samples.UserControls.CreateFAQ" %>
<fieldset>
    <label>Your Name</label>
    <asp:TextBox ID="_yourName" runat="server" />
    <br />
    <label>Question Title</label>
    <asp:TextBox ID="_questionTitle" runat="server" />
    <br />
    <label>Question</label>
    <asp:TextBox ID="_question" TextMode="MultiLine" Columns="30"
          Rows="10" runat="server" />
    <br />
    <asp:Button ID="_save" Text="Submit Question" runat="server"
        onclick="_save_Click" />
</fieldset>
```

In Listing 12-5 you may notice some hardcoded IDs for the parent page as well as the redirect page. This is not ideal as you must recompile the code if any of the nodes change. The section "Passing Data to .NET Through Macro Parameters" details how to add public properties and pass in data as macro parameters to .NET controls.

12. Create a macro called **FAQ Form** and point it to the newly created .NET user control. This time, remember to select the Use in editor check box, as shown in Figure 12-7.
13. In the FAQ Area node's Richtext Editor, add the FAQ From macro and publish the page. The page should render something similar to the top image in Figure 12-8.
14. Fill out the form and submit it. The Thank You page appears.
15. To verify that the question was added, simply reload the FAQ Area node and you should see an unpublished node with the title that you added in the form, as shown in Figure 12-9.

Notice here that you have, by not publishing the programmatically created node, added a small workflow. An editor or administrator will have to review the question, provide an answer, and then publish the FAQ entry to make it public.

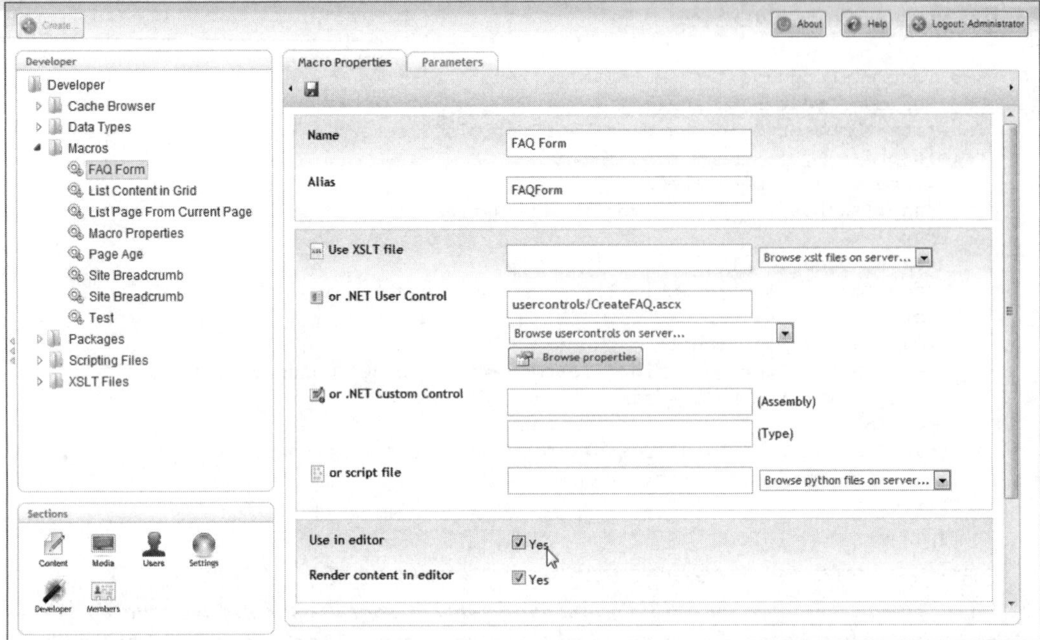

FIGURE 12-7

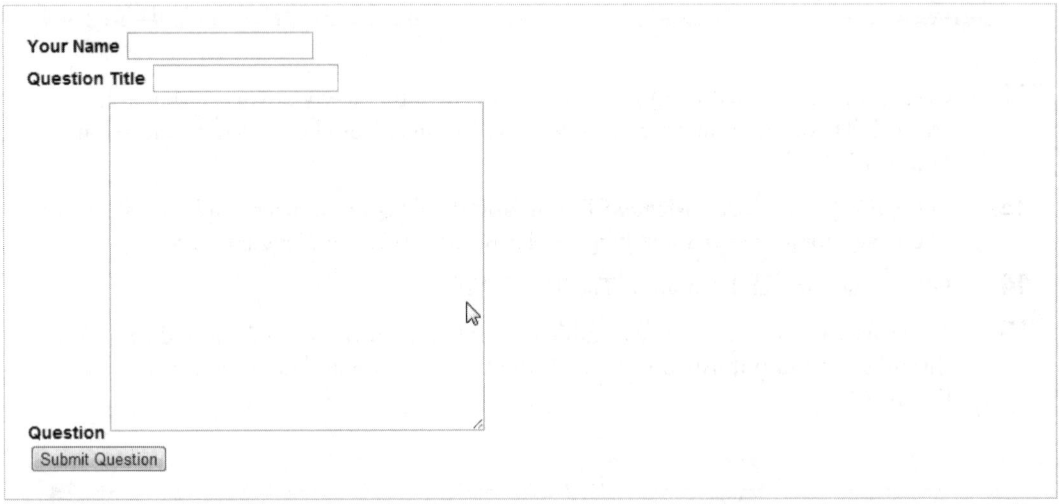

Your Name
Question Title
Question
Submit Question

FIGURE 12-8

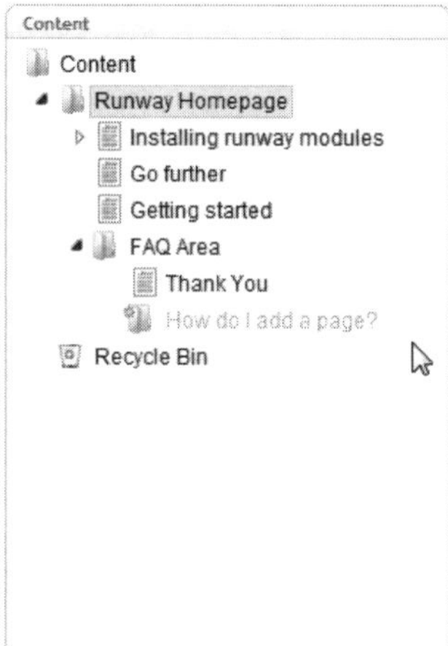

FIGURE 12-9

Creating a Custom Data Type

Umbraco ships with a lot of different data types and in most cases they are sufficient for standard content management fields. However, in some cases, like the FAQ example that you have been working with, a custom field may be required. Take for instance the category field that you added to the FAQ document type. As it stands now, the editor is forced to type in a value. That is not ideal because typos can be made and typically you want categories to remain standard across all the entries. A better solution might be to query for a set of categories that are stored in a custom table and outside of the Umbraco framework.

This next example shows you just how to do that. Here's the gist of what will go down:

- You set a manual list of categories in a DataTable and use it as data source for a standard `<asp:DropDownList />` control. Of course, in a real-world example you would probably be querying a database or get your data from some live source.
- You implement the `IUsercontrolDataEditor` interface to save the selected item as an Umbraco value. To implement this interface you must reference the `umbraco.editorControls.userControlGrapper` assembly. This interface only has a single member and you need only have a public object type called value with the associated getter and setter methods specified.
- You use a public class property to pass the selected value to the interface.

To set a manual list of categories, follow these steps.

1. Create a new user control in your project called `CategoriesDT.ascx`.
2. Add the code from Listings 12-7 and 12-8 to your new user control.

LISTING 12-7: CategoriesDT.ascx.cs

Available for download on Wrox.com

```
using System;
using System.Data;
using umbraco.editorControls.userControlGrapper;

namespace UmbUsersGuide.Samples.UserControls
{
    public partial class CategoriesDT : System.Web.UI.UserControl,
                                        IUsercontrolDataEditor
    {
        public string UmbracoValue = "";
        protected void Page_Load(object sender, EventArgs e)
        {
            if (!Page.IsPostBack)
            {
                // Wire up the dropdownlist and load the
                // data items
                _categories.DataSource = GetCategories();
                _categories.DataTextField = "Name";
                _categories.DataValueField = "ProductID";
                _categories.DataBind();
            }
            // if this is a postback, set the UmbracoValue
            // public property so we can reference the value
            // in the implemented interface below
            else if (Page.IsPostBack)
            {
                UmbracoValue = _categories.SelectedValue;
            }

            // If there is a saved value, always set it as the
            // [selected] value of the control
            if (!UmbracoValue.Equals(""))
            {
                _categories.Items.FindByValue(UmbracoValue).Selected = true;
            }
        }

        private DataTable GetCategories()
        {
            // Setup the data table columns so tha we can
            // populate them below.
            DataTable dt = new DataTable();
            dt.Columns.Add("ProductID", Type.GetType("System.Int32"));
            dt.Columns.Add("Name", Type.GetType("System.String"));

            // populate with static data
            DataRow dr = dt.NewRow();
            dr["ProductID"] = 1;
            dr["Name"] = "Technical Questions";
            dt.Rows.Add(dr);
```

```
            dr = dt.NewRow();
            dr["ProductID"] = 2;
            dr["Name"] = "Backoffice Interface";
            dt.Rows.Add(dr);

            dr = dt.NewRow();
            dr["ProductID"] = 3;
            dr["Name"] = "Permissions";
            dt.Rows.Add(dr);

            dr = dt.NewRow();
            dr["ProductID"] = 4;
            dr["Name"] = "Custom Functionality";
            dt.Rows.Add(dr);

            return dt;
        }

        #region IUsercontrolDataEditor Members

        public object value
        {
            get
            {
                // if there is no value, set the value to null
                // otherwise use the selected value
                return UmbracoValue;
            }
            set
            {
                // When the control is loaded in the backoffice,
                // check if there is a saved value. If so, set the
                // matching item in the dropdownlist to selected.
                if (value != null &&
                      !String.IsNullOrEmpty(value.ToString()))
                {
                    UmbracoValue = value.ToString();
                }
            }
        }

        #endregion
    }
}
```

LISTING 12-8: CategoriesDT.ascx

Available for download on Wrox.com

```
<%@ Control Language="C#" AutoEventWireup="true"
CodeBehind="CategoriesDT.ascx.cs"
Inherits="UmbUsersGuide.Samples.UserControls.CategoriesDT" %>
<asp:DropDownList ID="_categories" runat="server">
</asp:DropDownList>
```

All that is happening in Listing 12-7 is that the public object is getting the value and performing a save to the document type property (in this case, `category`*). Then upon loading of this custom data type, the public object value is returned and matched to an existing item in the dropdown (the list of items from the database).*

The only thing left to do is add the CategoriesDT user control as a data type in the backoffice and switch out the document type control with the new data type.

1. Navigate to the Developer section.
2. Right-click the Data Types node and click the Create menu item.
3. In the dialog that appears, name your new data type **FAQ Categories** and click the Create button.
4. In the resulting right-hand pane, select **umbraco user control wrapper** as the Render Control and click the Save button.
5. Leave the Database data type as Ntext and choose the new user control from the dropdown, as shown in Figure 12-10.
6. Save the data type again.

If you change the Database data type after values have already been saved using the data type, you will lose all the saved data. So, choose carefully when creating your new data types.

7. Navigate to the FAQ document type in the Settings section.
8. In the Generic Settings tab, change the Type of the Category property to FAQ Categories, and click Save.
9. Navigate to the Content section and open the submitted question; notice that you now have a handy drop-down control listing the categories.

As always with Umbraco multiple solutions exist. Other options to make this data type even more flexible in terms of data source would be:

- Populate the drop-down control with a set of nodes of a specific type. For example, you could create a document type for FAQ Categories that would have the Name and Id properties, then iterate over the nodes of that document type.
- For the FAQ Categories example, you could just as well have created a new data type based on the Dropdown List data type and hard-coded the prevalues.

In fact if you ask ten Umbraco developers how they would go about solving this problem, you would probably end up with at least eight different answers.

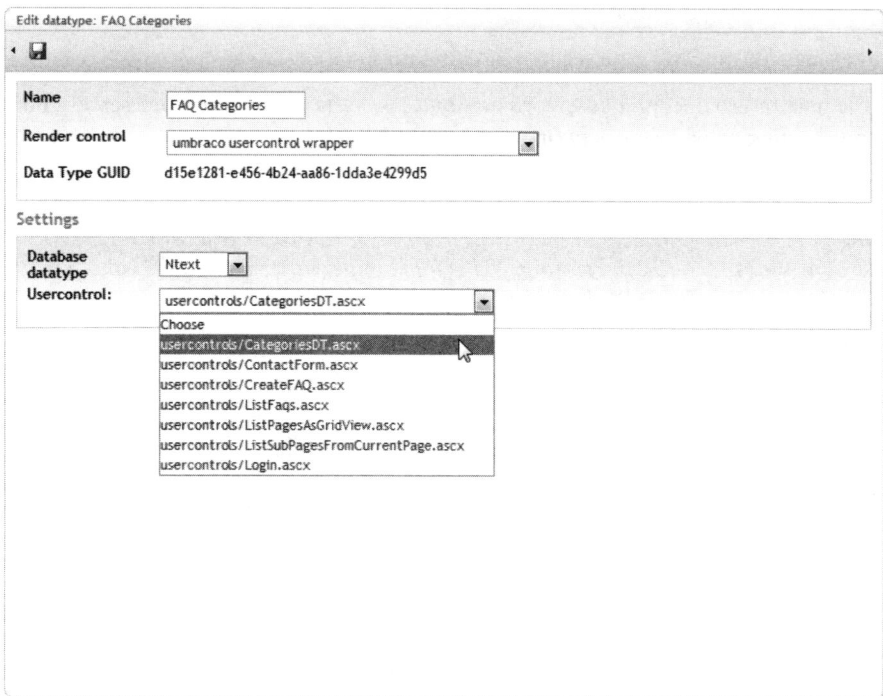

FIGURE 12-10

Sending Email with a Contact Form

This section's example is a very popular feature on most websites. It's a simple contact form that allows you to send an email to a specified email address with the contents of the form. As usual, Umbraco leverages the standard .NET mail classes and settings to accomplish this. It even comes with a handy library method called `SendMail` that you can use to send simple emails (as shown by the bolded code in Listing 12-9). All you need to do is set up an email server in the `Web.config`. The default installation is configured for `localhost`, as shown in the following.

```
<system.net>
    <mailSettings>
        <smtp>
            <network host="127.0.0.1" userName="username" password="password" />
        </smtp>
    </mailSettings>
</system.net>
```

To configure Umbraco to use your own *SMTP* (simple mail transport protocol) server, follow these steps:

1. Open up the web.config file located in `<install root>web.config`.
2. Find the settings for the SMTP server by searching for `<system.net />`.
3. Change the host, username, and password attributes to values matching your server and user (set by your hosting provider or network administrator).

For testing purposes in your development environment, you can configure the SMTP service with the following settings. This will simply write the results to a local file as specified in the `pickupDirectoryLocation` *path.*

```
<system.net>
  <mailSettings>
    <smtp deliveryMethod="SpecifiedPickupDirectory" >
      <specifiedPickupDirectory
         pickupDirectoryLocation="C:\testdropfolder\"/>
    </smtp>
  </mailSettings>
</system.net>
```

All you have to do is set it to an SMTP server that you have access to and authority to relay through. Without further ado, see Listings 12-9 and 12-10 for this example.

LISTING 12-9: ContactForm.ascx.cs

Available for download on Wrox.com

```
using System;

namespace UmbUsersGuide.Samples.UserControls
{
    public partial class ContactForm : System.Web.UI.UserControl
    {
        protected void Page_Load(object sender, EventArgs e)
        {
            if (Page.IsPostBack)
            {
                // hide the form
                _formView.Visible = false;

                // Show the Thank You Message
                _messageView.Visible = true;
            }
        }

        protected void _sendEmail_Click(object sender, EventArgs e)
```

```
            {
                // send an email using the Umbraco libray SendMail method
                umbraco.library.SendMail(_emailAddress.Text,
                        "youremail@domain.com",
                        "Someone filled out the contact form!",
                        _message.Text,true);
            }
        }
    }
```

LISTING 12-10: ContactForm.ascx

Available for download on Wrox.com

```
<%@ Control Language="C#" AutoEventWireup="true"
CodeBehind="ContactForm.ascx.cs"
Inherits="UmbUsersGuide.Samples.UserControls.ContactForm" %>
<asp:Panel ID="_formView" runat="server">
    <fieldset>
        <label>Your Name</label>
        <asp:TextBox ID="_yourName" runat="server" />
        <br />
        <label>Your Email Address</label>
        <asp:TextBox ID="_emailAddress" runat="server" />
        <br />
        <label>Your Phone Number</label>
        <asp:TextBox ID="_phone" runat="server" />
        <br />
        <label>Message</label>
        <asp:TextBox ID="_message" TextMode="MultiLine"
               Columns="30" Rows="10" runat="server" />
        <br />
        <asp:Button ID="_sendEmail" Text="Send Email" runat="server"
            onclick="_sendEmail_Click" />
    </fieldset>
</asp:Panel>
<asp:Panel ID="_messageView" Visible="false" runat="server">
</asp:Panel>
```

Passing Data to .NET Through Macro Parameters

Throughout all the examples so far you have probably noticed that a lot of hard-coding values have taken place. For example, when creating a document, wouldn't it be nice to pass in the `ParentId` of the node where you want to create the FAQs? Or, in the contact form, wouldn't it be great if the To Email address could be set dynamically, allowing you to reuse the form in multiple places for multiple reasons?

Chapter 5 discusses macro parameters and how to use them. Well, you can use these macro parameters to pass data to your .NET user controls via public properties.

To demonstrate, let's modify the preceding example where the FAQ question was created, and pass in the `ParentId` and the `ThankYouId` using macro parameters. The bolded code in Listing 12-11 shows the added or changed code.

LISTING 12-11: CreateFAQ.ascx.cs

```
using System;
using umbraco.BusinessLogic;
using umbraco.cms.businesslogic.web;

namespace UmbUsersGuide.Samples.UserControls
{
    public partial class CreateFAQ : System.Web.UI.UserControl
    {
        public int ParentId { get; set; }
        public int ThankYouId { get; set; }
        protected void Page_Load(object sender, EventArgs e)
        {
        }

        protected void _save_Click(object sender, EventArgs e)
        {
            // need to register a user to associate the newly created
            // document with. Since this is an anonymous user, we'll
            // use the admin account which always has an ID of 0
            User adminUser = new User(0);

            // create a new document using the Umbraco Document API
            Document faq = Document.MakeNew(
                _questionTitle.Text, // this will be the nodeName
                DocumentType.GetByAlias("faq"), // get the document type ID
                                                   by the alias we created
                adminUser,
                ParentId); // the parent ID where this new
                              page should live (the FAQ Area)

            // inject the user input into the document type properties
            // of the FAQ node that was just created above
            faq.getProperty("question").Value = _question.Text;
            faq.getProperty("author").Value = _yourName.Text;

            // We could optionally choose to publish the node here
            // In this case we're not going to as we don't want
            // unreviewed questions to appear on the site.
            //faq.Publish(adminUser);

            // This adds the created and published document to
            // the xml cache
            //umbraco.library.UpdateDocumentCache(faq.Id);

            // Redirect the user to a Thank You page that we created
```

```
                // in the content tree. We use Umbraco's NiceUrl helper
                // method to generate the URL by node id
                Response.Redirect(umbraco.library.NiceUrl(ThankYouId), true);
            }
        }
    }
```

When you have built the altered user control and deployed it to your Umbraco installation, adding these public properties as Umbraco macro parameters is a breeze:

1. Navigate to the Developers section and select the FAQ Form macro.
2. As shown in Figure 12-11, click the Browse properties button.

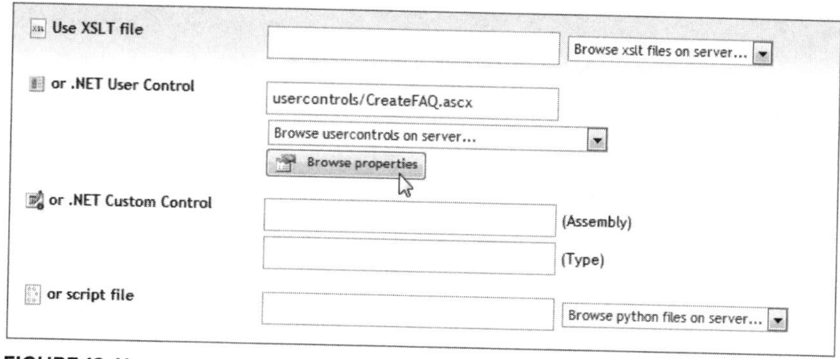

FIGURE 12-11

3. In the resulting dialog, you will see the two properties that you added—`ParentId` and `ThankYouId`—already preselected for your convenience. Simply click Save Properties and Umbraco will turn them into macro parameters automatically.
4. There's one more thing that you want to do before re-adding this macro to your page. Navigate to the Parameters tab and set the Type of the two parameters to contentPicker, as shown in Figure 12-12. This allows you to choose the nodes from the content tree instead of typing in the node Id of the page.

Now, when you go to re-add the FAQ form to the FAQ Area page, you will be prompted to select the corresponding Parent and Thank You pages, as shown in Figure 12-13.

You may also want to change the `Name` *attribute of the parameter to be more user friendly, but this is completely optional from a functional standpoint.*

The most obvious benefit of working with public properties and macro parameters is that you have now removed the requirements of code changes if you need to update where the submitted FAQs should be saved or what page to redirect the user to upon submission.

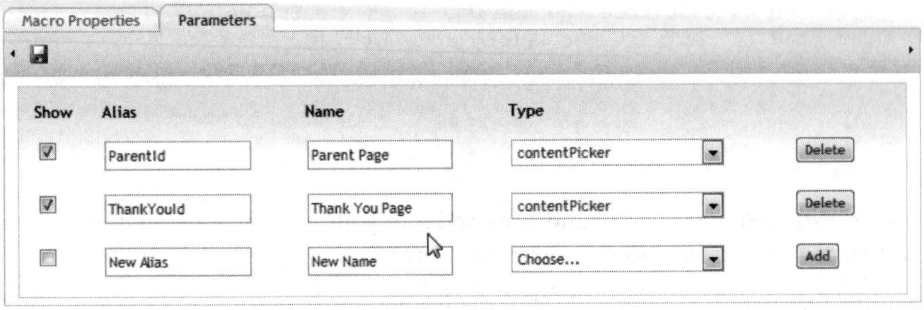

FIGURE 12-12

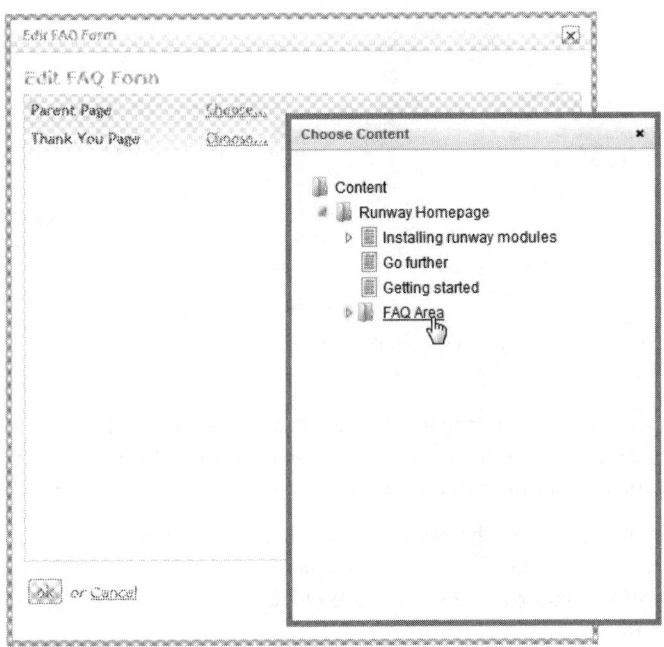

FIGURE 12-13

Creating a Login Macro

If you must deal with personalized or restricted content in your website, you need the ability to have users log in by providing member account credentials. As mentioned earlier in this book, Umbraco implements the standard .NET Membership Provider model. This means that you can pretty much just drag and drop the various login controls onto your user controls and be done! Well, at least theoretically. You need to perform a few configurations to get this working.

Chapter 2 provides details on how to work with members—adding member types, member groups, and the member details. To get the standard Umbraco Membership Provider to work, only two things need to happen:

1. Add at least one Member Type to the Members section.
2. Configure the UmbracoMembershipProvider key in `Web.config` to have the `defaultMemberTypeAlias` attribute match one of your configured Member Types.

You can find the membership providers configuration in the `<system.web> <membership /></system.web>` *node in* `Web.config`.

That's it! Now, all you need to do is add an `<asp:Login />` control to a user control and create a macro for it. See Listings 12-12 and 12-13 for an example (be aware that it is alarmingly simple).

LISTING 12-12: Login.ascx.cs

Available for download on Wrox.com

```
using System;

namespace UmbUsersGuide.Samples.UserControls
{
    public partial class Login : System.Web.UI.UserControl
    {
        // The default redirect page after logging in
        public int LoginRedirectPage { get; set; }
        protected override void OnInit(EventArgs e)
        {
            base.OnInit(e);
            _loginForm.LoggedIn += LoginUser_LoggedIn;
        }

        // When the user has successfully authenticated
        // redirect them to the specified page
        void LoginUser_LoggedIn(object sender, EventArgs e)
        {
            // Redirect the user to a specified page
            Response.Redirect(umbraco.library.NiceUrl(LoginRedirectPage));
        }

        protected void Page_Load(object sender, EventArgs e)
        {

        }
    }
}
```

The `OnInit` *override is not even needed here. It's simply there to provide an example of how to redirect users to a specific page upon login as a configurable item.*

LISTING 12-13: Login.ascx

Available for download on Wrox.com

```
<%@ Control Language="C#" AutoEventWireup="true" CodeBehind="Login.ascx.cs"
 Inherits="UmbUsersGuide.Samples.UserControls.Login" %>
<asp:Login ID="_loginForm" runat="server">
</asp:Login>
```

USING .NET FROM XSLT VIA XSLT EXTENSIONS

One of the coolest things with XSLT (as an opinion from a .NET developer) is the ability to consume .NET methods and rich functionality from within your XSLT templates. In most cases you won't need this functionality if the XSLT template is only working with outputting published data from content or media. However, in other cases, you may need to access external data or gain access to transformations that are simply not possible to accomplish with XSLT 1.1 alone.

Enter XSLT extensions! As with most custom functionality, XSLT extensions require a bit of configuration and coding to get started. The short of it is this:

1. You create a class with public access and some public static methods that return a value.
2. You add a line to the XSLT configuration file that indicates to the XSLT parser where to find your new extension methods.
3. You reference the class namespace and prefixes in the XSLT templates.

Sounds easy, right? It really is, because even the last item is done for you automatically when you create new XSLT templates from the backoffice (for ones that are created after you add an extension library). Roll up your sleeves and create a simple extension. Listing 12-14 covers the basics of the public class and has but one method in it for the purposes of this example. The use case for this example may be that you are trying to figure out how many days old a particular page is and display that in the footer of each page.

LISTING 12-14: XsltExtensions.cs

```
using System;

namespace UmbUsersGuide.Samples
{
```

```
        public class XsltExtensions
        {
            public static string DayDiff(string startDate, string endDate)
            {
                // Parse the passed in dates to DateTime
                // objects.
                var sDate = DateTime.Parse(startDate);
                var eDate = DateTime.Parse(endDate);

                // Subtract the start date from the end date
                // and return the number of days
                return eDate.Subtract(sDate).Days.ToString();
            }
        }
    }
```

Now, add the reference to the class in the `<install root>/config/xsltExtensions.config` file, as shown in Listing 12-15. This allows Umbraco to recognize that a class exists with public methods that are mapped to the specified alias. In this case, all the method calls from within the XSLT templates will be prefixed with `umbusersguide.library:MethodName`.

LISTING 12-15: xsltExtensions.config

```
<?xml version="1.0" encoding="utf-8" ?>
<XsltExtensions>
  <ext assembly="/UmbUsersGuide.Samples"
       type="UmbUsersGuide.Samples.XsltExtensions"
       alias="umbusersguide.library" />
</XsltExtensions>
```

To utilize this new method, create a new XSLT macro in the backoffice called `PageAge.xslt`, leaving both the Clean template selected and the Create Macro check boxes selected. You will notice that in the new XSLT template some automatically added attributes appear in the `<xsl:stylesheet />` element, as highlighted in bold in Listing 12-16. To use the new method in your XSLT template, simply follow these steps:

1. Click the Insert xslt:value-of icon in the toolbar, as shown in Figure 12-14.
2. Click the Get Extension button and select the umbusersguide.library item in the first drop-down list.
3. Select the DayDiff method in the second drop-down list.
4. Click the Insert button and click the Insert Value button.
5. Fill in the arguments, as shown in Listing 12-16.

If you thought XSLT templates were cool before, now there is virtually no limit to what you can accomplish with them (within technical design reasons of course).

Insert xsl:value-of button

Edit xsl

Insert xslt:value-of

Filename PageAge.xslt

Skip testing (ignore errors)

```
<?xml version="1.0" encoding="UTF-8"?>
<!DOCTYPE xsl:stylesheet [ <!ENTITY nbsp " "> ]>
<xsl:stylesheet
  version="1.0"
  xmlns:xsl="http://www.w3.org/1999/XSL/Transform"
  xmlns:msxml="urn:schemas-microsoft-com:xslt"
  xmlns:umbraco.library="urn:umbraco.library" xmlns:Exslt.ExsltCommon="urn:Exslt.E
  exclude-result-prefixes="msxml umbraco.library Exslt.ExsltCommon Exslt.ExsltDate


<xsl:output method="xml" omit-xml-declaration="yes"/>

<xsl:param name="currentPage"/>

<xsl:template match="/">

  This page is <b><xsl:value-of select="umbusersguide.library:DayDiff($currentPage
```

FIGURE 12-14

Available for download on Wrox.com

LISTING 12-16: PageAge.xslt

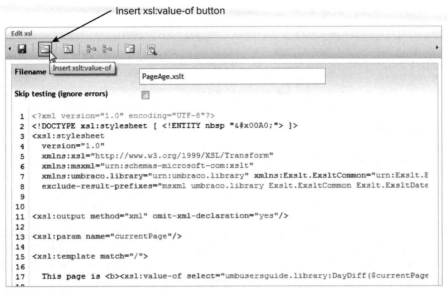

```
<?xml version="1.0" encoding="UTF-8"?>
<!DOCTYPE xsl:stylesheet [ <!ENTITY nbsp " "> ]>
<xsl:stylesheet
  version="1.0"
  xmlns:xsl="http://www.w3.org/1999/XSL/Transform"
  xmlns:msxml="urn:schemas-microsoft-com:xslt"
  xmlns:umbraco.library="urn:umbraco.library"
xmlns:Exslt.ExsltCommon="urn:Exslt.ExsltCommon"
xmlns:Exslt.ExsltDatesAndTimes="urn:Exslt.ExsltDatesAndTimes"
xmlns:Exslt.ExsltMath="urn:Exslt.ExsltMath"
xmlns:Exslt.ExsltRegularExpressions="urn:Exslt.ExsltRegularExpressions"
xmlns:Exslt.ExsltStrings="urn:Exslt.ExsltStrings"
xmlns:Exslt.ExsltSets="urn:Exslt.ExsltSets"
xmlns:umbusersguide.library="urn:umbusersguide.library"
  exclude-result-prefixes="msxml umbraco.library Exslt.ExsltCommon
Exslt.ExsltDatesAndTimes Exslt.ExsltMath Exslt.ExsltRegularExpressions
Exslt.ExsltStrings Exslt.ExsltSets umbusersguide.library ">


<xsl:output method="xml" omit-xml-declaration="yes"/>

<xsl:param name="currentPage"/>

<xsl:template match="/">

  This page is <b><xsl:value-of
  select="umbusersguide.library:DayDiff($currentPage/@createDate,
  umbraco.library:CurrentDate())"/></b> days old.
```

```
</xsl:template>

</xsl:stylesheet>
```

The possibilities are endless in terms of what you can return from an XSLT extension method. One other example worth noting is the `XPathNodeIterator`, which would be used to return structured (XML format, of course) data on which you could then run standard XPath statements.

THE UMBRACO EVENT MODEL

The event model that Umbraco employs is great for interacting with content and media and intercepting or injecting actions into the workflow as Umbraco's node lifecycle is executed. Again, the aim of this book is to introduce you to the concepts and not delve into granular details. In short, having access to these event hooks provides you with the ability to add workflows and integrate third-party and a host of other applications.

Event Hooks

Every action in the Umbraco process is covered by the event model, which makes subscribing to any of these events with just a few lines of code possible. Table 12-1 lists all the available event hooks and in what context they are relevant. This is a listing of all the events that you can tap into. For more specific examples of when these are used, see the sample code in the "Event Samples" section.

TABLE 12-1: Event Hooks

EVENT CONTEXT	EVENT NAME

Access
umbraco.cms.businesslogic.web.Access
	`BeforeSave`
	`AfterSave`
	`New`
	`BeforeAddProtection`
	`AfterAddProtection`
	`BeforeRemoveProtection`
	`AfterRemoveProtection`
	`BeforeAddMemberShipRoleToDocument`
	`AfterAddMemberShipRoleToDocument`
	`BeforeRemoveMemberShipRoleToDocument`
	`AfterRemoveMemberShipRoleToDocument`

continues

TABLE 12-1 *(continued)*

EVENT CONTEXT	EVENT NAME

Access
umbraco.cms.businesslogic.web.Access (continued)
	`BeforeRemoveMembershipUserFromDocument`
	`AfterRemoveMembershipUserFromDocument`
	`BeforeAddMembershipUserToDocument`
	`AfterAddMembershipUserToDocument`

BaseTree *umbraco.cms.presentation.Trees.BaseTree*	`BeforeNodeRender` `AfterNodeRender`

CMSNode
umbraco.cms.businesslogic.CMSNode
	`BeforeSave`
	`AfterSave`
	`New`
	`BeforeDelete`
	`AfterDelete`
	`BeforeMove`
	`AfterMove`

CreatedPackage
umbraco.cms.businesslogic.packager .CreatedPackage
	`BeforeSave`
	`AfterSave`
	`New`
	`BeforeDelete`
	`AfterDelete`
	`BeforePublish`
	`AfterPublish`

Content
umbraco.content
	`BeforeUpdateDocumentCache`
	`AfterUpdateDocumentCache`
	`BeforeClearDocumentCache`
	`AfterClearDocumentCache`
	`BeforeRefreshContent`
	`AfterRefreshContent`

EVENT CONTEXT	EVENT NAME
ContentControl *umbraco.controls.ContentControl*	`BeforeContentControlLoad` `AfterContentControlLoad`

DataTypeDefinition
umbraco.cms.businesslogic.datatype .DataTypeDefinition
	`Saving`
	`New`
	`Deleting`

Dictionary
umbraco.cms.businesslogic.Dictionary
	`Saving`
	`New`
	`Deleting`

Document
umbraco.cms.businesslogic.web.Document
	`BeforeSave`
	`AfterSave`
	`New`
	`BeforeDelete`
	`AfterDelete`
	`BeforeMoveToTrash`
	`AfterMoveToTrash`
	`BeforePublish`
	`AfterPublish`
	`BeforeSendToPublish`
	`AfterSendToPublish`
	`BeforeUnPublish`
	`AfterUnPublish`
	`BeforeCopy`
	`AfterCopy`
	`BeforeRollBack`
	`AfterRollBack`
	`BeforeAddToIndex`
	`AfterAddToIndex`

continues

TABLE 12-1 *(continued)*

EVENT CONTEXT	EVENT NAME

DocumentType
umbraco.cms.businesslogic.web.DocumentType
	`BeforeSave`
	`AfterSave`
	`New`
	`BeforeDelete`
	`AfterDelete`

Domain
umbraco.cms.businesslogic.web.Domain
	`BeforeSave`
	`AfterSave`
	`New`
	`BeforeDelete`
	`AfterDelete`

InstalledPackage
umbraco.cms.businesslogic.packager .InstalledPackage
	`BeforeSave`
	`AfterSave`
	`New`
	`BeforeDelete`
	`AfterDelete`

Macro
umbraco.cms.businesslogic.macro.Macro
	`BeforeSave`
	`AfterSave`
	`New`
	`BeforeDelete`
	`AfterDelete`

Media
umbraco.cms.businesslogic.media.Media
	`BeforeSave`
	`AfterSave`
	`New`
	`BeforeDelete`
	`AfterDelete`

EVENT CONTEXT	EVENT NAME

MediaType
umbraco.cms.businesslogic.media.MediaType
	`BeforeSave`
	`AfterSave`
	`New`
	`BeforeDelete`
	`AfterDelete`

Member
umbraco.cms.businesslogic.member.Member
	`BeforeSave`
	`AfterSave`
	`New`
	`BeforeAddGroup`
	`AfterAddGroup`
	`BeforeRemoveGroup`
	`AfterRemoveGroup`
	`BeforeAddToCache`
	`AfterAddToCache`
	`BeforeDelete`
	`AfterDelete`

MemberGroup
umbraco.cms.businesslogic.member.MemberGroup
	`BeforeSave`
	`AfterSave`
	`New`
	`BeforeDelete`
	`AfterDelete`

MemberType
umbraco.cms.businesslogic.member.MemberType
	`BeforeSave`
	`AfterSave`
	`New`
	`BeforeDelete`
	`AfterDelete`

continues

TABLE 12-1 *(continued)*

EVENT CONTEXT	EVENT NAME
Language *umbraco.cms.businesslogic.language.Language*	BeforeSave AfterSave New BeforeDelete AfterDelete
Stylesheet *umbraco.cms.businesslogic.web.StyleSheet*	BeforeSave AfterSave New BeforeDelete AfterDelete
StylesheetProperty *umbraco.cms.businesslogic.web .StyleSheetProperty*	BeforeSave AfterSave New BeforeDelete AfterDelete
Template *umbraco.cms.businesslogic.template.Template*	BeforeSave AfterSave New BeforeDelete AfterDelete
User *umbraco.BusinessLogic.template.Template*	Saving New Disabling Deleting FlushingFromCache

Event Examples

Hooking into an event requires you to simply create a class that derives from the `umbraco.BusinessLogic.ApplicationBase` class. Both the class and constructor must be public in order for the hook to be caught in the execution of the action.

Listing 12-17 provides an example of auto expiring a node on a particular date. This is useful for things such as news items, events, and other time-sensitive material. For the purposes of this example, assume that there's a business case to expire your FAQs after seven days from the original publish date.

Because code that's executed in an event hook is silent (meaning it's executed without any screen or process feedback), logging all steps religiously is important. If something unexpected happens, you can always refer to the umbracoLog table to track down whether one of your event hooks caused the issue.

LISTING 12-17: AutoExpireFaq.cs

Available for download on Wrox.com

```
using System;
using umbraco.BusinessLogic;
using umbraco.cms.businesslogic.web;

namespace UmbUsersGuide.Samples
{
    public class AutoExpireFaq : ApplicationBase
    {
        public AutoExpireFaq()
        {
            Document.BeforePublish += new
            Document.PublishEventHandler(Document_BeforePublish);
        }

        /// <summary>
        /// Event Handler that gets hit before an item is published.
        /// </summary>
        void Document_BeforePublish(Document sender,
                    umbraco.cms.businesslogic.PublishEventArgs e)
        {
            // log entry of event

umbraco.BusinessLogic.Log.Add(umbraco.BusinessLogic.LogTypes.Custom,
                     0,
                     "Document_BeforePublish: AutoExpireFaq STARTED");

            // Check to make sure that the node that is being published
            // is of Document Type FAQ
            if (sender.ContentType.Alias == "FAQ")
            {
```

```
umbraco.BusinessLogic.Log.Add(umbraco.BusinessLogic.LogTypes.Custom,
                        0,
                        "Document_BeforePublish: FAQ Doc Type matched");

                    // Check to make sure that that the expiration date
                    // is not already set.
                    // NOTE: ExpireDate corresponds to the Expiration
                    // date field in the properties tab
                    if (sender.ExpireDate != DateTime.MinValue &&
                      sender.ExpireDate < DateTime.Now)
                    {
umbraco.BusinessLogic.Log.Add(umbraco.BusinessLogic.LogTypes.Custom,
                        0,
                        "Document_BeforePublish: CANCELLED - FAQ
                         expiration date already set");
                        e.Cancel = true;
                    }
                    else
                    {
umbraco.BusinessLogic.Log.Add(umbraco.BusinessLogic.LogTypes.Custom,
                        0,
                        "Document_BeforePublish: FAQ expiration date set");

                        // Add 7 days to the current date and set that as
                        // the auto expiration date
                        sender.ExpireDate = DateTime.Now.AddDays(7);
                        sender.Save();
                    }
                }
            }
        }
}
```

LINQ TO UMBRACO

LINQ to Umbraco was developed to provide developers with an alternative way to work with Umbraco content nodes. It was designed from the start to provide an alternative to XSLT for developers who prefer working in a more traditional .NET environment using *POCOs* (*Plain Old CLR Object*) and *C#* or *VB.NET* syntax. As such, it's important to note that it's not meant to be a replacement for the `NodeFactory` or Document API (discussed earlier in this chapter). The default data provider for LINQ to Umbraco is the `NodeDataProvider`, which looks directly at the XML cache, much like the XSLT templates do. So, using LINQ to Umbraco out of the box means that you have access to the published nodes in a strongly typed read-only fashion.

If all you're trying to do is output a document type property on a page, then sticking with standard Umbraco display fields, namely the `<umbraco:item />` *tag that is covered in Chapter 4, is best.*

Getting Started with LINQ to Umbraco

To use LINQ to Umbraco in your project, you must export your document types to .NET. The process of exporting your document types is covered in Chapter 3. Doing this provides you with several data contexts from which to query the nodes you're looking for. Listing 12-18 goes back to the FAQ example and shows how to output nodes using LINQ method or query syntax.

Before you can dig into code samples, export your document types using the following settings, and add the generated class to your project in Visual Studio.

Use the following values for exporting the document types.

- DataContext Name: FAQ
- Namespace: UmbUsersGuide.Samples

LISTING 12-18: ListFaqs.ascx.cs

Available for download on Wrox.com

```
using System;
using System.Linq;
using System.Text;

namespace UmbUsersGuide.Samples.UserControls
{
    public partial class ListFaqs : System.Web.UI.UserControl
    {
        // Initialize a private FAQDataContext
        private FAQDataContext ctx;
        protected void Page_Load(object sender, EventArgs e)
        {
            // Tie the localized ctx variable to a new instatiation
            // of the Data Context
            ctx = new FAQDataContext();

            // Now, query the context using LINQ query syntax to
            // get some nodes. This returns an IEnumerable which
            // you can then use to loop over for display
            var techQuestionFaqs = from faq in ctx.FAQs
                                   orderby faq.UpdateDate descending
                                   where faq.Category == "1"
                                   select faq;

            var htmlOut = new StringBuilder();
            htmlOut.Append("<ul>");
            foreach (var faq in techQuestionFaqs)
            {
                htmlOut.AppendFormat("<li>{0}</li>", faq.NodeName);
            }
            htmlOut.Append("</ul>");

            // send the output to the view
```

continues

LISTING 12-18 *(continued)*

```
                _faqList.Text = htmlOut.ToString();
            }
        }
    }
```

Getting started using LINQ to Umbraco as an alternative to XSLT or the `NodeFactory` class is that simple.

Extending LINQ to Umbraco

LINQ to Umbraco was built with performance, flexibility, and testability in mind. So, although it's great as a potential replacement for XSLT or `NodeFactory`, it's also great for CRUD operations. Out of the box, it comes with a method called `SubmitChanges`, which are used to save changes to nodes in the database.

Trying to execute this method using the default `NodeDataProvider` *results in a* `System.NotSupportedException` *because this provider is read-only.*

To learn more about how to extend LINQ to Umbraco, including how to create your own providers, take a look at Aaron Powell's blog at `www.aaron-powell.com/`. Aaron is the father of LINQ to Umbraco and large part of the Umbraco core team.

TAKE HOME POINTS

This is a bog chapter and very heavy on programming concepts. Even if you're not an avid programmer with lots of experience, the examples in this chapter should start you on your way to creating new content and working with existing content in your Umbraco installation. Here's what you should have learned in this chapter:

- Creating a macro in the Umbraco backoffice to render your .NET controls.
- How to tweak the code examples to your needs (you're provided a full-blown Visual Studio solution and a project with code samples that you can download at www. `wrox.com`).
- Leveraging the power of .NET in your XSLT macros using XSLT extensions.
- Working with Umbraco's event model and examples on how you can implement custom hooks to work with your content, media, and more.

PART III
Deploying, Troubleshooting, and Sample Applications

13

Deploying to a Production Installation

- What should you consider when deploying to a production installation?
- How do you leverage the Umbraco packager?
- How do you handle media items?
- What are the steps for syncing databases between environments?
- What are the Courier tools and how do you use them?

Deploying your Umbraco website is going to be an important part of showcasing your hard work. You have a number of things to think about and steps to take in order to make sure that your installation goes smoothly. This chapter provides an overview of the options available to you when planning and executing your deployment. It also provides an overview of how to work with Courier, which is an Umbraco-licensed add-on for deploying to and syncing with multiple environments.

PLANNING CONSIDERATIONS

To make your deployment and management of multiple environments as worry-free as possible, developing a process and sticking to it is important. In short, you must think about basically four components for a first-time production deployment. In general, these align nicely with the installation of Umbraco because you are simply moving the entire site from your development environment to the production system.

1. **Move/copy the database:** This process varies slightly depending on what database you chose to install Umbraco on. This chapter gives you all the dos and don'ts for working with SQL Server Express.

At the time of this writing, SQL Server (including Express), SQL Server CE, MySQL, and Vista DB are supported database engines.

2. **Transfer the Umbraco installation:** Transferring your Umbraco installation to the new server is as simple as compacting the files in your *webroot* into an archive and exploding that archive on the destination server. This also moves your media items, of course.
3. **Set up an IIS website.** You want to point it to your Umbraco installation webroot.

It's strongly recommended that you utilize the `<appSettings .../>` *portion of the* `web.config` *to set any environment specific attributes as opposed to hard-coding such values in your code. This is standard best practice and not specific to Umbraco, but makes your deployment process that much easier.*

4. **Configure any environment-specific changes in your `web.config` file.** For example, you'd configure the SMTP server for sending emails, the connection string for the database, and any other custom settings you may have.

Refer to Chapter 1 for detailed installation instructions and to Chapter 14 for troubleshooting issues that may come up during your deployment process.

You also have more technical challenges to think about if your website is going to be experiencing heavy load or is very large in terms of the number of nodes. If you take that into consideration, you may need to load balance your installation, which Umbraco supports out of the box. The topic of this book does not cover load balancing, but if you are interested in this topic, go to `http://umbraco.org/help-and-support/video-tutorials/umbraco-fundamentals/load-balancing` for detailed videos on how to configure your Umbraco installation for load balancing.

Once you have your installation in production, you will want to perform partial deployments for updates throughout the life-cycle of the website. The remainder of this chapter analyzes the options and provides you with an overview of each option. It also provides an overview of the Umbraco PRO tools that are available to make your life as an administrator much easier.

USING THE PACKAGER

Chapter 10 introduced you to the power of the packager and how it can help you to share the functionality of what you are developing as part of the Umbraco ecosystem. It also does a lot more than that. It can be your friend when deploying your production website for the first time and even when deploying updates. It's especially useful in cases where you have limited access to the hosting environment where your production system lives in terms of FTP or remote desktop access. Again, refer to Chapter 10 for a step-by-step guide to creating your own packages.

For organization and planning purposes you should version your deployment packages in the name. Although the packager can be used for both initial production deployment and for updates, a recommendation is to use it only when deploying for the first time in a blank Umbraco installation. This avoids any potential for node duplication or node ID confusion and the potential to overwrite existing resources with unintentional changes.

Using Umbraco PRO tools, such as Courier, you can remove the ambiguities and risks of things such as node ID mismatches and overwriting critical assets during deployments. Check out the end of this chapter for more details on how to use Courier.

So, to use the packager follow these simple steps:

1. Navigate to the Developers section of Umbraco. Right-click the Packages node and click the Create menu item.
2. In the Create dialog, name your package, in this case something like what is shown in Figure 13-1. Click Create.

FIGURE 13-1

3. Click the Properties tab and fill in all the properties of the package, as shown in Figure 13-2.

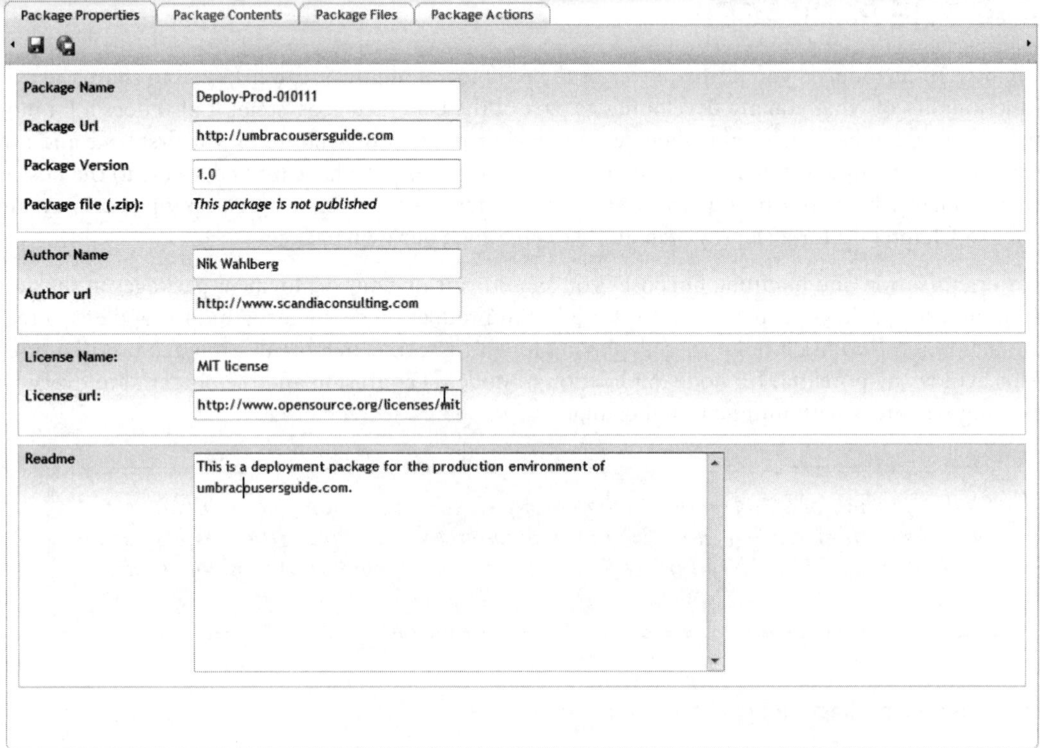

FIGURE 13-2

4. In the Package Contents tab, select *all* the checkboxes except the ones listed under Data Types, unless you have custom data types that need to be deployed as well. Your selections should look like those in Figure 13-3.

5. In the packager, media items are not treated as nodes of content. As such, you must manually include them by selecting the entire media folder along with any images and script files that make up the templates of your Umbraco website. Make all these selections in the Package Files tab, as shown in Figure 13-4.

6. Publish your package and download it to your computer by clicking the Download link, which becomes available in the Package Properties tab next to the Package file (.zip) field after you publish your package.

Deploying the content is now as easy as installing a local package in the Packages node of the Developers section. For details on installing local packages, see Chapter 10.

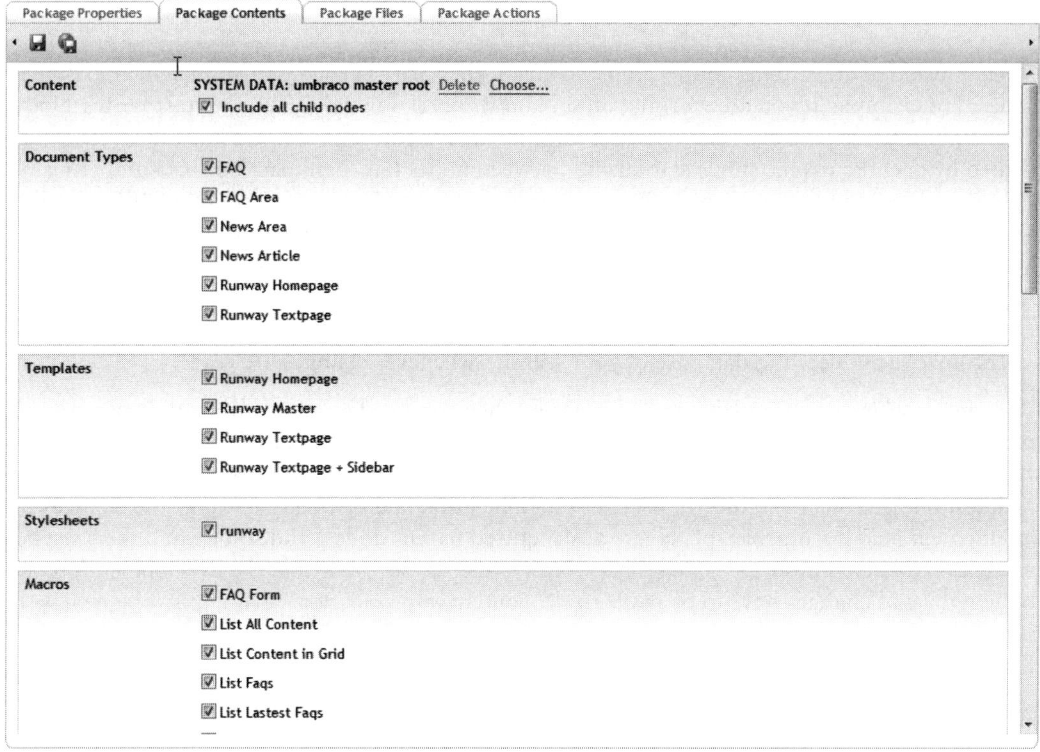
Package Properties
Package Contents
Package Files
Package Actions
Content
SYSTEM DATA: umbraco master root Delete Choose...
Include all child nodes
Document Types
FAQ
FAQ Area
News Area
News Article
Runway Homepage
Runway Textpage
Templates
Runway Homepage
Runway Master
Runway Textpage
Runway Textpage + Sidebar
Stylesheets
runway
Macros
FAQ Form
List All Content
List Content in Grid
List Faqs
List Lastest Faqs

FIGURE 13-3

Package Properties
Package Contents
Package Files
Package Actions
Remember: .xslt and .ascx files for your macros will be added automaticly, but you will still need to add assemblies, images and script files manually to the list below.
Absolute path to file (ie: /bin/umbraco.bin)
/media
Delete
/scripts
Delete
Add
Load control after installation (ex: /usercontrols/installer.ascx)

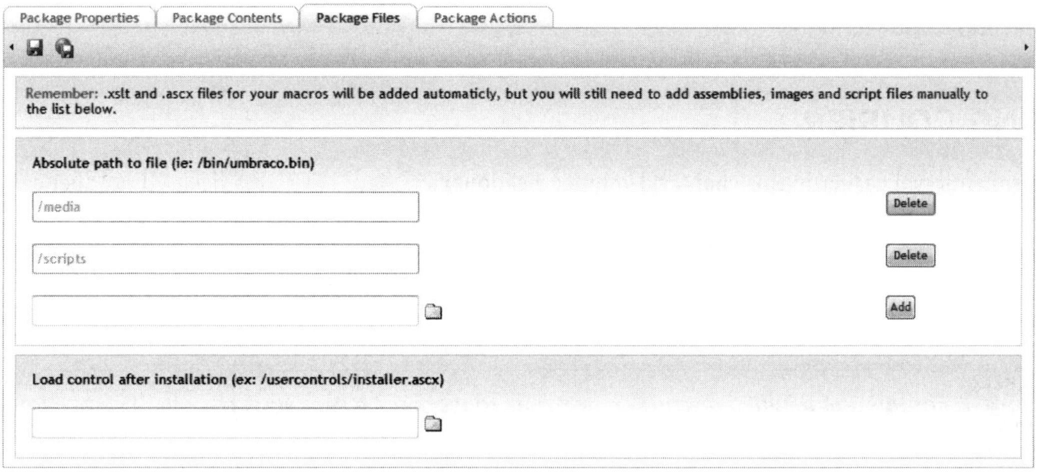

FIGURE 13-4

DATABASE SYNCHRONIZING

When you add content nodes to the Umbraco CMS, they are assigned unique incremental numeric values. For example, if you are working off a blank Umbraco install, you may start with a Node ID of 1070 when you create your very first node in the system. As nodes are added this ID is incremented by one; the parent/child relationship between nodes has no impact on this numbering. A child node could have an ID of 1100, whereas its parent node may have an ID of 1085. It all depends on when the node was created and what the max ID number was at the time of creation. When Umbraco relates nodes to one another and when it stores the path to each node, these IDs play a very important role to the hierarchy of the website. So, keeping the IDs in sync from one environment to the next is important. To preserve this hierarchical relationship, the best practice is to synchronize the underlying database of your website whenever changes are made.

An example where synchronizing makes sense is when you need to add additional document types to your installation but need to retain changes made to the content tree. To preserve the content structure of the production website, you must first synchronize your development database with the latest information contained in production. When that is done, you can make the changes in development (add document type, create any required parent nodes, and so on), and then resync the production database after the changes have been made. In the event that the development process is too lengthy and changes have to be made to the content in production during this time, you would have to keep track of the changes and use a combination of manual updates and the packager (see the previous section) to make the changes and make sure they are synced in both environments.

The best practice for performing a hot sync of the database is to create a full backup of the site using SQL Server Management Studio Express (or the full version if you have access to that). The process creates a `.bak` file that you can use to simply restore the database in the target environment. Synchronizing the environments using this method allows you to operate without causing any intentional downtime.

USING COURIER

As mentioned earlier in this chapter, Umbraco headquarters have released a licensed product called Courier. This tool takes the pains out of migrating content from a staging or development environment to a production environment. Courier is available for a small license fee. You can download this product, along with other PRO offerings, directly from the Umbraco repository found in the packages node in the Developer section of your Umbraco installation.

For tips and detailed instructions on how to work with packages, refer to Chapter 10.

In a nutshell, Umbraco Courier consists of the following features and benefits:

- **Right-click is all you have to learn.** Courier lets you deploy content directly from the context menu. All you need to do is right-click the content you want to transfer and select the

Transfer to Staging option. Courier will validate all dependencies and make sure that the transfer only happens if there are no conflicts between the two environments.

- **Detects all images.** Without any configuration needed, Courier will automatically discover any images associated with your content and transfer those without your needing to think about it. It even knows about any variations of the image you use and makes sure that the correct sizes and thumbnails are transferred.
- **No more ID conflicts.** Although content IDs between environments might change, it's not something you'll need to spend time on. Courier knows about your site structure and will automatically restore links and other ID-based references so they match the new environment.
- **Secure content deployment.** Courier makes it possible to have your develop and staging environments completely separated from production. This means that you can remove the backoffice from your website completely and manage your website from within the firewall and with a database completely separated from your live website.
- **Publish directly from staging.** Not only content and media transfer are supported, but secure publishing is in the package as well. This means that when your next big marketing campaign or product launch is ready and approved, it can go live with a single click.
- **Completely configurable.** Courier comes with a wide set of configurable options, which ensures that even highly sophisticated and custom-built data types can be supported and updated, too. Configuring Courier is as simple as updating an XML file once.

The obvious requirement for using Courier is that you have at least two environments to work with. The first is your source server and the second, where the content is being sent, is the host. Both of these environments must have Courier installed and configured for the transfer to take place. To install the product, simply follow these steps:

1. Navigate to the Developers section of the Umbraco backoffice and expand the Packages node.
2. Expand the Umbraco package Repository and click Umbraco PRO.
3. Click Courier in the resulting right-hand pane.
4. Click Download and Install Package and follow the instructions to install the product.
5. When the installer finishes, Courier asks you to set up the environment configuration by providing a host name (where the content should be sent) and an identifier of that environment. Figure 13-5 shows a sample setup.
6. Click Update Configuration, and you are done.
7. Repeat these steps for the production environment, skipping Step 5 because production will be the host and not the source server.

After the installation is complete, all you need to do is right-click the node that you want to deploy to the production environment and click Transfer to Production. Courier takes care of all the associated images and resources, gives you an option to publish the content on the host server, and displays a confirmation when the task is complete, as shown in Figure 13-6. Any transferred content is recorded as an edit and can be rolled back on the host as it would with a manual change.

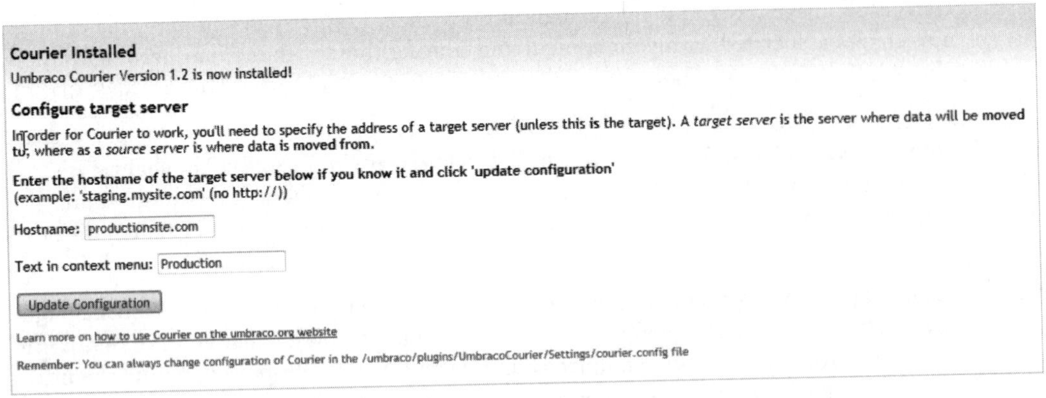

Courier Installed

Umbraco Courier Version 1.2 is now installed!

Configure target server

In order for Courier to work, you'll need to specify the address of a target server (unless this is the target). A *target server* is the server where data will be moved to, where as a *source server* is where data is moved from.

Enter the hostname of the target server below if you know it and click 'update configuration'
(example: 'staging.mysite.com' (no http://))

Hostname: productionsite.com

Text in context menu: Production

Update Configuration

Learn more on how to use Courier on the umbraco.org website

Remember: You can always change configuration of Courier in the /umbraco/plugins/UmbracoCourier/Settings/courier.config file

FIGURE 13-5

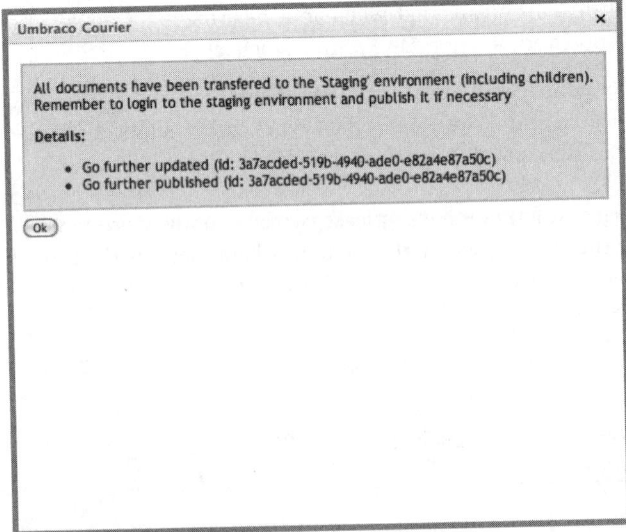

FIGURE 13-6

TAKE HOME POINTS

Deploying is probably the least glamorous aspect of working on websites, but a necessary evil nonetheless. Coming out of this chapter you should be comfortable with the following:

- Deploying your site for the first time to a production environment.
- Using the packager to move files between different environments.
- Working with your database to synchronize content and avoid node ID conflicts.
- Using Courier to deploy changes from one environment to the next.

14

Troubleshooting

- How do you troubleshoot installation issues?
- What should you consider when you use shared hosting?
- How does Umbraco handle and log errors?
- How do you use 404 pages and page redirects?

As with all complex, modern software, you are likely to encounter an issue or two along the way with your Umbraco experience. Almost without fail you will find the solution to the issue to be simple, but only after you understand what the issue is. In this chapter you'll learn techniques for identifying issues with Umbraco and how to determine whether the solution is a configuration-related change or a more involved solution.

With nearly 100,000 sites using Umbraco, and hundreds of thousands of installations, a very good chance exists that the issue you encounter will have already been encountered by other Umbraco users as well. Although this may be little consolation in itself, a strong likelihood exists that another Umbraco user has discovered the solution to the issue and has posted it on the Umbraco Community Forum found at `http://our.umbraco.org`.

INSTALLATION TROUBLESHOOTING

By the time you have arrived at this chapter you have probably already successfully installed Umbraco, perhaps even multiple times. Then comes the time when your Umbraco installation fails. What to do? A methodical approach to identifying the issue goes a long way toward a quick solution.

Unless the issue is very obvious, perhaps an error message that states the problem, review the following checklist to help identify the cause:

- Are file permissions set correctly?
- Is Umbraco configured in a virtual directory?

- Does the IIS application pool .NET Runtime version match the Umbraco .NET runtime version?
- Are all of the files present?

Each item of this checklist is examined in greater detail in the following sections.

Are File Permissions Set Correctly?

File permissions are by far the most common issue with Umbraco installations. The identity of the IIS application pool must have sufficient permissions to be able to read, write, and modify certain files in your Umbraco instance. For local and development installations, granting the IIS application pool identity read, write, and modify rights to all files located in your instance is sufficient. For production sites, best practice is to grant the IIS application pool identity more granular rights because not all files should have these permissions applied.

You can locate the identity of an IIS application pool by viewing the Advanced Settings of the application pool from IIS Manager (see Figure 14-1). On most IIS installations, the IIS Application Pool identity will be set to `ApplicationPoolIdentity` or `Network Service`. In the case of `ApplicationPoolIdentity`, IIS will dynamically create the account when an application pool is started, and therefore this account provides the most security for your applications.

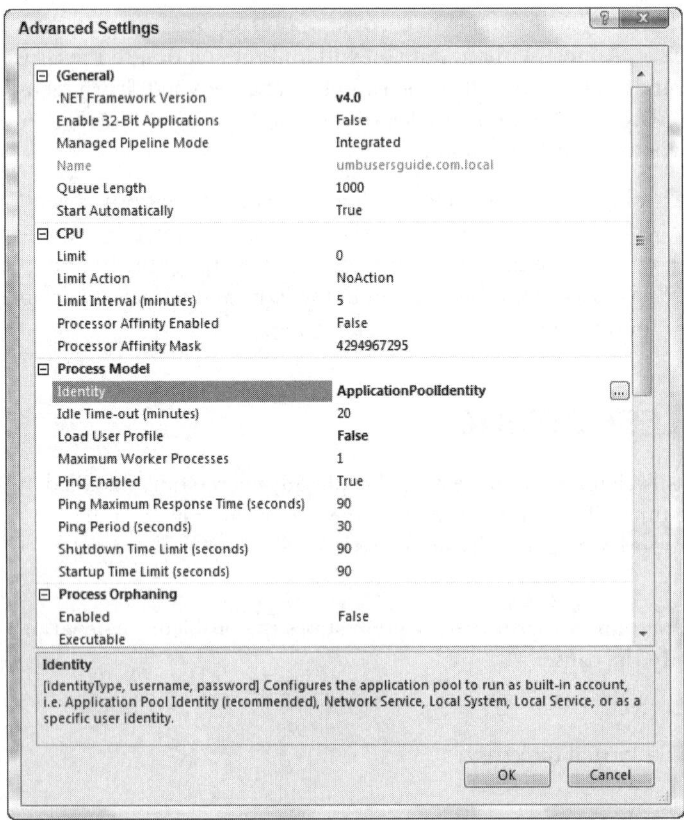

FIGURE 14-1

If you use the Microsoft Web Platform Installer to install Umbraco, these settings will be configured appropriately by the tool and you will not need to adjust the settings.

Is Umbraco Configured in a Virtual Directory?

Umbraco is not intended to be run from a virtual directory. From IIS Manager a virtual directory is easily identified as a subfolder under an IIS site. Although Umbraco may mostly function when configured in a virtual directory, you may encounter unexpected behavior with this configuration. You can remove the virtual directory from beneath an IIS site and create a new IIS site with the Umbraco installation location as the home directory.

Does the IIS Application Pool .NET Runtime Version Match the Umbraco .NET Runtime Version?

With the various versions of the .NET Runtime (1.1, 2.0, 3.5, 4.0) and the various .NET Runtime versions targeted by Umbraco (2.0/3.5, 4.0) it's no wonder some confusion surrounds this issue. A common symptom of this issue is a very generic error displayed in the browser, "Service Unavailable." The solution to this issue is very simple. Check the Umbraco version you have, which is clearly indicated by the name of the Umbraco Installation Package, and make sure it matches the .NET Runtime version. Typically the .NET Runtime version is indicated as the last part of the name, "Umbraco 4.5.2 for .NET 4." You can find the .NET Runtime version for the IIS application pool from the Basic Settings dialog of the application pool's settings (see Figure 14-2).

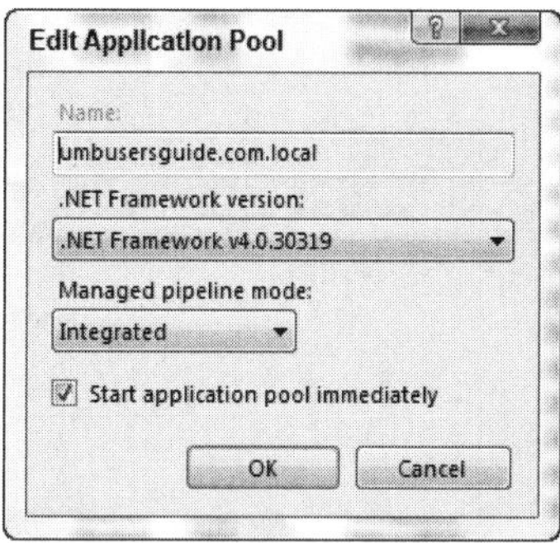

FIGURE 14-2

Are All the Files Present?

If you installed Umbraco with the Microsoft Web Platform Installer, then not having all the files is very unlikely. However, if you installed Umbraco from a downloaded installation package that you extracted to a local directory on your web server, this issue is very common. Some recent versions of Microsoft Windows with specific User Access Control settings restrict the type of files that can be extracted from a .ZIP file from an unknown source, such as a website. Although this behavior is designed to protect operating systems from malicious files, it also protects some operating systems from files you want, such as Umbraco installation files.

A common symptom is that the Umbraco user interface will load, but it will be missing some of the layout elements and not all items in the content tree will display. The solution is to simply unblock the Umbraco Installation package from the file properties dialog before extracting the files to the target location on the file system (see Figure 14-3).

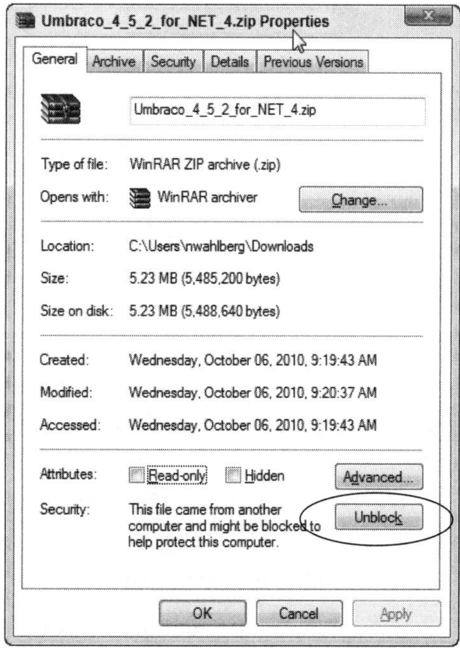

FIGURE 14-3

Database-Related Installation Issues

Fortunately, database-related installation issues are some of the easiest to identify and fix. Generally, an error message indicates that Umbraco cannot connect to the specified database and the Umbraco Installation Wizard checks for a valid connection before completing the installation. Umbraco expects the database, usually a Microsoft SQL Server database, to allow SQL authentication. However, the default installation settings for Microsoft SQL Server have SQL authentication disabled.

To enable SQL authentication, simply update the setting for Server Authentication to SQL Server and Windows Authentication Mode from the Server Properties dialog for the Microsoft SQL Server instance you are using (see Figure 14-4). To access this property dialog, follow these steps:

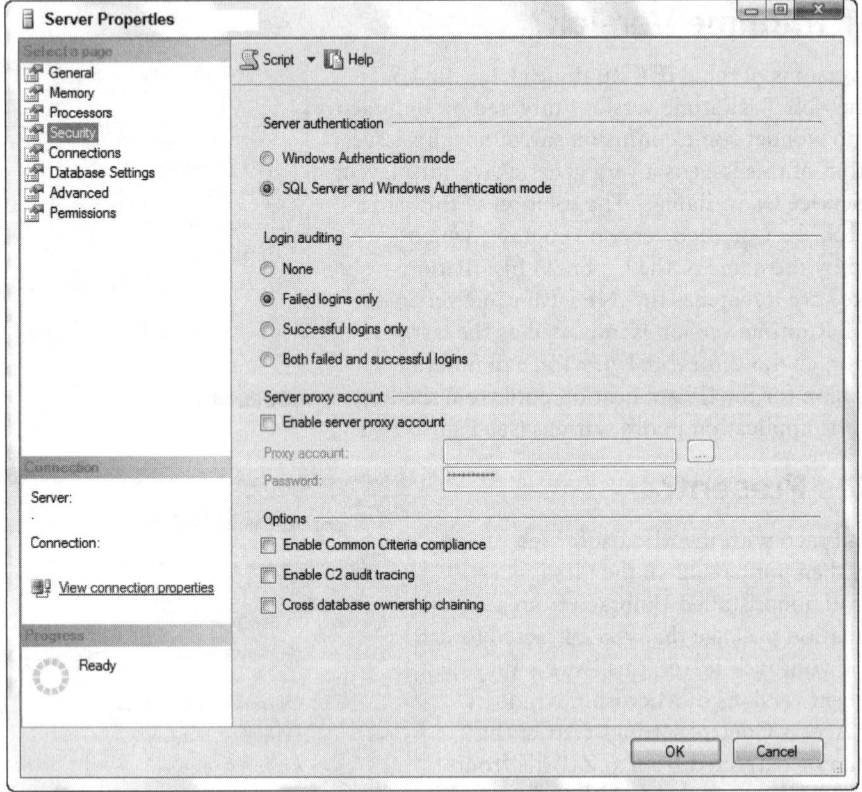

FIGURE 14-4

1. Open SQL Server Management Studio and login as a Server Administrator (usually this is the built-in Windows user account or the SQL "sa" account).
2. Right-click the SQL instance you are using, select Properties from the menu, and then select the Security option from the Select a Page list.
3. Make updates as required.
4. When you're finished, click the OK button to update SQL Server with your changes.

Umbraco stores database connection information in the `web.config` file, under the *appSettings* key *umbracoDbDSN*. A typical connection string value for this key is:

```
<add key="umbracoDbDSN" value="server=./SQLEXPRESS;database=umbDB;
user id=umbDBUser;password=secretPassword" />
```

This key must contain valid connection information in order for Umbraco to be able to connect to your database. Using the values from the key and Microsoft SQL Server Management Studio, you can connect to the specified database. If you cannot, Umbraco cannot connect either. Carefully check the values to make sure they are valid.

When you are installing Umbraco in an environment where you may not have complete control of the database settings and users, you may not have access to the database administrator password. In this case the input fields in the Microsoft Web Platform, and other tools, for the database administrator name and password will not be applicable. In this case, you will need a SQL Server login account that has rights to create a new database. In addition, you'll need a SQL Server login account that has rights to create a new login. If you do not have a SQL Server login account with these rights, which you may not in a shared hosting scenario, you should ask the host's support team to create an empty database and assign a login to the database for your use. After you have this information, you can update the input fields and successfully connect to your Umbraco database.

SHARED HOSTING CONSIDERATIONS

If you are using a shared web host for your Umbraco site, you will no doubt notice that most of the preceding troubleshooting tactics are not available to you. This makes your job of identifying the issue more difficult, but keep in mind that the issues are very likely the same even if the environment is not. Most hosts provide you with a control panel or dashboard to make changes to your website and database. Using these you can accomplish solutions discussed earlier.

Even if you are using a shared host for your Umbraco website, installing the Microsoft SQL Server Management Studio (full or Express version) locally on your PC is still advantageous because you'll find it invaluable when working with database issues. All hosts provide connection information to allow you to connect your Umbraco database remotely from your local PC.

ERROR HANDLING AND LOGGING

Umbraco has a reputation for generous error logging; some even say that Umbraco's verbose error and event logging is too much. When you have an issue with your Umbraco site, the error log is an invaluable tool in helping you discover the cause. By default, Umbraco creates a log entry for nearly all events, errors, and custom logging routines, but you can adjust what Umbraco logs by updating the log configuration.

As Umbraco is really an ASP.NET application at heart, errors that are generated within the ASP .NET runtime, and not handled by an error handling routine, will generate an entry (or two) in the Windows event log. This log can be hugely beneficial to developers creating custom code for

Umbraco and also for helping to identify issues in third-party packages and code used as part of your Umbraco site.

The Umbraco Error Log

The Umbraco error log is the table `umbracoLog` in your Umbraco site's database. Because the log is located in the database it offers another good reason to have the Microsoft SQL Server Management Studio installed because viewing the table is much easier. A number of Umbraco packages are also available that allow you to view and manage the contents of the `umbracoLog` table. You can find these packages in the Projects section of the Umbraco Community site (`http://our.umbraco.org/projects/`).

As mentioned earlier, the Umbraco error log creates entries for nearly all errors and events in Umbraco. You can change what Umbraco logs by updating the logging section in the `/config/umbracoSettings.config` file for your site. Here is the default setting for the logging section:

```
<logging>
    <enableLogging>true</enableLogging>
    <enableAsyncLogging>true</enableAsyncLogging>
    <disabledLogTypes>
      <!-- <logTypeAlias>[alias-of-log-type-in-lowercase]</logTypeAlias> -->
    </disabledLogTypes>
  </logging>
```

As a general rule, enabling logging in Umbraco is a good practice. However, in situations where a high-performing site is of the utmost importance you may choose to disable logging and gain a performance boost. To disable logging simply set the following key value to `false`:

```
<enableLogging>true</enableLogging>
```

For a production version of your site, disabling some of the types of entries that Umbraco logs is a good practice. Which you decide to disable will depend on your particular requirements and, especially, on the amount of errors your site may generate. The available log type aliases you may choose to disable include the following:

```
<logTypeAlias>assigndomain</logTypeAlias>
<logTypeAlias>copy</logTypeAlias>
<logTypeAlias>debug</logTypeAlias>
<logTypeAlias>delete</logTypeAlias>
<logTypeAlias>login</logTypeAlias>
<logTypeAlias>loginfailure</logTypeAlias>
<logTypeAlias>logout</logTypeAlias>
<logTypeAlias>move</logTypeAlias>
<logTypeAlias>new</logTypeAlias>
<logTypeAlias>notfound</logTypeAlias>
<logTypeAlias>open</logTypeAlias>
<logTypeAlias>packagerinstall</logTypeAlias>
<logTypeAlias>packageruninstall</logTypeAlias>
<logTypeAlias>ping</logTypeAlias>
<logTypeAlias>publicaccess</logTypeAlias>
<logTypeAlias>publish</logTypeAlias>
<logTypeAlias>rollback</logTypeAlias>
```

```
<logTypeAlias>save</logTypeAlias>
<logTypeAlias>scheduledtask</logTypeAlias>
<logTypeAlias>sendtopublish</logTypeAlias>
<logTypeAlias>sendtotranslate</logTypeAlias>
<logTypeAlias>sort</logTypeAlias>
<logTypeAlias>unpublish</logTypeAlias>
```

You will generally leave the following log type aliases enabled:

```
<logTypeAlias>system</logTypeAlias>
<logTypeAlias>error</logTypeAlias>
<logTypeAlias>custom</logTypeAlias>
```

The Windows Event Log

The Windows event log contains entries for errors generated by Umbraco, third-party code, and custom code that run in the .NET Runtime. Generally the errors are logged in the Application section of the Windows logs. You can view the Windows event log from the Windows Event Viewer, a Microsoft Management Console plug-in.

An especially helpful tactic is to create a filtered view of the Application log that displays only entries where the source is from the .NET Runtime and the ASP.NET Runtime version that your Umbraco site is using (see Figure 14-5).

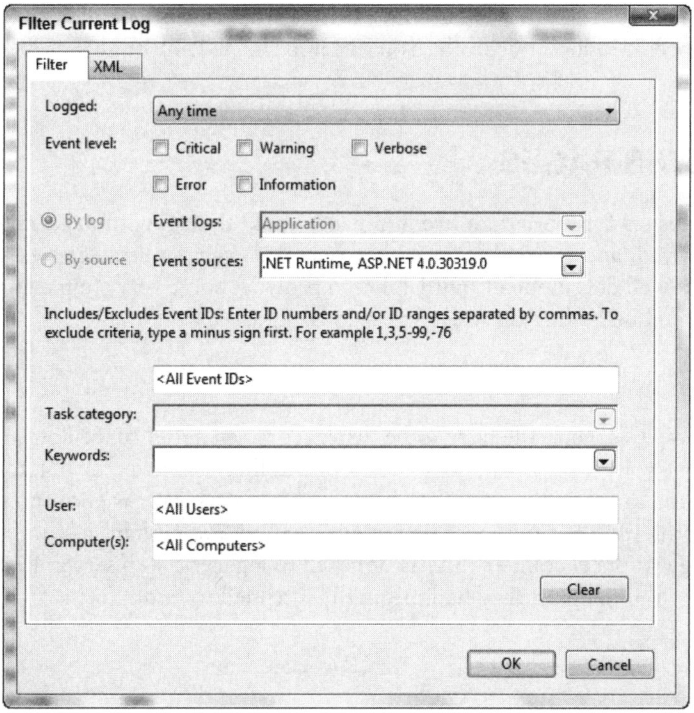

FIGURE 14-5

The most helpful information in a Windows event log entry is generally found in the Exception Information section of the entry's details. The following is an example entry that shows the error is originating from a failed attempt to load the `Umbraco.Forms.UI.Pages.FeedProxy` class:

```
...
Exception information:
    Exception type: HttpParseException
    Exception message: Could not load type 'Umbraco.Forms.UI.Pages.FeedProxy'.
...
```

A Note about XSLT and Errors

Both of the preceding sections about the Umbraco error log and the Windows event log deal primarily with errors that occur in the execution of .NET code. Although the Umbraco error log also contains entries for Umbraco events and will, generally, contain entries for Umbraco errors, errors encountered in the execution of XSLT are not captured by either of the logs. In the case of XSLT, an XSLT specific error will generally be output to the browser. By default, the error output from Umbraco is the rather unhelpful "Error parsing XSLT file: \xslt\somexslt.xslt."

Given the behavior of XSLT and errors, the best approach is to carefully create your XSLT so that proactive error handling is included, such as checking for empty values or unexpected input. Beyond what you can anticipate occurring, your XSLT might also contain a routine to output a default value if the expected behavior fails.

You can use the XSLT Visualizer from the Umbraco XSLT Editor to test negative input and verify that your XSLT will handle unexpected values gracefully. You can find the XSLT Visualizer on the toolbar of the Umbraco XSLT Editor.

MOVED AND MISSING WEB PAGES

Anyone who has been creating websites for more than five minutes has had to deal with pages that can't be found, pages that have moved, and pages that have been renamed. Various strategies exist for dealing with these constants in web development, but Umbraco provides some very simple and flexible methods for dealing with and managing these ever-present conditions.

404 Pages

Umbraco provides a very simple way to specify the page to be displayed when a 404 (page not found) error is encountered. In the `/config/umbracoSettings.config` file, set the `error404` key value to the ID of the Umbraco node to use as your page to display when a 404 error is encountered. A good practice is to create a helpful 404 page that contains site navigation and perhaps a search form for your site. When your site visitors encounter this, as opposed to a generic web server 404 page, they are much more likely to find the page they had originally intended to find.

```
<errors>
  <error404>1010</error404>
</errors>
```

The page specified in the `error404` key will apply to all sites within your Umbraco instance, regardless of the culture settings for each site. When you have multiple sites targeting different culture variants you can specify a unique page to be displayed for each site by setting the value of the associated `errorPage` key. The attribute culture defines which culture, and therefore which site, the page applies to. The culture value "default" indicates the key for sites that do not have an associated `errorPage` key.

```
<errors>
  <errorPage culture="default">1010</errorPage>
  <errorPage culture="en-US">2001</errorPage>
</errors>
```

Page Redirects

Umbraco provides several methods for handling page redirects when pages have moved or been renamed. One of the most flexible methods is to use the built-in URL rewriting feature provided by Umbraco's inclusion of the UrlRewriting.Net libraries. You create a redirect rule using UrlRewriting .Net by creating entries in the `/config/UrlRewriting.config` file. You have many options when using this method, all of which you can find at the project's website (`www.urlrewriting.net`). A sample 301 (permanent) redirect using UrlRewriting.Net follows:

```
<add name="301ReDirect"
          redirectMode="Permanent"
          ignoreCase="true"
          virtualUrl="^~/OldSection/(.*).aspx"
          destinationUrl="~/NewSection/$1.aspx" />
```

In addition to using UrlRewriting.Net and the associated entries in the `/config/UrlRewriting .config` file, Umbraco also has two built-in methods to manage page redirects. Both are enabled by creating Document Type properties with specific names and data types. Both enable 302 (temporary) redirects and, as such, are well suited to use by landing pages and content likely to be updated continuously. With both of these Umbraco redirect methods, the redirect will only occur if a value is supplied for the Document Type property, so you can safely create these properties for your document types and use them only as needed.

Using umbracoRedirect

To use `umbracoRedirect`, follow these simple instructions:

1. Create a property with the alias **umbracoRedirect** for the document type your page is using.
2. Select the Data Type of Content Picker.
3. Save your change.
4. From the Umbraco Content section, select the page from which you want to redirect and then set the value of the `umbracoRedirect` property by selecting the page to which you want to redirect.
5. Save and publish your changes.

The next time a site visitor loads the original page, a 302 redirect message is sent from the web server and the new page loads. With `umbracoRedirect`, the URL also updates in the visitor's browser.

Using umbracoInternalRedirectId

To use `umbracoInternalRedirectId` you follow the same procedure as with `umbracoRedirect`, except you should set the alias of the Document Type property to `umbracoInternalRedirectId`. In the case of `umbracoInternalRedirectId` the site visitor's browser will load the new page with a 302 redirect message sent from the web server. In this case, the URL will display the original URL in the visitor's browser.

TAKE HOME POINTS

In this chapter, you saw how to identify Umbraco issues and determine solutions. After reading this chapter, you should know how to:

- Use the installation issues checklist to quickly identify and correct installation related issues
- Use the Umbraco umbracoLog table and the Windows Event Log to identify issues with your Umbraco site
- For production sites, disable some of the default Umbraco logging by editing the `/config/umbracoSettings.config` file for your site
- Use the Umbraco XSLT Visualizer to verify that your XSLT works as expected and identify when it doesn't
- Set a default 404 page for your Umbraco site to give your site visitors a good experience when a page cannot be found
- Use the built-in Umbraco properties, `umbracoRedirect` and `umbracoInternalRedirectId`, to maintain your site's links when you make changes to page names or site structure

15

Sample Application: Classified Ads

- What will you get out of this chapter's sample application?
- What skills do you need going into this chapter?
- What features of Umbraco are implemented in this sample application?
- What does all this code do?

As a bonus to all the concepts that you learned reading through each and every chapter so diligently, this chapter gives you a take-home application that demonstrates a large number of the features that Umbraco supports. After all, some of you will be better at learning by looking at examples, and the sample application that you can download from the Wrox developer site will put the concepts to work using best practices and industry standards.

To download the code needed for this chapter please visit `www.wrox.com/WileyCDA/Section/id-105127.html` *and click the title of this book. The download page opens, where you can download both the Visual Studio solution for the underlying source of this sample application as well as the accompanying Umbraco 4.6.1 installation files needed to run the application on your local development environment. See the next section for more details.*

WHAT TO CONFIGURE FOR THIS EXAMPLE

This chapter provides you with a detailed walkthrough of what an Umbraco application might look like as a real-world example. The application is built to illustrate a lot of the features of Umbraco and is a classified ads submission and browsing application. You can apply the functionality demonstrated in this sample application to a variety of other implementations as well. The application should serve as a good example for you even if the Umbraco implementation that you are working on is not directly tied to classified ads.

You must configure three components to make this application run:

- Visual Studio Solution with all the code that supports the sample application.

If you do not have access to Visual Studio you can run and build this solution using Microsoft Webmatrix. You can find Webmatrix at `www.microsoft.com/web/webmatrix/`.

- Archives containing a complete install of Umbraco 4.6.1, including one of the freely available skins. This also includes all the customizations to installed templates, which are covered later in this chapter in "The Umbraco Installation Components" section.
- SQL Server database files for the Umbraco installation.

To get a refresher on how to deploy an Umbraco instance, see Chapter 13.

ASSUMPTIONS TO MAKE FOR THIS EXAMPLE

Although most of this book is not very technical, to get through this chapter, you must have a fair background in programming concepts. You should have working knowledge of the following concepts to get the most out of this sample application and accompanying code:

- C# .NET programming language and concepts
- XSLT for working with Umbraco macros
- XHTML and CSS
- Visual Studio integrated development environment
- General concepts such as installing and deploying web applications (including Microsoft IIS and Microsoft SQL Server)

In addition to these broader requirements, another assumption is that you have reviewed the totality of the chapters in this book. References to previous chapters are provided where necessary, but by now you should have a good foundation of the various Umbraco approaches and concepts.

VISUAL STUDIO FEATURES

The Visual Studio solution and associated project implement a wide array of the available Umbraco features to give you an example implementation that you can apply to concepts far outside the realm of classified ads. So, here's what the sample app covers in terms of Umbraco functionality:

- Nested master pages
- XSLT macros for outputting the content in various formats
- A custom .NET user control
- Document API for creating a node programmatically
- Event hooks to move and set node properties before the node is published
- Reading configuration files to avoid hard-coding values
- Custom data types in the backoffice and rendering them in your .NET user control

The functional features of the classified ads application are as follow:

- On the homepage a user can access the latest three submitted classified ads.
- The user can browse all the available classified ads grouped by the selected ad category and filtered by the expiration date (defaulted to 21 days from publication and set using the `BeforePublish` event).

For a list of all available event hooks, see Chapter 12.

- The user can submit a new ad to the system that you must first review in the Umbraco backoffice before it is published. When an editor clicks the Save & Publish button in the backoffice, the ad moves out of the unreviewed ads and then publishes.

THE UMBRACO INSTALLATION COMPONENTS

As you know by now an Umbraco installation is made from a series of components. In this section you'll read more about which ones make up this sample application and how they function in relation to your Umbraco installation.

Before you install, you need to configure your Visual Studio project to reference the following Umbraco libraries, as shown in Figure 15-1.

- businesslogic
- cms

- interfaces
- umbraco

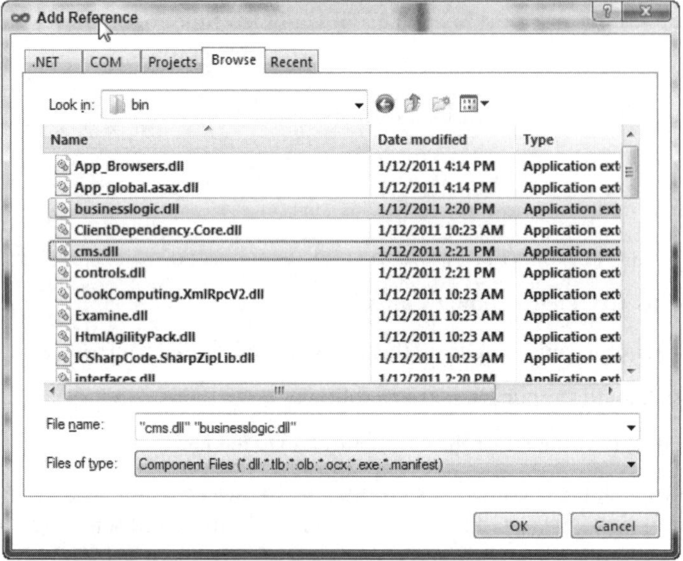

FIGURE 15-1

You can find the Umbraco libraries in your `<install root>/bin` *folder.*

Now that you have the libraries configured, you'll need to set up the document types, templates, macros, and event hooks that will run the example. These are outlined in the following sections.

Document Types

A few document types are needed to support the classified ads. This section shows how to use them and how they relate to the overall website. Table 15-1 describes each document type in detail.

Templates

Because you are leveraging one of the standard Umbraco skins, very little template work is involved in this sample application. Only one master page template is required in this case, and you use this master to output the details of a classified ad. Instead of starting from scratch and reworking the layout of the site, you can use the available Textpage template as a parent masterpage and inject the output from the `ClassfiedAdDetails.xslt` macro. Listing 15-1 contains the simple template code that was added to the `Textpage.master` file.

TABLE 15-1: Classified Ads Document Types

NAME	ALIAS	DESCRIPTION
Classified Ads	ClassifiedAds	This document type does not do very much other than act as a container for all the classified ads that are submitted via the custom .NET control or added in the Umbraco backoffice. Its function is to organize the content tree and make sure that classified ads are stored here and only in this particular content tree. The ClassifiedAds document type is set as an allowed child node of the Homepage document type, as shown in Figure 15-2.
Classified Ad	ClassifiedAd	This document type is the root of the classified ads and contains all the properties that you are asking the user to fill in as part of the submission process. This is also where the custom data types are used (this is covered in greater detail in the "Macros" section).
Unapproved Ads	UnapprovedAd	This tool is simply a container that houses ads when they are submitted using the custom .NET user control from the front-end of the website. This particular document type has one property set, which is one of the standard Umbraco properties `umbracoNaviHide` (you use this to hide the navigation).

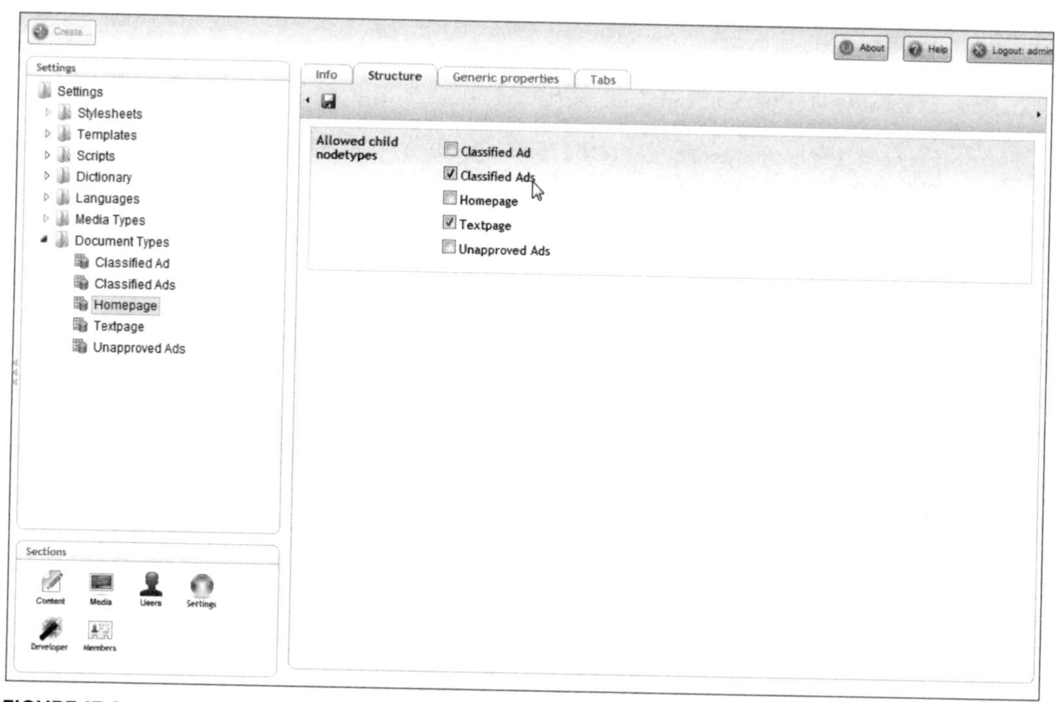

FIGURE 15-2

LISTING 15-1: Textpage.master

Available for download on Wrox.com

```
<%@ Master Language="C#" MasterPageFile="~/masterpages/umbMaster.master"
AutoEventWireup="true" %>
<asp:Content ID="Content1"
        ContentPlaceHolderID="cp_content" runat="server">
    <div id="subNavigation">
        <umbraco:Macro ID="Macro1" Alias="umb2ndLevelNavigation"
runat="server"></umbraco:Macro>
    </div>
    <div id="content" class="textpage">
        <div id="contentHeader">
          <h2><umbraco:Item ID="Item1" runat="server"
field="pageName"/></h2>
        </div>

        <umbraco:Item ID="Item2" runat="server" field="bodyText" />
        <asp:contentplaceholder id="ClassifiedDetails"
runat="server"></asp:contentplaceholder>
    </div>
</asp:Content>
```

The highlighted code snippet in Listing 15-1 shows what was added to the skin file. All this does is provide a target region to add the classified ad details to. Listing 15-2 shows what the added template, `ClassifiedAdDetails.master`, looks like.

LISTING 15-2: ClassifiedAdDetails.master

Available for download on Wrox.com

```
<%@ Master Language="C#"
   MasterPageFile="~/masterpages/umbTextpage.master"
   AutoEventWireup="true" %>
<asp:content ContentPlaceHolderId="ClassifiedDetails" runat="server">
    <umbraco:Macro Alias="ClassifiedAdDetails"
 runat="server"></umbraco:Macro>
</asp:content>
```

The key to this file is the inclusion of the `ClassifiedAdDetails` macro, which renders all the properties of the individual classified ad that is currently displayed to the user.

The code in Listing 15-2 could as well have been displayed using a bunch of `<umbraco:item .../>` *tags. But, because you have various fields that you must format (like dates and images), it's a cleaner separation and more readable format to output it in an XSLT macro.*

Macros

As mentioned, you need a number of macros to support this level of customization. The XSLT that you use is a straightforward output with various filters. The .NET user control is how the user submits an ad without logging into the Umbraco backoffice and how you can instruct Umbraco to programmatically create a node using the Umbraco document API. Table 15-2 describes the features and functionality of each of the XSLT-powered macros.

For more details on using XSLT-powered macros, see Chapter 11.

TABLE 15-2: XSLT Macros

MACRO	DESCRIPTION
`ClassifiedAdDetails.xslt`	This macro displays each document type property from the Ad Detail tab. In addition to simply displaying straight values, it also formats the publication date and formats the optionally submitted ad image.
`ClassifiedAdsLatest.xslt`	To display the three latest ads that were added and approved, this XSLT macro does a few things. It used the `<xsl:sort ../>` tag to sort the retrieved nodes by the updated date in descending order (newest to oldest). It also restricts the output of the top three nodes of the nodeset that was returned from the `xsl:for-each select` statement by comparing the `current position()` in the loop to make sure that it is less than or equal to 3. Notice, too, that the selection of the original nodeset includes the XSLT extension `GetXmlAll()`. This means you can place this macro anywhere on the site and it always returns the classified ads without having to worry about where they live in the content hierarchy. The returned nodeset is also filtered by specifying that the `name()` should be equal to `ClassifiedAd`. This ensures that you are only returning classified ad nodes.
`ClassifiedAdsListing.xslt`	This macro is the most complex of the three because it uses what is referred to as the Muenchian method for grouping the output of classified ads by the specified ad category. This list is not filtered other than to compare the ad expiration date to today's date to make sure that it is greater than or equal to today. Any ads older than today should not appear. The output of the list also includes a thumbnail version of the optional ad image. A bit of jQuery shows and hides this image. The jQuery code is available in the `scandia-bll.js` script file, which you can find in the Visual Studio solution in the `scripts` folder.

To get more details on the Muenchian method, see Chapter 5. For more on grouping, see Chapter 11.

The .NET portion of this application takes care of creating the submitted classified ads and uses the Umbraco document API to accomplish this task. Table 15-3 provides an overview of what each component does in the `ClassifiedAd` .NET user control–powered macro.

TABLE 15-3: ClassifiedAd .NET Macro

USER CONTROL FILE	DESCRIPTION
`ClassifiedAd.ascx`	This file displays the classified ad submission form and contains nothing Umbraco specific at all. The code in this file is standard .NET controls and form validation. The Submit button executes the `PostBack` event, and the code-behind takes it from there.
`ClassifiedAd.ascx.cs`	This file is also known as the code-behind file. It is where all the business logic is executed and, more importantly, where the Umbraco-specific logic takes place.

You must pay attention to several things in the `ClassifiedAd ascx.cs` file:

- **Public Properties:** The properties defined in the class scope of this file are used to capture the macro parameters that are set in the Umbraco macro. The code uses these values for storing the submitted classified ad in the right place in the content tree and also for storing the accompanying image if one is uploaded.
- **Reading Configurations:** Lines 30–44 are all about reading the configuration file that is located in the `<install root>/config` folder.
- **Display Custom Data Type Values:** Lines 46–78 query Umbraco for the custom data types and loop over the returned XML to parse and set list items for the HTML form.
- **Creating the Classified Ad:** The `submit_click` method does all the heavy lifting for creating the Umbraco node. Line 87 calls the document API and creates the document using the public properties passed in using the macro parameters, as well as locally set parameters. Each property is then saved to the newly created document via the `getProperty` method. You then skip the publishing of the new document because you want it to be reviewed in the backoffice first. Finally, you see a redirect to the Thank You page, which was also passed in using the macro parameters.

See Appendix D for details on how to work with Umbraco data types.

Event Hooks

Chapter 12 covers the Umbraco event model. In the sample application, you tap into the event hooks made available to you when a node is published (or in this case before it's published).

The code folder in the sample application Visual Studio project contains the code that executes when a node is published, as shown in Figure 15-3.

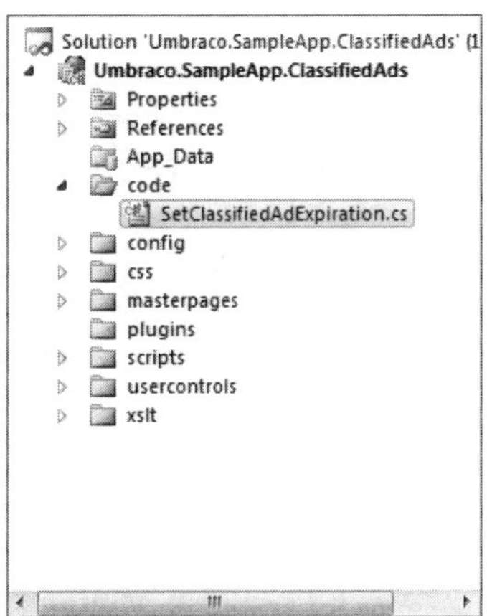

FIGURE 15-3

A couple of things to note when you open this file:

- The `SetClassifiedAdExpiration` class extends `umbraco.BusinessLogic.ApplicationBase`. Extending this class forces Umbraco to run it every time an action is performed in the Umbraco backoffice. This is what allows you to tap into the Umbraco event hooks and inject functionality to the backoffice without rewriting or changing the Umbraco source code. Cool, huh? The code in this case attaches to the `umbraco.cms.businesslogic.web.Document.BeforePublish` event.
- Make sure that the published node is of document type `ClassifiedAd`. If it's not, then the process continues.
- Make sure that the parent of the published node is currently the Unreviewed Ads node, as shown in Figure 15-4.

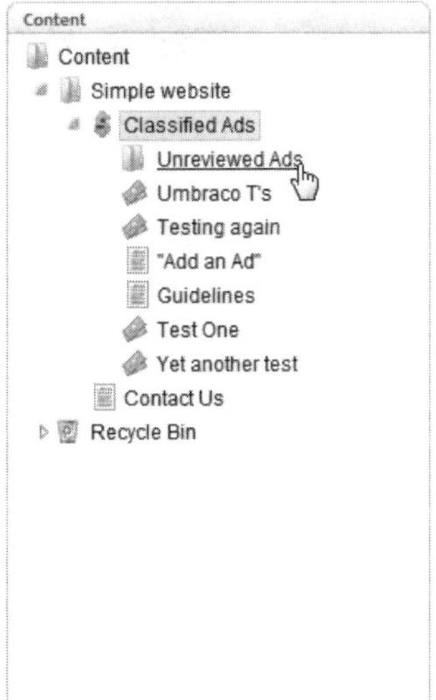

FIGURE 15-4

All this code executes when a user clicks the Save & Publish button located in the top toolbar in the Umbraco backoffice.

Leveraging the `umbraco.BusinessLogic.Log` *class when working with events is very important. This registers entries in the umbracoLog table with messages that you specify. Without these log table entries, troubleshooting an event issue is difficult because you have no indication of the event taking place just by looking at the backoffice. You can find an example of this on line 28 in the* `SetClassifiedAdExpiration.cs` *class.*

Of course, many other things can happen in this type of event hook that have not been implemented here; for example, sending an email notification to the user who submitted the ad with a message that the ad is now live.

PUTTING IT ALL TOGETHER

All these moving parts are put together in the sample Umbraco site used in this chapter. Figure 15-5 shows the result of the classified listing.

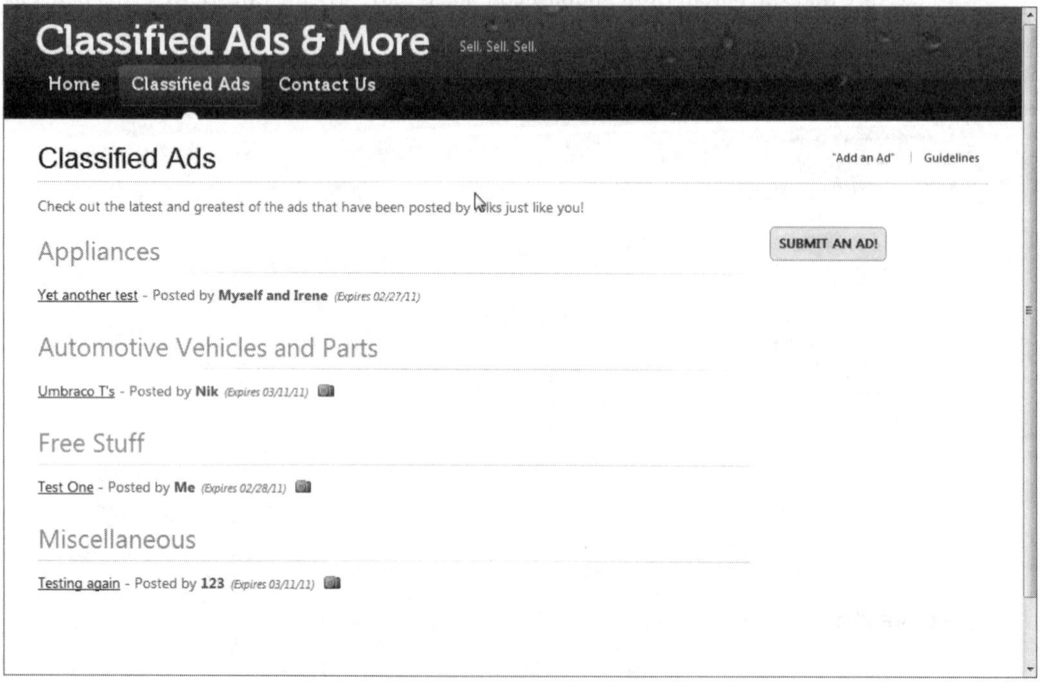

FIGURE 15-5

To run your application, follow the instructions in Chapter 13 to deploy the downloaded Umbraco installation and associated SQL server database. Don't forget to check out Chapter 1 for references on how to configure your IIS website and other installation tricks.

TAKE HOME POINTS

This final chapter ties together all the functionality and features that have been discussed throughout the book. The sample Visual Studio solution and the complete Umbraco website should serve as a blue-print for you when you build your first few projects. In short, here's what you have learned in this chapter.

- Working with Umbraco in Visual Studio
- Leveraging the Umbraco event model to extend the backoffice functionality
- Creating Umbraco content nodes using the Document API
- Outputting content via XSLT files and .NET masterpage templates

PART IV
Appendixes

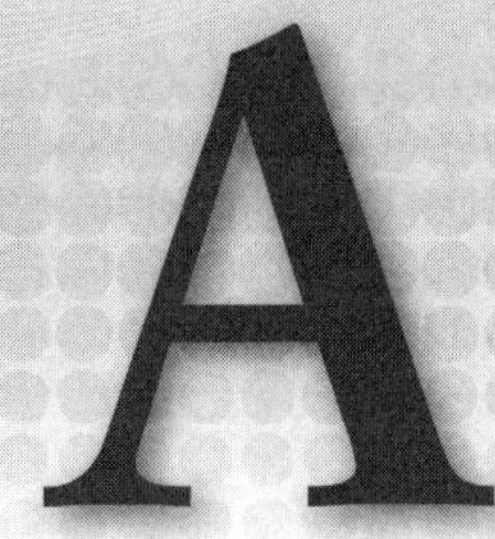

Upgrading an Existing Installation

- What are the steps for upgrading?
- How do you back up your existing installation?
- How do you check package compatibility?
- How do you copy the right files?
- How do you properly test and troubleshoot your installation?

Umbraco releases updates on a relatively regular basis. These frequent releases are typically minor updates to address bug fixes found by HQ and the community, and the upgrade process is usually made up of copying a few files. However, sometimes major releases come out that require a more diligent and detailed process. This appendix can guide you through this process as it applies to the current version of Umbraco. At the time of this writing, the current version is 4.6.1.

OVERALL STEPS TO UPGRADE

The following steps should serve as a roadmap to perform the upgrade. Performing these steps in the order in which they are outlined is important. Most of these steps are self-explanatory, but steps 1, 3, 5 and 7 are discussed in greater detail throughout this appendix.

This may be obvious to some users but, first and foremost, never upgrade a live site directly without first running the upgrade in a development environment.

1. **Back up your files and database:** Copy down all of your files (including the Umbraco-specific files) and back up and restore the production database in development.

2. **Navigate to `http://umbraco.codeplex.com` to grab the latest version of Umbraco.** You can always find the latest version in the upper-right corner of the webpage, as shown in Figure A-1. If you use the built-in Microsoft Windows Compression tool, make sure to unblock the archive to make sure that Windows does not remove any files during the unarchive process.

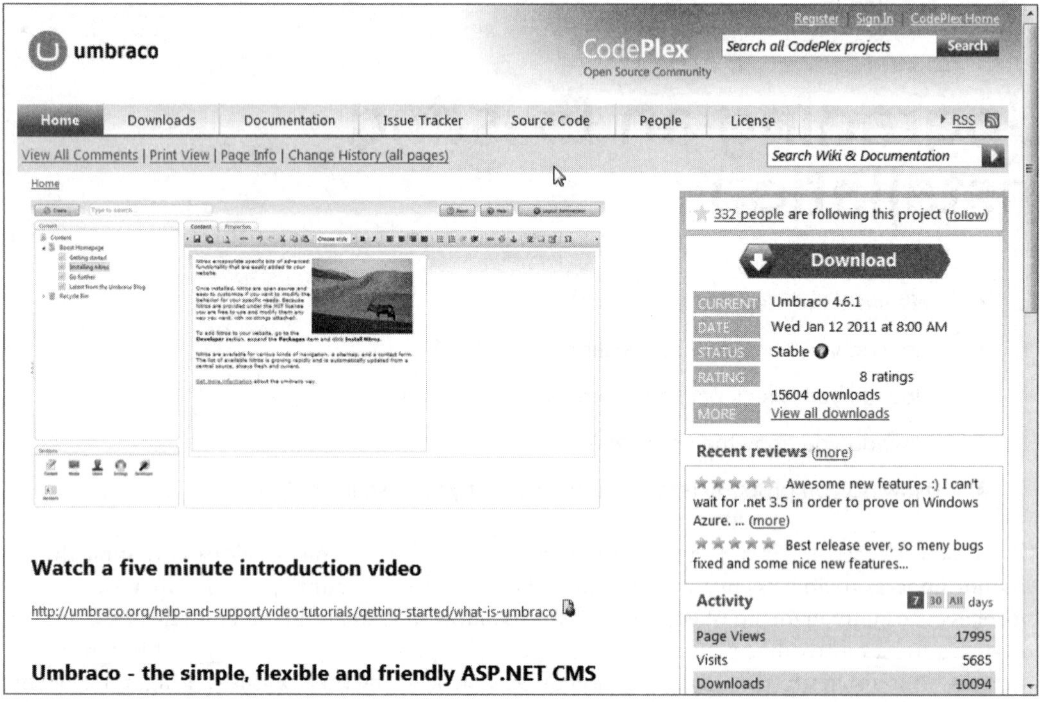

FIGURE A-1

3. **Check Package Compatibility:** Go through all the installed packages and make sure that they are compatible with the new version.

4. **Check all the configuration files for any changes particular to your installation.** Files to look through are `web.config`, files in the `/config` folder, and any other custom files you may have.

To ensure that you are catching all the changes in the configuration files, you can use a tool such as ExamDiff, which you can download from `www.prestosoft.com/edp_examdiff.asp`.

5. **Copy the right files:** Transfer any changes to the new configuration files in the new version folder that you downloaded in Step 2.
6. **Follow the upgrade wizard:** Navigate to the URL of your development installation and follow the steps outlined in the upgrade wizard.
7. **Test and troubleshoot your upgrade.**

BACKING UP YOUR FILES AND DATABASE

You must back up a few items as part of the upgrade process. After you have created the backups of the following items, restore them into your local development environment. For more details on the deployment process, refer to Chapter 13.

- **Installed files.** Archive all the files in your production installation root and overwrite your development environment. This includes all the files in the installation.
- **Database(s).** You should do a hot backup of your database and restore it over your local development database to ensure that the most recent content, media, and configurations are backed up. To make sure that changes are not made during the upgrade process, you can disable editor accounts temporarily.

For a guide on performing a database backup for SQL Server, see `http://support.microsoft.com/default.aspx?scid=kb;en-us;Q314546#10`. *For a guide on performing a database backup in MySQL, see* `http://dev.mysql.com/doc/refman/5.0/en/copying-databases.html`.

CHECKING PACKAGE COMPATIBILITY

Some third-party packages may have been developed for a specific version of Umbraco. This is typically only a problem between major versions, but is something you must keep in mind when performing the upgrade. As of Umbraco 4.5, the package repository lists what versions are supported by the particular package, as shown in Figure A-2. It is up to the developer to indicate this value, so make sure to test before deploying a package in production.

To check already-tested packages and the status of their compatibility, see the Wiki entry available on the developer's community site at `http://our.umbraco.org/wiki/reference/packaging/umbraco-45-compatibility/umbraco-45-package-testing`. If you have any questions, contact the package developer or see the package-specific forums (shown in Figure A-3) that are typically available for comments and bug reports.

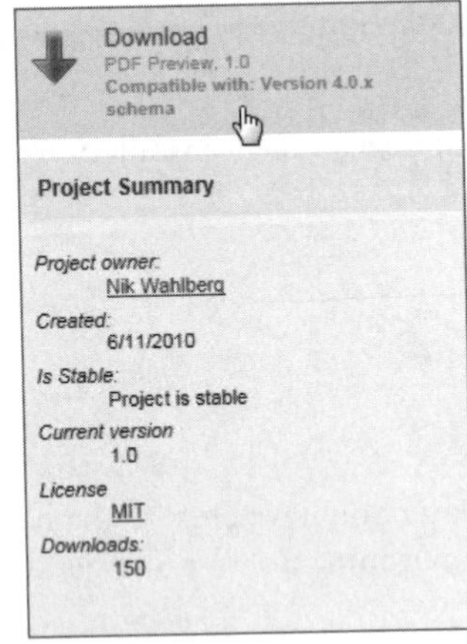

FIGURE A-2

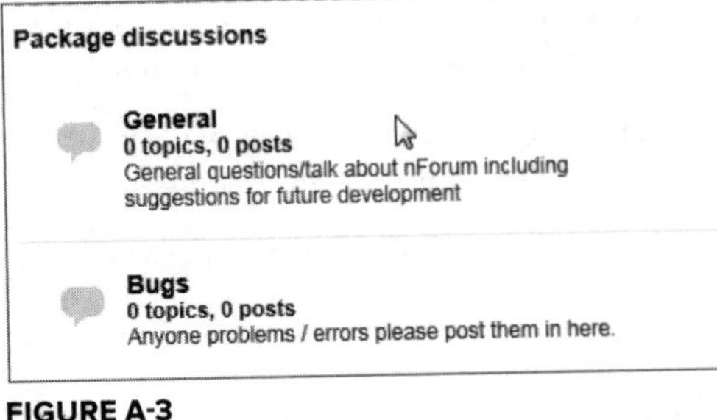

FIGURE A-3

COPYING THE RIGHT FILES

After you have restored the production environment to the development environment, it's time to upgrade the installation. To ensure that you are copying all the necessary files, reference the following file list:

- `/app_data`
- `/app_browsers`
- `/app_code`
- `/bin`
- `/config *`
- `/data`
- `/install`
- `/umbraco`
- `/umbraco_client`
- `web.config *`
- `default.aspx`

The asterisk (*) items in the previous list indicates that you need to remember to copy any configuration file updates as well.

After you have finished copying and overwriting all the files, you can simply run your development installation by calling its URL; Umbraco automatically launches the installer and walks you through the upgrade process.

TESTING AND TROUBLESHOOTING

Now it's time to test, test, test! You must test all the functionality that is specific to your application. As far as Umbraco basic functionality is concerned, you should:

- Run sample pages and make sure that templates and layouts look consistent.

- Check all the package functionality that you are using to make sure it is rendering correctly and that backoffice functionality is correct.
- Publish a node in the content tree to make sure that all of your permissions are set correctly on the file system.

The following are some common issues that you might run into, but if you are having issues beyond what is listed here, see the developers' forum at `http://our.umbraco.org`:

- **No content is showing up or is showing out-of-sync content from production.** This probably means that you need to republish the content to refresh the content XML cache. To rectify this situation, simply right-click the Content node in the Content section of the Umbraco backoffice, and select the Republish entire site menu option as shown in Figure A-4.

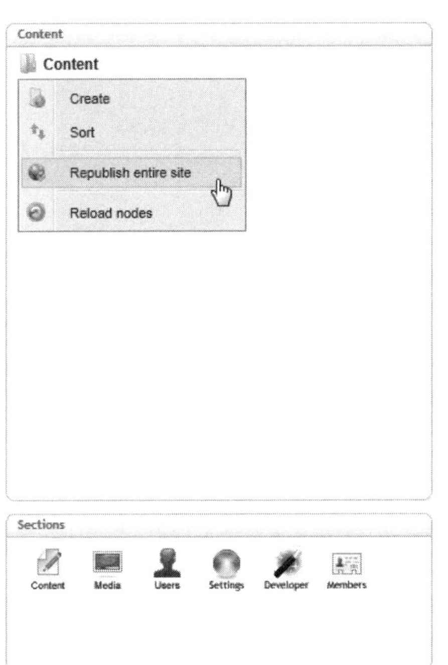

FIGURE A-4

FIGURE A-5

- **The .NET version configured for your website may not be the same as the Umbraco version you downloaded.** Check your IIS website's application pool to determine what version it is running, as shown in Figure A-5. The application pool can be changed by clicking the Basic Settings action from the right-hand action pane in IIS manager. Umbraco 4.6.1 is available in both .NET 4.0 and .NET 3.5.
- **The ASP.NET AJAX library might be missing.** Umbraco 4.5.x and higher are not dependent on the ASP.NET AJAX library. However, some third-party packages may be. Copying the AJAX libraries to the `<install root>/bin` directory of your Umbraco installation should resolve this issue.

B

Setting Up Your Visual Studio Environment

- How do you mimic the Umbraco folder structure?
- How do you set up build events?
- How do you reference the Umbraco libraries?

Editing templates, styles, scripts, and other resources within the Umbraco backoffice is certainly possible, as you have seen throughout the book. However, working with all of these assets and custom code outside of Umbraco is best practice. Luckily, Visual Studio provides you with plenty of toolsets to accomplish this. But why would you want to? Here are a couple reasons:

- **Multi-developer environments.** If you are working on a team and sharing a single development installation, deployment and code syncing is much easier if the assets are worked out outside of Umbraco.
- **Source control integration.** As you may know, Microsoft Visual Studio allows you to source control your code with your favorite source control system, such as Subversion, CVS, or Visual SourceSafe.

The instructions in this appendix are specific to Visual Studio 2010 but also apply to Visual Studio 2008. Earlier versions also support similar functionality, but the approach is different.

SETTING UP THE UMBRACO FOLDER STRUCTURE

There are a few folders in the Umbraco install that you must have access to, and a few that you will want to include in the event that you are extending Umbraco's functionality or working with configuration files.

Table B-1 lists all the Umbraco folders that you should include as part of your Visual Studio project and how they map to your Umbraco installation. See Figure B-1 for a view of the project structure.

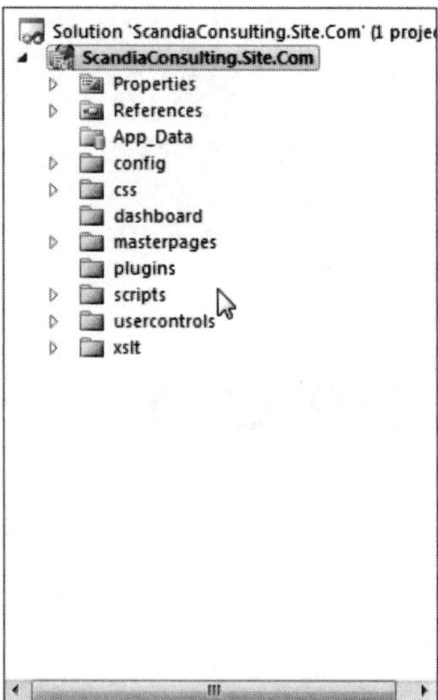

FIGURE B-1

TABLE B-1: Visual Studio Project Folders

VISUAL STUDIO FOLDER	UMBRACO PATH
config	<install root>/config
css	<install root>/css
dashboard	<install root>/dashboard This is a custom folder that you should create in your installation directory; you can use it to create a custom dashboard made up of .aspx files presented to your users in the right-hand pane of the Umbraco backoffice. See <install root>/config/Dashboard.config for an example.
masterpages	<install root>/masterpages
plugins	<install root>/umbraco/plugins
scripts	<install root>/scripts
usercontrols	<install root>/usercontrols
xslt	<install root>/xslt

SETTING UP THE BUILD EVENTS

Build events enable you to add actions either before or after the project build operation. In Umbraco, you use these events to trigger several `XCOPY` commands to transfer the compiled DLLs as well as any other files to your Umbraco installation. Without these actions, you would have to manually copy the compiled files to your Umbraco installation after every build in order to see the changes reflected on your website.

You manage build events in the project properties. To open the properties, simply double-click the Properties node in the Solution Explorer, as shown in Figure B-2.

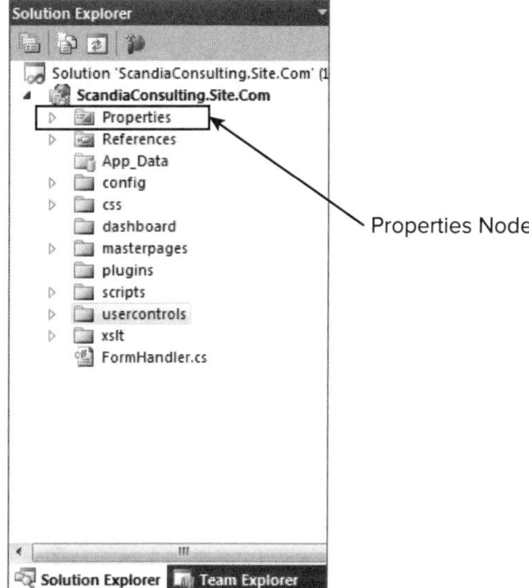

FIGURE B-2

After you're in the project Properties page, follow these steps to add the build events:

1. Click the Build Events tab along the left-hand side of the page, as shown in Figure B-3.
2. Click the Edit Post-build button located under the Post-build text area, also shown in Figure B-3.
3. In the Post-build Event Command Line dialog that appears, shown in Figure B-4, add the `XCOPY` commands that will ultimately copy your project files and assets to your local or network-accessible Umbraco installation. Listing B-1 shows a sample set of `XCOPY` commands that you can use as a template for your own environment. Remember to change the target paths (`<install root>`) and point them to your specific environment.
4. Click the OK button in the Post-build Event Command Line dialog and then save the project properties.

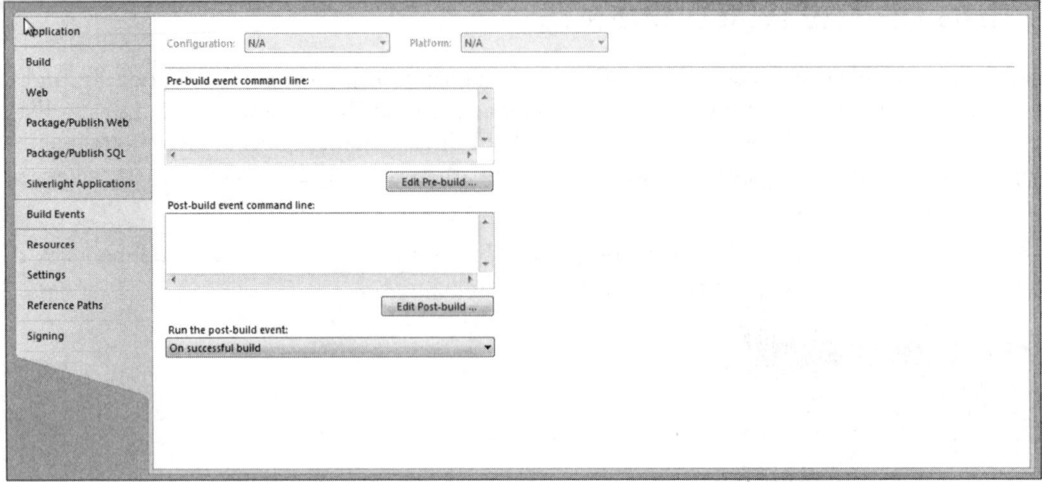

FIGURE B-3

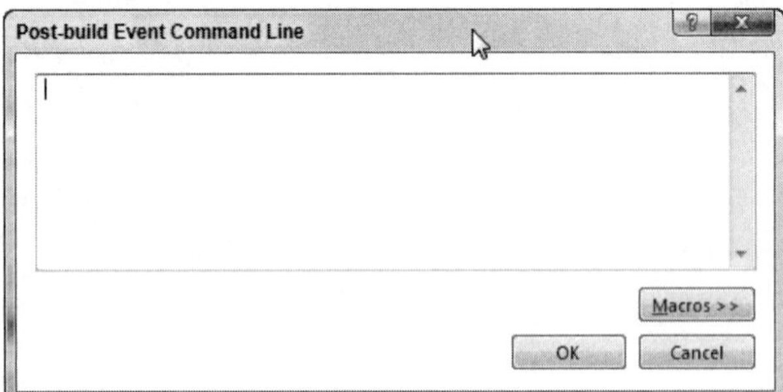

FIGURE B-4

The variables preceded by a dollar ($) sign in Listing B-1 are known as macros in Visual Studio. You can select from a predefined list of macros by clicking on the Macros >> button in the Post-build Event Command Line dialog, and insert them into your command line.

LISTING B-1: XcopyCommands.txt

```
XCOPY "$(ProjectDir)bin\$(TargetName).*" "<install root>\bin" /Y
XCOPY "$(ProjectDir)usercontrols\*.ascx" "<install root>\usercontrols" /Y
XCOPY "$(ProjectDir)css\*.*" "<install root>\css" /Y
XCOPY "$(ProjectDir)dashboard\*.*" "<install root>\dashboard" /Y
XCOPY "$(ProjectDir)scripts\*.*" "<install root>\scripts" /Y
```

```
XCOPY "$(ProjectDir)xslt\*.*" "<install root>\xslt" /Y
XCOPY "$(ProjectDir)masterpages\*.master" "<install root>\masterpages" /Y
XCOPY "$(ProjectDir)config\*.*" "<install root>\config" /Y
```

REFERENCING THE UMBRACO LIBRARIES

If you are interacting with the Umbraco document API or referencing other Umbraco functionality in your user controls, you must reference the appropriate Umbraco DLLs so that your code will compile and Visual Studio IntelliSense will work.

To include references to these core Umbraco libraries, simply follow these steps:

1. Right-click the References node in the Solution Explorer and select the Add Reference menu item, as shown in Figure B-5.

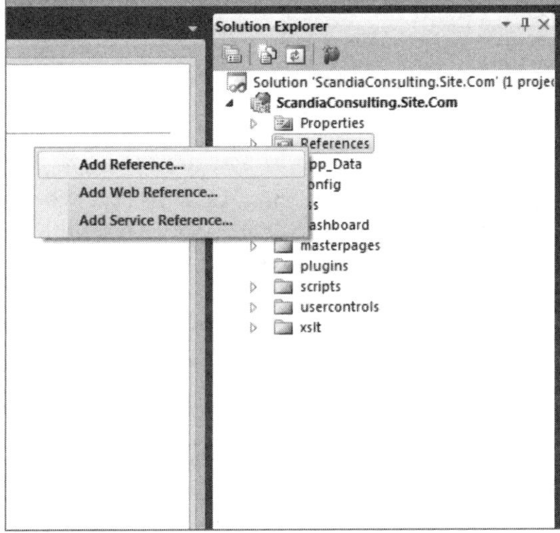

FIGURE B-5

2. In the Add Reference dialog, select the Browse tab and locate your `<install root>/bin` folder. As shown in Figure B-6, select the necessary DLLs. The core DLLs that you should include are:

   - `businesslogic`
   - `cms`
   - `controls`
   - `umbraco`
   - `umbraco.editorControls`

3. Click the OK button.

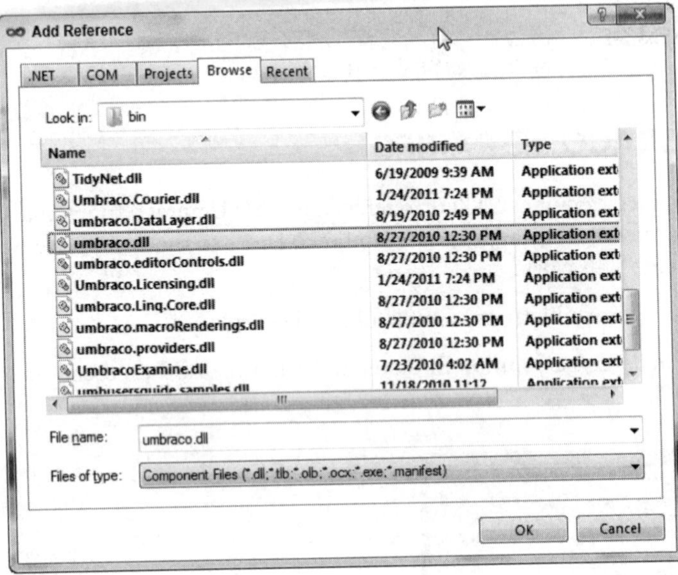

FIGURE B-6

You can include others, as well; for example, the `UmbracoExamine` DLL if you are working with Examine for searching, and so on. However, the preceding list is enough to work with the document API and other core Umbraco functions, if you have a need for that.

For examples on how to work with the document API, see Chapter 12.

Resources

- Where do you find Umbraco source and installation files?
- What should you know about the Umbraco community?
- What services and products does the Umbraco Headquarters offer?

Umbraco is, as you may know by now, an open source project with a large developer and user community. Successful open source projects invite users of the product to give feedback, report bugs, and encourage others to get involved in helping new users of the product to get started. Umbraco is known as the "Friendly CMS" because the core team has been very successful in engaging users and developers to contribute their time to support and evangelize the product.

You can get involved in the Umbraco open source project in several ways. The resources listed in this appendix should point you in the right direction for gaining access to all the available Umbraco products, as well as show you how you can contribute.

SOURCE AND INSTALLATION FILES

Because Umbraco is available under the MIT license, you can download the full source of the product and modify it to your heart's content. However, in most cases, you want to download the installable binaries to install Umbraco from Web Platform, as covered in Chapter 1. Use the following links to download the source and installation archive.

- **Source:** `http://umbraco.codeplex.com/SourceControl/list/changesets`
- **Installable archive:** `http://umbraco.codeplex.com/`

COMMUNITY

The Umbraco project is supported by a very strong community of developers and users alike. Because of the active user base support, answers are typically just a few minutes away as soon as you post a problem on the community support site. You can access this site at `http://our.umbraco.org`.

The community site also contains a lot of development documentation and, of course, the ever-growing package repository where you can download plug-ins for your Umbraco installation.

The coolest thing about participating in the Umbraco community is earning what's known as Karma. The *Karma* will increase your rating on the community site and if you earn enough you will be featured under the People section. Karma increases the more you participate and can be earned by all sorts of actions. These actions include answering questions that people may post on the forum, adding to the wiki where you identify holes, sharing your development in the form of packages, and more. We encourage you, as an Umbraco user, to participate on the forums as it is where most of the users get started.

UMBRACO HEADQUARTERS

The Umbraco team provides a series of services and products to help you get started and grow your Umbraco initiatives. As an organization Umbraco is, first and foremost, committed to the development of the product, but its main focus is also on giving the community and users the tools they need to success.

- **Umbraco PRO:** Umbraco is not in the business of consulting or providing package development but the organization sells licensed software and support services in a number of areas. To learn more about the Umbraco PRO products and services, visit the corporate website at `http://umbraco.org`.
- **Umbraco TV:** Umbraco TV is a subscription service that the Umbraco organization offers to users and developers. It's a suite of recorded videos that provide in-depth instructions on how to accomplish everything from working with content to leveraging the Umbraco API. Check it out at `http://umbraco.tv`.
- **Umbraco Training and Certifications:** The Umbraco organization has set up several levels for certification programs to allow developers and companies to become recognized in the industry. To receive certification, the individual or organization must first attend one of two training courses that Umbraco conducts in many parts of the world. For more information on training and certification, see `http://umbraco.com/help-and-support/training`.

Data Type Definitions

- What's a data type again?
- What does each data type do?
- How do I configure my own data types?

Working with and creating your own data types for the Umbraco backoffice will undoubtedly enhance the flexibility and versatility of your Umbraco installation. Umbraco comes with a whole stack of built-in data types to solve the most common data entry and manipulation tasks. The section "Definition of Built-in Data Types" provides a detailed description of each of these built-in types. Did you know that you can also create your own variations of some of the built-in data types? You can read more about that in the "Configuring Your Own Data Type" section.

As a matter of recommendation, the authors suggest installing and using the community-driven package uComponents. You can download this package directly from the package repository in the Developer section ⇨ Packages ⇨ Umbraco Package Repository ⇨ Backoffice Extensions. See Chapter 10 for details on how to work with packages.

THE DATA TYPE'S PURPOSE

What is a *data type* in the realm of Umbraco? In short, it's an interface for editors to use to manipulate, save, and publish data for any given document type field in Umbraco. In technical terms, it's an input type used to store data in a particular format. Umbraco allows you to store this data in four predefined database data type formats. Table D-1 lists the supported database data types.

TABLE D-1: Supported Database Data Types

DATA TYPE	DESCRIPTION
`Date`	Use this data type for date and time stamp, such as event start date and so on.
`Integer`	Use this data type if you are recording the number of available spots for an event or to store a node ID, for example. Only numbers are allowed when using this data type.
`Ntext`	In terms of size, `Ntext` is the most flexible but also the data type that will take up the most space in your database. Any number of characters can be stored in this data type. The suggested use is for the Richtext Editor or other large input field.
`Nvarchar`	This data type is most useful for simple text strings because it grows with the number of characters as needed, up to a maximum of 500 characters.

One critical thing to keep in mind is that when you create an Umbraco data type and specify, for example, `Integer`*, and then decide to change it to* `Nvarchar` *at a later time, the data that was stored in the* `Integer` *field will not remain when the data type is changed. This is because data is stored in separate columns in the database depending on the database data type that is selected during the creation of the Umbraco data type. If you need to make this sort of change after data has been saved using the data type, manual database changes are required in order to copy the original values to the new data type column.*

DEFINITION OF BUILT-IN DATA TYPES

A number of data types come with the basic install of Umbraco. Most of the data types listed in the following sections also allow you to create variations of them to fit your own needs. For example, the Ultimate Picker data type allows you to specify which type of HTML input control should be rendered as well as indicate which node to start with.

The fields that allow you to set additional configurations require you to add either *prevalues* (predefined values for the user to select from), or set other settings like HTML control type and so on. The steps that follow describe how this is done. Each field, however, is made up of at least three attributes. This includes a Name to identify the data type; the Render Control, which specifies which HTML control is used to enter or interact with the data; and finally, a system-generated GUID (globally unique ID).

1. As shown in Figure D-1, enter the desired value in the Add prevalue field and click the Save button in the toolbar toward the top of the screen.
2. Repeat step 1 for the remainder of the values that you need to add.
3. You can edit a prevalue value by clicking the value. This reveals an editable field, shown in Figure D-2, that auto-saves when you click outside of the field.

Name	Checkbox list
Render control	Checkbox list
Data Editor GUID	b4471851-82b6-4c75-afa4-39fa9c6a75e9

Settings

Database datatype	Nvarchar
Add prevalue	Value to show

FIGURE D-1

Settings

Database datatype	Nvarchar	
Text	Value	
Value to show	29	Delete sort
Add prevalue		

FIGURE D-2

More complex data types will ask for more details. See the section "Ultimate Picker" for an example.

Approved Color

The Approved Color data type allows you to create a field that presents a color picker with a predefined list of colors from which the editor can select. Simply add the hexadecimal colors you want the editor to have access to in the Add prevalue field, as shown in Figure D-3. Figure D-4 shows what the end result looks like when you use the data type in the Content section.

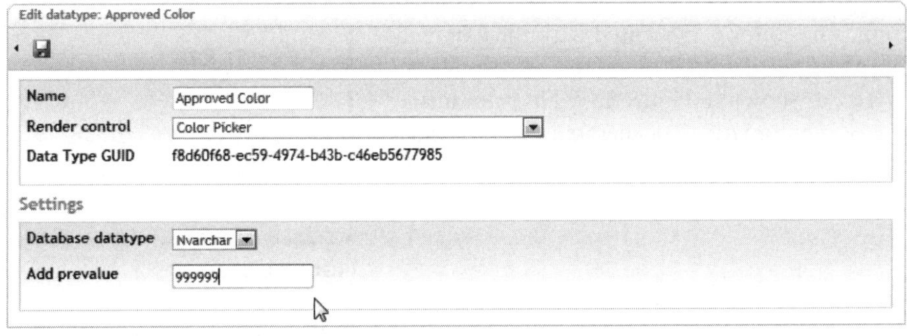

FIGURE D-3

Approved Color
Select a color by clicking a square. The selected color is shown in the first box.

FIGURE D-4

The saved result will be a string of the selected color value as you defined in the prevalue list.

Checkbox List

As the name implies, Checkbox List allows you to render a list of checkboxes with the values you define in the prevalue list, shown in Figure D-5. The view in the Content section is shown in Figure D-6.

Database datatype Nvarchar

Text	Value	
Value to show	29	Delete sort
Another selection	32	Delete sort

Add prevalue

FIGURE D-5

Checkbox List
Value to show
Another selection

FIGURE D-6

The saved result of the checkbox list datatype is a comma-separated list of the selected values. The following code snippet shows how to work with the saved values in XSLT:

```
<xsl:variable name="items"
     select="umbraco.library:Split($selectedCheckboxItems,',')" />
<xsl:for-each select="$items//value">
   <xsl:value-of select="umbraco.library:GetPreValueAsString(current())"/>
</xsl:for-each>
```

Content Picker

The Content Picker is a replica of the content tree shown in the Content section. The editor is presented with the Content Tree view that he or she has permission to see and can select a node from this tree, as shown in Figure D-7. No prevalue is here because the tree is automatically generated based on the user's permissions.

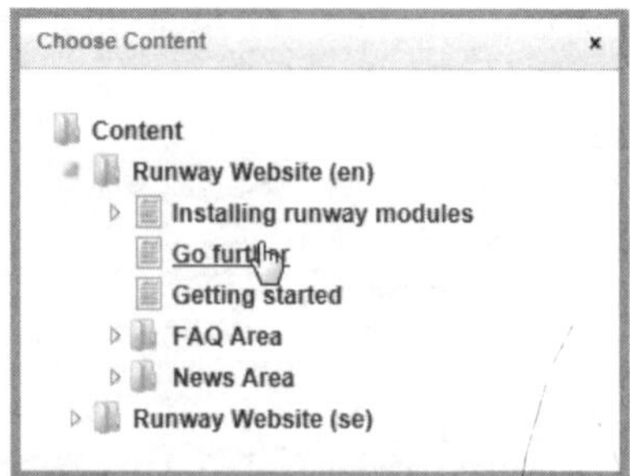

FIGURE D-7

To provide a Content Picker with a specific start node, see the "Ultimate Picker" section later in the chapter.

Date Picker with Time

A Date Picker with Time presents your user with a calendar control to pick a date and select a time (consisting of the hour and minute). Figure D-8 shows the view that the editor sees. Use this data type to specifically set a time *and* a date. If you are only interested in the date, use the Date Picker data type.

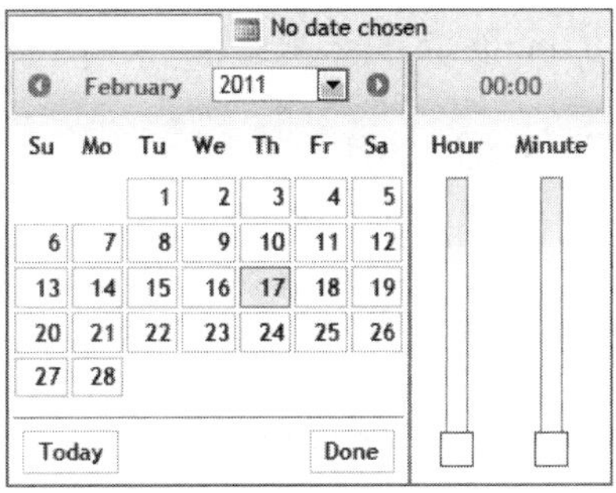

FIGURE D-8

The saved result for this data type is a date object. To put the value in a human-readable format, you can use the available date format function from the `umbraco.library` extension methods, as shown in the following code snippet. Any valid date format can be supplied.

```
<xsl:value-of
   select="umbraco.library:FormatDateTime($dateNode, 'MM/dd/yyyy')"/>
<xsl:value-of
   select="umbraco.library:FormatDateTime($dateNode, 'hh:mm')"/>
```

Date Picker

The Date Picker presents a user with a calendar control to pick a date. Figure D-9 shows the view that the editor sees.

The saved result for this data type is a date object. To put the value in a human-readable format, you can use the available date format function from the `umbraco.library` extension methods, as shown in the following code snippet. Any valid date format can be supplied.

FIGURE D-9

```
<xsl:value-of
   select="umbraco.library:FormatDateTime($dateNode, 'MM/dd/yyyy')"/>
```

Dropdown Multiple

The Dropdown Multiple data type allows you to present the editor with an HTML select box to pick multiple values from. As with other data types, simply add the prevalues you want, and the editor will see something similar to what is shown in Figure D-10.

FIGURE D-10

Similar to the saved result of Checkbox List, the saved result is a comma-separated list of values. For an example of how to output the selected values using XSLT, see the section "Checkbox List" earlier in the chapter.

Dropdown

The Dropdown control simply displays a standard HTML select box, giving the editor the option to select one and only one value from the list. Again, add your values using the Add prevalue field, repeating for all the values that you need to display in the dropdown field.

Image Cropper

The Image Cropper control is very useful if you have editors uploading images to the Media section of the Umbraco backoffice. This particular data type only applies to the Image media type. It allows you to specify predefined crop sizes for images that are uploaded, which restricts the user to publishing images in a specific format. To add crop sizes and behavior specific to your needs, follow these steps:

1. In the Property alias field, enter **umbracoFile**. This stores the file that you're uploading to the Media section.
2. Select the Save crop images checkbox. A Quality input field appears. In this field you can specify the DPI (dots per inch) with which the resulting cropped image should be saved. Figure D-11 shows an example of the image cropping result.

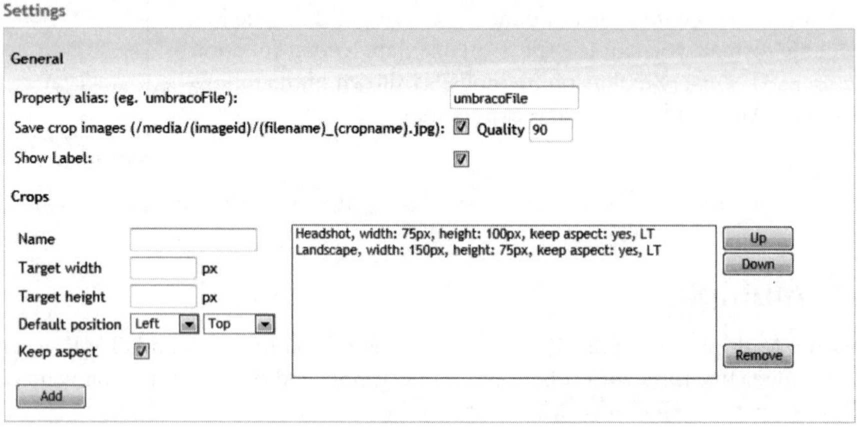

FIGURE D-11

3. Select the Show Label checkbox. Doing this will display the name of the crop in the Media section.
4. Fill in the name of the crop region. This example has a headshot format available for users to use when cropping images.

5. Fill in a target width and height. These values set the maximum dimensions of the crop.
6. Set the default position of the crop. This setting determines where the crop region is placed when the crop action is first initiated.
7. Click the Add button.
8. Repeat step 1 through 7 for the number of different crops that you want to make available to your editors.
9. Save the data type by clicking the Save icon in Umbraco's main toolbar.

Before you can use the cropper, you must add the data type as a property for the Image media type. To do this, follow these steps.

1. Navigate to the Settings section in the Umbraco backoffice.
2. Expand the Media Types node and click Image.
3. Click the Generic Properties tab at the top of the screen.
4. Click the "Click here to add a new property bar" option toward the top of the right-hand pane.
5. Fill in the name of the property. In this example, the property name is **Crop**.
6. Select Image Cropper as the Type.
7. Save the Image media type by clicking the Save button in Umbraco's main toolbar.

Your media library is now set up to show the cropper when an Image is uploaded. See Figure D-12 for an example of what the cropping plugin will look like. Now you can use the corner handles on the defined regions to specify what portions of the original image should be shown in the crop.

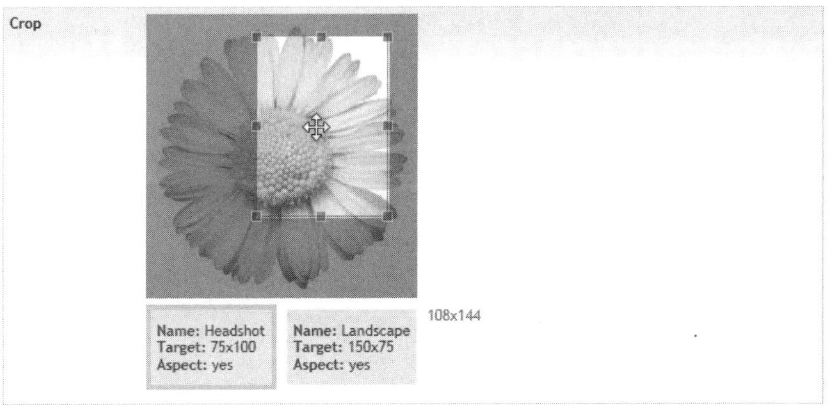

FIGURE D-12

To access these images in your XSLT, simply output the image using the following code snippet:

```
<!-- get the image from media library usign GetMedia -->
<xsl:variable name="pic"
    select="umbraco.library:GetMedia($img1, 'true')/umbracoFile" />
<-- Create an image object -->
<img>
    <!-- add the src attribute to the image tag -->
    <xsl:attribute name="src">
        <xsl:value-of select="$pic/crops/crop [@name='headshot']/@url"/>
    </xsl:attribute>
</img>
```

Macro Container

The Macro Container allows you to give your editors a way to add macros to the Content node. This provides a way for editors to include custom functionality from any macros that you have developed (see Chapter 5).

As shown in Figure D-13, you must specify which macros your users can select, how many they can select for any given node, and what the dimensions of the control should be in the Content section.

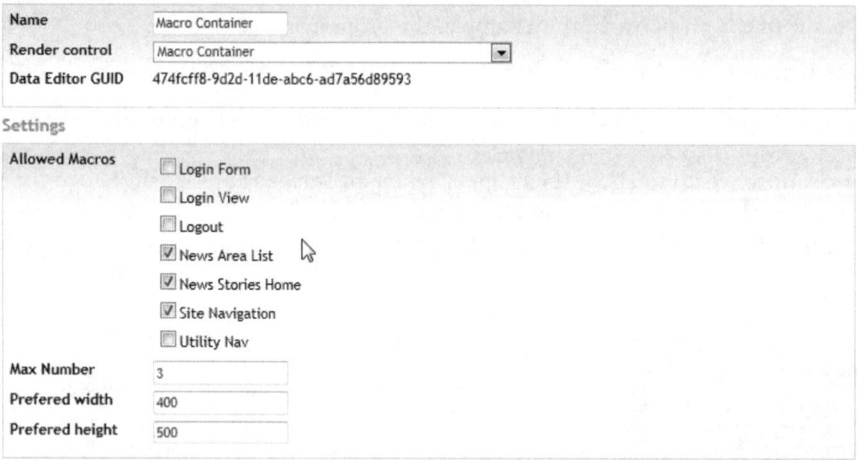

Name: Macro Container
Render control: Macro Container
Data Editor GUID: 474fcff8-9d2d-11de-abc6-ad7a56d89593

Settings

Allowed Macros: Login Form, Login View, Logout, News Area List (checked), News Stories Home (checked), Site Navigation (checked), Utility Nav
Max Number: 3
Prefered width: 400
Prefered height: 500

FIGURE D-13

The saved result of this selection is a list of Umbraco macro tags. A sample of this output is shown in the following code snippet:

```
<macroContainer>
    <![CDATA[
        <?UMBRACO_MACRO  macroalias="NewsAreaList"  />
        <?UMBRACO_MACRO  macroalias="SiteNavigation"  />
    ]]>
</macroContainer>
```

Media Picker

The Media Picker is just what the name suggests. This data type allows editors to select a media item from the media library. Permissions and access for the individual editor applies here just like in the Content Picker. So, if an editor has a specific start node set, that's all he or she will see when using this control. Figure D-14 shows what the editor sees when working with the Media Picker in the Content section of the Umbraco backoffice.

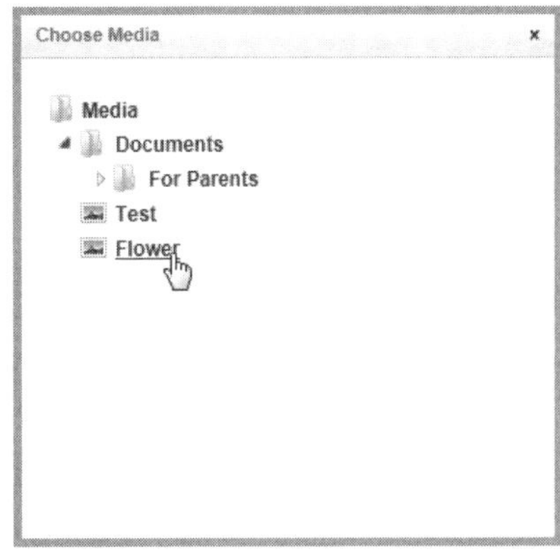

FIGURE D-14

The saved result for this data type is the ID of the media item. An example of how to get the path of the file is shown in the following code snippet:

```
<xsl:value-of
    select="umbraco.library:GetMedia(imageFieldName, 'true')/umbracoFile" />
```

Member Picker

The Member Picker simply shows a list of any members that have been added to the Members section of the Umbraco backoffice. The saved result of this data type is the member ID.

Radiobox

Similar to the Checkbox List data type, Radiobox displays a list of the added prevalues in a list with HTML radio buttons. As is expected with HTML radio buttons, an editor can only select one value when using the data type.

Related Links

This data type is very useful when you need to display a list of internal or external links associated with a particular page. As shown in Figure D-15, the control allows you to add as many related links as you need for any given node. When you add an internal link, you are asked to select a node using the Content Picker. When you add an external link, you simply enter the URL. In addition, you can indicate whether the particular link should open in a new window.

The saved result of this data type produces XML that you can parse using simple `XPath` statements.

Umbraco ships with an XSLT template to output related links. See Chapter 5 for more details on how to use the built-in XSLT templates.

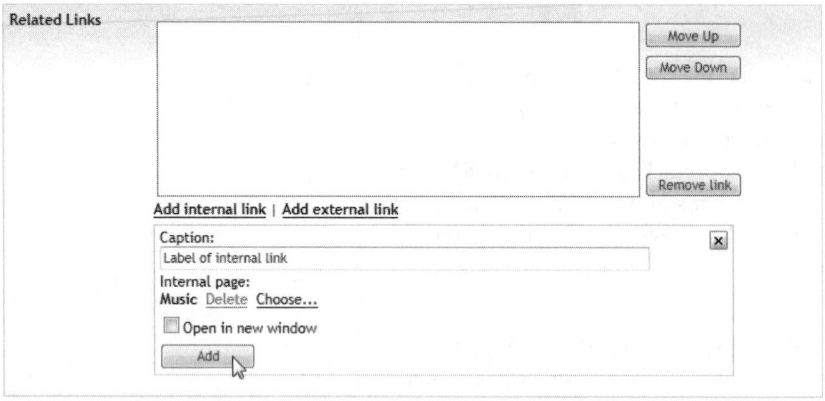

FIGURE D-15

Richtext Editor

The Richtext Editor data type is the foundation of the Umbraco WYSIWYG (what you see is what you get) editor and what allows editors to manage content in a non-technical fashion. As shown in Figure D-16, you can toggle quite a number of settings for this data type. As you can see, this data type is based on the TinyMCE plug-in, which is an open source WYSIWYG editor that Umbraco has elected to implement.

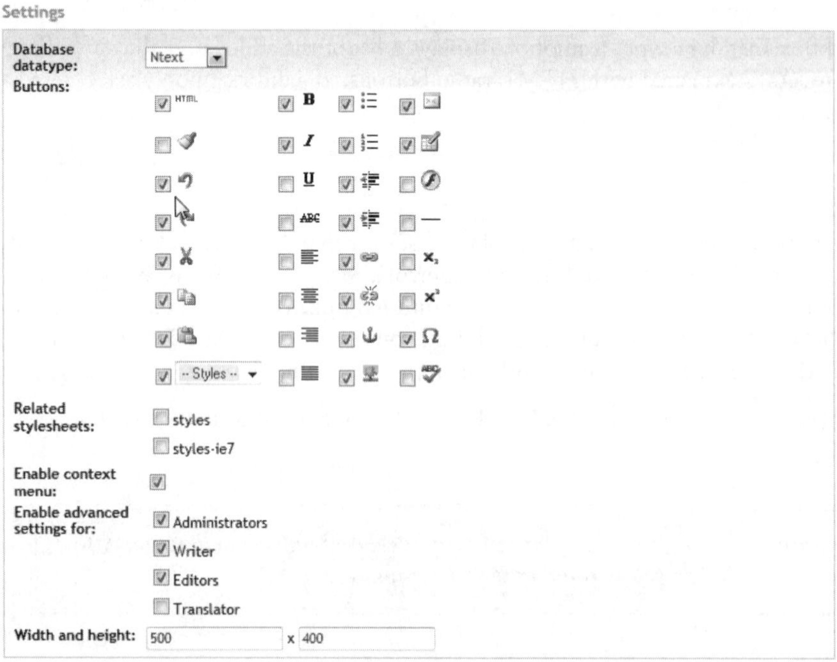

FIGURE D-16

The options for this data type are fairly obvious, and the default settings are a good standard for your editors. The most important setting to note here is the Related Stylesheets setting, which allows you to specify stylesheets that you want to apply when rendering the content in the richtext editor control. For example, if you want the paragraph tag to look a certain way within the editor window, you can specify that in the stylesheet that applies.

See Chapter 4 (in the "Styles and Scripts" section) for more details on how to work with styles for the editor window.

The saved result of this data type produces standard and XHTML-compliant HTML.

To configure the behavior of the TinyMCE WYSIWYG control, you can make changes to the `<install root>/config/tinyMceConfig.config` *file. You may be specifically interested in the* `<validElements />` *node, which specifies which HTML elements are allowed in the editor markup.*

For advanced settings and instructions on how to configure TinyMCE, check out `http://tinymce.moxiecode.com/`.

Simple Editor

Again, the name kind of gives away what Simple Editor is. It's a multi-line text field that allows very simple editing, such as inserting HTML bold, italic, and link tags into the text. Figure D-17 shows an example of the editor.

FIGURE D-17

Tags

The Tags data type (see Figure D-18) provides editors with an auto-suggest control so that tags are not added multiple times for any given field across multiple pages. For example, if you add the string *cars* to this field on a particular page, and then go to edit the same field on another page, you'll see "car" as a suggestion as soon as you type the letter c in the textbox.

FIGURE D-18

As of Umbraco 4.6.x, you can also specify a tag group for the data type. This means you can keep separate lists of tags for different data types so as not to cross-contaminate the lists between different types of fields.

The saved result of the Tags data type is a comma-separated list of values. See the section "Checkbox List" earlier in the chapter for an example of how to work with this data in XSLT.

Textbox Multiple

Textbox Multiple is simply a multi-line text input in the form of the HTML element `<textarea />`. By default, this data type is based on `Ntext`, which allows you to put in an unlimited amount of data (or as much as your database can store).

Textstring

The Textstring data type is a standard one-line text HTML input field that allows you to save simple strings.

True/False

The True/False data type presents the editor with a checkbox to indicate a true or false value for a field. You use this data type for something like determining whether a node appears in the navigation.

The saved result of this data type is a 1 if the checkbox is selected and a 0 if the checkbox is not selected.

Ultimate Picker

The Ultimate Picker data type is a powerful control that allows you to provide editors with a means of selecting nodes from your content tree. Options for the render controls include: Auto Complete (like the Tags data type), Checkbox List, Dropdown List, List Box (like the Dropdown Multiple data type), and Radiobutton List (like the Radiobox data type). In addition, you can specify where in the content tree the nodes should start. This means that you can limit the view of a certain subset of the nodes in the content tree. Combine this data type with a document type filter capability, and you have a very flexible content picker.

Here's an example. In the website example in this book two separate sites are set up with two different languages. If you want to create a content picker with only the FAQs from the English website, you can configure the Ultimate Picker data type to look something like Figure D-19.

Similar to the Checkbox List and other multi-select data types, the Ultimate Picker saves the values in a comma-separated value list.

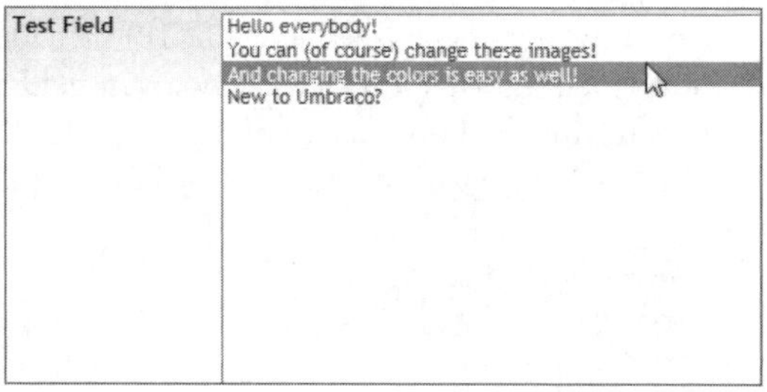

FIGURE D-19

Upload

The Upload data type enables you to attach a file to a page. This field is different from using the Media section in that the file you upload is not accessible from the Media section. If you know the path to the file, the file is only accessible from the scope of the `currentPage` in your XSLT.

The saved result from this data type is the path to the uploaded file as a string.

CONFIGURING A DATA TYPE TO YOUR NEEDS

You have seen the extreme flexibility of the built-in data types that ship with Umbraco. But what if you need to create your own variation of one of the data types described in the previous section? For example, you may need a rich text editor but you don't want all the bells and whistles that are in the standard one. You can easily create a new data type based on the TinyMCE control type (just like the built-in Richtext Editor data type). Just follow these steps:

1. In the Developer section, right-click Data Types and click the Create menu item.
2. Provide a name for your new data type, something unique, as shown in Figure D-20.

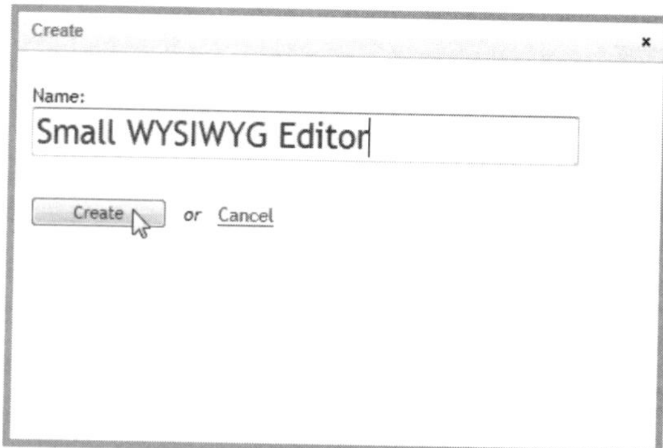

FIGURE D-20

3. In the resulting right pane, select TinyMCE v3 wysiwig as the Render Control.
4. Click the Save button in the top toolbar. The settings specific to the TinyMCE control are revealed in the pane at the bottom.
5. Configure the control to your needs and save it once again.

Now you can use the newly created data type in your document types, and it is rendered for editors in the Content section.

This process can, of course, be implemented with all the data types and each one will have its own settings and variations.

If you need to create a new data type with your own custom input control, see Chapter 12.

INDEX

Symbols and Numbers

A

E

I

J

K

L

M

N

O

P

R

U

X